Beyond Exemplar Tales

NEW PERSPECTIVES ON CHINESE CULTURE AND SOCIETY

A series sponsored by the American Council of Learned Societies and made possible through a grant from the Chiang Ching-kuo Foundation for International Scholarly Exchange

1. Joan Judge and Hu Ying, eds., *Beyond Exemplar Tales: Women's Biography in Chinese History*
2. David A. Palmer and Xun Liu, eds., *Daoism in the Twentieth Century: Between Eternity and Modernity*

Beyond Exemplar Tales

Women's Biography in Chinese History

Edited by
JOAN JUDGE and HU YING

Global, Area, and International Archive
University of California Press
BERKELEY   LOS ANGELES   LONDON

The Global, Area, and International Archive (GAIA) is an initiative
of the Institute of International Studies, University of California,
Berkeley, in partnership with the University of California Press,
the California Digital Library, and international research programs
across the University of California system.

University of California Press, one of the most distinguished
university presses in the United States, enriches lives around the
world by advancing scholarship in the humanities, social sciences,
and natural sciences. Its activities are supported by the UC Press
Foundation and by philanthropic contributions from individuals
and institutions. For more information, visit www.ucpress.edu.

University of California Press
Berkeley and Los Angeles, California

University of California Press, Ltd.
London, England

Library of Congress Cataloging-in-Publication Data

A catalog record for this book is available from the Library
of Congress.

20   19   18   17   16   15   14   13   12   11
10   9   8   7   6   5   4   3   2   1

ISBN: 978-0-520-28973-4

For Antigone, Avital, and Brenna,
in celebration of friendship
across the generations

Contents

Illustrations

Acknowledgments

This volume began to germinate over a decade ago. At that time, first-rate work on Chinese women's history was appearing like "spring bamboo shoots," and we realized that a number of us shared an interest in the Chinese women's biographical tradition. Elated by what we found in our sources and eager to share our ideas on how to handle the unique challenges presented by this rich and diverse material, we conversed over several workshops (at the Southern California Center for Chinese Studies) and conference panels (at annual meetings of the Association for Asian Studies).

This conversation led to an international conference on Chinese women's biography held in March of 2006, in the idyllic setting of Laguna Beach, California. The conference was generously supported by a number of foundations and programs: the ALCS/CCK New Perspectives on Chinese Studies Series, the University of California Pacific Rim Program, the University of California Humanities Research Institute, and three divisions of the University of California, Irvine: The Center for Asian Studies, The Humanities Center, and the Office of Research and Graduate Study.

We are extremely grateful to the discussants and participants at the conference for their incisive comments on individual papers and their contributions to discussions of broader conceptual issues. The final product bears traces of their valuable insights, even though their names may not be attached to the chapters. We particularly want to acknowledge JaHyun Kim Haboush, who pushed us to think of biography as a cultural project, and whose silent and valiant battle with cancer ended on January 30, 2011. Other good colleagues include Suzanne Cahill, Eileen Cheng, Stephen Durrant, Hsiung Ping-chen, Dorothy Ko, Wai-yee Li, Michael Nylan, Lisa Raphals, Song Shaopeng, Yi Jo-lan, Anne Walthall, and Xia Xiaohong.

Our special thanks to Anne Walthall, colleague and devoted friend, who from the planning stage of the conference, gave unstinting moral support and intellectual guidance. The conference would have been impossible without the logistical support of the ever-resourceful staff person in the Department of East Asian Studies at UC Irvine, Mindy Han, and the help of graduate students at Irvine at the time, Zhen Zhang, Hsin-chieh Li, and Han Li. We also thank Michelle Cho for her help in copyediting the first draft and preparing it for submission to the press.

Our greatest debt is ultimately to the authors in this volume. They not only gave us extraordinary material to work with but willingly endured countless rounds of revisions before and after the book was accepted. They also offered invaluable suggestions on the conceptualization of the volume, and on the introduction and epilogue.

The book could not have materialized without the assistance of Steven C. Wheatley, vice president of the ACLS, and Kelly Buttermore, the grants coordinator for the ACLS, who facilitated publication by, and provided a generous subsidy to, the Global, Area, and International Archive at the University of California, Berkeley, and the University of California Press. Our editor, Nathan MacBrien, the publications director for the Institute of International Studies at the University of California, Berkeley, has been an absolute pleasure to work with: encouraging at every stage in the process and a meticulous copyeditor, highly responsive to our many queries. We are also deeply grateful to Nathan for securing such excellent readers for the manuscript. We heartily thank those two anonymous readers for their detailed and penetrating comments on individual essays, and for their suggestions on how to transform a collection of essays into a coherent book.

Our personal debts are also weighty. We owe the origin of this book to Michael Phelan, who first suggested the collaboration, having witnessed the convergence of our interests over the years. We thank both Michael and Josh for their forbearance as "the co-edited volume" made repeated incursions into our lives at various points over the last several years. It is to our daughters, who were more or less conceived alongside the project, that we dedicate this work. While their childhood may have delayed the publication date of the book, like so many women recorded and unrecorded in biographies, our lives are immeasurably enriched by theirs. Their friendship has been among the greatest pleasures of our collaboration.

J. J. and H.Y.

Introduction

Joan Judge and Hu Ying

In a story from the *Biographies of Women* (*Lienü zhuan*) compiled by Liu Xiang (77–6 BCE), a woman of the town of Qishi in the state of Lu laments: "The King of Lu is old and the prince too young." When a neighboring woman responds that this is "the officials' concern," not theirs, the woman of Qishi protests: "In the past, a stranger on horseback trampled our farmland, causing us to go hungry all year. If the country of Lu is faced with disaster, the King, the officials, fathers and sons will all suffer. Can women alone be spared?"[1]

About two thousand years after the compilation of this story, a woman revolutionary, Qiu Jin (1875–1907), wrote the following poem:

> War flames in the north—when will it all end?
> I hear the fighting at sea continues unabated.
> Like the woman of Qishi, I worry about my country in vain;
> It's hard to trade kerchief and dress for a helmet.[2]

The story of the woman of Qishi thus furnishes the modern poet with an apposite allusion to comment on her own times. It allows her to voice her concern for China's early-twentieth-century national crisis and her critique of the gender constraints that prevented her from full political participation. Qiu Jin herself would in time "trade" women's clothing "for a helmet" as she led the planning of a military uprising against the Qing government, an act that would cost her her life. At the founding of the Republic in 1911, she would be exalted as a nationalist martyr. Qiu's life was hence transformed into a modern exemplar story for later readers to draw upon and emulate as she herself had drawn upon the tale of the woman of Qishi.

1

THE CHINESE WOMEN'S BIOGRAPHICAL TRADITION

We begin our introduction with a modern citation of the ancient *Biographies of Women* because it is the urtext of the Chinese women's biographical tradition and, as such, provides the ideological and historical scaffolding for all of the essays in this volume. Liu Xiang's collection of 125 biographies generated a major tradition that dominated Chinese writing and thinking about womanhood from the time of its compilation in 34 BCE through and beyond Qiu Jin's day at the turn of the twentieth century. It served as the template for the women's biography section in dynastic histories—the earliest extant example being Fan Ye's *History of the Later Han (Hou Hanshu)*—for local histories, and for a plethora of genres of didactic texts and literati writings for over two millennia.

The *Biographies* has been translated into English, and in recent years Liu's text and the traditions of official women's biographies it spawned have been the subject of at least two book-length studies in English.[3] With the exception of this scholarship, however, to date scholars who have studied China's rich tradition of life writings and given authoritative definitions of Chinese biographical genres have largely based their analyses on men's biographies.[4] The specificities of women's biography and its place within the Chinese historical tradition have yet to be systematically examined.[5]

This volume is the first to attempt such a systematic study. It heralds the emergence of Chinese women's biography as a field with its own historical significance and scholarly integrity, its own methodological protocols and research possibilities. Nurtured by the now well-established field of Chinese women's history and literature, the essays that follow bring together a critical mass of scholarship on women's biography that spans the two millennia of the Chinese women's biographical tradition and represents a diversity of disciplines and interdisciplinary approaches.[6]

WOMEN'S BIOGRAPHIES AS SOURCES
FOR CHINESE HISTORY

Narratives of women's lives discussed in this volume are valuable sources not only for Chinese women's history but for Chinese history as a whole. Essays by authors using different approaches and divergent materials uniformly reveal that women's biographies force us to rethink certain of our scholarly assumptions and revise our understanding of broader historical trends.

While the explicit purpose of the *Biographies of Women* and its later rescensions was to describe, contain, and regulate women's lives, the ultimate objective of these various texts was to mold Chinese culture and morality. Liu Xiang originally compiled his collection to promote empire-wide—not gender-specific—cultivation in Confucian values. Late imperial scholars followed Liu in using tales of upright women to decry decadent social customs and promote a moral vision of politics in their own day. The practice of using women's biography as a means of moral cultivation further extended beyond Confucians. Buddhists, Daoists, and modern nationalists all utilized exemplary narratives as pedagogical tools.

Just as Confucians did not have a monopoly on the use of instructive biography, neither did the admittedly highly influential *Biographies of Women* serve as the exclusive moral template for women in imperial China. Significant challenges to the *Biographies'* ideological hegemony within the tradition of Chinese life writing reflect the often unacknowledged challenges to the philosophical hegemony of Confucianism in Chinese culture. Several chapters in this collection unearth alternate traditions of womanhood and draw on unorthodox genres of "biography." The former include the tradition of "virtuous and talented ladies" (*xianyuan*). Initiated by Liu Yiqing in his fifth century *A New Account of Tales of the World (Shishuo xinyu)*, this tradition developed alongside the lineage of righteous exemplars generated by Liu Xiang's *Lienü zhuan* and brings into sharp relief elements of the Chinese cultural realm that defied Confucian feminine and social norms. In a similar vein, biographical records in a number of the alternate narrative forms examined in this volume offer insights into aspects of private and affective life that are typically ignored in *lienü*-style texts. Tang dynasty epitaphs, for example, shed light on private aspects of women's—and men's—lives, such as emotional bonds and Buddhist piety, that remain largely invisible in canonical biographies more constrained by Confucian precepts.

Most important, this volume collectively demonstrates that Chinese culture, often heralded for its millennia of continuity, was as dynamic as it was continuous. In fact, it was this very dynamism that enabled such continuity. Even the *Lienü zhuan* tradition, which prevailed over challenges to its hegemony and endured for over 2,000 years, was never static. Its most canonical of biographies functioned as media for the ongoing process of cultural self-reproduction in China rather than as immutable cultural artifacts. Those who supported the status quo legitimated themselves by citing ancient precedents and appropriating their own interpretations of familiar exemplar tales into their expanded editions of the *Biographies of Women*. Likewise, critics of the status quo, including Qiu Jin, resignified ancient stories in ways that sanctioned their challenge to contemporary cultural and political authority.

The fluidity of this biographical tradition both reflected and constituted shifting cultural and gender norms over time. While biography's generic purpose—to instruct—remained constant through history, the lessons it was used to impart varied significantly, from promoting multigenerational families in antiquity to increasing cotton production in the communist era, from celebrating chastity martyrs in the late imperial period to eulogizing revolutionary martyrs in the early twentieth century. It was because of the rich interpretive possibilities within each life story that a modern reader such as Qiu Jin could meaningfully appropriate the ancient story of the woman of Qishi and link her own thwarted revolutionary aspirations to this early paragon's keen political frustration. The ways various historical actors like Qiu Jin deployed or contested the biographical tradition at a particular moment in time reveal more about the complexities of that moment than about the enduring influence of a set of unchanging values identified with Liu Xiang's text.

WOMEN'S BIOGRAPHIES AND THE CULT
OF FEMALE CHASTITY

The dynamic nature of the Chinese tradition of women's biography is most dramatically illustrated by a radical shift in its normative emphasis between the tenth and fourteenth centuries, which gave rise to what became known as the late imperial cult of female chastity. Biographical material produced before this shift features multifocal representations of laudable female qualities—including eloquence, public-mindedness, and economic ingenuity. Material from the later periods, in contrast, increasingly emphasizes the strict regulation of female virtue and sexuality in accordance with a highly prescriptive reading of the *Biographies of Women*.

The narrowing of the repertoire of sanctioned female qualities from a wide range in Liu Xiang's original text, which included, in Lisa Raphals's language, "intellectual virtues," to the singular value of wifely fidelity was the product of broader historical forces.[7] These forces included geopolitical anxieties in the Northern (960–1126) and Southern Song dynasties (1127–1279) that were generated by both the political-military threat posed by the Liao, Jin, and Mongol forces, and the social threat posed by these northern nomadic people's sharply contrasting gender norms—threats that became dramatically real when the Northern Song fell to the Jin and the Southern Song was conquered by the Mongol Yuan (1260–1368).[8] These externally generated anxieties were compounded by internally generated ones as rates of female literacy increased over this period, particularly in the late Ming dynasty (1368–1644).[9] A second conquest dynasty, the Qing (1644–1911) further—if often ambivalently—developed the system of imperial rewards for faithful maidens and widows by successfully extending it to commoners in a period of rapid demographic growth and social instability. The result was a continued intensification of the chastity cult.[10]

The increasingly strident, public, and official endorsements of wifely fidelity from the Song through the Qing dynasties, as well as the plethora of exemplar tales it spawned in literati writings and in dynastic and local histories, underline the effectiveness of women as vessels of the symbolic and of women's biographies as vehicles for normative pronouncements. This symbolic and normative role was particularly pronounced in times of political and cultural crises that often coincided with dynastic or regime transitions. Changes in definitions of female virtue were, thus, both reflections and constituents of wider historical trends.

GENRE CONSIDERATIONS

In our examination of the historical complexity and significance of Chinese narratives of women's lives, we proceed from the assumption that "biography" is a shorthand term, a convenient, conventional English translation. It carries its own generic expectations, including, for example, chronological structure and psychological development, that are not fulfilled by the Chinese material. Rather, this material is composed of a variety of traditional forms, usually brief sketches of at most a few pages in length. These sketches serve particular social and cultural functions that require them to detail only some facets—rather than the complete unfolding—of an individual's life. To clarify this distinction and outline the distinguishing characteristics of Chinese biographical forms, we briefly describe the chief subgenres in the Chinese tradition of life writing here (the interested reader will find a full list of genre terms in appendix A).

The masterpiece of official, formal biography (*zhuan*) is found in Sima Qian's *Records of the Grand Historian* (*Shiji*). Written from 109 to 91 BCE, it includes seventy chapters of individual or linked lives. Except for one chapter on the reign of Empress Lü, there is no counterpart for women's biography in Sima Qian's magnum opus.[11]

Collected biographies of women's lives began in 32 BCE with Liu Xiang's *Lienü zhuan*, as previously noted. While the women's biographical tradition overlaps with men's to some extent, its outstanding characteristic is its organization by chapters devoted to specific virtues. The overwhelming majority of women's *zhuan* attached to dynastic histories or local gazetteers "are line items devoid of narrative detail, even though they appear under headings that are conventionally translated as 'biography' (*zhuan*)" (Mann, this volume). These highly formulaic entries are not meant to narrate a life but to highlight the important deeds that demonstrate a specific woman's exemplary virtue.

Parallel to the official biography is the private biography, a popular genre since at least the eleventh century. This genre includes biographical sketches typically written by family members, close friends, or private scholars not appointed by the government. Often written to attain or demonstrate literary merit, these sketches were frequently commissioned by the family of a recently deceased individual and would ultimately be included in the author's collected writings. In other instances these informal biographies were written as draft versions to be submitted later as material for official biography. They typically contain records of the deceased's virtuous behavior similar to those found in more formal *zhuan*, but also intimate anecdotes that would be inappropriate in more official biographies.

The Chinese obituary/mortuary tradition also contains rich biographical material, including epitaphs, eulogies, and funerary essays. These materials are either carved in stone, buried with the deceased, or erected in front of the tomb. While this memorial culture is generally conventional and didactic, it often renders a fuller picture of women's lives than does formal biography.

Just as Chinese and Western notions of biography differ radically, Western autobiography does not have a ready corollary in the Chinese tradition until modern times. The most apposite counterparts are found in the Chinese poetic tradition and in posthumous literary collections. These collections represent the individual's literary corpus and were understood as a reflection of his or her internal landscape. They typically include prefaces and postscripts written by notable writers that supply both biographical information on the author of the collection and autobiographical information on the author of the preface.

METHODOLOGICAL APPROACHES

The generic particularities of Chinese women's life narratives have obliged us to develop our own research methods and reading strategies, and the dynamism of the Chinese women's biographical tradition has required us to craft carefully historicized tools of analysis.

The modes of biographical analysis elaborated by scholars of China thus far have, as previously noted, focused on biographies of men and are only applicable on the most general level to the study of biographies of women. Feminist scholarship on Western women's biography, which has yielded impressive textual discoveries and often inspiring theoretical reflections over the past decades, has also been of limited value for our project.[12] More recent innovations in scholarship and critical theory on the Romanticism-inspired Western biographical tradition, while of great interest, again rarely offer methods applicable to the Chinese tradition.[13] The need to formulate methods versatile enough to encompass the richness and distinctiveness of the Chinese women's biographical tradition is what has brought us together in this volume.

A key issue that emerged from our research as central to the study of Chinese women's biography concerns how to understand the subjects in these life stories. Some of us understand the scholar's task as principally to recover any vestiges of a historical actor's subjecthood while remaining mindful of the discursive parameters within which this subjecthood was formed. When the biographical record is limited or formulaic, as it most often is in the Chinese case, we must both interpret the silences and omissions in orthodox texts and find new, unorthodox sources that may provide access to fragments of the subject's story. In contrast, a number of us, faced with the elusiveness of any kind of unified authentic self in these biographical materials—whether formal or informal—abandoned the quest for the interiority of our biographees altogether. We focus instead on examining the cultural projects that were so ubiquitous in the production of Chinese women's biography.

Our research thus led us to the heart of an important debate in Western feminist philosophy concerning subjectivity, selfhood, and agency. This debate was at its most acute in the mid-1990s when the troubled relationship between feminism and postmodernism was at its apex. To summarize schematically: in the postmodern critique the subject is an effect constituted through a chain of linguistic signification, while feminist critical theory insists on autonomy and self-reflective subjectivity as crucial to its political goals.[14] Judith Butler, as a postmodern feminist, stakes out a theoretically promising position with recourse to both critiques: "To be constituted by language is to be produced within a given network of power/discourse which is open to resignification, redeployment, subversive citation from within and interruption and inadvertent convergence within such networks."[15] Could a biographical subject, such as the late imperial faithful maiden who is constituted by the cultural project of female chastity and the prevalent literati discourse, still be—as Butler suggests—a critical subject?

Bearing these key issues in mind and confronting the unique challenges of their historical materials, the contributors to this volume employ three, often overlapping and mutually inclusive, reading strategies. Any one author often relies on more than one strategy.

The first is a close interpretive and contextually situated reading of various types of formal biographies. The premise of this strategy is that most biographical writing on Chinese women's lives is convention-bound and highly formulaic. The only voices that can possibly be recuperated are not those of the biographical subjects but of the biographies' authors, who were generally male. Rather than lament these limitations, we attempt to overcome them by focusing on what these texts can fruitfully reveal about the larger cultural and world making projects that informed the representation of women's lives at a particular point in time.

Our second strategy circumvents the silences in and limitations of formal biographical texts by seeking out new, noncanonical sources of information on women's lives. These sources include fiction, whose boundaries with nonfiction were more porous in imperial China than they are in our contemporary world; personal letters, which add new dimensions to our understanding of officially recorded lives; epitaphs, which can serve as countertexts to either more or less canonical sources; poetry, with its above-mentioned autobiographical tendencies; prefaces to poetry collections; and oral interviews.

The third strategy involves seeking out texts authored *by* women. Unearthing materials in which women express themselves in their own words allows us to overcome at least some of the limitations of typical *lienü*-style narratives in which women are exclusively represented through their actions. While such female-authored biographical—or autobiographical—texts are less abundant than historians of women would hope and often remain bound by existing gender scripts, researchers familiar with the rich Chinese source base and not bound by strict generic definitions can locate and fruitfully analyze such documents.

STRUCTURE OF THE VOLUME

These three reading strategies structure the volume: the first is most intensively used in Part II, "Biography as Cultural Project," the second in Part III, "Alternative 'Biographical' Sources," and the third in the final subsection of Part III, "In Her Own Voice." Part I highlights the key meth-

odological and philosophical issue that is implicit—to differing degrees—
in each of the subsequent chapters.

Methodological and Philosophical Reflections: Probing Silences, Questioning Interiority

In Part I, Susan Mann urges us to find new modes of accessing fragments
of a biographical subject's story. Using her own close reading of a number of Qing dynasty texts as an example, she asks us to scrutinize, as she
herself does, a range of sources, from less formal biographical sketches or
"records of deeds" (*xinglüe, xingshu, xingshi*) to inscriptions on paintings
and birthday greetings. Mann encourages us not merely to interpret the
"noise" that the authors of these various materials want us to hear but to
use our own historical knowledge and imagination to fill in the gaps and
silences in biographical narratives. Certain of these silences are the result
of convention—authors rarely described furniture and home decoration,
for example, details of daily life that are of intense interest to scholars of
material culture today. Other omissions are the result of prevailing norms
that discouraged frivolous discussions of clothing, fashion, and personal
appearance in biographies of upright exemplars. The most glaring dearth
of information for scholars of the early twenty-first century, however, is
the product of Chinese cultural and generic taboos against the discussion
of family discord or of matters pertaining to the body and sexual practices.

In contrast, Gail Hershatter calls "into question the existence, or at
least the presumed shape, of interiority itself" and suggests that the effort
to reconstruct a unified authentic self is more a reflection of our own
late-twentieth- and early-twenty-first-century sensibilities than it is of
the concerns of the authors or the reality of the subjects of our various
biographical texts. She is driven to this conclusion not by the noises or
silences she encountered in biographical texts but by the oral interviews
she conducted with communist labor models in the People's Republic of
China. In probing these women's self-narrated tales with their emphasis
on service, self-sacrifice, and sexual purity, Hershatter uncovers vestiges
of the chastity cult—one of the most powerful forces in the constitution
of the late imperial female subject—and draws telling parallels between
these mid-twentieth-century labor models and self-effacing Ming-Qing
exemplars of female virtue.

The tension between the approaches highlighted in these two essays—
the scholar's urge to "know" the subject of her inquiry, and the skeptic's
awareness of the limitations both of our ability to fully apprehend the past
and of the sources we rely on for access to that past—informs much of the

volume. While the three reading strategies according to which the rest of the collection is shaped do not resolve this tension, they highlight it in productive ways.

Biography as Cultural Project

Five chapters focus not on accessing the personal subjecthood of their biographical subjects but on identifying and probing the logic of the world-making projects that framed those subjects at a certain point in time.

Harriet Zurndorfer's chapter opens Part II, which is otherwise organized chronologically, because it offers the reader elemental insights into the tradition of Liu Xiang's *Biographies of Women*, a crucial point of reference for the entire volume. Zurndorfer discusses different editions of the text and the commentarial tradition it spawned. She then reads an early–nineteenth-century annotated version of the *Lienü zhuan* against the life of its female author, Wang Zhaoyuan, as presented in Wang's chronological biography and other sources. In Zurndorfer's retelling, Wang is able to assert agency in what one would expect to be a highly prescriptive realm of scholarly inquiry. Rather than be limited in her research by the ideological parameters of the canonical *Lienü zhuan*, she was able to resignify the ancient compilation of biographies as a site of evidential scholarship (*kaozheng*) and use it to assert her own abilities as a *kaozheng* scholar.

In chapter 4, Nanxiu Qian offers a historical comparison of the *Lienü zhuan* tradition with the *xianyuan* tradition or genre of women's biographies advanced in the *Shishuo xinyu* and in later *Shishuo* imitations. In so doing, she highlights rarely acknowledged elements of the Chinese cultural realm that directly challenged Confucian orthodoxy. While Qian's focus is on the early imperial period, her essay contributes to our understanding of the context for the narrowing of conceptions of women's virtue in the late imperial period. She suggests that this contraction reflects a broader retrenchment of cultural resources available to represent women. Whereas in the early and medieval periods *xian* was defined as "virtuous and talented" and served as an alternative to the already more restrictive *lie*, she argues, by the late imperial period the definition of *xian* had been confined to the sense of "worthy" with an exclusive focus on "virtue."

Weijing Lu maps debates over the propriety of the actions of Ming and Qing dynasty faithful maidens (*zhennü*)—young women who sacrifice their lives for their sick, dying, or dead fiancés—onto debates over Confucian ritual propriety. She shows how biographies of this unique category of woman became a complex site for discursive debates and metaphorical identification among *male* scholars and intellectuals, and she uncovers a world where ritual, philosophical, ethical, and gender meanings were heatedly contested rather than uniformly accepted.

Joan Judge offers a close reading of the textual filiations and paratextual frames of a 1908 expanded edition of the *Biographies of Women* by a male scholar, Wei Chengbo (Xiyuan, Lianshang, fl. 1908). Wei's collection is evidence of how the "end" of the *lienü* tradition of women's biographies figured in the early-twentieth-century politics of culture: the same faithful maidens examined in Weijing Lu's chapter, for example, remained potent instruments for moral and political critique in the context of late Qing constitutional reforms. Read in tandem with his reformist writings on law and his more conventional palace poetry, Wei's commentaries on the lives of exemplars further demonstrate how easily Confucian cultural ideals and national reform agendas coexisted at a distant remove from the rising revolutionary fervor.

Hu Ying's chapter brings us closer to this revolutionary fervor in its rereading of three historical and ideological phases in commemorative writings on Qiu Jin's life from the immediate aftermath of her execution in 1907 to the New Culture period and the 1930s and 1940s. Tracing the profound historical and philosophical taproots of these biographies, Hu demonstrates that modern martyrology can only be understood by grasping the complex ways traditional morality was recuperated within it. As she negotiates the cultural byways through which her famed historical subject was transformed into a spectacular revolutionary martyr, she also struggles to make sense of—and to better understand how Qiu's biographers made sense of—China's revolutionary moment.

Alternative "Biographical" Sources

The eight essays in this section probe the gaps between formal biographies and the greatly varied and largely untapped aggregate of texts on women's lives that do not readily conform to our expectation of a full-length biography.

Epitaphs and fiction. Ping Yao demonstrates that recorded and transmitted, as well as newly excavated, epitaphs provide invaluable insights into certain aspects of the daily lives of elite women—and men—in the capital and urban regions of the Tang dynasty. These sources include discussion of the emotions and Buddhist practice, topics that are silenced in Confucian narratives. Yao distills information on everyday life gleaned from several thousands of epitaphs and maps it to form larger social and demographic patterns. She also finds that while the epitaphs underscore features of the

Tang polity and society that are familiar to us such as the monopoly on power of the great clans and the prevalence of Buddhism, they also raise new questions about, for example, the nature of the social devastation caused by the mid-eighth-century An Lushan Rebellion.

Beverly Bossler's essay delineates one aspect of the radical shift in conceptions of women's virtue that began in the mid- and culminated in the late imperial period. Creatively using sources that blur the lines between fiction and nonfiction, she argues that that the circulation of (fictional) biographies/stories of courtesans in the Northern Song helped legitimize the public circulation of writings on upper-class faithful wives. She further demonstrates that courtesan tales provided new generic models for, and introduced new elements of romance into, narratives of wifely fidelity.

Katherine Carlitz contrasts mid-Ming epitaphs for women to the vernacular fiction that they may have read or heard. She draws materials from the Chenghua (1465–1488) through Jiajing (1522–1567) eras, a century that saw the maturation and hegemony of the civil-service examinations. Epitaphs, which were in their own way fictions, described model lives that would contribute to a family's rise within the imagined community of examination-takers. Apparently playful stories, by contrast, allowed society to express the inherent tensions in the family model that women were charged to uphold: problems of sexual attraction, disobedient daughters, competition between wives and concubines. All of the stories that Carlitz analyzes have roots in earlier dynasties, showing us that women faced durable problems requiring repeated attempts at imaginative resolution.

Diaries and letters. Two chapters demonstrate the usefulness of supplementing official biographies with more private sources where they can be found. Patricia Ebrey reads the official Song biography of the Empress Xiang against the diary of a member of the Council of State. This document describes otherwise muted aspects of Empress Xiang's domestic life and sheds light on the intrigues of Northern Song court politics.

Ann Waltner juxtaposes two genres related to the life of the female Buddhist and Daoist mystic Tanyangzi—a formal biography *of* her and recently discovered letters *by* her—to demonstrate that chaste widowhood, family loyalty, and religious practice appeared to her as a seamless whole. Waltner's careful reading highlights the differences between these sources and allows her to draw tentative conclusions about genre and gendered voice. The case of Tanyangzi further underlines that Buddhists and Daoists—not only Confucians—used biography as a social pedagogical tool: Tanyangzi transmitted her teachings not by disseminating her doctrine but by publishing her biography.

In her own voice? The authors of chapters 13–15 examine women's self-narration in three different genres: poetry, prefaces to poetry collections, and oral interviews. Questioning how women constituted themselves and other women as historical actors, they attempt to draw closer to the ever-elusive interiority of the historical female Chinese subject.

Wilt Idema taps a major but as yet underused biographical and autobiographical source on women (as on men) throughout Chinese history—poetry—to bring the late Ming woman, Bo Shaojun, to life. He examines a series of 100 of Bo's poems (only 81 of which are extant). While Bo wrote these poems to mourn her husband's death, Idema probes what they reveal about her own unique mode of self-expression.

Ellen Widmer also turns to a genre that is rarely associated with biography but, nonetheless, often highly biographical: prefaces to poetry collections. She begins by observing that women were rarely the authors of texts formally labeled *zhuan* or biography. She nonetheless goes on to argue that women did write biographies and autobiographies in the form of prefaces to other women's poetry collections. She analyzes the gendered insights these texts offer by comparing them to male-authored prefaces.

Yu Chien-ming uses interviews and oral history to gain access to three mainland women's subjective experiences of the Sino-Japanese War and its aftermath when they followed their husbands to a new life in Taiwan. This methodology allows her to challenge received narratives on the impact of the Sino-Japanese war on women's subjectivity and on mid-twentieth century notions of identity. When Yu's essay is read in tandem with Gail Hershatter's, the pair underline the diverse results that one research tool—in this case oral history—can yield. While Hershatter concludes that the flat responses coaxed from the labor models she interviewed reveal no traces of subjective interiority, Yu's interviewees provide us with intimate details of women's romantic and daily lives. Whatever the source of this discrepancy—geography (Hershatter's interviewees are in mainland China, Yu's in Taiwan), interviewing techniques, the ideological overlay of mainland society—it reveals that the outcome of a single method of approaching women's lives can be as varied as the lives themselves.

We now invite the reader to turn to the individual chapters. Each makes a unique contribution to the emerging field of Chinese women's biography and all are in conversation with each other. At the same time, every contribution is a scholarly work with its own integrity, rich in details and arguments that go beyond the scope of this brief introduction. Each essay intersects with other fields of inquiry—whether *Lienü zhuan* scholarship, late imperial poetry, Buddhist and Daoist practice, or oral history. Singly and collectively, all demonstrate how the analysis of biographical narratives on Chinese women adds new dimensions to feminist scholarship, raises innovative questions about the methods of and sources for historical scholarship, and deepens our understanding of Chinese culture.

PART I

Methodological and Philosophical Reflections

Probing Silences, Questioning Interiority

1. Biographical Sources and Silences

Susan Mann

The rich Chinese biographical record is full of silence on many subjects. Details of furniture and home decoration, clothing and fashion, and personal appearance, for example, receive little attention in accounts of individual women's lives. These aspects of a visual culture, so necessary to lively biography in English-language narratives, were not so important to Chinese readers and writers of biography. What they wanted to hear about were *deeds*. From the sublime to the mundane, a woman's deeds were the measure of her moral character. Talent also drew comment, at least in some times and places. In narrating a woman's life, and describing her talent, her own words are often quoted as if verbatim, in patches of brisk monologue or dialogue, and lines from her poems may be precisely reprinted. These records of deeds, talent, and words can make noisy biographical sources, especially when the historian juxtaposes as many sources as possible and listens closely.

BIOGRAPHICAL MATERIALS IN CLASSICAL CHINESE: NOISE AND SILENCE

When writing about Chinese women's lives in English, a contemporary historian is on one level quite spoiled. Biographical writings on women in classical Chinese sources are abundant. These range from the meticulously documented short records of "exemplary women" appended to every local history and dynastic history to much more detailed accounts in family memoirs and eulogies. Women's published literary collections include poems written by and exchanged with the poet, along with prefaces and other encomia composed for the printed edition. Women's lives and their writings also come in for comment in books of poetry criticism (*shihua*).

As a bonus, a woman's published poetry collection often includes margin notes by the compiler or editor, who was usually a male relative (father, brother, son, nephew, grandson). These cryptic asides elaborate the circumstance of the poem, the feelings of the author at the time, or the nostalgia represented by the events described. Such sources open a door into a woman's intimate private world of family and friends, with a kind of intense but quiet noise that can be mesmerizing.

Ironically, by contrast, the formal biographical records of women's public honors—particularly the award of imperial inscriptions of merit (*jingbiao*) for chaste widowhood or martyrdom, or the receipt of posthumous honorific titles—produced some of the least interesting prose and the most cavernous silences in the genre of biography. Announcements of these honors, with vital statistics about the women who won them (natal surname, marital family, native place(s), offices and/or titles of close male kin, famous sons, etc.) appear ad nauseam in local gazetteers and genealogies, as addenda to biographies of male relatives, and in official histories. The overwhelming majority of them, however, are line items devoid of narrative detail, even though they appear under headings that are conventionally translated as "biography" (*zhuan*). To be sure, some collections of women's short biographies—anthologies such as Wanyan Yun Zhu's mid-nineteenth-century *Langui bao lu*—present lively little tales of martyred and heroic and virtuous women, some of which (in the case of Yun Zhu's anthology) hint at gossipy subjects such as spousal or in-law abuse.[1] But standard-issue "exemplary women's biography" (*lienü zhuan*) drew bitter complaints from the mid-Qing historian Zhang Xuecheng, who satirized their formulaic quality.[2]

Arthur Wright, an admirer of the "exemplary woman" biography, praised the original *Lienü zhuan* by the Han scholar Liu Xiang. Wright admired the way stories of exemplary women dramatized *choices* among roles that a biographical subject makes, and also *role performance* and *shifts in roles* resulting from aging, political crisis, or other ruptures or challenges.[3] The plot line of the best of these women's biographies begins with her life as a young girl, then tracks crucial choice-points that arise as her life proceeds through marriage (or not, in the case of faithful maidens or nuns), wifely duties, childrearing, service to in-laws, widowhood, and death. Following Wright's analysis of role performance and role shifts and choices in women's biographies, we find several themes. Role performance may feature work, especially embroidery and spinning and weaving, but also saving and spending (that is, frugality and generosity), or service, especially care for a mother-in-law or teaching fatherless sons. Role performance may foreground childhood precocity as well as mature wisdom, and talent in reading or writing. For role shifts, betrothal/marriage and life crisis events (landmark birthdays and deaths, especially death of a spouse or, less frequently, child) supply turning points that biographers seize upon to structure their narratives.

All kinds of biographical material can be plumbed for these themes: not only standard biographies (*zhuan*) and formal eulogies (*muzhiming*) but also (or especially) less formal biographical sketches or "records of deeds" (*xinglüe, xingshu, xingshi*). Critical notes on poetry, inscriptions on paintings, prefaces to poetry collections, and birthday greetings are stuffed with biographical detail, sometimes closely observed.[4] Moreover, as Beverly Bossler has noted, biographical narratives of women's lives were often written by men whose deep emotional attachment inspired unusual candor.[5] Male writers also liked to use women's lives as a forum for examining problems of their own, and they often held up women as an example to underscore men's shortcomings.[6]

Biographical materials on women's lives can surely be noisy spots in the Chinese historical record. Still, reconstructing a woman's biography too often hinges on the fortuitous discovery of a text that makes unexpected noise, as the following discussion will show. The examples below illustrate the importance of juxtaposing different sources to create noise where silence might otherwise reign. The themes represented include womanly talent and womanly work, the virtue of widows, and other inspiring examples of women caught in family crises that try their virtue. As these stories show, biographical sources sometimes make noise when one least expects to hear it. The historian needs to pay attention.

PRECOCITY AND MARRIAGE

Observations about childhood precocity are almost *de rigueur* in stories of elite women whose lives are preserved in the historical record, creating a noisy drumbeat that reveals much about the conditions of learned women's lives. Precocity meant that many a young girl entered early into the fray of literary acclaim and reputation, where her work was judged and discussed. The eyes of the literary world followed closely the literary progress of the daughters of notable writers, both male and female, applying pressure that was not unlike the pressure suffered by sons as they were groomed for the civil-service examinations. Thus, who gets mentioned and who is left out lends a barb to seemingly offhand remarks, such as these by the nineteenth-century poet and critic Shen Shanbao (1807–

62), commenting on the talented daughters of the poet Zhang Wanying (1800–after 1861): "Wanying's daughters Wang Caipin and Wang Cailü [misprint for Caifan] stood out from the others in their cultivation and intelligence. At the age of eleven or twelve, they were able to create proper rhymes . . . "[7] This innocuous conventional praise, which we might dismiss as a puff for the nieces of a friend (Shanbao was closely associated at that time with Wanying's eldest sister, Qieying), instantly discounts the writings of Wanying's other three daughters, two of whom are known to have produced poetry collections. An interesting detail also emerges in an error: Caipin, Wanying's eldest daughter, achieved some acclaim in her lifetime and her collected poems survive. Cailü, on the other hand, was the youngest daughter and the only one whose birth mother was not Wanying but a concubine. A reader familiar with the courtesy name (*zi*) of Wanying's girls would have caught Shen Shanbao's mistake: she obviously meant to refer to Caifan, the second eldest.[8] At the time of writing Shen Shanbao was living in Beijing, far away from the Changzhou home of the Zhang and Wang families, but since her critical opinion carried great weight among Jiangnan women writers, one suspects that this error would have been caught and rectified in a subsequent printing, had the Taiping rebellion not disrupted flows of information and communication during the time Shen's work first circulated.

Shen's innocent mistake and the singling out of two of Wanying's five daughters remind us that commentators facing sibling sets of many talented women were challenged to mention and praise all, in order to avoid slighting some. This makes one appreciate Bao Shichen's (1775–1855) evenhanded remarks on the writing of Zhang Qi's (1765–1833) four daughters (the youngest of whom was Wanying, named above, the mother of Wang Caipin and her sisters):

> Guanying's is detached and lofty (*youjun*). Lunying's is edgy and vigorous (*pai' ao*). Wanying's is harmonious and elegant (*heya*). In other words, each partakes of some element of their father's genius. As for Qieying, her writing is exceedingly sentimental (*chanmian feice*) without being trite (*bushi yu yu*). In choosing her words and in describing events (*zhuci bishi*), she always expresses her deepest beliefs. Coming as she does from a family of eminence and influence, she nevertheless produces poems that are highly original. Their form is beautiful yet they attain great heights.[9]

Bao Shichen here gives a bow to Qieying, as the oldest of these four talented daughters. He finds something distinctive to say about the work of each of the siblings, while explicitly linking the four daughters' talent to their *father's* learning, in contrast to Shen Shanbao, who stressed the transmission of talent from mother or aunt to daughter.

In other words, comments on precocious young women can serve simultaneously to silence or foreground other women and to compliment one or more of the parents. Praise of a young girl's precocity could also be used to comment on her unfulfilled promise as an adult:

> She was innately intelligent and an excellent poet even without
> any training. By the time I was seven or eight *sui*, she had already
> completed a portfolio full of poems. After she married (in 1815), her
> household duties prevented her from composing poetry, and so most
> of the poems in this collection date from before that year.[10]

This brother's observation about his elder sister's lapse into literary silence at marriage encodes several female virtues: devotion to familial service, loyalty to spouse and family, and even self-denial. What may be implicit, and cannot be known without reading more into a particular family's records, is whether or not this is also a kind of gossip implying criticism of the spouse or in-laws, who have somehow failed to nurture or stood in the way of a young woman's continued literary accomplishment. Notice that in this rhetorical strategy, the natal family is the family nurturing "family learning" (*jiaxue*), while the marital family inadvertently (perhaps) silences it.

On hearing this kind of noise in the sources, a historian suddenly understands the pressures that beset young women of upper-class families where education was the norm and poetic talent the expectation. A girl with many sisters was in competition with them from the time she began to read. Family contests where poems were exchanged, or "linked" using the same rhyme pattern, or where a "thing" was named and a "poem on the thing" (*yong wu shi*) produced, were occasions for sibling rivalry. Collected "poems on things" by several cousins were sometimes published together in family collections, where readers could draw their own conclusions about who excelled and who was mediocre. Moreover, as a young poet's work drew attention beyond her family, anthologists outside the family intruded as arbiters of in-house family competition, suggesting that comments in poetry criticism must have been as eagerly (or anxiously) awaited as a book review. By the same token, the same noise exposes pressures on anthologists and writers of poetry criticism (*shihua*) who, like the compilers of local gazetteers, had to contend with their obligations to friends and powerful patrons as well as with their own awareness of the delicacy of their judgments and the weight they carried in the context of family dynamics as well as beyond the family in the form of cultural capital. Sisterly pride, implicit hierarchies of age and talent, and the author's own felt need to produce appreciative phrases that are just right—balanced precisely to the occasion and the sensibilities of his audience—all sound in the noise from such sources.

WOMANLY WORK

Maureen Robertson has shown how work and writing were linked in women's self-presentations, such that poems were written only when work was done.[11] But we can also find examples of women for whom womanly work became a displacement for writing, as in the case of Zhang Qi's wife Tang Yaoqing (1763–1829), who—despite her evident talent, we are told by her biographers—did not write poems until she was past her fortieth year. As her daughter Qieying recalled:

> My mother was extremely clever. She was a genius with bits of colored silk, which she could fashion into flowers, birds, and landscapes that were utterly realistic. Once when she was amusing herself, she created a lantern out of an eggshell and decorated it with a pieced-silk painting titled *Streams and Mountains*. The lofty mountains reached into the clouds and overhanging cliffs towered above. Atop the mountains was a Buddhist temple with seven levels, and on the left side a multistory pagoda. The vista was brilliantly clear, with golds and azures glowing like jewels. The mountainous rocks supplied shade from the glare of the variegated profusion of color. At the foot of a hill on the east lay the green leaves of great slant-cut trees, a comely woodcutter wandering, singing, in their midst. Along level banks and twisting torrents, hanging willows and blue-green peach trees gleamed around a small village. A tiny boat came into view, bobbing along the water as if seeking directions from the ferryman on a distant bank. Layers of mountain peaks and high cliffs surrounded the stream on three sides, as if they were a ladle out of which the stream poured into the sea. There was also a long bridge on the east which hung down over vast forests, deeply shading a mountain kiosk as if to shelter it. By the tips of the tree branches, an imposing pavilion rose. The stream's clear water flowed fresh and free among duckweed and rocks. All of this was brilliantly captured in just a few inches of space. There were eighteen mountains, eleven dwellings and buildings, five persons, two bridges, two fish, seven rocks in the water. The vista was surpassing, as if you were lying on your back gazing at the sky, as if you were viewing a heavenly scene, brilliant and delightful to the spirit, overwhelming to the eye, so that you could not begin to spell out all of its detail.[12]

This lush expressiveness in cloth and color contrasts with Tang Yaoqing's slim surviving written work, a single *juan* of 32 short poems.[13] Another striking thing about this daughter's memories of her mother's handwork is Qieying's attention to the aesthetic, even spiritual, qualities of her mother's silk creations. This kind of noise is rare in women's biographies or memoirs, which stress labor and the long late hours of spinning or weaving, rather than the beauty of the product. Taken together, this juxtaposition of noise (about embroidery) and silence (about poetry) invites the historian to ponder a telling detail of Tang Yaoqing's biographical narrative: the fact that she did not begin to write poetry until she was in her early forties. Perhaps embroidery was the only creative outlet that felt comfortable to a young woman with a strict upbringing (other sources tell us that Yaoqing's father was a notorious stickler for the proper rituals).[14]

TALENT

Talented women's poems receive more attention in prefaces and biographies than do women's arts in other media, particularly music, painting, and calligraphy. Here is an arresting account of the art of the calligrapher Zhang Lunying (1798--after 1868), Zhang Qi's third daughter, written by her younger brother:

> Every morning when she rose, she would wash and then, leaning on her desk, she would write several hundred characters. Whether her door was open and she was dressed for the day, or whether her door was closed and she had retired for the night, she would still be writing hundreds of characters. Even when she had gone to bed, if she did not fall asleep, she would get up and write some more. When her family chided her for not getting enough rest, she said, "If I let a day go by without writing, I feel that I have lost something [or, that I am somehow remiss]. I cannot stop myself [*wu yi ri buzuo shu ruo you suo shi yu ba buneng yi*]."[15]

And:

> My sister had a mild disposition and she was so slight that she barely filled her clothes. Yet when she applied her brush, she became strong and robust, with bold and weighty strokes that could not be contained. She could execute big square characters with a spirit and talent that were overwhelming; her work was grave and sedate, yet of exalted beauty. When she wrote in the *li* style "official" script, her style was vigorous and free, and the force of the brush was steady and deep . . . [16]

Just as Tang Yaoqing's silk work may have been an alternative outlet for aesthetic expression she could not release in poetry, so Zhang
Lunying's calligraphy seems to have played multiple roles in her own
psychic and social development. Elsewhere in her brother's memoirs of
his sister, we learn that Lunying did not begin composing poetry until
after she passed the age of thirty, that her obsession with calligraphy was
a way of dispelling her grief at the death of her elder sister Guanying,
and that at the height of her success, "not a day passed without people begging for some of her work." Lunying, it turns out, became the
housekeeper and household manager for her brother after she was left
a widow and he a widower. She instructed her nieces and nephews and
adopted children in calligraphy and poetry, and (family writings imply)
her income kept the family afloat during the years while her brother
Yuesun was still trying to establish his own career. Lunying's obsessive
productivity, in other words, might have been driven not only by love of
her art, but also by her awareness of its economic value to her struggling
relatives.

In juxtaposing accounts of Lunying's calligraphic genius against biographical accounts of her spouse's life, we learn further that her husband
did not believe that calligraphy was a suitable pursuit for a woman,
and that he was only brought around to an appreciation of his wife's
art after some years of persuasion, as described (again) by Lunying's
younger brother in a biography of his brother-in-law: "My father personally instructed [my sister Lunying] in the calligraphy of the Northern
Dynasties. Sun Jie [her husband] was at first displeased by this, believing
that it was unseemly for a woman to do [*fei furen shi*]. But when my sister
had completed her studies, he reluctantly pronounced that she was worthy
of continuing her father's teachings. He would often take out her poems
and calligraphy to show his friends, always with great delight."[17] Here
we see a subtle comment on the lingering vestiges of prejudice against
women's arts within the ranks of the scholar class, perhaps even a slight
criticism of Sun Jie's own upbringing, in this case successfully overcome
by prolonged exposure to more enlightened values. It is also worth noting
that Sun Jie himself was a failure as a scholar. After his father's death, he
took up residence in his wife's family, where he was employed at home as
a tutor for his nephews and nieces. Praise of Lunying's art and her success may thus point silently to her husband's lack of talent. The telling of
women's lives to criticize men is a biographical strategy to which we shall
return below.

WIDOWHOOD

The trauma of widowhood, a worn-out theme in writings celebrating women's lives, was often described in the evocative but cryptic image of the cedar boat from the *Shijing* (Classic of poetry). But biographies of widows were sometimes splendid venues for melodrama. Here is an excerpt from Zhang Qi's elder brother Zhang Huiyan's (1761–1802) memoir for his paternal grandmother, née Bai, illustrating the artful use of direct quotation:

> My grandfather was a fine scholar but he had difficulty passing the lowest level of the examinations, so his own father sent him north to sit for the Shuntian exams registered as a merchant in Tianjin. Unfortunately, while he was there he became ill and died in the capital. He was thirty-five *sui* at the time. When news of his death reached my grandmother, she was distraught and suicidal. Her father-in-law, my great-grandfather, who was seventy-one *sui* himself, shouted at her: "Heaven! My son and his wife both dead??!" She immediately recovered herself. Then her father-in-law said: "I am old. The children are young. Do you mean to die?" My grandmother wept and begged his pardon, saying: "I dare not." The following year her father-in-law grew ill. As he neared death, he gazed at my grandmother and said tearfully, "I am dying. You and the children share a common fate (*ming*). For every day you live on, they will live too." He paused for a long time, coughed, and said: "Our poverty is dire. We have no one to depend on. If I die, can you survive?" My grandmother wept and replied, "I will live and die with my children." With that, her father-in-law drew his last breath.[18]

But wait, it gets better. Zhang Huiyan's grandmother persevered. She had two daughters, aged twelve and thirteen *sui,* and she put them to work sewing and weaving to bring in money for food. She taught her three sons (aged eleven [Huiyan's father], nine, and six) herself because she could not afford a teacher, saving questions about passages she could not understand for the occasional visit from her late husband's brothers. Then we learn the following:

> Some people said to my grandmother, "Your family is so poor. You should let your sons pursue some other occupation that will support you. If you make them study now, you'll starve before they get anywhere." To which my grandmother replied, "Since the time of my father-in-law and five generations before him, the men in the Zhang family have been scholars. My late husband was following in their footsteps. If my sons end this tradition, I will not be able to face my late father-in-law, who on his deathbed charged them to study."[19]

These words, preserved forever in the family's writings (and first recorded by what means we shall never know), became the mantra celebrating the life of Huiyan's grandmother, and his memoir of her remains one of Zhang Huiyan's best known writings.

Lady Bai's dramatic life as a widow must have been on Zhang Huiyan's mind when he composed his biographical sketch (*shilüe*) for his mother, née Jiang. Recorded with vivid total recall are the following details:

> My mother was nineteen when she married my father. In the ten years that followed she bore four children, two boys and two girls. The second one of each died, leaving only my elder sister and me. Then my father died, and four months later my mother gave birth to my younger brother. My father himself had been orphaned young, and he and his two brothers had worked as teachers to support their own mother, my grandmother. After her death they went their separate ways, and my uncles lived in separate homes in the city. But when my father died, my uncles said: "Our younger brother has died tragically, leaving two young sons. This is our responsibility." But they were poor, too, so they saved what they could and every New Year they would give us money and grain. Meanwhile, my mother and my sister took in sewing and made clothing to support us.
>
> When I was nine my uncle ordered me into the city to study with my elder cousins. After a month I went home for a visit. I arrived in the evening and there was no evening meal; everyone went to bed on an empty stomach. The next morning I was so hungry I couldn't get up. My mother said, "You are not used to being hungry? Your sister and brother and I face this every day." I cried then and my mother cried too. Just then one of my female cousins begged some cash and bought me a sticky rice cake to eat . . .
>
> I lived with my uncle and studied there for four years. When I returned home, my mother had me teach my little brother. My mother and my sister taught embroidery. They would always count their thread to be frugal. Every morning they would start with thirty threads. Then they would steam some rice, and they would continue working at night under a single lamp. My mother and sister sat facing each other; I and my brother would hold our books and lean up against them. The sound of the needles and the sound of reading blended together and echoed each other. After the fourth watch, my sister, my brother, and I would go to bed, and then my mother would retire. . . . [20]
>
> I recall that when I was five, my mother wept constantly for nearly a month. Then suddenly one day she lay down and was very still. I was playing at the foot of her bed and I remember thinking that she must have cried herself to sleep. In a little while my grandmother came and only then did I realize that she had tried to strangle herself with her sash. Fortunately, they were able to revive her. [21]

The slippage in this biography is hard to ignore: the contrast between Huiyan's mother's fortitude and determination (in which she was constantly compared to her mother-in-law) and her despairing recourse to suicide (recalling her mother-in-law's own brief capitulation). Perhaps these slippages or contrasts are introduced by the author precisely to heighten our appreciation for the obstacles overcome, but they are striking in their candor and almost obtrusive in their revelation of human frailty. Equally interesting is the framing of the entire story, which is told through the lens of Zhang Huiyan's guilt. It is a kind of self-remonstrance that, as we see in the following examples, appears often in men's memoirs of women.

FRUGALITY AND GENEROSITY

In his memoir for his late wife, Tang Yaoqing, Zhang Qi recalled her privations and hardship during his long absences from home:

> When I took up my writing implements to travel, first to Zhejiang, later to Anhui, then to Henan and Shandong, and finally to the capital, my earnings were exceedingly thin. I might return once a year, or once every three to five years. Whether or not the family ate during that time was entirely up to her. Between 1808 and 1809, when I was in Shaanzhou and my letters were delayed, winter came and my wife had no padded cotton clothing and nothing at all to get her through the season. The four girls did embroidery and exchanged what they made for rice, and they ate one bowl of gruel a day. I did not reach home again until my fiftieth birthday, in 1813.

Zhang Qi goes on to say that after passing the *juren* exam in 1814, he spent ten years away from home working in the capital. "As for my late wife and my three married daughters, all of them worked cooperatively without the slightest conflict, and when the situation grew dire, my late wife turned to her sons-in-law Zhang Zhengping and Sun Jie and relied on income from assets they pawned so that they could support themselves."[22]

In Zhang Qi's son's biography of his father, the son complains (one would have to call it a complaint) that when he took his mother's body home to be buried after she died (in Guantao, Shandong, where his father was serving as a county magistrate), the family had no house and no land even though his father had held an official position for eight years. "When I spoke to my father about this," wrote Zhang Qi's son, "he responded: 'When a proper gentleman manages his household, his first priority is an ancestral shrine. For decades I have focused on the fact that our family has no shrine. You must go back and arrange for one. Once that is ready, we can think about a house.'"[23] So in his biography of his father, the son recounts how he dutifully built a modest shrine (mostly of straw, he tells us, and not exactly complete) that his father would visit often. In concluding his account of his father's life, the son comments: "My father, who was not good at managing his assets, died without leaving even the means to transport his body home. A gentleman in a nearby city who did not know my father, along with many others [carefully lists names], sent me money so that I could take his body home for burial."[24]

In another memoir for Tang Yaoqing, the relationship between Zhang Qi's inadequacies and his wife's competence is cast somewhat differently by their close family friend (later in-law, who married his daughter to Zhang Qi's surviving son) Bao Shichen:

> In his later years, when Zhang Qi traveled widely, his wife supported herself with her needlework [he mentions her prowess, especially in the appliqué techniques described in more detail above] while also instructing her children, each of whom established a reputation for learning. Then when her husband sought a government office, she took out loans to establish a shrine honoring her mother-in-law as a chaste widow and to bury her mother-in-law properly, so after some years she was able to carry out both of these obligations. She was always abstemious and frugal in feeding and managing the family so that her husband did not have to worry about family matters and could devote himself to pursuing his own goals. As the wife of an official [after she joined Zhang Qi in his posts in Shandong], she shunned fine jewelry and adornment and saved carefully, so that her husband did not have to worry about the family and could achieve his objectives in office. She constantly saved her husband's income, so that she could share what they had with her husband's relatives. When she visited the elderly and the sick, she would take them clothing for summer and winter, always thinking ahead for the long term. All of this was well known to those in her neighborhood.

Bao Shichen makes this point partly to chastise himself for being so slow to grasp the family's straitened circumstances. He enjoyed the Zhang household's hospitality for a long time, even spending six months there at one point, before he finally became aware of Tang Yaoqing's difficulties. Only during a visit to the family home while Qi was sojourning in the capital, when Tang Yaoqing greeted him in the dead of winter wearing thin cotton clothes and pretending nothing was amiss, did the problem dawn on Bao Shichen.[25]

Here Bao Shichen tells a familiar story. How many times must we read about a success-driven scholar whose wife manages the household in his

absence so that he is not "burdened with family matters"? Bao's story could
have carried sharper barbs. He was, after all, not only an old friend but (by
the time he composed the eulogy) also related to Zhang Qi by marriage,
and his gentle criticism of Qi's wooly thinking about money is as kindly as
the comments of Qi's own son. Yet Bao does seem shocked and sobered by
his winter encounter with the shivering Tang Yaoqing ("can any suffering
be greater than this?" he asks himself), perhaps stricken as much by his
own guilt at having taken advantage of the family as by his sympathy for
her. Be that as it may, all of these stories about Tang Yaoqing's savings and
spending are clearly part of a larger and quite noisy critical commentary
on her husband's improvident ways. This use of women's biography to
criticize men (or as self-reproach) is a strikingly familiar one, dating at
least to the earliest stories of Mencius and his mother. Here Bao also gives
us insight into tensions affecting men's relationships with each other, aris-
ing out of their interactions with wives, mothers, or—as in the following
case—daughters of friends or relatives.

For harsher and less allegorical biographies of indirect criticism, Zhang
Xuecheng's (1738–1801) memoirs of the women stand out. One of my
favorite examples is Zhang's short biographical sketch of his two young
female cousins, composed sometime after each died an untimely—and, in
his view, tragic—death.

> My cousin . . . [Zhang's father's brother's son] had two daughters, both
> born to his wife Lady Xun. The elder married a "student of the Imperial
> Academy" [*jiansheng* degree holder] . . . , the younger was betrothed to
> a tribute student [*fusheng*]. . . . Both girls were wise and filial, in keep-
> ing with their upbringing. Yet both, confronting circumstances beyond
> their control, grew depressed, languished, and died. How pitiful!
>
> When I went to the capital for the first time, in 1760 [Zhang would
> have been a young man of about twenty-two at the time], I stayed in
> my cousin's home. His wife served me food and drink with utmost
> solicitude, and their two daughters came out to pay their respects.
> At the time, the elder was thirteen *sui* [i.e., she was about ten years
> younger than Zhang], the younger barely ten. Their bearing was
> severe and upright; although they had been reared in the women's
> apartments, they acted like students in an academy. Their mother,
> who was by then in her fiftieth year, had borne no sons. When we
> male relatives came over to visit her, if the two girls were practicing
> reciting poetry while we were there, the sounds we heard would be
> so elegant and refined that all of us would sit back and sigh.
>
> The next time I returned to the capital, five years had passed. The
> elder daughter had been married into the Hu family as a successor wife
> [i.e., her husband's first wife had died]. The Hu family had grown rich

and influential by procuring salt monopoly privileges for clients in exchange for a handsome fee. The elder daughter was an irreproachable daughter-in-law who waited on her husband's parents with utter reverence; she also looked after the daughter of his late first wife and was kind to his concubine. In time, however, the Hu family moved to Fengrun county, some distance away from the capital. The girl grew despondent longing for her parents. A year later, when she made a trip back to see them, she forced herself to smile and laugh in order to reassure her mother, and when she was asked about her husband's family, she said nothing. Not long afterward, however, she became ill after giving birth to a child, and died. She was barely twenty *sui* [in years, barely nineteen or possibly eighteen]. After her death, her personal maid returned to her natal family and told them that when their daughter waited on her mother-in-law, the younger woman would sometimes gently criticize the older by her own example. Once, for instance, her mother-in-law took the grain she had cooked and exchanged it for melons, then offered some melon to her daughter-in-law. The girl thanked her but declined to eat, saying she feared there would not be enough to serve the rest of the family. [The import of this story appears to be that the mother-in-law had selfishly exchanged the family's staple food for an expensive fruit; by declining to share it, the daughter-in-law was subtly remonstrating with her for her selfishness and possibly, too, for her extravagance.] Her mother-in-law usually accepted what she said, but sometimes she laughed at her for being so extreme, at which times the girl would say that she was far from her parents and dare not be remiss. When she died, bereft and longing for her parents, the Hu family members, young and old, wept bitterly until they lost their voices.

The second daughter, meanwhile, was betrothed in her eleventh year to a man surnamed Zhao. The Zhao had been farmers for generations, and [her fiancé] was the first in his line to receive an education and win the lowest degree of *shengyuan*. When he came to pay his respects to my cousin and his wife, I happened to be visiting. He appeared to me to be a man who was educable, and so I congratulated my cousin and his wife on the match. When in 1767 the elder daughter died in the Hu household, my cousin's wife was so grief-stricken that she became ill and lay in bed day and night. Her younger daughter, who was living with her parents together with her husband, comforted and watched over her mother vigilantly for months, but to no avail— the following year, she died. In the meantime, the family's fortunes declined steadily and my cousin threw himself on anyone who would help him to survive. His younger daughter, by then in her eighteenth year, took charge of the household with great dignity and composure, which only made my cousin love her more dearly than ever. Sometimes when there wasn't enough cooked grain in the house, he wanted the servants to eat less and sip gruel instead. But she would always take gruel before the servants did, saying that they had been together so long that they should always share both the hard times and the good times equally.[26]

Zhang goes on in this vein, explaining how this young cousin was like a granddaughter to his mother when he brought her to visit, and noting freely what a ne'er-do-well her husband was. In the end, inevitably, the younger daughter dies too, like her sister, lonely and unappreciated, and worse, scorned by her in-laws who could not even understand her. Zhang recounts with great bitterness how they made fun of his cousin's devotion to proper family rituals and of her dignified conduct. Perhaps the most telling line in this doleful story, however, is Zhang's homily at the end:

> My cousin's two daughters died before their time and never got what they deserved. Their parents adored them. . . . They were utterly pure (*baixi*). [27] My grandnephew . . . knows the art of physiognomy, and he once said: "These two girls are certain to bring glory upon their families. How unfortunate that they are not boys!" He had no idea that they would come to this. Since ancient times people have known that marrying out a daughter and selecting a son-in-law is a matter that must be approached with the greatest caution![28]

Zhang uses the refracted mirror of these young women's lives to comment on a man's, through elaborate coding. References to salt merchants and license procurement, comments on a farm family's first son to be educated, on the "successor wife" status of the elder daughter and the uxorilocal marriage of the younger daughter, and on the silent grieving of the bereaved mother—juxtaposed against vignettes dramatizing the superior ritual sensibilities of the Zhang girls—all reveal that the Zhang girls married beneath themselves. Who shows up in the mirror as the morally culpable person? Not mother, whose heartsick death is intended as a dramatic critique of her daughters' fate. Clearly the unhappy lives of these two young women reveal to every reader that their father failed them: it was he who decided to marry them into questionable circumstances, obviously—in the case of the elder daughter—ignoring the reputation of the family in the interests of making a powerful connection. In the case of the younger daughter, the father's foremost concern was to "bring in a son-in-law" because there was no male heir in the family. He paid no heed to the considerations that usually governed such arrangements among members of his own circle.[29] Salt merchants and the politics of procuring a salt monopoly privilege were powerful signals of influence and inferior social status in the eyes of the scholar-gentry class. And in Zhang's eyes, marrying out a daughter as a second wife, like engaging a young man from a farm family to enter your own household as a son-in-law, meant a marriage "down" for the bride.

Zhang Xuecheng never wrote a biography of his male cousin, the father of those girls. Instead, as we see, he did something much more telling: he composed not only the daughters' biography above—itself unusual for its detailed attention to the short lives of two otherwise unremarkable young women—but also an extremely long biography of his cousin's wife (the girls' mother—the one who died of grief). That biography holds up an even clearer mirror image of his cousin as a ne'er-do-well—irresponsible, unreliable, self-indulgent, incompetent, and—above all—utterly dependent on the resources of the women in his family to make his way in the world.[30] Zhang's biographies of women supplied a venue where he could noisily skewer his improvident cousin.

Zhang's stories of women's lives tread a fine line between commentaries on ritual propriety and gossip—malicious gossip at that, written to damage its target. Beyond gossip, moreover, in the larger context of Zhang Xuecheng's philosophical writings, his biographies of women and an essay on "Women's Learning" served as a forum to dramatize and showcase his criticism of the decadence and self-serving pretensions of his contemporary world of letters.[31] Such biographies are a subtle example of the biography-as-soapbox, familiar to anyone who has studied Wei Yuan's eulogy for the hapless magistrate killed in the Zhong Renjie rebellion, now an infamous Qing document in Philip Kuhn's textbook.[32]

As Zhang Xuecheng's noisy memoirs show us, the suffering of female relatives could inspire male writers to excessive detail, in their zeal to record their own judgments of human character and foible. A rather different example of a similarly gossipy memoir appears in a gravestone inscription (*cuozhi*) written by a local scholar for Bao Mengyi (1808–44). The adopted daughter of the aforementioned Bao Shichen, Bao Mengyi married the only son of Bao's friend Zhang Qi, and she died an untimely death at the age of thirty-seven after bearing two children. The wrinkle in her story is the unusual composition of the household into which she married. Her husband was the younger brother of the four Zhang sisters introduced above. Two of the four sisters had uxorilocal marriages. Thus at the time of her wedding, Mengyi faced the unusual challenge of cohabiting with two of her husband's married sisters and their spouses. This alone constituted a significant departure from patrilineal family norms, which assumed that any bride would move into the household of her husband's parents. A further complication faced Mengyi, however. Mengyi's husband had had an elder brother who died in his mid-teens, just before being capped, but after he had been betrothed. This deceased elder brother's fiancée, née Fa, had also joined the Zhang household as a faithful maiden (*zhennü*).[33] In other words, the marital household Bao Mengyi entered included her husband's elder brother's chaste fiancée, two of her husband's elder sisters, and their married-in husbands. As the spouse of the household head, whose parents were both deceased and who was the sole surviving male heir, Bao Mengyi should have enjoyed that status of superior female in the Zhang household. But her circumstances were complicated. She was younger than her sisters-in-law by some years, and—as we discover from her noisy biographer—faithful maiden Fa had claimed the rank of senior daughter-in-law, on the grounds that she was the spouse of the [deceased] elder brother.

Managing this scenario would qualify any woman for sainthood, in Confucian terms or otherwise, but Bao Mengyi's particular trials and triumphs are revealed to us in detail by the delicately chosen words of her gravestone inscription. Its author, Fang Junmo (fl. 1861), realized (or was coached to understand) that he could freely discuss every detail of Bao Mengyi's situation if he fastened on a problem of ritual propriety and used her life to illustrate its workings. The problem he chose was the ritual hierarchy separating the wife of a first-born son (*zhongfu*) from the wife or wives of the younger sons (*jiefu*). (The text on which the case rests is a passage in the *Li ji* (Book of Rites): "when the father-in-law dies and the mother-in-law is old, the wife of the eldest son makes sacrificial offerings and waits upon guests; concerning every particular, she must consult with her mother-in-law, and the wife or wives of the younger sons will consult with her" (*jiu mo ze gu lao, zhongfu suo jisi binke, mei shi bi qingyu gu, jiefu qingyu zhongfu*). In his epitaph, Fang explains that Bao Mengyi's situation in light of this injunction from the classics was not merely delicate. Faithful maiden Fa, he reveals, was mentally ill (*xinji*). She flew into uncontrollable rages that she vented on Bao Mengyi. In the face of these rages, Fang explains, Mengyi was unfailingly deferential, meeting faithful maiden Fa's every demand, quietly weeping while accepting responsibility for whatever had displeased her sister-in-law, and then finding some way to resolve the anger and calm her down. So successful was she, Fang reports, that the faithful maiden herself said proudly: "My younger sister-in-law respects me." Fang's own comment at the end of the epitaph is worth translating in full:

> Lady Bao's wise actions and constant rectitude are confirmed by the testimonial of her family members, all of whom describe her this way with no exception. Truly she was a splendid person, but what truly

distinguished her wisdom was the knowledge of the foundation of the rites that she displayed in her submissive service to faithful maiden Fa. According to the rites, parents-in-law must make sure not to set the wife of a younger son in a position of rivaling the place of the wife of the first-born son: they must not walk together, nor be given the same charge, nor sit together. The ancients made a clear distinction between the wife of the first-born and the others so that everyone would know the proper hierarchy and follow it . . . In later times, the *zongfa* has been lost . . . , such that every individual pursues her own ends and competes with others within the same family, even to the point where a daughter-in-law will boast of her husband's wealth and status and use it to dominate the other women in the household, never consulting with the wife of the first-born about such things as the sacrifices or receiving guests. The result is discord and sharp words, which put the family in jeopardy and create the potential for great disaster. Faithful maiden Fa's illness was severe and beyond her control. Only by faithfully adhering to the standards governing the conduct of a junior wife was Lady Bao able to correct her heart. If we imagine how she bore her tribulations in silence and resolved her difficulties by herself, we can expand upon the meaning of that to understand other things: as she honored her sister-in-law so she filially serve her parents; as she treated her sister-in-law with intimate concern, so she supported her husband—and lived in harmony with other members of the household, and treated the servants and concubines with motherly kindness. It cannot be otherwise. If we deeply examine the meaning of the ritual systems established by the ancients, we see that only this kind of conduct truly fulfills the meaning of the "wifely way [*fudao*]"—yet there was no hint of self-aggrandizement to be found in her anywhere. For this reason, whether she was interacting with those above her or those below her, she made them all happy; and when she was carrying out a duty, she was always mindful of the essential principles behind it. The orderly state of governance of all under heaven is based entirely on just such conduct. Alas! We must tell this to all the wives of future generations! Therefore I say: truly this woman knew the foundation of the rites.[34]

Faithful maiden Fa herself is a biographical subject shrouded in silence. For most faithful maidens, whose position in the family system was anomalous, a cryptic reference to an imperial *jingbiao* is all the historical record will reveal. As a faithful maiden honored by the imperial government, faithful maiden Fa's life was relatively well documented, being mentioned in a total of five cryptic references. Some of these references, like Fang's own comments above, were intended to stress the virtue of others who tolerated or indulged her excessive devotion to ritual propriety. For instance, the brief observation dropped by Zhang Qi into the middle of his epitaph for his late wife, Tang Yaoqing, mentions her only by way of further praising his wife's virtue: "My wife took pity on her and welcomed her into our household so that she could fulfill her vow as a faithful maiden."[35] A notice in the *lienü zhuan* chapter of the Changzhou local history of 1879 says only: "In 1848, the 28th year of Daoguang, an imperial commendation (*jingbiao*) was conferred on the faithful maiden Fa, from Yanghu." An appended note adds: "She was betrothed to Zhang Juesun."[36] Faithful maiden Fa also appears in one-line references in the Zhang family's genealogy (twice) and in a birthday greeting for one of her sisters-in-law, where she is the subject of a discussion about an heir.

Since I had spent years trying to find out more about faithful maiden Fa when I stumbled upon Fang Junmo's grave inscription, my joy in his noisy revelations knew no bounds. But I was also struck by the contrast between Fang's exposé and the heavy silence surrounding this faithful maiden in every single public and private document relating to the Zhang family and Bao Mengyi's marriage (Bao Shichen had ample opportunity to comment and he never said a word). The silence was precisely where the noise was supposed to be: in stories celebrating the young Fa woman's faithful maidenhood, especially the reasons for the *jingbiao* she was awarded. It is that silence that made me aware of the taboos Fang Junmo was breaking, and that also made me appreciate how deftly he made his way through the moral thickets of what to say and how to say it.

Fang Junmo's grave inscription shows how biographical narratives can slip from moral commentary and dutiful chronicle into gossip reminiscent of *People* magazine. Some biographies let readers find out—or permit writers to reveal—secrets, breaking the silences surrounding famous or highly placed private persons who kept their lives out of public view. I once envied Matthew Sommer and Janet Theiss because the court cases they study reveal so much about the inner workings of ordinary people's lives.[37] Court records are closed doors for those of us who study elite families, who were usually able to keep their private lives out of the magistrate's courtroom. But reading biography has given me a new perspective. Although silence is a great problem in published records of elite women's lives, many biographical sources are so noisy that they make up for it.

2. Getting a Life

The Production of 1950s Women Labor Models in Rural Shaanxi

Gail Hershatter

The Chinese 1950s is now long enough ago and remote enough from current political configurations to be regarded as a legitimate topic for historians. Scholars pursuing events from that time encounter a substantial paper trail, the artifact of an ambitious state that issued directives, demanded reports, and sought to publicize its achievements and exhortations for a wider and wider public. What we get to read, however, is not ever completely congruent with what we want to know, and nowhere are the gaps more frustrating than with respect to rural women. Addressed by state policies about literacy, marriage reform, and above all mobilization for collective production, Woman as state subject is ubiquitous in the written record. Women, however—named women with personal histories, individual trajectories, and staying power beyond the occasional expression of enthusiasm for Liberation and its aftermath—are scarce.

The only rural women who consistently appear as individuals in the written record were those selected by the Party-state as examples for the wider population to emulate: labor models. Labor model reports and publicity created by local cadres and news reporters in the 1950s are, arguably, one type of biography. The retrospective self-narrations of former labor models and former cadres, collected in the 1990s, are another (and here I am using the term "biography" loosely, since these are oral narratives rather than written memoirs). The possibility of using both types of sources as biographical materials, and fashioning a biography closer to our commonsense understanding of the term, invites exploration.

This essay explores the collective production of women labor models, focusing on the blurry boundaries between state activity, community self-narration, and individual lives. It draws principally on interviews, published accounts, and archival materials about three Shaanxi women labor models who grew high-yield cotton—Zhang Qiuxiang of Weinan, who became a national labor model and member of the Chinese People's Political Consultative Conference and the provincial People's Congress; Shan Xiuzhen of Tongguan, selected as a national labor model in 1962; and Cao Zhuxiang of Weinan, a provincial labor model—as well as a model cooperative leader named Lu Guilan who became a provincial labor model in 1951 and a national model in 1957.

The reader looking for a coherent account of a specific life, or for that matter a dense account of rural collectivization that features actual people, will be disappointed. These are worthy projects, but before they can be attempted, we need to examine the processes by which labor models, and the sources that record their exploits, were generated. These processes include the placement of women within particular lineages of virtue, the ways that they learned to speak of their labor, the work of writing down and publicizing their exploits, and the task of remembering and narrating their lives from the vantage point of a radically different present. Each involves many human agents, not just the labor model or her amanuensis. This is not biography in the common sense of the term: a story of a person moving through time. Rather, labor model stories compel attention to the social production of a woman's life for particular purposes, and to its circulation, transformation, and recollection as the product of many different people and interactions.

What, then, of the revelations we have come to expect from biography, particularly knowledge of a person's inner thoughts and emotions as revealed by the full range of sources and memories? Labor model stories call into question the existence, or at least the presumed shape, of interiority itself. I conclude with some thoughts about whether extant labor model materials combined with oral narratives can be used to construct biographies, whether biography is possible or desirable in the wake of a major state project such as collectivization, and whether we should perhaps be asking other kinds of questions about the lives of rural women in this period.

LINEAGES OF VIRTUE

Stories of rural women labor models in the 1950s echoed many themes of older tales about virtuous women: industriousness, suffering, attention to the welfare of others, self-sacrifice (albeit for the collective rather than the patriline), and, interestingly, chastity or at least absence of sexual controversy. Like the virtuous widows and exacting devoted mothers in late imperial stories (see part II of this volume), labor models were active and determined. In the imperial era, publication of the biographies of virtuous women had brought glory to their families and communities, even as it promoted models of good behavior for the wider reading and listening public. Something similar can be said of the 1950s, when a village or production team that produced a famous labor model often saw their achievements publicized, first across the liberated areas and later across the province or even the nation. Labor models, like virtuous women in an older regime, became sources of community social capital. At the same time, they embodied and furthered the aims of the state. Like the imperial officials who encouraged the production of gazetteers, PRC officials hoped to promote emulation of labor models by promulgating the record of their heroic activity.

Of course, the differences between older tales of virtue and their 1950s counterparts were substantial. Virtuous women in early China were often lauded for their sage and sometimes audacious advice to rulers,[1] but paragons from the late imperial era were more commonly praised for their activities in the domestic realm. PRC labor model stories recombined and transformed elements from both of these eras. Like the women in early Chinese texts, and unlike late imperial women, the PRC labor model was typically involved in a political project—building socialism. Unlike the early Chinese heroines, she did not pursue this project through catching the ear of a powerful man, although encounters with powerful men became part of the story for the labor models who met Zhou Enlai and Mao Zedong. Rather, like the late imperial paragons, the labor model achieved political goals through the careful performance of quotidian labor, performed in this instance outside rather than within the domestic realm.

In the early years of the People's Republic in Shaanxi, virtuous women were not merely called forth by the state and named by their neighbors. They had to be created. Labor models were, as a 1951 set of instructions from the Civil Administration Bureau to local officials put it, to be both "trained and discovered."[2] Party or government cadres were the implied agents in the production of labor models. Assigned to rural Shaanxi villages to live and work for months on end (a process known as *dundian*, literally "to squat in a spot"), cadres identified potential leaders, cajoled them to take up leadership roles, trained them in the necessary skills, supported them if they met opposition, and recommended them for state recognition.

Women in central Shaanxi villages had not routinely engaged in full-time fieldwork before 1949, although it was common for them to help out during planting and harvest seasons. In some villages, Women's Federation cadres found women who had learned to farm because of family misfortune. Cao Zhuxiang, widowed in the 1940s at the age of twenty-four, was one such woman. At Liberation she was thirty-two and had been taught a full range of farming skills by her brother, going to the fields to plow at night so that the neighbors would not see her making crooked furrows. Her poverty and family circumstances, which marked her as a dangerously exposed and vulnerable person in the old society, made her available as a skilled leader of women when the new state turned its attention to bringing women into the fields. At the same time, her reputation as a faithful widow meant that she had the local prestige to be effective as a model. As Li Xiuwa, a former "squatting" cadre, explained:

> Cao Zhuxiang was widowed very young, and was restrained by the remnants of feudalism. She could not remarry, because she had a son. She had to remain as a widow in that family. From the time she was in her twenties, she devoted her youth to that family. Cao Zhuxiang could carry loads on a shoulder pole, push a cart, plow, and urge a draft animal on with shouts. She had all the skills of plowing, sowing, raking, milling, and winnowing. Cao Zhuxiang was extremely capable, and so she had prestige in the village. Not prestige in our current sense, but rather prestige given to her by feudal remnants. They said, this woman is capable, honest, can eat bitterness, and on this basis we [the provincial Women's Federation] can spread a new prestige, not only by having her join in production, but by having her join in political movements. She will not only lead her own small family, but will also lead the bigger [collective] family.[3]

Women were chosen as models for their role in production, not for virtue of the faithful wife/chaste widow variety. Nevertheless, if a woman was to be an effective model, she had to have the respect of her neighbors; shrewish wives and lascivious widows would not have served that purpose. Particularly when the objective was to pull women out of the domestic sphere and into collective agricultural production, a move that jostled uneasily against village notions of respectability, the labor model doing the persuading also had to be a model of probity. In that respect, Cao's faithful widowhood—and her refusal to consider proposals that she remarry even after 1949—kept her domestic life uncontroversial, unencumbered by wifely duties, and available for collective projects.[4]

Living and working side by side with labor models, sometimes eating in their homes, Women's Federation cadres were well aware that not all labor models had conflict-free domestic lives. And yet, one did not see in print—although one might hear it forty years later from a Women's Federation cadre—stories such as the one about a labor model whose husband opposed her work and who got so exasperated that she chased him around the household millstone with a stick, threatening to beat him, until the cadre pleaded with her to stop.[5] Instead, reports on labor models tended to list their domestic achievements side by side with evidence of high production and advanced political consciousness. A 1952 report on Shan Xiuzhen, for instance, included in her Plan for Patriotic Activities her intention to complete the following tasks: promote women's literacy, organize labor for fieldwork, console soldiers' families, donate grain to the state, produce cloth for her whole family, attend to her children's studies, and not quarrel with her husband.[6]

Lu Guilan, whose relationship with her husband was intermittently stormy, told of making a calculated assessment that divorce would undermine her credibility as a leader, even though local cadres wanted her to seek redress for his treatment of her:

> [During the land reform] my husband hated that I was not home all day long. He got mad at me. Look what a big bitterness I had back then. At night when I came back I had to sit on the *kang* to spin. I ran out during the day and I had to do housework at night when I came back. I behaved as usual. I couldn't hold myself above him even though the Communist Party had liberated me.
>
> One day my husband got mad and yelled at me that I ran around the whole day. He cursed, "If you are going to run around like this, just get out of here. Let's go to the township seat. We can't live like this. Let's divorce." I said, "I won't go with you. So shameful. I don't want to lose face. I never thought of divorcing you. I want to live with you. I never wanted to leave you." He was so angry that he pulled my arm and I hurt my head. I struggled not to go with him. I didn't want to bother the [officials at the] township seat. I didn't want to lose face. You were the head of women! Look, your husband treated you like this. I also had feudal thoughts back then. I just refused to go. He pulled me and I hurt my head on the doorsill and my face swelled this big. Two of the land reform cadres were irritated and wanted to criticize my husband. I disagreed. Why did I disagree? I was afraid the old people around there wouldn't accept it. They would say, "Look at her. She has just been a director of the women's committee for a few days and she pulled her husband to a meeting to struggle against him." It would definitely be harmful to mobilizing women.
>
> Finally the work team head of the administrative village got so mad. . . . He said, "I won't bother to care about you even if you are killed. You are so sympathetic to feudal thinking." But feudal thoughts had been there for thousands of years. It's impossible to make old people and young people accept it all at once. You have to be an example so that

you can liberate other women. In order to liberate the whole country, the communists climbed snowy mountains and went through grasslands. So many of our forebears died. Compared to that, my contribution and my hard work were nothing.

So I set myself an example to others. I was very kind to my parents-in-law. I never quarreled with my sister-in-law all these years. I just wouldn't divorce my husband. . . . This made it much easier for me to mobilize other women. . . . For the sake of liberating women, the bitterness I ate was nothing.

During the Marriage Law Movement Month [in 1953] men and women accused each other of sexual misconduct (*zuofeng wenti*). I set myself as an example to others. There was no gossip about me on this issue, although I worked together with men.[7]

Here Lu Guilan negotiates the complicated intersection of virtue, revolution, and political efficacy. Although she refers to herself as having been "feudal" in her thinking, she clearly communicates her sense that she did the right thing, both politically and ethically. What emerges here in memory, a source that scholars have sometimes regarded as more "authentic" than the written accounts generated under activist state regimes, is an account of layered historical virtue. As a faithful wife and dutiful daughter-in-law, Lu sacrifices herself for the collective liberation of women, a sacrifice that is itself a virtue consciously modeled on the Long Marchers, even though the behavior in question entails refusing to divorce a violent husband.

SPEAKING

By the mid-1950s, increasing cotton production was a national priority, and at Party instigation, various government units cooperated to involve women in growing it. This involved an adjustment in the gendered division of labor, as men gradually moved—not always willingly—out of cotton farming and into sideline production. Cotton growing was suddenly discovered to be suitable work for women, because it required dexterous fingers and meticulous attention to detail.[8] Yet few women were involved in all stages of cotton production.

One exception was Zhang Qiuxiang of Shuangwang Village in Weinan County, whose skill at cotton cultivation had already come to light at the first provincial cotton meeting, held in Weinan in April 1954. Women's Federation cadres thought she would be a promising model, and set out to get her cooperation: "From this point, we led Zhang Qiuxiang by telling her that "if only one person is red, there is only one dot of red; if all the people are red, there will be a wide swath of red."[9] Zhang was an experienced farmer from an extremely poor family; her revolutionary loyalties were profound. For her to be an effective model, however, more was required: she had to learn to speak in public, explain policies, hold people's attention, and fire their enthusiasm.[10] In spite of her cotton-growing skill, Zhang Qiuxiang was inarticulate. Undaunted, the Women's Federation cadres set to work:

> Zhang Qiuxiang could not read or make a speech, could not sum
> up her own experience. When we asked about her cotton growing
> experience, she just said "you plant, hoe regularly, top the cotton plants
> well." It was our comrades from the Women's Federation who picked
> up important content from her words and drew out the important
> points. After this, she experienced a lot and got to know the world,
> and found her wings. This shows that our Women's Federation put
> out considerable labor and hard work to cultivate these models, and
> carefully helped them, hand in hand.[11]

As Zhang's fame grew, "squatting" cadres acted as her secretarial staff. They remained in her village, joining in the cotton-growing work, and helping the illiterate cotton-growing champion reply to the dozens of letters that arrived daily from all over China, asking for cotton seeds, advice, and encouragement.[12]

Once the credentials and prestige of a labor model had been established, her main task in speaking publicly was no longer to testify to her past, but rather to mobilize efforts for the next task at hand. Thus we find Shan Xiuzhen in a 1961 speech to Weinan County commune members, reporting on a recent meeting of cotton producers and reminding everyone of the importance of pest control ("the bugs are just like enemies who attack us fiercely"), weeding, flood prevention, and manure application.[13] By this point in her career, a labor model's effectiveness depended on a shared social understanding of what she had accomplished and why she was worth listening to. Overt evocation of her background was no longer necessary; her life story was public property, framing the way in which her exhortations to labor were to be understood and heeded.

WRITING

From the early years of the PRC, local cadres were instructed to write accounts of labor model achievements. A 1951 Shaanxi provincial government directive specified that such accounts should first clarify what sort of model the person was: "The basic types can be divided into pest-control model, flood-fighting model, manure accumulation model, intensive cultivation model, disaster relief and famine fighting model, production model, . . . ordinary model, and other kinds of model mutual-aid groups, model villages, and so on." Second, the writer should include concrete experiences: How much manure had the model applied to the soil? How deep was the plowing? How often were crops rotated, irrigated, fumigated? What was the average output? By how much did it surpass the average output in the area? Third, what was the makeup of the village, its method of organizing labor and keeping accounts, its output, its penchant for production competitions? Fourth, what were the patriotic activities and improvements in political consciousness fostered by the labor models? Finally, the writers were exhorted, "Try your best to be comprehensive, material, and detailed."[14] Material about women labor models, necessarily gendered because women were being mobilized for tasks that they had not routinely performed before, was a subset of this larger bureaucratically defined genre.

Models were typically lauded for their hardscrabble origins and suffering in early life, allegiance to the Party after 1949, technical skill, political awareness, and contribution to current campaigns. A handwritten piece on Cao Zhuxiang probably written in 1954, for instance, identified her as a thirty-five-year-old widow who had of necessity learned fieldwork skills in the old society but had been despised because she had to perform field labor. Her first accomplishment in 1951 did not transgress the conventional gendered division of labor: she organized women into a spinning and weaving co-op. But within several years, the document continued, she had moved on to fieldwork tasks, leading the villagers in repairing wells. In keeping with point 4 (patriotic activities and political consciousness), the document has her inspiring reluctant villagers by invoking China's international role:

> But during the well fixing, some people said that the weather was too cold and they could not keep warm. At that time, Cao Zhuxiang said bravely, "The volunteer army beat the American devils in a world of ice and snow without any fear of death. They protected our good life. Now Chairman Mao called us to dig wells and prevent drought in order to increase the output. How can we be afraid of cold weather? We must overcome the difficulties and struggle against the weather in order to complete wells." After her encouragement, people expressed the opinion that, "We won't lower our head because of difficulties. We should increase our production in order to support the volunteer army."

The document goes on to describe how she organized a village "patriotic pact" to complete the summer wheat harvest, and then learned and applied

advanced techniques of seed selection, planting, hoeing, and pest prevention. It concludes with an account of her concern about "current affairs,
political study, and productive knowledge," which led her to organize group
newspaper readings and encourage her group members to attend winter
literacy classes. Matter-of-fact in tone, full of technical detail, and selective in its deployment of reconstructed dialogue or cinematic description,
this six-page document contains in compressed form all the important elements of a labor model narrative.[15]

By 1956, when advanced producers from across Shaanxi Province gath-
ered for a meeting, the documentation of labor model exploits had grown
more elaborated and refined. Archival records of the meeting contain a
file on each attendee.[16] The stories told in these 1956 files have a visual
specificity and an element of human conflict missing in the earlier reports,
although the virtues of the labor models are similar. Shan Xiuzhen, then
the forty-three-year-old head of an advanced producer's cooperative (APC),
had three heroic moments. In the first, an upper middle peasant who
wanted to withdraw from the collective in 1955 tried to embarrass her
by kneeling to her in public and demanding money the collective owed
him. Drawing on her Party education and her communist commitments,
Shan defused the situation with gentle words and patient explanations.
The second incident dated from 1954, when the collective decided to send
fifteen laborers into hilly territory to cut green fertilizer for the cotton
crop. The men doing the cutting needed to have steamed bread and noodles
delivered to them each day, but women were reluctant to take on the task
for fear of being gossiped about. (Sexual misconduct in the hills was the
implied content of the gossip they feared.) Keeping her eye on production
targets and her hands on the cooking pot, Chair Shan personally prepared
and delivered the food, leading to record output in crop production. In
the third anecdote she noticed that one of the draft animals was sick, got
speedy attention for the animal from the veterinarian, meticulously boiled
water and hand-fed medicine to the animal, and thus saved the life of a
collective resource valued at 300 *yuan*.[17] Together, these three incidents
showcased the virtues of a woman labor model: gentle and patient, but firm
in her communist commitments to the collective; unafraid of hard work
and immune to sexual gossip, in part because her conduct was irreproachable; meticulous and tender in caring for collective livestock, on which she
lavished maternal levels of attention.

When material on labor models was published for a wider audience, it
tended to be organized not around the narrative of a life *tout court*, but
rather according to the completion of specified tasks or the performance

of desired virtues. Sometimes the tasks were technical. In a 1956 publication of reports by labor models to a province-wide meeting on cotton field management, Zhang Qiuxiang, assisted by a Women's Federation cadre who served as her scribe and editor, presented tasks in cotton cultivation as a series of handy maxims about carefully preparing the soil, spreading fertilizer, selecting and preparing the seeds, planting early, thinning, weeding, irrigating at the right moments, topping the plants, battling pests, and using improved techniques to harvest the bolls.[18] Government agrotechnicians were the originators of some of these techniques, but they did not publicize their innovations directly. Rather, they used the stories of labor heroines to communicate specialized information. Centered as they were on hard work, group cooperation, and sacrifice, these stories had a solidity that, as Gao Xiaoxian puts it, "could be seen, touched, and studied," and thus made accessible to farmers across the cotton belt.[19]

By early 1958, the name "Zhang Qiuxiang" had become a shorthand way of talking about raising cotton production in Shaanxi.[20] In April, just prior to the formal launch of the Great Leap Forward,[21] the Women's Federation publicized the slogan "Study Qiuxiang, catch up with Qiuxiang." Innovations such as Qiuxiang fields[22] (experimental cotton plots), learn-from-Qiuxiang labor contests and, in 1959, "Go all out, catch up with Qiuxiang again" events soon followed. Zhang Qiuxiang herself was lauded in a national Women's Federation publication as "the first woman researcher of peasant origin" (*diyige nongmin chushen de yanjiuyuan*).[23] Pamphlets introduced by Women's Federation cadres and published by the Shaanxi Provincial Press, bearing titles like *"Silly Girls" Launch a "Cotton Satellite"* and *We Caught Up with Zhang Qiuxiang*, encouraged the spread of Qiuxiang fields across the cotton belt.[24]

Shortly after Zhang Qiuxiang was named a scientific researcher of peasant origin, the *Shaanxi ribao* reported, Vice Chair of the National Women's Federation Kang Keqing paid her a courtesy call, sloshing through a rainstorm to visit the storied experimental cotton plot.[25] She was followed four months later, the same newspaper reported, by a Soviet expert stationed in Xi'an, also braving a drizzle. The Soviet visitor was reported to have told Zhang Qiuxiang that the Chinese Great Leap Forward was unprecedented anywhere, past or present, and that the Soviet people were extremely happy at the achievements attained by the Chinese people. When he asked her how her high level of output had been attained, she modestly smiled and replied, "It is mainly the result of the Party's leadership and everyone's Communist mode of daring to think, daring to speak, and daring to act, along with our learning from the Soviet elder brother." The emissary, astonished, is said to have replied, "Your experience is very rich, and the Soviet people should learn from you and from all Chinese agricultural experts. When I return to the Soviet Union, I will tell the Soviet people in detail about the miracles you have created. The Soviet people are very concerned with the construction of China." And with that conversation concluded, Zhang Qiuxiang presented him with a five- or six-*jin* turnip and a cotton stalk with more than fifty bolls as a memento of his trip.[26]

This sort of political fantasia became more stylized as the Great Leap wore on and began to founder. By early 1959, Zhang Qiuxiang was quoted speaking in verse about the connection between politics and cotton:

The General Line is a beacon	*Zong luxian shi dengta*
It illuminates the peoples' hearts and they flower	*Zhaode renxin kaile hua*
In recent years since the General Line	*Jinnian youle zong luxian*
The cotton has bloomed bigger than the clouds.[27]	*Yao mianhua kaifang bi yun da.*

The moralistic tone of labor model discourse lingered well into the difficult years that followed. In the aftermath of the Leap, the Shaanxi Women's Federation continually referred to the prestige and achievements of Zhang Qiuxiang, citing cotton production as one area that had continued to grow and, it seems, using talk of this success as a means of salvaging the wreckage left by the Leap. (Whether the claims of increased cotton production were accurate—and given Shaanxi's overall situation, they are not necessarily fabrications—requires further investigation.) One such article, published in early 1960, ended with a "folk song" that linked Qiuxiang contests to the establishment of people's communes:

The People's Communes, a spray of blooms	*Renmin gongshe yizhi hua*
The sweet smell fills ten thousand rooms	*Huakai shili xiang wanjia*
In each place women strive and vie	*Funü daochu nao jingsai*
Qiuxiang's red flag everywhere flies.[28]	*Qiuxiang hongqi biandi cha.*

Labor models, exhibiting thrift and industry, were to lead the way to economic recovery without sacrificing political fealty. A 1962 pamphlet about Shan Xiuzhen published by the Women's Federation as a study guide for grassroots women's cadres took political virtue, not agriculture, as its organizing matrix. Entitled *Shan Xiuzhen, Glorious Proletarian Fighter,* this thirteen-page work was divided by subheads that distilled the essence of her achievement in ethical rather than technical terms: "High Aspirations,

Great Zeal" (*zhiqi gao, ganjin da*), "Consider the Big Picture, Advance in the Face of Difficulties" (*gu quan daju, ying nan er jin*), "Diligent, Conscientious, and Honest; Hard Work and Plain Living" (*qinken laoshi, jianku pusu*), and, finally, "A Red Heart Turned Toward the Party" (*yike hongxing xiangzhe dang*).[29] Each section began with a summary of Shan's quality of virtue as summarized in the subhead, followed by an illustrative anecdote or two, enlivened with retrospectively recreated dialogue. The pamphlet ended with an inspirational editorial about Shan reprinted from the *Shaanxi ribao*, advising the readers that if only they adopted her revolutionary ideals and spirit, no success was beyond their grasp.

Written accounts about labor models, then, were not biographies in the sense of a narrative about people's lives. Rather, these accounts did one of two things. Some presented material that otherwise might have been published in a technical manual in relatively colorful, sprightly form by using labor models and their cotton-growing apprentices as an organizing device. Others, in a manner similar to accounts of exemplary figures from the time of Liu Xiang's *Lienü zhuan*, "focused . . . on a particular type of extreme moral behavior," and like the *Lienü zhuan* as well as later exemplar texts studied by Beverly Bossler,[30] they often signaled "the critical virtue" of the labor model in the title. As the content of these stories became more explicitly entwined with dedication to communism, the specificity of the women became less important than their status as vessels for revolutionary virtues.

REMEMBERING

As the 1950s crescendoed into the Great Leap Forward, written accounts of labor model lives became simultaneously more colorful and more flat—full of heroic exploits and retrospectively imagined politicized dialogue, but increasingly devoid of surprise or depth. The historian in search of biographical insight is tempted to look elsewhere, in the liveliness of in-person interviews, but the results are mixed. In a series of life-history interviews, Cao Zhuxiang gave an account of one meeting after another, a story that caused the listener to wonder why, for instance, she appeared not to regret missing her daughter's wedding because she was attending a meeting, but also did not evidence any enthusiasm for the public activities that took her away from home. Zhang Qiuxiang, too, was opaque about her labor model career, whether from age, fatigue, or irritation at our persistent questioning about difficulties in organizing other villagers.[31] Ironically, however, it was precisely when the labor models grew most animated—in their stories of seeing Chairman Mao—that the puzzle of how to understand their relationship to modelhood and the state seemed most unsolvable. Far from a source of transgressive, disgruntled, or even reflective stories, memory seems to be the place where labor model discourse, currently discarded by a reform-era world with scant regard for these women, survives most intact. Consider two such memories.

For Lu Guilan, the chance to be a delegate to a meeting in Beijing offered community and, away from home, a giddy sociality with other women from similar backgrounds. Lu Guilan mocked her own country bumpkin naïveté amidst Beijing grandeur:

> Oh, my goodness. The food, the lodging! It was the Beijing Hotel. Look, when you walk in, the door turns. People go in the empty space and it turns automatically. I didn't understand it. There was even a joke. Shan Xiuzhen was a representative from Tongguan. She went to the Beijing Hotel. Here's a mirror, there's a mirror in the room. She entered and said, "Oops! How come here's me and there's me too?" We were very close when we went to meetings at the province. Zhang Qiuxiang, Shan Xiuzhen, Cao Zhuxiang . . . At night we sang opera [and accompanied ourselves] with dishes, bowls and chopsticks. We sewed shoe soles. . . . We chatted all day long. . . . They called me the director of the chat office. . . . It was so much fun. I still miss those big sisters now.[32]

The pinnacle of attendance at any national meeting was proximity to the Party-state's top leadership, an experience that produced intense emotions in the retelling. Here the informal hilarity of a woman-only opera party in a Beijing hotel room was replaced by the solemn joy of drawing close to the Party's acknowledged heart. As a delegate to the second meeting of the First National Women's Congress, Shan Xiuzhen saw Chairman Mao in 1953:

> No one slept the first night. The second day, I don't remember where we stayed, we were happy all evening. We took baths and washed our clothes and everything was clean and tidy. . . . In Huairen Hall, everything was in order. . . . The Shaanxi representatives were in the middle and I was in the front. After the representatives were seated, Chairman Mao, the Premier [Zhou Enlai], Chairman Liu [Shaoqi], the Chief Commander and other leaders of the central government came in, over fifty people. . . . When Chairman Mao came, the correct thing for you to do was welcome him. We weren't to move, because if we moved there would be chaos. People would say that women had no consciousness and didn't comply with rules. We didn't dare to pull on Chairman Mao to shake hands. We were supposed to love and protect Chairman Mao. "All you people, if Chairman Mao shook hands with all of you, wouldn't you be

worried about Chairman Mao?" They talked to us in advance. I was sitting there properly. Chairman Mao came. There were many people and we sat in a circle. Chairman Mao was smiling and took off his cap. The only thing I did was clap. [Chairman Mao] walked around twice. If he didn't walk around twice, the women on this side would have been able to see him, but those on that side would not. People were so happy that they were crying.

This was the first time, in Beijing, I had my picture taken with Chairman Mao. It was a pity that among the Shaanxi representatives, only director Yan and I were from the countryside. The picture was seven feet long and five feet wide, and it cost seventeen *yuan* and was unaffordable. I didn't have money and didn't have a copy printed. When the meeting was over, I came back. . . .

What I regret is this. At the third women's representative meeting in 1957, Chairman Mao received us and took pictures with us. [Zhang] Qiuxiang and [Cao] Zhuxiang were in the picture. Each of us got a copy. But the pity is that it was taken away and lost in the Cultural Revolution in 1966. This is the thing I regret the most.[33]

Meetings—occasions for workaday reporting and listening, for occasional out-of-town camaraderie and hilarity—were also the place at which labor models were most thoroughly interpellated as political subjects. Even at a distance of almost half a century, even given the personal and political effects of unhappy intervening events, the moment of sighting Chairman Mao seems untarnished. It is in their personal stories, even more than in the writings meant to publicize their achievements and laud their political consciousness, that these women emerge most completely as full participants in the political moment that produced them.

AFTERTHOUGHTS: BIOGRAPHY AND INTERIORITY

Labor model stories were a form of biography-in-process intimately connected to the social, intended to communicate, inspire, and mobilize in their own time, during the period of early socialism in China. The question is how we might make use of such stories as historical material—how they might function in historical time.

In spite of the prominence of rural China in state initiatives and state propaganda in the 1950s, the changes wrought by socialism in the everyday existence and consciousness of peasants remain frustratingly opaque. What is the connection between grand state goals, energetic local initiatives, social transformation, and what rural dwellers remember as important half a century later? The massive state-generated paper trail has little to say on this question. Rural labor models, as some of the few women who have names and trajectories in that paper trail, offer one way to explore these questions.

And yet, in spite of the heft of the sources and the possibility of interviews with women who recall those years, the prospects for historically illuminating biography are complicated—perhaps no less complicated than they are for the virtuous women of Liu Xiang's *Lienü zhuan* or the chaste widows in Ming-Qing gazetteers. Certain aspects of labor model lives—sexuality, some political conflicts, sources of retrospective bitterness—remain inaccessible, unaddressed or incompletely addressed in print, and unasked or unanswered (although not always absent) in interviews.

Interviews also suggest that emergence as a labor model, with its accompanying public activities, profoundly shaped these women's sense of who they were and their memories of that time. As revealing as oral narratives can be about struggles and compromises invisible in the written sources, women recalling their past as labor models do so in language provided by the historical process they are recalling. Their stories sometimes call that past to account, sometimes use it to call the present and its insufficiencies to account, sometimes narrate their virtue and value to a world that currently neglects them. What they never do is stand apart from that past and reject the subject positions that collectivization offered them, even though those positions have long since ceased to exist. Their intense relationship to their labor modelhood is as evident in their memories of singing in a Beijing hotel room or meeting Chairman Mao as it is in their accounts of their heroic exploits in the cotton fields. Their memories, in short, are neither in opposition to, nor even separated from, the project of state-building or the language of official history.

Put in contemporary parlance, many of these women came to inhabit the subject position of labor model to such a degree that their subjectivity cannot be apprehended independent of it. Indeed, these stories call into question the idea—already under fire in many disciplines, but generally sacrosanct in historical research—that if we could just dig far enough, the authentic person with an interior persona distinct from the public model would be waiting to reveal herself. Pure interiority, tales of non-normative personal change, life apart from or in resistance to state discourse, the truth of the self or selves, cannot be recovered through research on the 1950s. Indeed, the 1950s materials, and memories of the 1950s as recounted more recently, suggest that the whole project of a search for the real selves of a real past is chimerical. What the 1950s offers us is the possibility of constructing an account of how new women were brought into being, not by state fiat, but by the labor of cadres, the women themselves, their village communities, and regional or national reading and listening publics. These life stories direct our attention, not to hidden inner truths or the sort of life writing engaged in by contemporary biographers and historians, but to shared world-making projects. They suggest that the interior self is itself a historically situated and peculiar idea, and that our attachment to it as historians deserves a gaze as skeptical as any we turn on our source materials. They do not tell us what we want to know, but perhaps they offer us lessons we need to hear.

PART II

Biography as Cultural Project

3. The *Lienü zhuan* Tradition ar
Zhaoyuan's (1763-1851) Product.
of the *Lienü zhuan buzhu* (1812)

Harriet T. Zurndorfer

During the Han dynasty, two kinds of texts which were to serve as guides for women for the next 2,000 years first appeared: Liu Xiang's (77–6 BCE) *Lienü zhuan* (Biographies of women), and Ban Zhao's (ca. 48–ca. 118) *Nüjie* (Precepts for my daughters).[1] In the subsequent centuries, men issued numerous editions of Liu's collection to communicate desirable characteristics of women, while women, emulating Ban, authored and/or revised moral tracts to instruct correct female behavior and comportment.[2] Although three female-authored annotations to the *Lienü zhuan* did appear before the Tang dynasty, it would take more than a millennium before another woman, Wang Zhaoyuan (1763–1851), would venture into what had become a male prerogative: compilation of and/or commentary on the *Lienü zhuan*. This essay attempts to unravel the textual scholarship of the women's biographical tradition. It then examines the changing conditions that encouraged later editions of the *Lienü zhuan*, focusing on Wang Zhaoyuan's *Lienü zhuan buzhu* (Commentary on the *Lienü zhuan*). While modern scholars have demonstrated the fallacies of treating Liu Xiang's text and its successor editions as "a catalogue of timeless virtues," or evidence of an "unchanging," "traditional" Chinese womanhood, less attention has been paid to the distinct conditions under which individual editions of the *Lienü zhuan* have been generated.[3] My goal in the second part of the essay is to situate Wang Zhaoyuan's accomplishment within the history of *Lienü zhuan* compilations, *kaozheng* (evidential research) scholarship, her particular life story, and the history of modern biographical study.

ABOUT THE *LIENÜ ZHUAN*

The original edition of the *Lienü zhuan* contained 104 biographies of women organized thematically into seven categories and chapters: "Muyi zhuan"

xemplars of mothers); "Xianming zhuan" (the capable and intelli-
t); "Renzhi zhuan" (the benevolent and wise); "Zhenshun zhuan" (the
etermined and obedient); "Jieyi zhuan" (the principled and righteous);
"Biantong zhuan" (those able in reasoning and communication): and "Niebi
zhuan" (the pernicious and depraved).[4] According to both contemporary
and modern scholars, Liu Xiang may have composed the *Lienü zhuan* in an
effort to counter what he saw as the pernicious influence of palace women.
In his biography of Liu Xiang in the *Hanshu*, the Han historian Ban Gu
(32–92) wrote that Liu compiled the *Lienü zhuan* "to admonish the Son
of Heaven."[5] Liu attended the imperial court as a chamberlain and in that
capacity was able to witness the regimes of four emperors, three of whom he
served. Ban Gu's biography attributes Liu's observation of Emperor Cheng's
(r. 32–7 BCE) indulgence of the Zhao sisters (empress and consort) as the
principal reason for the *Lienü zhuan* compendium. While many modern
scholars accept Ban Gu's standpoint that Liu meant to forewarn Emperor
Cheng of the potential threat of low-born female courtiers, it remains
uncertain whether admonition was indeed Liu's principal purpose.[6]

Sherry Mou contends that Liu Xiang adapted the biographies section
of the *Shiji* (Records of the grand historian) into the *Lienü zhuan* format
"to appraise women within the tradition of men."[7] But unlike the *Shiji*
biographies of real historical persons, Liu made the women in the *Lienü
zhuan* into "paradigms" of "integrity and principles," and thus, Liu Xiang
created a new historical genre.[8] Mou maintains that Liu Xiang meant to
demonstrate the possibility of women being judged within the Confucian
humanist tradition that idealized the Confucian gentleman scholar striving for self-cultivation.[9] Other modern scholars view the *Lienü zhuan* as
reaffirmation of the centrality of marriage and its ritual protocols to the
Confucian social structure. Lo Yuet Keung focuses on the connections
between the *Shiji*'s emphasis on the husband-wife relation, the position
of women in pre-Han society, and Liu Xiang's *Lienü zhuan*.[10] His study
highlights how Liu Xiang projected the importance of the husband-wife
relation into his text. And Catherine Gipoulon also links the importance
of marriage to Liu Xiang's project.[11] She interprets the *Lienü zhuan* in
terms of an analogy between the role of a wife in her family and that of an
official or minister to his ruler: both the husband/wife and the sovereign/
minister are bound by obligations of reciprocity.

Like other works he assembled to edify Han emperors, such as the *Shuo
yuan* (Garden of persuasion) or *Xin xu* (Newly arranged anecdotes), Liu
Xiang drew upon various sources to create the *Lienü zhuan*. In this case,
he excerpted from the *Zuo zhuan* (Zuo's commentaries), *Gongyang zhuan*

(Gongyang's tradition), and the *Guliang zhuan* (Guliang's tradition), and appended quotations from the *Shijing* (Book of songs) to his biographies.[12] This conforms to the early Han state trend toward actively sponsoring the collection and compilation of pre-Han Confucian texts. Although some modern scholars have challenged the consistency and effectiveness of these efforts at codification,[13] it seems Liu Xiang's endeavor to preserve narratives from earlier texts into the *Lienü zhuan* did prove successful.

Liu's *Lienü zhuan* inspired imitation, but the first extant work to incorporate its format was Fan Ye's (398–445) *Hou Hanshu*. Thereafter, other dynastic histories, and later, many local gazetteers contained a section devoted to "biographies of women."[14] In the official histories, the lives of "ordinary women" (as opposed to female imperial relatives with their own sections in dynastic histories) were confined to this arena. Sherry Mou suggests that this development led ultimately to the restricted focus in later imperial dynastic histories on biographies of chaste women, as opposed to biographies of various women.[15] Fan Ye's "biographies of women" already marked the transformation of biographies of women as exemplars, with the emphasis on virtue and (bodily) chastity. Moreover, Mou adds, Fan Ye also set the precedent of having women's biographies come after all other biographies——usually directly before accounts of foreign tribes—thus relegating them to a subordinate position.[16]

The *Suishu* "Jingji zhi" (Bibliography) recorded ten works with the title *Lienü zhuan* and variations.[17] These include four versions of *Lienü zhuan* by four authors (Liu Xiang, a certain Gao, Huangfu Mi, and Qi Wusui); a sequel to *Lienü zhuan* by Xiang Yuan, entitled *Lienü hou zhuan;* a three-chapter summary of the essentials of *Lienü zhuan,* called *Lienü zhuan yao lu;* one introductory text, *Lienü zhuan zan* by Miao Xi; and three eulogies, including one by Cao Zhi, *Lienü zhuan song,* and two by Liu Xin (50–20 BCE), Liu Xiang's son. The best known of these encomia was Liu Xin's *Lienü zhuan song* (later known as *Lienü zhuan songyi*). By the time this list was composed during the Tang period, two versions of Liu Xiang's *Lienü zhuan* were circulating: an eight-*juan* edition alleged to be the original and a fifteen- to sixteen-*juan* variant that resembled the earlier edition in both structure and fundamental contents but included biographies of women from later dynastic eras added by later compilers. The eight-*juan* version was made up of the original seven chapters plus, according to some scholars including Lisa Raphals, a *juan* of basic argumentation about the contents of the *Lienü zhuan,*[18] or, according to others including Bret Hinsch, an expanded collection of Han and post-Han stories about women, with or without illustrations.[19]

In contrast to the *Suishu* bibliography, the *Jiu Tangshu* bibliography claimed that Liu Xiang's *Lienü zhuan* consisted of two *juan* only.[20] Hinsch postulates that the abridged text is related to Emperor Tang Taizong's (599–649) project to provide an illustrated version of the *Lienü zhuan* fitted on palace screens for court ladies to view, enjoy, and consume. However, the bibliography in Ouyang Xiu's (1007–72) *Xin Tangshu* recorded the existence of Liu Xiang's *Lienü zhuan* in fifteen *juan*, with annotations by Ban Zhao.[21] This documentation is also in agreement with another contemporary source, Wang Yaochen's (1001–56) *Chongwen zongmu* (Chongwen [Library] catalogue).[22]

The "metamorphosis" of the original seven- to eight-*juan Lienü zhuan* into a fifteen- to sixteen-*juan* compilation caused alarm among some Song literati who saw the need "to recover" the authentic text. In their analyses of the *Lienü zhuan*'s publication history, both Hinsch and Raphals consider the Song era a turning point in the reproduction of the text. During the first one hundred years of the Song, the *Lienü zhuan* circulated only in manuscript, and even then its transmission was restricted to the literati elite. Both modern scholars recognize the prefaces by Zeng Gong (1019–83) and Wang Hui (1049–1101) to the *Lienü zhuan* (which are both extant) as important clarifications about the text's evolution. They also both credit the literatus Su Song (1020–1101) with the official restoration of the *Lienü zhuan* to eight *juan*, entitled *Gu Lienü zhuan* (Old biographies of women). Most modern editions have emanated from Su Song's collated version. Hinsch argues that Su Song reconstructed Liu Xiang's original text using Liu Xin's *Lienü zhuan songyi*.[23] Su removed materials from the first seven *juan* that postdated Liu Xiang and remitted all these later materials to a single chapter at the end. In addition, Hinsch notes that Su Song's contemporary Lü Jinshu, who served the Song dynasty Zhimige, a government agency that dealt with the editing and publication of texts, also worked on the *Lienü zhuan*.[24] Finally, both Hinsch and Raphals emphasize the significance of the Jian'an, or Jianyang (Fujian) Yu family publishing enterprise, responsible for the first printing and distribution of the revised Song text.[25]

Raphals and Hinsch disagree on the date of the preface to the first Jianyang print (either 1036 [Raphals] or 1063 [Hinsch]), yet they nonetheless agree that widespread distribution of the printed *Lienü zhuan* did not take place until the Yuan dynasty.[26] The Yuan emperors favored the ideals of loyalty and fidelity that the *Lienü zhuan* espoused and thus stimulated the publication and circulation of the text.[27] In her study of Jianyang publishers, Lucille Chia has discovered a "beautifully produced" *Gu Lienü zhuan* in *shangtu xiawen* (running illustration) format originating from the Yuan period and printed by the Yu family's Qinyou tang.[28]

THE *LIENÜ ZHUAN* IN THE LATE IMPERIAL ERA

With the onset of the Ming dynasty, illustrated versions of the *Lienü zhuan* became the norm. As a number of modern scholars have demonstrated, a new reading public, which included women who "craved the instant gratification" that pictorial illustration delivered, had emerged in this period, thus stimulating the illustrated *Lienü zhuan* boom.[29] With "fidelity [becoming] more and more beautiful to look at,"[30] publishers vied with one another to deliver editions that could fetch high prices both from connoisseurs and from social-climbing "nouveau riche" anxious to demonstrate their appreciation of the Confucian ideals of women's behavior.[31] In some locations such as in Huizhou (Anhui), the "craze" for the *Lienü zhuan* manifested itself at a time when self-styled "Confucian literati" propagated the importance of female chastity, especially in relation to the behaviour of widows. What resulted was a highly prized Huizhou printing tradition of the *Lienü zhuan* and related female-instruction texts like Lü Kun's (1536–1618) *Gui fan* (Female exemplars; 1618), which reified the ideals of the chastity cult but downplayed other qualities endorsed by the *Lienü zhuan*.[32]

As Raphals has shown, the *Huitu lienü zhuan* (Illustrated biographies of women; 1610–20?) exemplifies this bias whereby the illustrations blemish the value of many of the *Lienü zhuan* stories. While this particular text retained almost all the biographies of the original Han-Song *Lienü zhuan*, the illustrations themselves minimize other virtues elaborated upon in the Han-Song editions of *Lienü zhuan* chapters and thus "change the flavor of the text as a whole."[33] Illustrated stories of suicide and extremes of filial loyalty made the *Lienü zhuan* more marketable but also undermined the *Lienü zhuan*'s complex presentation of desirable female qualities.[34] To argue her viewpoint that the Ming illustrated *Lienü zhuan* editions helped discourage interest in and understanding of the "intellectual virtue stories" in the *Lienü zhuan*, Raphals has made an extensive comparison of the illustrated *Gui fan* and *Huitu lienü zhuan* with passages in Han-Song *Lienü zhuan* editions.[35] Both Ming texts, she shows, venerate the quality of filiality while disregarding the virtues of wisdom and rhetorical skill.[36] As she observes, "illustrations of women engaging in admonition or discussion" were subsumed by those representing "women dying in flaming buildings or resisting rape."[37]

Ming editions of the *Lienü zhuan* were not the first to be illustrated. Ban Gu's original title to Liu Xiang's work was *Lienü zhuan song tu* (Biographies of women with encomia and illustrations).[38] The Tang compendium *Chuxue ji* (Initiation to learning) confirms that Liu Xiang's original edition had included illustrations.[39] The most celebrated of all illustrated versions to the *Lienü zhuan* was the one attributed to the Jin dynasty painter Gu Kaizhi (ca.345–406). Although Gu's paintings were lost, the fame of his illustrations endured for centuries. Publishers of later illustrated editions such as that one printed by the Jianyang Yu family claimed that the drawings in their editions were those of Gu Kaizhi.[40] Bussotti rightly argues that it is near impossible to establish a certain link between these pictures and the book illustrations.[41] And yet, well into the eighteenth century scholars would claim illustrations accompanying the *Lienü zhuan* were in fact reproductions of Gu Kaizhi's original representations.[42]

Such assertions confirm a well-known tendency of the Chinese literati elite to covet the art of antiquity, particularly that of Gu Kaizhi, who along with three others (Lu Tanwei [460?–early sixth century]; Zheng Sengyu [active late fifth–early sixth century]; and Wu Daozi [710–c. 60]) were "must-haves" for Ming-Qing collectors.[43] Even the invading British forces, during their pillage of the Summer Palace in 1860, could not resist the lure of a Gu Kaizhi painting: they looted the handscroll *Nüshi zhentu* (Admonitions of the imperial instructress to court ladies; late fifth century by Gu Kaizhi), which now survives in the British Museum in London. Modern scholars have traced the *Nüshi zhentu*'s previous history to a collection of four handscrolls that Emperor Qianlong (r. 1736–96) had obtained from the former collection of Gu Congyi (1523–88) and which he named *Simei ju* (All four beauties complete).[44]

The other artist that Qing connoisseurs of illustrated *Lienü zhuan* editions coveted was the Ming master Qiu Ying (ca. 1498–1552). A facsimile edition exists of the 1779 reprint of Qiu Ying's supposed illustrations to the aforementioned sixteen *juan Huitu lienü zhuan*.[45] This 1779 edition belonged to Bao Tingbo (1728–1814), the celebrated bibliophile and sponsor of the printed series "Zhibuzu zhai" (Know-your-deficiencies Studio).[46] As is well known, many a Ming or Qing aesthete falsely attributed various courtly style paintings that were imitations of Qiu Ying's work to the great artist.[47] Such claims aside, the significance of the illustrated Ming *Lienü zhuan* editions in the long term is their role in the general shift of cultural norms which became apparent during the last decades of the Ming dynasty.

In the late Ming, the *Lienü zhuan* became an instructional text, fixated on a woman's capacity to demonstrate chastity, loyalty, and reverence in her roles as wife and mother. Raphals claims that these illustrated *Lienü zhuan* "reflected the complexity of the interactions between Neo-Confucian canon, didactic literature, and social practice."[48] It could further be argued that the almost obsessive preoccupation with the female virtues espoused in these late Ming *Lienü zhuan* texts was connected to the literati's fixation with the concept of *qing*. This term is most commonly associated with emotion and feeling, which may also carry a sexual connotation.[49] The multivalent discourse that flourished during the last decades of the Ming prompted intellectuals to critique contemporary mores, and to evoke the *qing* ideal in their search for ways to revitalize Confucian values.[50] For example, Feng Menglong's (1574–1646) *Qingshi leilüe* (A classified outline of love), which purports to elevate the place of the educated courtesan in Ming society, records stories of "chaste courtesans" who defended themselves, much in the same manner as the heroines of the *Lienü zhuan* had done.[51] By bringing these morally "marginal" women to the "center" of the Confucian moral universe, Feng stressed the possibility of invigorating the world in which he lived according to Confucian doctrine.

By the close of the Ming dynasty, such efforts at moral revitalization had proved less than successful,[52] but members of the elite continued to see a real need to regenerate values that would support order, regularity, and security. Underlying these values was the stable kinship system.[53] The *Lienü zhuan* conception of womanhood which emphasized loyalty, chastity, and duty to family fitted perfectly to the "'new' conservatism of the late Ming, with its emphasis on ritualism, female sexual purity, and its male equivalent, the purity of dynastic loyalty."[54]

The status of the *Lienü zhuan* as an "instructional text" endured one hundred years after the Ming downfall. As *kaozheng* scholarship, with its emphasis on the reconstruction of the sources of antiquity and the clarification of Confucian textual legacies, attracted more adherents during the last quarter of the eighteenth century, the *Lienü zhuan* became the focus of scholarly query. Two distinguished *kaozheng* scholars applied their knowledge of textual criticism to comment on and reconstruct the Song edition of the *Lienü zhuan*. Wang Shaolan (1760–1835), well known because of annotations to the *Shuowen* dictionary and *Qianfu lun* (a collection of thirty-six essays by Wang Fu [c. 90–165]), wrote a one *juan* work, *Lienü zhuan buzhu zheng'e* (Corrections to commentaries on the *Lienü zhuan;* reprinted in the *Xuetang congke*) which the modern classicist Luo Zhenyu (1866–1940) rediscovered. Gu Guangqi (1766–1835), a Suzhou-based member of Ruan Yuan's (1764–1849) extensive literati network, and an accomplished scholar of epigraphy, textual criticism, and bibliography, published *Gu Lienü zhuan fu kaozheng* (An appendix of evidential research verifications to the old *Lienü zhuan*) in 1796.[55] This unillustrated edition became particularly popular in literati circles, and was the direct inspiration for Wang Zhaoyuan's own supplementary annotations to the *Lienü zhuan*.

We now turn to Wang's biography. Our discussion is based on the *nianpu* (chronological record) of her marriage to one of Qing China's leading *kaozheng* scholars, Hao Yixing (1757–1825). Prepared by the twentieth-century classicist Xu Weiyu (1905–51), this *nianpu* was based on the various collected works compiled by Wang and Hao, printed by their descendants, and entitled "Hao Lan'gao (Xixing) fufu nianpu" (Chronological record of Hao Lan'gao [Yixing] and his wife; 1936).

A PERSONAL HISTORY OF WANG ZHAOYUAN

Wang Zhaoyuan was born on October 4, 1763, in the village of Hebei, Fushan District, Dengzhou Prefecture, which is located on the northern side of the Shandong peninsula.[56] This locale, which one may consider a kind of "cultural backwater" (especially in comparison with Jiangnan), was where Wang Zhaoyuan, the only child of two locally well-known teachers, grew up. At the age of five, her father died. Thereafter she and her mother (surnamed Lin) began to subsist on the latter's earnings as a teacher.[57] Through her mother, Zhaoyuan developed literary skills and prepared herself to follow her mother's example as a "teacher of the inner chambers." It was in her capacity as a female instructress to Hao Yixing's only daughter Gui that Zhaoyuan entered her future husband's life. Yixing's first wife, also née Lin (b. 1758), had died in 1786. Although the *nianpu* does not make clear whether Zhaoyuan had served in the Hao household before the wife's demise, by late 1787 at the age of 25 *sui* (twenty-four years old), she became Hao's second wife in what proved to be a companionate marriage.[58]

Yixing represented the fifteenth generation of the Hao lineage in Qixia (also the birthplace of Zhaoyuan's mother), an inland district of Dengzhou Prefecture. At the time of his marriage to Zhaoyuan, Yixing was in the throes of the cycle of examination success and failure. A year into his second marriage he gained his *juren* degree, but it would take some eleven years before he passed his *jinshi*.[59] During the decade of the 1790s, a crucial period in the intellectual and social development of the couple, Yixing encouraged Zhaoyuan to use her literary talents to write poetry and prose commentary.

In 1794 the great scholar and official Bi Yuan (1730–97) became governor and Ruan Yuan director of education in Shandong.[60] These eminent men persuaded local scholars to engage in one of the specialities of *kaozheng* research, epigraphical study, which both Yixing and Zhaoyuan began to pursue. Ruan Yuan probably first became aware of Yixing's local reputation as poet and scholar, and of Zhaoyuan's literary talent at this time.

The relationship between Ruan and the couple intensified in 1799 when Yixing passed (after two previous attempts) the metropolitan exam for which Ruan served as director.[61] Zhaoyuan, accompanied by other Hao family members, journeyed to Beijing to join in the celebration of her husband's achievement. On that occasion she met Ruan, along with other *kaozheng* luminaries. The happiness of this period was short lived, however. The couple went into mourning at the death of Yixing's father in 1800, and shortly thereafter, of their second son (they had suffered the loss of their first son in 1792).[62] Although Zhaoyuan gave birth to a third son in 1801, she remained profoundly distressed at the death of her eldest two children.[63] With so much death and sorrow in the family in such a short period of time, she turned to annotating the *Liexian zhuan* (Biographies of [Daoist] transcendants), also attributed to the *Lienü zhuan* compiler Liu Xiang, apparently taking refuge in this collection.[64] When news spread in literati circles that Zhaoyuan was engaged in a meticulous and critical exegesis of the *Liexian zhuan*, the renowned bibliophile Hong Yixuan (1765–1837) immediately offered to write a preface. His encomium was incorporated into the final version, the *Liexian jiaozheng* (Corrections to the *Liexian zhuan*), first printed in 1812, some eight years after Zhaoyuan had embarked upon the project.

Zhaoyuan may also have been interested in this specific Han work because of its resonances with the text Yixing had been studying and revising around the same time, the *Shanhai jing* (Classic of mountains and seas), in particular its images of immortals. Also, in early 1805 Yixing was collaborating with Gu Guangqi on lexicographical and phonological research to the *Erya* (Examples of refined usage).[65] Zhaoyuan assisted Gu and Yixing, and it was probably through her acquaintance with Gu that her appreciation of his 1796 publication *Gu Lienü zhuan fu kaozheng* led her to consider formulating her own annotated edition to the *Lienü zhuan*. The Tongcheng scholar Ma Ruichen (1782–1853) wrote in the first of the two prefaces to the *Lienü zhuan buzhu* that Zhaoyuan's research on the *Erya* might have inspired her annotations. He commended her abilities "to examine (what was) counterfeit and to substantiate errors, to expand on existing evidence, and to document (that) in writing . . ."[66]

WANG ZHAOYUAN AND THE *LIENÜ ZHUAN BUZHU*

It took Zhaoyuan almost seven years to complete her annotations to the *Lienü zhuan*, which modern scholars consider an exemplary piece of scholarship. As the epilogues to the various editions of the *Lienü zhuan buzhu* attest, Zhaoyuan was aware that she was not the first woman to offer exegesis on the *Lienü zhuan*.[67] Fragments of three major sets of annotations known as the *sanjiazhu* (three schools of annotations), all authored by women, of the pre-Song editions of the *Lienü zhuan* have survived, but only in fragmentary form.[68] The three commentators were Ban Zhao, Zhao Mu or Mother Zhao, and Yu Zhenjie, whose notes were still available when Wei Zheng (580–643) compiled the bibliography section for the *Suishu*. Zhaoyuan at the end of her own annotations briefly discussed her predecessors.[69]

Wang Zhaoyuan's collated edition of the *Lienü zhuan* followed the Song edition eight-*juan* arrangement, with the first seven *juan* of biographies attributed to Liu Xiang, and the last chapter adding twenty biographies of women from the Zhou to the Han dynasties. Throughout this eight-*juan* compilation, Zhaoyuan appended notes to each of the biographies. These comments revealed her affinity for contemporary linguistic controversies among *kaozheng* scholars and her superior knowledge of early texts. As a *kaozheng* scholar, Wang Zhaoyuan approached the *Lienü zhuan* with the same kind of methodology her male counterparts utilized in evidential study.[70] She strove to explicate, annotate, and expurgate passages in the *Lienü zhuan* in order to restore what could be "proved" by evidential research to be Liu Xiang's original text. Thus, Zhaoyuan's aim was not to revitalize the moral nuances of the *Lienü zhuan* but rather to establish, as far as possible, the "original" language of Liu Xiang's text. However, in some of her annotations, as for example, in the story "The Wife of Zhao Shuai of Jin," where she clarifies passages that emphasize the marital duties of both men and women, the moral message is more explicit.[71]

In general, Zhaoyuan's remarks and notes expose three kinds of scholastic negligence: inaccuracies of transmission, omissions, and insufficient textual research. Examples of the first type of deficiency may be seen in her notes to the eighth story in *juan* 1 "The Governess of the Lady of Qi." Zhaoyuan records that the character *jiao* in the text, meaning "to exchange," should have been *jiao* indicating pretty or handsome, thus reading, "Lady Jiang was pretty," rather than "Lady Jiang was exchanged."[72] Similarly, she found transmission mistakes in the thirteenth story in *juan* 8, "The Wife and Daughter of Wang Zhang." Wang Zhang's difficulties with those at court is recounted here, and Zhaoyuan writes that the matter of those who betrayed him, which led to this detention, was not simply an affair (*shi*), but in fact a crime (*zui*).[73] Her annotations here make clear how the readings of the stories were affected by these misprinted characters.

Her notices of omissions include remarks to the first story in *juan* 1, "The Two Royal Consorts of You Yu [Shun]." Here she demonstrates that an entire sentence from another text, the *Shiji suoyin* (Commentary on the Records of the historian), was expurgated.[74] Significantly, the deleted expression, " . . . that Yao's daughters taught Shun the skill of a bird to go up into a granary, and the art of a dragon to go into a well," reveals the remarkable talents of these two women. In other words, Zhaoyuan restores passages in the *Lienü zhuan* that highlight female ability. The same observation about Wang and female talent may be drawn from her exegesis of the ninth story in *juan* 1, "Her Serenity Ji of Lu," where she directs attention to the original passage in the *Guoyu* (Discourses of the states) that conveyed that it was the wife of the Duke of Lu—not an official—who spoke for him.[75] By indicating that the expression *dafu* is a mistake for the correct wording *furen*, Zhaoyuan is able to indicate once again the importance of the portrayal of talented women in the *Lienü zhuan*.

Finally, we observe another occasion when Zhaoyuan displays her knowledge of pre-Han texts. According to the fifteenth story in *juan* 6, "The Daughter of the Taicang of Qi," there were five kinds of corporal punishments. But Zhaoyuan counters this statement with citations from the *Shiji* and *Hanshu* which state that there were only three kinds of punishments at the time the story took place.[76]

Ma Ruichen's introduction to the *Lienü zhuan buzhu* was complemented by that of another well-known *kaozheng* scholar, Zang Yong (1767–1811). Zang Yong, also a member of Ruan Yuan's inner circle and acquainted with Hao Yixing already in 1794, had lodged at the Hao home in the autumn of 1810 to assist Yixing in the second edition of the appendices to his commentaries to the *Shanhai jing*, the *Shanhai jing jianshu*.[77] Zang was aware of how Zhaoyuan helped Yixing correct more than 300 misprinted graphs and provided an updated count of the graphs for each chapter and for the book as a whole. Observing the working relationship of Yixing and Zhaoyuan, Zang Yong compared them to another famous scholarly pair, the father and son Wang Niansun (1744–1832) and Wang Yinzhi (1766–1834): *Gaoyou Wang fuzi, Qixia Hao fufu* (In Gaoyou, there are the prominent father and son [scholars from the Wang family]; in Qixia, there are the distinguished husband and wife [scholars from the Hao family]).[78]

At this point, in the second decade of the nineteenth century, news of Zhaoyuan's erudition and intellectual prowess was becoming widespread. No less than seven prominent scholars commented at length on her particular amendments to the *Lienü zhuan*: the encomia of Wang Niansun, Wang Yinzhi, Ma Ruichen, Hu Chenggong (1776–1832), Hong Yixuan, Mou Ting (1759–?), and Wang Shaolan were all included in an appendix and printed in the 1879 edition of the *Lienü zhuan buzhu*.

Wang Zhaoyuan's *Lienü zhuan buzhu* may be viewed not only in the context of *kaozheng* scholarship but also from the perspective of women's writing and publishing during the first decades of the nineteenth century. Ellen Widmer has assessed Wang Zhaoyuan's 1812 *Lienü zhuan* publication in the light of two contemporary trends, that is, commercialism and didacticism.[79] Although Zhaoyuan's text was a "family production," first printed in Hao and Wang's *Saishu tang waiji* (Secondary works of the Studio for Airing Books in the Sun),[80] its popularity was sufficient to attract commercial interest. Widmer holds such commercial interest in women's literary production responsible for "fuelling the increase in energy, quality, and complexity of women's writings at this time," in the early nineteenth century, developments that distinguished earlier achievements of writing and reading women in the seventeenth century.[81]

While the aim of early–nineteenth-century publishers was increasingly to capture "a faceless female reader" who may have been lower in social class, as yet we know little about the reception of Wang's *Lienü zhuan*.[82] We do know, however, that the success of Zhaoyuan's *Lienü zhuan buzhu* directly inspired another female author to annotate the *Lienü zhuan*. In 1825, shortly before her death, Liang Duan (?–1825), completed her collation to the *Lienü zhuan*, entitled *Lienü zhuan jiaozhu* (Commentary to the *Lienü zhuan*).[83] It was published in 1831 by her husband, Wang Yuansun (1794–1836), with the title *Lienü zhuan jiaozhu duben* (Annotated reader to the *Lienü zhuan*). Liang Duan's great aunt, the famed Hangzhou woman scholar Liang Desheng (1771–1847), wrote a preface.[84] The elder Liang was married to Xu Zongyan (1768–1819), who was also a member of the 1799 *jinshi* class. It is therefore likely that Zhaoyuan's accomplishment was known through her husband's network of fellow students, many of whom were linked to Ruan Yuan.

Despite the rise of networks of female writers and readers in this period, then, male networks remained integral to the production and dissemination of women's writings. Zhaoyuan in Shandong could connect to Ruan from Yangzhou, Gu from Suzhou, and Zang from Changzhou, revealing both the degree to which women's literati networks extended in the early nineteenth century and the degree to which they remained dependent on male connections. Male involvement in Wang's literary production further demonstrates that it was possible for women to gain acceptance within male intellectual circles. Zhaoyuan apparently had no problems pursuing her literary skills or accepting male scholarly appreciation of her talents. Her classical knowledge and *kaozheng* skills allowed her to assert in public space her authority as a *cainü* (talented woman), and permits us to consider the implications of gendered scholarship in China prior to the twentieth century.

AFTER WANG ZHAOYUAN'S *LIENÜ ZHUAN BUZHU*

In 1883 Wang Zhaoyuan's *Lienü zhuan buzhu* also received imperial recognition. At the behest of the Shuntian official Bi Daoyuan (?–1889; *jinshi* 1841), who had memorialized the Guangxu Emperor, to consider the importance of the writings of both Yixing and Zhaoyuan, the Emperor issued an edict praising their scholarship on January 14, 1883. Guangxu further requested that a selection of their works (including the *Lienü zhuan buzhu*) be housed at the Beijing palace's Nanshu fang (Pavilion of the south) for consultation by members of the Hanlin Academy. This edict, as well as Bi's memorial, were printed in one of Wang's posthumous collected writings, *Shishuo* (Poems and commentary).[85]

Although some fifteen years later, Wang Zhaoyuan's reputation, along with that of the other woman *Lienü zhuan* commentator, Liang Duan, were vilified by the reformer Liang Qichao (1873–1929),[86] the *Lienü zhuan* tradition endured in various forms into the twentieth century. Even with the onset of lithography and other new printing techniques made popular through the publication of illustrated courtesan guides and connoisseur books in Shanghai such as *Jingying xiaosheng chuji* (Mirror reflections and flutes sounds, first collection; 1887), which presented "model mores" for courtesans, the *Lienü zhuan* format remained the standard arrangement for conveying desirable female qualities, including those prized for enjoyment in the pleasure quarters.[87]

Around 1904, Xiao Daoguan (1855–1907) from Fuzhou (Fujian) compiled a new set of annotations to the *Lienü zhuan*, entitled *Lienü zhuan jijie* (Collected annotations to the *Lienü zhuan*), using a *kaozheng* approach resonant with that of Wang Zhaoyuan and Liang Duan.[88] The preface to this work proclaimed Daoguan's affinity to the earlier *Lienü zhuan sanjiazhu* and, notably, her appreciation of Zhaoyuan's own edition. Like Zhaoyuan, Daoguan intended her revision to be a model of *kaozheng* scholarship.

Daoguan's interest in etymology culminating in her study *Shuowen chong-wen guanjian* (Views on duplicated characters in the *Shuowen*) and her compatible marriage to Chen Yan (1856–1937), an accomplished poet and later a professor of literature at Beijing University, liken her life to that of Zhaoyuan. The similarity of these two women's intellectual pursuits, although spaced some 100 years apart, implies that despite the nineteenth century vicissitudes in women's learning, the contents and format of the *Lienü zhuan* also remained a serious tradition.

Men continued to engage in this tradition as is evident in an expansion of the *Lienü zhuan* written in 1908 and examined by Joan Judge in chapter 6 of this volume. While Wei Xiyuan's collection, as well as that of Xiao Daoguan, were direct textual descendents of Liu Xiang's *Lienü zhuan*, new-style texts—-from women's journals to modern textbooks—-continued the *Lienü zhuan* tradition in dramatically new forms. These new media advanced the aims of the new women's education in the late Qing and early Republic by celebrating exemplars from the *Lienü zhuan*, using the female biographical narrative form, and even integrating foreign women into the repertoire of Chinese female paragons.[89]

CODA: CHINESE WOMEN AND MODERN BIOGRAPHICAL WRITING

The *nianpu* by Xu Weiyu of the Hao-Wang marriage, which allows us to understand the circumstances behind Zhaoyuan's *Lienü zhuan buzhu*, was itself the product of new innovative biographical writing initiated in the Republican era.[90] This *nianpu*, first published in the journal of Qinghua university, appeared at a time when Chinese scholars were just beginning to collaborate and lay the foundations to create the first English language model "biographical dictionary," *Eminent Chinese of the Ch'ing Period*. This work marked a shift away from the kind of "praise and blame" writing that had dominated the Chinese biographical tradition for so long, and focused instead on the "personalities" of the 800 men and women chosen for inclusion in the study. That the *Eminent Chinese* acknowledged the importance of women (wives, daughters, daughters-in-law, mothers) was in itself a novelty. Contrary to what Liang Qichao had written about *cainü*, Xu's and other scholars' published studies of the 1930s illuminated the respected position learned women had enjoyed in the High Qing.[91]

Central to that groundbreaking work on women's biographies were the contributions of Chen Yinke (1890–1969) who was the first historian to probe the personalities of women in Chinese history. Beginning with portraits of the Tang figures, Empress Wu (Wu Zetian [r. 690–705]) and Yang Guifei, continuing with studies of "long-suffering genteel wives of impoverished literati," and culminating in his "magnum opus," *Liu Rushi biezhuan* (An ulterior biography of Liu Rushi [1618–44]; 1959?), Chen's historical work gave a prominent place to women.[92] This biography of Liu Rushi, together with his later study of the woman writer Chen Duansheng (1751–96), communicated Chen's appreciation of women's literary proficiency and entrance into circles of male literati discourse.[93]

It has only been in the last few decades that modern scholars in East Asia and Euro-America have built upon the legacies of Chen Yinke and the literary scholar Hu Wenkai to investigate women's lives and writings.[94] That task has not been easy since, as we have attempted to demonstrate, the *Lienü zhuan* model itself has dominated the historical record for so long that crucial aspects of women's subjectivities have been submerged or obscured. As we analyze the 2,000-year-long *Lienü zhuan* tradition today, as one of the cultural institutions that contributed to the regulation of life during the imperial age, we need to examine the various purposes this tradition served and the nature of its influence over the writing of women's biography.

4. *Lienü* versus *Xianyuan*

The Two Biographical Traditions in Chinese Women's History

Nanxiu Qian

Liu Xiang's (77–6 BCE) *Lienü zhuan* (Biographies of women) gave rise to two major female biographical traditions: *lienü* (exemplary women) and *xianyuan* (virtuous and talented ladies). As Harriet Zurndorfer notes in chapter 3 of this volume, Liu Xiang's text led to the inclusion of a *lienü* chapter in fourteen of the twenty-six extant Chinese dynastic histories, as well as in numerous gazetteers (see appendix B). What is less well known is that it also inspired the chapter "Xianyuan" in the *Shishuo xinyu* (A new account of tales of the world), compiled by the Liu-Song (420–479) Prince Liu Yiqing (403–44) and his staff. The *Shishuo xinyu* (*Shishuo* for short) characterizes over 600 diverse late Han (ca. 150–220) and Wei-Jin (220–420) historical figures in its 1,130 anecdotes, each categorized under 36 personality types. So structured, the *Shishuo* inspired numerous imitations in later periods: Eighteen out of the thirty-five works of the *Shishuo* genre that I have located each contain a "Xianyuan" chapter. There are also two *Shishuo* imitations exclusively devoted to women (see appendix C). Both the *lienü* and *xianyuan* traditions emulate Liu Xiang's *Lienü zhuan* in accentuating women's roles in family and in society. Each, however, has a specific orientation in representing women's lives and guiding their behavior. *Lienü* records, being incorporated into official history writing, became increasingly reflective of Confucian norms. Conversley, accounts of *xianyuan*, rooted in the free-spirited Wei-Jin intellectual aura and written by private scholars, featured strong-minded, self-sufficient literate women.

To be sure, the *Shishuo* genre is primarily anecdotal, yet it has also had a strong biographical component since its formation. For one thing, all the works of the *Shishuo* genre depict historical figures. Each work deals with a specific time period, past or present; in all, the authors consciously filled out all the dynastic spans and thus formed a complete counterpart to the twenty-six histories (see appendix C for the time period covered in each *Shishuo* work). Furthermore, the circulation of *Shishuo* from its very beginning included Liu Jun's (462–521) extensive commentary that provided, among other things, biographical information about most of the characters in the text. Some authors of later imitations consciously followed this template and added their own commentaries, showing a willingness to increase the biographic authenticity of their respective contributions: Nine out of the eighteen *Shishuo* works that contain a *xianyuan* chapter feature such content (see appendix C for the *Shishuo* works with commentaries). Finally, even without being supplemented by regular biographical data, a *xianyuan* entry usually exposes more individual qualities of a woman's life vis-à-vis a *lienü* entry, which was often formatted by court sanctioned values.

Yet the study of Chinese women's history has so far emphasized the role of the *lienü* tradition while largely ignoring the recurring dissenting voice of its *xianyuan* counterpart. Late imperial versions of *xianyuan*, for example, offer a strong counternarrative to that of the chastity cult that has dominated understanding of the Ming and Qing eras in modern Chinese historiography. This chapter attempts to correct this bias by demonstrating the coexistence of *lienü* and *xianyuan* in China's historical writing on women. Reconstructing these two traditions and their relationship will be conducted through historicizing the sociopolitical and intellectual context surrounding their formation and transmission. Against this backdrop, this chapter tries to explain why and how an author chose one genre over the other between dynastic history and the *Shishuo* style, and what these choices would imply about Chinese women's history and Chinese culture.

This chapter first examines the formation of the *lienü* and *xianyuan* traditions that interacted with each other throughout China's history. In a very general sense, the two had more or less kept a complementary relationship until the fourteenth century, as the second section demonstrates. From the Ming on, as Raphals, Carlitz, and others have noted, there was a marked shift towards the concept of the chastity cult in the *lienü* texts. At the same time, the *xianyuan* tradition most strongly asserted itself in valorizing free-spirited writing women. The third section probes this late imperial discrepancy between the two traditions. The final section briefly surveys how the last works of *lienü* and *xianyuan* transformed themselves in accordance with the rapid sociopolitical changes at the turn of the twentieth century.

THE FORMATION OF THE *LIENÜ*
AND THE *XIANYUAN* TRADITIONS

Scholars continue to debate whether Liu Xiang compiled the *Lienü zhuan*, and whether its earliest extant version, edited by Song scholars, reconstructs Liu's original text. Here I follow the historical tradition established by Ban Gu (32–92) in the *Hanshu* (History of the Former Han) that ascribes the *Lienü zhuan* to Liu Xiang.[1] As Zurndorfer notes in chapter 3, Ban Gu claimed in his biography of Liu Xiang that Liu had compiled the *Lienü zhuan* to aid his ruler in establishing Confucian order, beginning with disciplining the imperial harem.[2] In the *Lienü zhuan*, Liu invoked two types of female models: "virtuous and talented royal consorts, and righteous and chaste wives" (*xianfei zhenfu*).[3] The two moral codes signified by these models, *xian* and *zhen*, deserve closer scrutiny, as do their continually evolving meanings in the Han contexts. Both codes would each occupy a central place in the later writing of Chinese women's history.

A widely used moral category in the works that were conventionally designated "Confucian classics" in the Han period, *xian* depicts those who possess both *de* (virtue) and *cai*, the ability and/or talent to actualize virtuous qualities.[4] The meaning of *zhen* in the pre-Qin and Han texts is more complex. According to Xu Shen (30–124) in *Shuowen jiezi* (Interpretation of words): "*Zhen* [means] query through divination (*zhen, buwen ye*)", a definition that is extended to include *zheng* (correctness, righteousness) and constancy.[5] These various meanings were used to describe both men and women in pre-Qin and Han texts. Whereas for men *zhen* retained the same connotations throughout the imperial period, for women it gradually became focused on a sense of "chastity."[6]

In the discursive context of Liu Xiang's *Lienü zhuan*, however, *zhen* carries a much broader meaning than "chastity," as is evident in the equation of *xianfei* and *zhenfu* in the quotation above from Liu Xiang's biography in the *Hanshu*. I believe these two terms are mutually referential (*huwen*); *fei* and *fu* share the same set of modifiers *xian* and *zhen*. Only by possessing these combined qualities—virtue, talent, righteousness, and chastity—could these women make "the state prosperous and their families illustrious" (*xingguo xianjia*)[7]. "Chastity" alone could not fulfill such grand tasks.

Liu Xiang's *Lienü zhuan* gave rise to the *lienü* and the *xianyuan* traditions at precisely the same time. The first dynastic history to include a chapter entitled "Lienü zhuan," Fan Ye's (398–445) *Hou Hanshu* (History of the Later Han [25–220]), was compiled in the 430s.[8] Liu Yiqing's *Shishuo* featuring the chapter "Xianyuan" was also completed around 430. The profound differences between the two traditions (at this historical point) can be attributed to two factors: the sociopolitical backdrop of the time in which the stories were set, and the scholastic and ideological orientations of the respective authors.

Stories included in the *Hou Hanshu* "Lienü zhuan" take place during the later Han period, in which Confucianism was esteemed as the state ideology and Confucian moral codes were considered guiding principles for human behavior. The *Shishuo* "Xianyuan" stories are set in the Wei-Jin period, which was characterized in part by *Xuanxue* (Abstruse learning). In this era, human capacity, talents, and the individual's true inner self were at the center of attention, in accordance with *Xuanxue* ideals. In terms of the scholastic trends of the fifth century, therefore, while Liu Yiqing's work was representative of the fields of *Xuanxue* and *Wenxue* (Literature), Fan Ye's was representative of *Ruxue* (Confucian learning) and *Shixue* (Historiographic learning).[9] These scholastic affiliations would have also reflected political preferences.

A prince of the Liu-Song royal clan who had held important positions, Liu Yiqing was, however, "by nature unceremonious and plain, with few desires but a love of literature" (*weixing jiansu, gua shiyu, aihao wenyi*).[10] Zhou Yiliang (1913–2001) maintained that Liu Yiqing retreated into literature because of Emperor Wen's (r. 424–53) suspicious nature. The paranoid emperor killed several important ministers, including his brother Liu Yikang (409–51), causing his courtiers to live in constant fear.[11] Liu Yiqing found refuge in literature and the relatively aloof *Xuanxue*. Both learnings culminated in his compilation (with the aid of his staff) of the *Shishuo xinyu*, including the "Xianyuan" chapter.

Fan Ye, conversely, was by nature ambitious. He had served on the staff of Liu Yikang and was deeply involved in Yikang's power struggle with the emperor. He further extended his political aspirations to historical writing, with a clear purpose of "rectifying a dynasty's gain and loss" (*zheng yidai deshi*).[12] Both of his fields of interest—governing the state and writing the history of a Confucian dynasty—required his focus on the *Ruxue* learning that guided his compilation of the *Hou Hanshu*, including the "Lienü" chapter.

Fan's preface to this chapter emphasizes the importance of *xian* and *zhen* that Ban Gu had highlighted in his biography of Liu Xiang. The entries in the chapter further stress *xian* over *zhen*. Of the twenty women's life stories Fan Ye has included, two-thirds praise women's advice to their husbands or demonstrate how their learning and eloquence have guided their families; only seven of the cases exemplify *zhen*. Of these seven, six are about the virtue of chastity, while only one concerns the original meaning of *zhen*, constancy. In its formative stage, therefore (as argued in chapter 3 of this volume and in Lisa Raphal's *Sharing the Light*), the *lienü* tradition emphasized both ability and virtue. As Fan Ye states in the preface: "The selection brought together women of particularly outstanding talent and lofty behavior (*caixing gaoxiu*), without focusing on one specific virtue."[13] This is evident in the two most lengthy entries on Ban Zhao (45–120?) and Cai Yan (fl. late Han) respectively.

Ban Zhao is the perfect agent of the values Fan Ye advocates in his preface. Using her "erudite learning and outstanding talents" (*boxue gao-cai*), she has completed her brother Ban Gu's unfinished *History of the Han*, assisted Empress Deng in governing the state, and compiled *Nüjie* (*Instructions for women*) for inner chamber discipline.[14] Cai Yan also uses her extraordinary "learning, talents, and capacity of reasoning" (*boxue you caibian*) to make significant cultural contributions. In a period of great political chaos, she has restored her family library collection from memory and composed poems to lament the people's suffering; hence her cultural contributions to the country, the people, and her family. While her case would prove problematic to later scholars because of her three marriages, for Fan Ye, Cai's unfortunate marital life only intensifies her personal sorrow in a chaotic time.[15]

Fan Ye departed most from Liu Xiang in removing Liu's category of "pernicious favorite women who caused disorder and ruin" (*niebi luan-wang zhe*) and erecting the "Lienü zhuan" as a "shrine" to exemplary women. He consequently shifted Liu Xiang's purpose from "putting the son of Heaven on guard" to "glorifying the history of our women" (*zhao wo guantong*).[16] This new purpose articulated by Fan Ye would foreshadow the compilation of later dynastic "Lienü zhuan."

Liu Yiqing and his staff also departed significantly from Liu Xiang's archetype, glorifying women in the *Shishuo* "Xianyuan" chapter for very different reasons. While Liu equated *xian* with *zhen*, the *xian* in "Xian-yuan" was detached from the Confucian moral code and was evoked in the context of the Wei-Jin *Xuanxue* value system. The best way to understand the meaning of *xian* in "Xianyuan" is through its central figure Xie Daoyun (ca. 335–after 405). In comparing Xie with another remarkable young woman, Nun Ji describes her as deeply imbued with the "Bamboo Grove aura" (*linxia fengqi*), which renders her far superior to the other woman, a mere "flower of the inner chamber" (*guifang zhi xiu*) (19/30) (chapter 19, "Xianyuan" / entry 30 of the *Shishuo xinyu*).[17] Here *linxia fengqi* refers to the aura of the "Zhulin Qixian" (Seven virtuous and talented men of the bamboo grove), who have embodied the most esteemed Wei-Jin characteristics: philosophical depth, poetic talent, and artistic expertise, combined with a carefree and lofty lifestyle.[18]

Thus the *xian* in *xianyuan* refers to the *xian* in the *Zhulin qixian*, and transcends its Han connotation that combined Confucian *de* (virtue) with *cai* (talents, abilities). Consistent with the Wei-Jin *Xuanxue* redefinition of *de* as potency, potentiality, and efficacy, the Wei-Jin concept of *xian* denotes persons with the "ability and potential to act according to the *Dao*."[19] The *Dao* here also transcends the Confucian realm to include the Ways of other schools of thought. The "Seven Virtuous and Talented Men" were named *xian* because they followed the Daoist Way of defying ritual bondage. Their "spirit of freedom and transcendence" created the Bamboo Grove aura.[20] Similarly, the "Virtuous and Talented Ladies" were named *xian* because they, like the "Seven Men" and their *Dao*, transcended the Confucian virtues of obedience and submission that the male world had imposed upon them. In one *xianyuan* example, Mother Zhao (d. 243) invokes the Daoist principle of nonstriving (*wuwei* or *buwei*)[21] in warning her soon-to-be-married daughter against unnecessary striving (*wei*) that might expose her to public scrutiny (19/5). Mother Zhao is *xian* because she guides her daughter to self-protection following the *Dao* of Laozi and Yangzhu.

According to the *Shishuo* "Xianyuan" chapter, the Wei-Jin standards for judging a virtuous and talented woman include the ability to analyze human character, literary talent, composure in the face of difficulties, a commitment to protecting her family, and the courage to criticize and challenge her husband, brothers, and sons. Overall, the women who merit inclusion in the *Shishuo* "Xianyuan" manifest their *de* primarily through their roles as protective and loving mothers, wives, sisters, and daughters, and their *cai* as creative talents and iconoclastic thinkers. *De* and *cai* are thus woven into their *xian* behavior.

In protecting their families and coping in times of chaos, these virtuous and talented women often surpass their men in courage, wisdom, composure, and judgment.[22] Xu Yun's (d. 254) wife, Lady Ruan, is one example, as depicted in the *Shishuo*. On their wedding night, when Xu refuses to consummate the marriage because of Lady Ruan's "extraordinary homeliness," she seizes his robe, scolds him for betraying Confucius' teaching about loving virtue more than sensual beauty, and shames him into fulfilling his responsibility (19/6). Throughout their marriage, she gives Xu political advice (19/7). When she realizes that Xu is doomed to his tragic fate, she calmly shelters her two sons during the crisis. All the while her "spirit and facial expression remain unchanged" (*shense bu bian*), sustained by a mental strength (19/8).

The women in *Shishuo* display their *cai* in a variety of ways—as poets, writers, pure conversationalists, and housewives—thereby earning great respect and admiration from their spouses, male relatives, and the broader society.[23] They are often more adept than men at the major Wei-Jin intellectual practice, *renlun jianshi*, or judgment and recognition of human (character) types, succinctly translated as "character appraisal."[24] Shan Tao's wife, Lady Han, for instance, evaluates three men among the famous "Seven Men": Ji Kang, Ruan Ji, and her own husband. Although Shan himself was the most prominent character-appraisal adept of the time,[25] he accepts Han's judgment when she ranks him lower than his two friends. This sort of story, thus, not only praises women's talent but their courage to challenge the highest authority in a male-dominated practice (19/11).[26]

While earlier historical writings generally overlook the inner world of women, the "Xianyuan" chapter explores their *qing* (feelings, emotions, passion, affection, sentiments, etc.). The women are loving but rarely tender or subservient. Their talents signal their sensitivity, in literature and art particularly. Public recognition of their capabilities further encourages their self-esteem. This self-esteem, combined with their sensitivity, often complicates their relationships—particularly their relationships with their husbands—and causes emotional turmoil. The most talented women, thus, often seem to be the most unhappily married.

When the talented and cultivated first-rate poet Xie Daoyun openly expresses her unhappiness with her mediocre husband by comparing him to the men in her natal family (19/26), she is actually comparing him unfavorably with herself.[27] In a famous passage, the *Shishuo* describes how Xie Daoyun rises to the challenge of describing a flurry of snow more successfully than one of her male cousins. As his "salt-scattering" analogy lacks poetic imagination and natural vitality, her description of the snow as "willow catkins on the wind rising" (*liuxu yinfeng qi*) brilliantly brings fluffy, warm spring into gloomy, cold winter. Xie Daoyun's exceptional talent and resulting resentment of an intellectually disappointing husband—inferior even to the cousin she so clearly trumped in this poetry contest—initiated a new literary theme of inner chamber lament in her day and would inspire a great number of bitter episodes in later "Xianyuan" chapters.

Most of the women the *Shishuo* celebrates defy Confucian social conventions. Xie Daoyun defies the Han Confucian decree that a woman's husband is her Heaven.[28] Lady Han puts men, including her husband, under close, critical scrutiny, stealthily observing two male strangers all night in order to appraise their character.[29] Xu Yun's bride scolds her husband, breaking the principle of obedience from the very start of their marriage. The modern scholar Yu Jiaxi, therefore, questions whether the women featured in this chapter are true *xianyuan*, and quotes Jin historians in condemning Wei-Jin men for not disciplining their women.[30] Indeed, the *Shishuo* demonstrates that a supportive male relation—a father, uncle, husband, son, or brother—stood behind almost every daring woman and openly or tacitly endorsed her unconventional behavior and remarks. Xie An comforts his niece Daoyun's marital resentment (19/26), and Shan Tao accepts his wife Han's character appraisal. This man-woman solidarity, formed upon the *Xuanxue* belief in equality of human nature, would extend its influence into the late imperial *xianyuan* tradition and set up a sharp contrast to the gender relationship in the *lienü* tradition.

THE PRE-MING RELATIONSHIP BETWEEN *LIENÜ* AND *XIANYUAN*

Later "Lienü zhuan" compilers acknowledged their indebtedness to Liu Xiang but altered his fundamental purpose. No longer "putting the son of Heaven on guard" by, for example, including pernicious female exemplars who were a danger to the court, their aim was to "glorify the history of our women" by collecting women's stories that had been "neglected in the previous historical writings."[31] Each of the prefaces to the dynastic "Lienü zhuan," starting with Fan Ye's, reiterated this purpose. The Yuan minister Tuotuo (1313–55), for instance, stated in his preface to the *Songshi* (History of the Song [960–1279]) "Lienü zhuan": "Men who dispatch their ambition in the four directions can achieve merit through close ties with mentors and friends. Women, however, who remain confined within the inner chambers have difficulty leaving their good deeds in history. How, therefore, can we abandon the records of exemplary women from previous dynasties?"[32]

Just as the purpose of writing "Lienü zhuan" shifted, so did the standards for selecting the *lienü* entries, which became increasingly moralistic. But before the Ming, this moral approach had been solidly grounded in an emphasis on women's talents and abilities. As noted above, the first dynastic "Lienü zhuan" in the *Hou Hanshu* applauded women's capability and talents over chastity. The second (in the compiler's time sequence), in Wei Shou's (506–572) *Wei shu* (History of the [Northern] Wei [386–534]), increased the number of virtue entries while asserting that women's virtuous behavior was dependent on their "discernment" (*mingshi*). From the Tang onward, moral categories and entries increased and those emphasizing talents decreased. The *Jinshu* (History of the Jin [265–420]), compiled by the Tang minister Fang Xuanling (578–648) and others, expanded the *lienü* categories of *zhen* in the *Hou Hanshu* and *liecao* (various virtues) in the *Wei shu* into twelve moral categories, including: *zhenlie* (chaste and heroic), *gaoqing* (lofty feelings), *junjie* (rigorous integrity), *huilie* (good and heroic), *roushun* (tender and docile), *gongjian* (obedient and frugal), *yishu* (virtuous and gentle), *shijie* (avowed integrity), *qiuren* (pursuing humanity), *yueli* (ritual adherence), *yinzhi* (living in reclusion), *fuze* (women's rules), and *muyi* (maternal deportment). Still, among them *gaoqing* is derived from the *Hou Hanshu* "Lienü" category *gaoshi* (lofty female scholars) that elevates virtue and talent, and *caishi* (talent and judgment), although not listed in the *Jinshu* "Lienü" preface, is clearly the focus of at least fourteen of the thirty-three "Lienü" entries.

In subsequent dynastic "Lienü zhuan," categories related to talents and abilities were still lingering, such as *mingshi yuantu* (discernment and insight) and *zhongzhuang* (loyalty and strength) in the *Suishu* (History of the Sui [581–618]), by the Tang minister Wei Zheng (580–643) and others.[33] *Zhongzhuang* also appeared in Tuotuo's "Lienü zhuan" for *Songshi* and *Jinshi* (History of the Jin [1125–1234]). Tuotuo's preface to the *Liaoshi* (History of the Liao [947–1125]) "Lienü zhuan" asserts that "it is better to have virtuous and talented women" who live as their husbands' companions than to have "heroic women" who martyr themselves after their husbands' deaths.[34] Therefore, Tuotuo labeled two of the five *Liaoshi* "Lienü" entries *xiannü*: women as learned scholars and excellent poets whose talents had important political and cultural ramifications. In brief, although moral categories already proliferated in the pre-Ming *lienü*, in general this tradition had boasted both talents and virtues to this point, and in this overlapped with its *xianyuan* counterpart.

Since the very beginning the *xianyuan* tradition shared with the *lienü* its purpose to "glorify the history of our women," as exemplified in the following *Shishuo* episode. Xie An asks Lu Tui why his father-in-law, Zhang Ping, composed an obituary for his mother but not for his father. Lu Tui replies, "Surely it must be because a man's virtue is displayed in his conduct of affairs, while a woman's beauty (*furen zhi mei*), unless depicted in an obituary, would never be made public" (4/82). The *Shishuo* author set up a "Xianyuan" chapter clearly for making women's beauty public. His standards for selecting the *xianyuan* entries therefore expounded his understanding of "beauty" through conceptualizing *xian* as virtue and talent within the Wei-Jin cultural context. Later *xianyuan* chapters followed this purpose and standards, except that the connotation of *xian* was molded to fit the specific cultural purpose of each *Shishuo* imitator and the social reality surrounding each *Shishuo* imitation.

The two extant Tang *Shishuo* imitations, Feng Yan's (*jinshi* ca. 756) *Fengshi wenjian ji* (Feng's memoirs) and Liu Su's (fl. 806–820) *Da Tang xinyu* (New account of the Great Tang), emerged in the mid-Tang, just as the dynasty had survived the devastating An Lushan rebellion (755–757). The intellectual elite invoked various literary genres to rebuild the moral order so as to restore the Tang imperial glory. Among them were the *Shishuo*, which, the authors hoped, could offer model personalities to form a strong bond between the subject and the ruler. Authors of the Tang imitations, especially the author of the *New Account of the Great Tang*, therefore changed the aesthetic and psychological orientation of the *Shishuo* to fit a new ethical scheme, and only chose role models from among Tang gentlemen, such as Wei Zheng (580–643), a paragon of loyalty, and Zhang Yue (667–730), the epitome of Tang cultural achievements. Women were excluded, except for Empress Wu Zetian (r. 684–704) and a number of royal consorts who helped establish Tang imperial authority. No *xianyuan* chapter appears in extant Tang *Shishuo* imitations.

Only two Song *Shishuo* imitations exist today: Kong Pingzhong's (*jinshi* 1065) *Xu Shishuo* (Continuation of the *Shihshuo*) on the Southern and Northern to Five Dynasties (ca. 420–960), and Wang Dang's (fl. 1086–1110) *Tang yulin* (Tang forest of accounts) on the Tang (618–907). The two authors both belonged to the intellectual circle headed by the famous scholar-official Su Shi (1036–1101), and they proceeded with the imitation of the *Shishuo* as a result of a scholastic debate between Su Shi and Cheng Yi (1033–1107).[35] The fundamental difference between the two scholars and their followers, to put the matter somewhat starkly, lies in their respective approaches to the *Dao*.

Cheng Yi, one of the moral philosophers who established *Tao-hsüeh* [*Daoxue*] (Learning of the Way, Neo-Confucianism in a narrow sense),[36] equated the *Tiandao* (Way of Heaven) with the *Tianli* (principle of Heaven), the *Tianming* (mandate of Heaven), and *xing* (human nature).[37] He argued: "Learning is to make one seek [the *Dao*] from one's inner [nature]. If one seeks [the *Dao*] not from inside but from outside, then one is not conducting the Sage's learning."[38] He thus asserted that "literature harms the *Dao*" (*zuowen hai Dao*), for it turns scholars' attention away from their inner nature toward the examination and depiction of external trifling things.[39] Su Shih, on the other hand, understood the *Dao* in a Daoist fashion, viewing it as what "the myriad things rely upon to be themselves" and what "the myriad principles are confirmed by."[40] This *Dao* could only be "brought on" by the close study of all things. Literature provided the best way to "bring on" the *Dao*—by capturing the subtleties of the phenomenal world in words so that the reader might intuit the *Dao* embodied in all things.[41]

For Su Shi and his followers, the *Shishuo* genre offered an ideal literary means to express a person's self as bred from the *Dao* of Nature.[42] Kong and Wang both turned away from the more didactic Tang imitations and went back to the original, aesthetically oriented *Shishuo* scheme that more authentically rendered subtle human nature, including that of women. Due to the Tang dynasty's lingering moral momentum, however, the Song *Shishuo* "Xianyuan" was crafted to celebrate women who combined moral strength and artistic/literary talents: intelligent imperial consorts who gave advice on state affairs; worthy mothers who shaped their son's moral behavior; virtuous wives who killed themselves after their husbands' deaths; and talented women well versed in the classics and poetry.[43]

Emphasis on virtue and talent in both the *lienü* and the *xianyuan* traditions hence resulted in their often sharing common sources of women's stories. The *Jinshu* "Lienü zhuan" offers a most obvious example. Its Tang compilers presented an elaborate list of moral categories for the lives of Jin women; yet fourteen accounts, representing about 41 percent of the women included, praise their scholastic and literary talents and their expertise in "character appraisal."[44] Among them, some of the most defiant cases against Confucian norms are taken from the *Shishuo xinyu*, the product of the Wei-Jin free spirit. For instance, the *Jinshu* compilers adopted word for word from the *Shishuo* Xie Daoyun's complaints about her mediocre husband.[45]

The Tang historian Liu Zhiji (661–721) attributed such disjunctions to the *Jinshu* compilers' lack of discernment in picking and choosing among archives.[46] In fact, the compilers had their own specific moral focus in appropriating stories from the *Shishuo* and other sources. They chose stories that valorized women's efforts in protecting their families, whether or not their behavior might fit Confucian norms. This standard was consistent with the general emphasis on the power of hereditary clans during the Six Dynasties and the early Tang. This is apparent in an episode also about Xie Daoyun that appears in the *Jinshu* "Lienü" but not in the *Shishuo*: Xie Daoyun's talented younger brother-in-law Wang Xianzhi is trapped in a *Xuanxue* philosophical debate. Covering her face with a gauze veil and walking into the all male-member *Xuanxue* club, Daoyun takes Xianzhi's place and defeats his opponent.[47] Thus, by breaking the gender demarcation, Xie Daoyun defends the intellectual pride of her family. This Xie Daoyun is as defiant against Confucian decorum as the one in the *Shishuo* "Xianyuan."

By the same token, the *xianyuan* chapters in the two Song *Shishuo* imitations—the only two before the Ming—quote from the dynastic "Lienü zhuan." For instance, "Xianyuan" in Kong Pingzhong's *Continuation of the Shishuo* relates the most virtuous account from the "Lienü zhuan" of the *Jiu Tangshu* (Old history of the Tang [618–907]) by Liu Xu (887–946) and others, in which a woman mutilates her body to protect her chastity.[48] In brief, a common emphasis on both virtue and talent created a complementary relationship between pre-Ming *lienü* and *xianyuan* writings. Significant differentiation of the two would have to wait until the beginning of the Ming dynasty.

CONFLICTING TRADITIONS IN THE MING AND QING

Late imperial dynastic "Lienü zhuan," beginning with the *Yuanshi* (History of the Yuan [1260–1368]), compiled in the early Ming, became increasingly dominated by morality, as reflected in the fine discrimination among behaviors with *jie* (integrity, chastity) and *xiao* (filial piety). The *Yuanshi* and the *Mingshi* (History of the Ming [1368–1644]) "Lienü zhuan" more specifically defined *jie* as *xunjie* (to die for keeping *jie*) and *kujie* (to forbear bitterness for keeping *jie*), and *xiao* as *chunxiao* (full devotion to parents and/or in-laws) and *sixiao* (to die for parents and/or in-laws). These specifications were further institutionalized in the Qing dynasty, when the Ministry of Rites sanctioned the honor system for women that distinguished *xiaofu* (filial daughters-in-law), *xiaonü* (filial daughters), *liefu* (heroic women), *lienü* (heroic girls), *shoujie* (to maintain widowhood), *xunjie* (to die for keeping *jie*), and *weihun shoujie* (faithful maidenhood)[49]. The *Qingshi gao* "Lienü zhuan" based its long list of moral categories—*xianmu* (worthy mothers), *xiaonü, xiaofu, xianfu* (worthy wives), *jiefu* (wives of integrity), *zhenfu* (chaste wives), *zhennü* (chaste girls), *liefu,* and *yixing* (righteous behavior)—on the rubrics set up by the Ministry of Rites.[50]

In addition to categories evolving, their definitions also underwent significant changes. *Lie* had a broad meaning from the *Hou Hanshu* to the *Jinshi,* indicating a woman who either died resisting violence or avenged a wrong done to her state and/or her family. Beginning with the *Yuanshi, lie* became firmly associated with *zhen,* referring only to a woman protecting her chastity against violent assault. Similarly, *yi,* which had covered a broad range of righteousness, was reduced in the *Mingshi* and the *Qingshi gao* to protecting other people's children. And *xian*, which had described virtuous and talented women who instructed and advised their fathers, husbands, and sons on sociopolitical issues, was reduced to its domestic function. For this reason, I have translated *xian* in the *Qingshi gao* "Lienü zhuan" as "worthy."[51]

This heightened moralism was reflected in a greater emphasis on female self-sacrifice. The *Hou Hanshu* "Lienü zhuan" tells of 7 women who died for moral causes, about 30 percent of the total; the *Yuanshi* reports on 154, about 75 percent; the *Mingshi* 322, more than 90 percent; and the *Qingshi gao* more than 92 percent. The actual figures were certainly much higher. The preface to the *Qingshi gao* "Lienü zhuan" announces that each year there were thousands of exemplary women whose stories merited reporting, while "those who died in war atrocities often numbered in the hundreds of thousands."[52] Toward the later imperial period, the primary unnatural cause of death for women overwhelmingly became suicide to protect chastity.

What caused the *lienü* tradition to shift from its early emphasis on "outstanding talents and lofty behavior" to late imperial valorization devoted only to the "martyrdom of chastity" (*jielie*)?[53] The *Yuanshi* "Lienü zhuan" was the first to single out *xunjie*, or a woman's suicide after her husband's death, as the most prominent virtue, and thereby inaugurated the late imperial chastity cult.[54] *Yuanshi's* celebration of *xunjie* is certainly grounded in Yuan social norms honoring chaste women.[55] Composed by the early Ming historians, *Yuanshi* also reflects the social decorum of that time, which is further exposed in the preface to the *Mingshi* "Lienü zhuan." The compilers cited, in a rather critical tone, historical tradition, state policy, local customs, and literati provocation as jeopardizing women's well-being in the name of *zhengqi*, or righteous spirit. Compiled in the early Qing dynasty, *Mingshi's* criticism of the recently fallen Ming is incisive. Yet the Qing regime needed to appeal to the existing cultural tradition in establishing its own political legitimacy. The compilers thus reluctantly ended their preface with an assertion of the importance of the *zhengqi* discourse in differentiating human beings from beasts.[56]

A sharp divergence between the two traditions occurred with the late imperial profusion of *Shishuo* imitations, mostly published from the mid-Ming to the early Qing (see appendix C). These texts were the product of growing resentment among certain segments of the literati over the narrow-minded and repressive orthodoxy of the civil-service examination system. The Yuan-Ming establishment of the Cheng-Zhu *Lixue* (Learning of Principle) as the center of the state's educational and administrative systems, as well as the rapid expansion of the number of lower-level degree holders in Ming society, deprived many talented and free-spirited literati of the opportunity to hold office. At the same time, the growth of a commodity economy offered literati the possibility of making a living from their literary and artistic talents. Under the circumstances, certain literati separated their identity from the mainstream values of degree and office-holding and embraced an artistic lifestyle made possible through economic independence. These dissident literati purposely chose the free-spirited *Shishuo* genre to voice their well-wrought discourse against the Cheng-Zhu *Lixue* and to assert their newly fashioned self-identities.

Almost all the late imperial *Shishuo* imitators included a "Xianyuan" chapter, and two even devoted their entire works to women. Together they consciously integrated *xianyuan* into women's history as a strong counter-discourse to the Cheng-Zhu *Lixue*-oriented *lienü* reincarnations. He Liangjun (1506–73) clearly stated in his *Yulin* (*Forest* of accounts), the first Ming *Shishuo* work, that despite "Confucian decorum [being] what women should value," he would concentrate on their "profound discernment and lofty behavior" (*shenshi gaoxing*). As a result, his "Xianyuan" chapter highly applauds talented, capable, outspoken and strong-willed women from the Han to the Yuan (ca. 206 BCE–1368), with no record of female docility, obedience, or suicide. Wang Shizhen (1526–90) further reinforced He Liangjun's "Xianyuan" principle by linking it to its Wei-Jin origin in the *Shishuo xinyu bu* (Supplement to the *Shishuo xinyu*), which Wang compiled through extracting episodes from the *Shishuo xinyu* and He's *Forest of Accounts*.

The late Ming radical scholar and literary critic Li Zhi (1527–1602) played a crucial role in formulating the *xianyuan* tradition into an anti-*Lixue* discourse. He composed his own *Shishuo* work, *Chutan ji* (Collection on the pond), by extracting episodes from the *Shishuo xinyu* and his close friend Jiao Hong's (1541–1620) *Leilin* (Taxonomic forest), which is a collection of historical anecdotes from antiquity to Yuan (ca. 3000 BCE–1368). He also added extensive comments based on his commentary on Wang Shizhen's *Supplement to the Shishuo*. Believing that the Wei-Jin spirit could be transmitted only through depicting human relations,[57] Li Zhi classified the *Collection on the Pond* not according to the *Shishuo* categories, but rather the five Confucian social relationships: *junchen* (ruler and subject), *fuzi* (father and son), *xiongdi* (brothers), *fufu* (husband and wife), and *shiyou* (mentor and friend).[58] Li Zhi, however, turned this original sequence over, putting husband and wife first and ruler and subject last, he argued that husband and wife were the beginning of people, just like Heaven and Earth were the beginning of myriad things, and therefore challenged the *Lixue* assertion that Heavenly principle was the origin of all.[59] He contended that the "natural" relationship between husband and wife was more important than the moral-political obligations stressed by the Cheng-Zhu school. This theoretical frame allowed Li Zhi to arrange the *Shishuo* "Xianyuan" episodes in the opening category of "Husband and Wife," in which he emphasized women's pivotal role in marriage and repeatedly praised talented and courageous women as "real men" or "better than men."[60] In contrast to the chastity cult in the late imperial *lienü* tradition, Li Zhi grouped stories about women's suicide in the subcategory of "Kuhai zhuao" (Women in the miserable sea), in lamentation rather than celebration.[61]

He Liangjun, Wang Shichen, Jiao Hong, and Li Zhi were among the most influential Ming thinkers, and their writings, Li's *Collection on the Pond* in particular, were highly popular during the Ming period.[62] Their dissenting *xianyuan* voice thereby penetrated into the following *Shishuo* imitations and culminated in two *Nü Shishuo* (Women's *Shishuo*): one by a male writer, Li Qing (1602–83), which was compiled in the early 1650s and covered women from antiquity to the Yuan (ca. 3000 BCE–1368), and the other by a woman, Yan Heng (1826?-54), which was published a decade or so after her death and focused on Qing women only. The two authors concurred on the *xianyuan* qualities that should constitute a female value system.[63] Central to this were *ru* (milk) and *xiang* (scent), two fluid and penetrating essences that connected the female body to the outside world. *Ru* links a mother to her child in the process of *ju* (nurturing) and signifies the maintenance of life and hence the symbol of humanity. *Xiang* emits women's beauty and talents. The two have mutually defined, refined, and reinforced each other.[64]

The late imperial *lienü* and *xianyuan* also signified sharp differences in gender relationships. *Xianyuan* continued *Shishuo's* equal gender status, whereas *lienü* featured increasing female docility and submissiveness. For instance, when women berate their husbands in the *xianyuan* the men respond to the women's admonitions and better themselves—to the woman's credit. In the *lienü*, the women remain tragically unable to change the situations they are in.

THE LAST WAVE OF *LIENÜ* AND *XIANYUAN*

The last wave of *lienü* and *xianyuan* appeared in accordance with the sociopolitical and intellectual turmoil at the turn of the twentieth century. The last dynastic "Lienü zhuan" in the *Qingshi gao* was composed between 1914 and 1927 in clear opposition to rising nationalism, which, the compilers argued, subverted the current state order by promoting the national interest over that of each household.[65] To correct this "fallacy," the *Qingshi gao* "Lienü zhuan" reemphasized women's conventional roles and therefore represented the culmination of the genre's moralistic thrust; an unprecedentedly high 92 percent of the 617 women included died protecting their chastity. However, the compiler of the *Xin Yuanshi* (New history of the Yuan; 1922) applied a nationalistic approach to his rewriting of the Yuan history. While the original *Yuanshi* "Lienü zhuan" made no reference to the dynasty's ethnic identity, the *Xin Yuanshi* "Lienü zhuan" highlighted the Mongol origin of the Yuan royal house in order to promote the idea that "using Chinese [culture] to transform barbarians should start with the relationship between husband and wife" (*yongxia bianyi bi zi fufu zhi lun shi*). Thus the compiler reinstalled a moral approach and brought the number of women martyrs from the original 159 to 226, adding a number of Mongol chaste widows.

The last "Xianyuan" chapter in Yi Zongkui's (b. 1875) *Xin Shishuo* (New *Shishuo*, completed in 1918) reflected tensions of this period between "New" and "Old," Western and Chinese values. The author returned to the forever fresh and unorthodox *Shishuo* narrative framework, wondering whether its free spirit could be aligned with Western individuality, and whether it could yield a productive middle ground between old and new.

Well before the *Xin Shishuo* appeared, however, the late Qing woman writer Xue Shaohui (1866–1911) had already proposed a solution to the problems Yi Zongkui would later raise. She did so by merging the *lienü* and the *xianyuan* traditions in the *Waiguo lienü zhuan* (Biographies of foreign women; hereafter *WGLNZ*), arguably the first systematic introduction of foreign women to the Chinese audience, so as to advance edification and self-strengthening for Chinese women. Foreign women's lives in the *WGLNZ* therefore both served as a model, elements of which could be used to educate contemporary Chinese women, and constituted a site where different visions of ideal womanhood were contested. Borrowing experiences from foreign women, Xue aimed at establishing an ideal, universalized womanhood. Using foreign agents to paint an alternative picture of virtue yet relating it closely to the Chinese tradition, Xue carefully sorted through and modified the *lienü* and the *xianyuan* traditions to create her own system. It combines *ci*, motherly love, with *xue*, learning. *Ci*, which had once been a major moral code in the *lienü* tradition, had long been eclipsed by the virtue of *zhen*, chastity. Replacing *zhen* with *ci*, and combining *ci* with *xue*, the central value of the *xianyuan* tradition, Xue elevated the significance of *ci* from maternal love to nurturing the people and the culture.[66]

Sherry J. Mou has criticized the *lienü* tradition in dynastic history, writing that it "is neither by nor for women." "Rather than providing truthful pictures of how women lived," Mou observes, "these biographies provide norms by which readers [primarily gentlemen, as Mou also notes] could measure current events."[67] Here we can see the necessity and the significance of reconstructing the *xianyuan* tradition and its relationship with the *lienü* tradition.

First, a study like this will manifest that the writing of women's history in traditional China is multivocal, as opposed to the relatively single-voiced narrative in modern Chinese historiography. This narrative can easily mislead students to believe, among other things, that the late imperial cult of chastity has always been an obsession in China. A chronological comparison of these two contrasting traditions shows that this is indeed not the case. The *lienü* became increasingly chastity-abiding only from the Ming onward, and the continuing presence of the dissident *xianyuan* discourse resisted such trends of the times.[68]

Second, to be sure, the *xianyuan* narrative, like its *lienü* counterpart, was mostly written by men, hence the reasonable doubt as to whether it could provide "truthful pictures of how women lived." Formed upon the Wei-Jin free spirit and choice for private scholars including women, however, the *Shishuo* genre has conveyed dissident opinions against mainstream values, as typified especially in its late imperial incarnations. Its *xianyuan* component, a conscious counter-discourse against the *lienü* norms, would therefore go beyond what Mou terms "gentlemen's prescriptions for women's lives," offering later generations alternative, if not more authentic, accounts of women's lives. Moreover, *lienü* and *xianyuan* have co-existed for the past 1,600 years. Each has established its own trajectory, but the two have also been mutually interactive. The dynamic tension between them would give rise to multiple readings and offer rich perspectives on women's lives that are as suggestive in what they conceal as in what they reveal.

Third, this study can help broaden our vision of other genres and versions of women's lives. For instance, Chang Qu's (fl. mid-fourth century) regional history *Huayang guozhi* (State records of Huayang), compiled between 348 and 355, contains a chapter about the lives of exemplary men and women. Each account starts with a brief comment on the subject's personality, showing the clear influence of Wei-Jin character appraisal, and might have foreshadowed the *Shishuo* genre.[69] In the late Ming, another genre on women's lives emerged, the *Baimei tu* (Portraits of one hundred beauties), when literati emphatically promoted women's accomplishments. In a very general sense, the *lienü* tradition focuses on *de*, virtue; the *xianyuan* on *cai*, talent; and the *Baimei tu* on *se*, beautiful appearance.[70] While *lienü* and *xianyuan* rely primarily upon historical records, the *Baimei tu* draw from both historical and legendary sources, and it combines biographical accounts with pictorial and poetic portrayals. Expanding our research sources, both textual and visual, will add new dimensions for understanding women, including women active during the later imperial period.

Last but not least, writing on women has closely interacted with every aspect of China's social, political, and cultural life. A study of various traditions of women's history will add a gender dimension to our understanding of Chinese social and political history, as well as Chinese culture. This gender-based history and cultural analysis will in turn enrich our understanding of Chinese women's history.

5. Faithful Maiden Biographies

A Forum for Ritual Debate, Moral Critique, and Personal Reflection

Weijing Lu

The faithful and righteous Wang Yuan is from Siyuli of Chong'an, Jianning Prefecture, [Fujian]. Her father, Yuanbao, is a government student. When Yuan was eighteen years old, a young man named Yu Kong from the same area presented betrothal gifts [to her family]. Yu Kong's father, Tingliang, was also a government student. Three years later, Yu Kong died of illness. Yuan's father concealed the news and did not let her know about it. After a while, when Tingliang buried his son, the funeral procession passed through Siyuli. Yuan's family all went out to see the precession. Realizing what had happened, Yuan was overcome by grief. She removed her hairpins and jewels, put on mourning clothing, and said to her parents: "Father taught me to read. One principle for a woman is that she should not remarry after her husband's death. Although I have not married, in my heart I have promised myself to the son of the Yu family. Now that he has died, I should go to the Yu family to preserve my fidelity." Her father did not listen. Retiring [to her own room], Yuan wanted to kill herself. Her mother, who loved her dearly, took precautions day and night. Yet, still, she almost succeeded several times in committing suicide.[1]

SHEN DACHENG (1696–1777), "Biography of the Faithful and Righteous Wang Yuan"

During China's late imperial period (1368–1911), thousands of young women defied parental authority in order to pledge themselves to life-long celibacy in honor of a living or deceased first betrothed.[2] Known to their contemporaries as *zhennü* or faithful maidens, these women followed a number of different paths.[3] Some lived out the rest of their lives with their own parents and brothers; a majority of them, including Wang Yuan, married into their deceased fiancé's families through a spirit wedding known as "holding the tablet to marry" (*bao zhu chengqin*), and adopted sons to carry on their betrothed's line of descent.[4] Still others took their own lives to follow their fiancés in death.[5]

The earliest faithful maiden was acclaimed in Liu Xiang's *Lienü zhuan* (Biographies of Women).[6] The practice was popularized only after the thirteenth century, however, and its appeal peaked during the eighteenth and nineteenth centuries.[7] Faithful maidens came from diverse socioeconomic backgrounds. A score of them were daughters of the political and intellectual elite who had been educated in classics and literature. There were also many from the lowest echelons of society, including girls from peasant or petty merchant families, those who did not "have a father or brother to teach them the 'Songs' or the 'History,'" to borrow a common expression from the biographers.[8] While faithful maidenhood was an empire-wide phenomenon, the majority of reported cases occurred in the South, in the Lower Yangzi region—the heartland of the late empire.

The faithful maiden cult represented an extreme form of what had become a late imperial Chinese obsession: female chastity. It developed in tandem with the widespread widow chastity cult, in which young widows refused remarriage or killed themselves upon the deaths of their husbands. But the faithful maiden cult was even more extreme. Whereas prevailing gender norms deemed remarriage for women a disgrace, a second betrothal was not against Confucian moral teaching and carried no social stigma. Young women who deliberately chose faithful maidenhood thus became sources of frustration and conflict in their homes and subjects of controversy and debate in society. While in a typical faithful maiden saga the parents tried in vain to dissuade their daughter from pursuing a life that they foresaw would only bring suffering, the Confucian elite reached no clear agreement on how to assess the young maiden's behavior. The prominent contemporary source that recorded their intense ritual and moral controversies was female biography.[9]

Faithful maiden biographies thrived for two key reasons: faithful maidens were powerful moral symbols, and their acts embodied profound ideological tensions.[10] A woman's personal decision not to remarry had long been politicized in Confucian moral philosophy. The chaste wife was homologous to the loyal minister. "A loyal minister does not serve two rulers;" according to an ancient saying, and "a righteous woman does not marry two husbands."[11] This time-honored representation of the chaste widow as a symbol of political loyalty found its most powerful expression in the image of the faithful maiden. Exemplifying extraordinary virtue, a betrothed young girl who took on a grave moral obligation that was not expected of her put morally crippled men to shame.

This metaphorical usage of the faithful maiden became particularly prominent at times of political crisis and national trauma. During the late Ming political disorder and the seventeenth-century Manchu conquest, for example, literati poignantly alluded to faithful maiden suicides to criticize corrupt officials or men who shifted their loyalty to the new dynasty, to lament the fallen Chinese dynasty, or to announce their own moral conviction. Sun Qifeng (1584–1675), a leading Neo-Confucian, remarked in his biography of a certain faithful maiden Fan in the mid-seventeenth century:

> There are differences in wifely fidelity. To die to preserve fidelity is more heroic than to live to preserve it. Moreover, it is more heroic for an unmarried woman to die to preserve fidelity than for a married woman to do so. The relationships that bind a ruler to his country, a minister to his ruler, a son to his father, and a wife to her husband are designated by Heaven and rooted in human feeling. To die to fulfill the responsibilities attached to one's relationships is obligatory in terms of *li* (universal principle), which should not be misunderstood, and in terms of *yi* (righteousness, honor-bond duty), which one should not avoid. For a woman who has never seen her fiancé, dying for him is comparable to the deed of a man who dies for his ruler without ever having served him. This is most heroic![12]

The faithful maiden ideal was subjected to sharply different interpretations, however. The questions concerning its ritual legitimacy engendered perhaps the most widespread, polarizing, and prolonged debate on female virtue in Chinese history. While the government and supporters sang the praises of the faithful maidens,[13] the critics denounced their choices as serious violations of Confucian rituals and teachings. Ambivalence, meanwhile, marked the positions of many other scholars. For scholarly fathers who did not agree with the choices their daughters made, the ideological collision caused emotional pain for both fathers and daughters. Faithful maiden biographies became in this context a forum of debate. Writers wove ideological perspectives and personal feelings into their poignant discussions of the virtues of their biographies, even turning life-story narratives into passionate defenses of the faithful maiden cult. This unique manipulation of the genre suggests that women's biography was neither a static nor a unified moral discourse. Divisions among the literati who authored these texts rested as much on their different understandings of Confucian texts as on their conflicting sense of moral responsibility and their deeply personal emotions.

Thus, at a fundamental level, faithful maiden biographies encapsulate a number of key issues that connect gender, emotion, and intellectual history in the late imperial period. They dramatize the great metaphorical power of faithful maidens as moral exemplars; they reveal the profound ideological divide among the Confucian elite concerning ritual and female chastity; they bring to the surface the ambiguity and struggle among evidential scholars, who could not always abide by its academic principles; and they open the window into the deep tensions between ritual, emotion, and morality.

THE CONTESTED MEANINGS OF FAITHFUL MAIDEN PRACTICE

As early as the Yuan period (1279–1368), the emergence of faithful maiden suicide sparked concerns about the extreme nature of the practice.[14] The criticism that faithful maidens "exceeded the middle path" (*guo zhong*) grew stronger over the course of the Ming, when the practice spread and the court began to bestow imperial honor regularly on faithful maidens, particularly those who had committed suicide.[15] The debate became most intense in the Qing dynasty, however, in the context of the renewed intellectual interest in ritual and the rise of the new scholarship of evidential research. During this period, as Kai-wing Chow has demonstrated, ritual was considered "the most effective method for cultivating Confucian virtues and a reliable way to exclude heterodox practices." [16] The question whether Confucian ritual sanctioned the faithful maiden practice figured in the core of the controversy. The development of evidential scholarship—which engaged the female scholar Wang Zhaoyuan discussed by Harriet Zurndorfer in chapter 3 of this volume—in the same period further inflamed the debate. A revolutionary reorientation of academic research and scholarship, the evidential school utilized the method of empirical study to recover the original meaning of the classics and reexamine all accepted knowledge.[17] Within this context, Confucian ritual was put at the forefront of academic inquiry and faithful maiden practice came under intense scrutiny, bringing the empire's best minds into direct confrontation.

Was the faithful maiden practice in accordance with Confucian ritual? The critics held that for a betrothed girl to die for her fiancé, or even to remain celibate, violated the rituals prescribed in the classics. In his landmark denunciation of the practice, Gui Youguang (1507–71) argues that, according to the classical marriage rites, a woman could not go to her fiancé's home without first completing all six steps of the marriage rites and receiving instruction from her parents. Otherwise, it would be called an "elopement." Even if she has completed all of the marriage rites except the last one, *miaojian* (a ceremony of offering sacrifice to a deceased parent-in-law at the family shrine, performed three months into a woman's marriage), she was still not to be considered a member of her husband's family. In making his point, Gu cites an excerpt from "Zengzi Asked" (*Zengzi wen*) in the *Book of Rites* (*Liji*):

> Zengzi asks: "If a woman dies before she has performed the ritual of *miaojian*, what should be done?" Confucius says: "Her coffin should not be placed at the ancestral temple. Her tablet should not be positioned next to that of her mother-in-law [to receive sacrifice]. At the funeral, her husband should not hold a cane, nor wear shoes of straw, nor have a (special) place (for wailing). She should be returned to her own family to be buried. This is to show that she has not yet become a wife." If she has not yet become a wife, she is not tied to her husband.[18]

Citing another excerpt from the same text, Gu further states that whereas it violates the marital ritual for a woman to preserve fidelity for a dead fiancé against her parents' wishes, it is in accordance with the marital ritual for her to marry another man.[19]

As the debate persisted throughout the seventeenth through the nineteenth centuries, critics of the faithful maiden cult drew on additional evidence and conceived new arguments to assert that the faithful maiden act ran counter to the teachings of the ancient sages. Both Mao Qiling (1623–1716) and Wang Zhong (1745–94) argued, for example, that taking one's life upon a fiancé's death made no sense in light of Confucian principles.[20] Mao Qiling wrote:

> In human society, a person's most revered bonds are the bonds with his/her ruler and parents; it is toward them that a person directs his/her ultimate loyalty and love. If it were appropriate to die to follow one's ruler or parent in death, then, there would be no one left in this world, because every person has a ruler and two parents. With a ruler and two parents for everybody, even a person with three lives would still have no life left over to commit suicide for a spouse.[21]

While Mao's argument had a Confucian humanist tone, Wang Zhong anchored his view on the moral principle of filiality. He argued that the faithful maiden's choice not only violated Confucian teaching about cherishing human life, it was also unfilial. According to mourning rituals, he pointed out, a married woman wears the mourning garment of *zhancui*, the highest grade of all, for her husband, and she wears the *zicui* mourning garment, which is a grade lower than *zhancui*, for her parents. However, in the case of the faithful maiden, she has not married and yet she rushes to mourn her fiancé wearing *zhancui* garment. In so doing, she places the status of a man whom she never married above that of her parents. "For her fiancé, this makes no sense; for her parents, this is unfilial."[22]

The textual and ideological evidence and pointed analyses made by these scholars, however, did not settle the controversy; they only provoked even more controversy and drew into debate persistently more scholars with widely divided opinions. For many of the supporters, biography became the most convenient and effective means of delivering their voice. The traditional genre for extolling female exemplars took on an entirely different meaning. It was not only for praising their virtue, but also to defend a moral icon who, in their view, was under attack unjustifiably.

BIOGRAPHY: A WEAPON IN DEFENSE OF FAITHFUL MAIDENS

In the Qing, the faithful maiden controversy made its way into the private studios of scholars and the public offices of government; into conversations and writings; and into poetry and commentaries on Confucian classics. But the most common site for scholars to engage the issue was in the biographies of faithful maidens. It is understandable that critics of the practice of faithful maidenhood would not write biographies celebrating faithful maidens, although authors holding ambivalent positions did not shy away from the task. Faithful maiden biography was thus dominated by supporters for whom the biographical narrative form became a powerful weapon in the late imperial controversy. Cai Shiyuan (1682–1733), for example, wrote a biography for a daughter of a close colleague and friend, Zhu Shi (1664–1736), grand secretary of the Kangxi and Yongzheng reigns. Zhu's daughter married into her deceased fiancé's home and died of illness eleven years later. In the biography, Cai includes a lengthy discussion demonstrating that she was a moral equal to the most celebrated heroines in ancient history. Citing evidence from the Confucian classic the *Spring and Autumn Annals* and other texts, he concludes that her action was appropriate, not extreme. He further calls her "a female equivalent of Boyi and Shuqi," referring to two male paragons of political loyalty.[23]

To confront the critics head-on, some scholars adopted a "question-answer" format in their biographies, virtually transforming supposedly eulogistic pieces into analytical essays of rebuttal. For example, when a certain faithful maiden Dai married into her deceased fiancé's home, Zhu Yizun (1629–1709) was asked to contribute a piece of writing in honor of the young girl. Zhu accepted the request, but he described her story in only two lines. He devoted the remainder of his essay to addressing four questions to make his point that what the girl did was ritually appropriate.[24]

In 1665, a seventeen-year-old peasant daughter, Song Dian, hanged herself following her fiancé's death. Wang Wan (1624–90), a friend of Zhu Yizun, was approached to write a commemorative piece in her honor. Wang opened his "Biography of the Martyred Girl Song" with this statement: "The rituals say a girl obeys her father and brother while young and she listens to her husband after marriage. Yet here are women who die for their fiancés before they are married. Some people are suspicious, and think that it goes too far." Wang then addresses the skepticism with a long rebuttal:

> The ruler-minister relationship and husband-wife relationship are the same. The common people who have not served a ruler are just like women who are betrothed but have not yet married. A man leading an army should die if the army is defeated; a man in charge of a country should die if the country is endangered. However, if people are not officials or they are not in charge of the army or country, even if they hold official posts, the early kings would not [casually] expect them to take their own lives when their army or country were defeated . . . However, when they did die, Confucius did not regard their actions as too extreme . . . Why, therefore, should we have doubts about a betrothed girl who follows her fiancé in death?[25]

Going on to argue from the ritual perspective, Wang stressed that there is no breach of morality in the faithful maiden action because, according to the ritual, once the betrothal process has started—that is, when a matchmaker has first engaged the two parties—a woman is connected to her fiancé. Thus, "when the fiancé is alive, they have defined their relationships and contacts; when he dies, she puts on *zhancui* morning garment to mourn for him. As such, what is extreme about a woman following her fiancé in death?"[26]

Wang Wan also wrote a faithful maiden biography for a young woman he knew personally. She was the daughter of Song Shiying (1621–1705) and had been engaged to the son of Ji Dong (1625–76). Both men were friends of Wang Wan. When Ji Dong's son was still a boy, Ji Dong brought him along to visit Song Shiyin. The boy's manner was so impressive to Song that he betrothed his little daughter to him. Ji's son died when he was fifteen years old. Although Song's daughter, who was only thirteen, expressed her resolve not to marry another man, Ji Dong was hesitant to allow her to move in with his family because "he was worried that she was too young."[27] Over the next ten years, she remained on a vegetarian diet and rejected makeup and fine clothing as if she were a widow. She finally starved herself to death when someone proposed a marriage. Deeply regretful, Ji Dong wept: "You are truly my daughter-in-law. I disappointed you!" He came to the Song family in person, took her coffin home, and buried it in his son's grave.[28]

In his epitaph for faithful maiden Song, Wang Wan directly confronts the ritual evidence cited by Gui Youguang:

> Someone asks: "If a woman who has not yet been presented at the ancestral hall dies, her tablet should not be put at the grand ancestral hall to receive sacrifice, and she should be buried with her own family. How can [the faithful maiden Song] be buried together with her fiancé?" I say: "You are wrong. The ritual has regularities and variations. If the fiancé dies after an auspicious day for marriage has been selected, the woman wears *zhancui* to mourn him. After the burial, she takes it off. This is normal. If the woman preserves her loyalty and does not marry someone else, this is a variation. What Jiting's [Song Shiying] daughter did for Ruzi [her fiancé] varies still further from this variation: at the beginning, she did not put on makeup, and did not drink wine and eat meat; later on, she did not hesitate to starve herself to death. She was already a daughter-in-law of the Ji family; how could we judge her with the ritual requirements for an unmarried woman?

Here Wang Wan relies on a "regularity and variation" scheme to refuse Gui Youguang's evidence, thus turning the ritual text to his advantage. He seems to suggest that, since faithful maiden Song acted as a grieving widow and daughter-in-law all along, she should be considered as such. Wang Wan's defense of the Song daughter is most noteworthy in that he was sensitive to the young woman's self-identity. His depiction of her behavior allows the readers to catch a glimpse of not only her determination but also her emotional ordeal.

In looking into faithful maidens' self-identity and emotions, Zhu Yizun argues more explicitly that there was some kind of emotional connection between a faithful maiden and her deceased fiancé that was nurtured by betrothal rites. "'Sending the birds (from the groom's family)' and 'accepting the pure silk (by the bride's family)'[29] is a process like connecting the energies of the mountains and the water, building a profound foundation for their mutual feeling."[30] Indeed, as we see in the Wang Yuan biography excerpted in the beginning of this chapter, faithful maiden biographies frequently portray young women as having regarded themselves as members of their deceased fiancés' families, and that it would violate *yi* if they married someone else. The depictions are of course through the lens of male authors, still they illuminate female subjectivity, allowing us to go beyond the moralist discourse of female chastity and glimpse faithful maiden's self-understanding of their actions. Faithful maidens themselves expressed similar views in their own writings. Their suicide notes and poetry, preserved in various anthologies and other contemporary sources, reveal their tremendous emotional ordeal as well as strong beliefs about honor and disgrace: betrothal for them stood as a commitment to a lifelong relationship, and marrying a man other than their first betrothed was a shame they could not face.[31] Faithful maidens' own poetry and male authors' biographies, therefore, provided mutual context for reading into their emotions and convictions. Although there is little doubt that the Chinese female biography is often formulaic, the genre does communicate much about female subjectivity.

Writers like Jiao Xun (1763–1820), an eminent evidential scholar and adamant supporter of faithful maidens, openly declared that his writing of faithful maiden biography was to clarify the confusion of those who followed Gui Youguang's view. He wrote four essays in faithful maidens' defense. When he was approached by a solicitor for a biography of a certain young woman Gao, he took the opportunity to condemn again the faithful maidens' critics. He targeted a man named Zhang Liangyu, a *jinshi* degree holder from his native town about a generation older than he, who believed that "only when a man and a woman live in one room is their husband-wife relationship established. When there is no husband-wife relationship, there is no reason that a woman should preserve fidelity until she dies."[32] Jiao Xun calls his opinion most "absurd."

In the emotionally charged debate, men did not refrain from openly chastising the opponents of the faithful maiden cult, and faithful maiden biographies forthrightly expressed their feelings. Writing much later in the Qing dynasty, Li Ciming (1830–95) was also direct and terse in his message, calling critics of faithful maiden practice "petty pedants." He wrote a biography of a certain faithful maiden Yang, who lost her fiancé at the age of eighteen and wanted to hang herself when someone tried to talk her out of her resolution not to marry. Five years later, she married into her late fiancé's home. Li Ciming commented:

> Sages did not expect people to practice the most difficult virtuous acts. Therefore, ritual does not prohibit women from remarriage, let alone a second betrothal. Yet petty pedants do not understand this, and they regard those who refuse to be engaged a second time as going to extremes. What kind of hearts do they have! Look at the faithful maiden. She cut off her hair and disfigured her appearance (*jiefa limian*) for five years [before she married into her late fiancé's home]. Can this kind of deed be done by someone who is not determined?!"[33]

Li Ciming not only disagreed ideologically with the critics of faithful maidens. He was deeply disturbed that men of learning lacked an understanding of these young women's actions as tremendously difficult human deeds.

As seen from the examples above, ritual evidence, although stated clearly, could be interpreted in vastly different ways. Supporters reinterpreted the passages in a way that would make sense to them, while combing ritual texts for other statements that could lend legitimacy to their position. In that process, they called into question some of the most revered commentaries on ritual texts, implicitly dismissing their authority. What is most striking, perhaps, is that many of these supporters, including Jiao Xun, were preeminent evidential school scholars. Yet, in the reading and rereading of ancient texts, even they would struggle to stretch or discredit the ritual texts in order to back up a stance to which they were determined to commit. Some even went to such an extent as to deemphasize the relevance of ancient rituals as guidance in social interactions. For example, both Jiao Xun and Zhang Xuecheng (1738–1801), another important figure in the evidential school, argued that contemporary institutions such as marriage differed from those of antiquity and, therefore, not all ancient rituals remained applicable.[34] These cases provide us with a unique look into the acclaimed evidential scholarship. They reveal a deep tension in the evidential movement: despite its rigid principle of verifying truth through textual evidence, when it came to a social issue that scholars held dear, textual evidence did not have the final word.

BIOGRAPHY: A SITE OF AMBIVALENCE

The sharp divisions among leading scholars did not mean that they or others were not ambivalent. Even Gui Youguang, the pioneering critic, did not hold firmly to his position. In a biography he wrote later in his life, he called the faithful maiden practice "an excessive deed performed by the virtuous and the wise." Although it was not in accordance with the teachings of the sages, he states, gentlemen would still love to talk about it.[35] Ambiguity can also be sensed in other biographies where, while the authors affirmed the faithful maidens' actions, they nevertheless went on to stress that the young women did so because of their special circumstances.[36]

The eighteenth century scholar Wu Ding (1744–1809) perhaps showed this ambivalence most revealingly. The Wu family claimed two faithful maidens, a grand-aunt of Wu Ding who killed herself to follow her fiancé in death at the age of seventeen, and an aunt who cut off her own hair to make pledge not to be betrothed again after her fiancé's death. Wu

Ding wrote accounts of their deeds and praised them profusely, and he also crafted an essay defending the faithful maidens.[37] His ambivalence was revealed, however, in two places. In his essay, he proposes that a line be drawn between two situations: if a young woman vows to be a faithful maiden after the rite of *nazheng* (presenting betrothal gifts to the woman's family) has been performed, which in his view signifies the completion of the betrothal process, then her deed is legitimate in terms of ritual; on the other hand, those who "preserve fidelity before the *nazheng* rite are surely stupid."[38] Wu also injected a subtle voice of criticism in his biography of the daughter of a fisherman named He. The young woman had committed suicide when her parents refused her request to marry her deceased fiancée. Wu praised her act, but he nevertheless commented that if He had been born into a family of learning and had had the opportunity to hear about the Confucian rituals, she would have more closely followed the "middle and appropriate way" upheld by the ancient sages.[39]

Wu Ding's ambivalence may be interpreted as his not being without reservations about the extreme nature of the faithful maiden practice, but he was at the same time obliged for personal and familial reasons to honor and defend the commitment and sacrifice young women like his grand-aunt and aunt made. More generally, the ambiguity detectable in other scholars' opinions could be traced to a conflicted sense of moral responsibility and even a sense of guilt. As members of the social elite, they were responsible for defending what they believed to be the true meaning of the Confucian teachings that guided social behavior. At the same time, even though the young women may be said to have overstepped what was prescribed in these teachings, they surpassed men of Confucian education—like the authors of the biographies themselves—in their courage and moral integrity. Educated men could not bear to silence or criticize these young girls who were willing to suffer to fulfill their moral conviction. In the conclusion to his "Biography of Faithful Maiden Wu," Liu Dakui (1698–1780) first concedes that Gui Youguang made a sound argument that it was against ancient ritual principle to marry a deceased fiancé, but then he stresses that "time changes and people possess different dispositions," and that what his biographee chose to do was deeply touching.[40]

Qian Daxin (1728–1804), a highly respected historian of his day, similarly argues in a biography of a local faithful maiden:

> The early kings made the rituals, and they originally did not require unmarried women to observe the principle of "following one's husband to the end." Yet in later times, there are women who remain unmarried all their lives [after their fiancés' deaths], or go to their fiancés' homes

to serve their fiancés' parents, or even kill themselves to follow their fiancés' in death. Although this type of action is not in the rituals, gentlemen do not necessarily disapprove of it. This is because they understand the depth of these women's resolve.[41]

Qian's remarks end on a note of sympathy: even though the faithful maidens did not act in accordance with ritual, they followed their heart's desire and resolved to embrace a moral ideal that was difficult for an ordinary person to achieve. In another biography Qian stated: "A gentleman will not force people to accomplish things that are difficult for them, but if they do accomplish a difficult thing, he still loves to tell about it."[42] A faithful maiden went beyond what was required and held herself to a higher standard. Her deed was, therefore, essentially commendable.[43]

As suggested in these arguments, the debate was as much about the Confucian gentlemen's conscience as it was about ritual propriety. It went against their moral conscience to decry an act that they perceived as noble self-sacrifice. This uneasiness was intertwined with their general view of the decadence of current social customs. A common claim of scholars in any historical period was that in times when social customs are in decline and social relationships in disarray, virtuous deeds—even excessive virtuous deeds—such as the faithful maidens' serve as great moral examples. Fang Bao acknowledged, for example, that Gui Youguang made a convincing argument that faithful maidens violated ritual. He nonetheless called faithful maidens "extraordinary women," contrasting them with the "countless people" who had no sense of morality.[44] In his biography of a faithful maiden Chen who hanged herself, Peng Duanshu (1697–1777) declares: "How heroic! Hasn't she accomplished something difficult for people to do? Her act would certainly shame women who remarry!"[45]

Similar feelings might have underlay the ambivalent position of Liu Taigong (1751–1805), a good friend of Wang Zhong. Liu believed that Gui Youguang made his point "gently yet persuasively," and thought Wang Zhong's essay was beneficial to classic studies and social custom.[46] One day, however, he received a letter from a friend which mentioned how a Yangzi River storm capsized all the boats but miraculously left the one that carried faithful maiden Hu unturned. Hu was on her way to marry her deceased fiancé. Deeply touched and believing that her remarkable virtue invoked protection from Heaven, Liu wrote an account about the story, in which he also praised two other faithful maidens with whom he had some kind of personal connection.[47]

It is important to bear in mind that the "ambivalent" men discussed above were leading evidential scholars whose fundamental methodology was "verifying with textual evidence" rather than interpreting with subjective understanding. Such scholarly conviction was compromised in the debate on the faithful maiden practice, however. Conflicting notions of moral and social responsibility, rather than textual evidence alone, conditioned positions in the debate.

SCHOLARLY FATHERS OF FAITHFUL MAIDENS

The faithful maiden debate was a distinctive public event that involved educated elite across the empire throughout the late imperial period. Yet it also had an intimate side that bridged the inner and outer spheres: many of these scholars had personal connections to faithful maidens as fathers, brothers, adoptive sons, close relatives, or family friends. The debate for them was not simply about ritual propriety but about an ideal for which girls from their own families sacrificed their lives.

Scholarly fathers seldom wrote biographies for their faithful maiden daughters themselves. Instead, they entrusted close friends with the writing. One reason, it seems, was ideological conflict, which pitted father and daughter against each other. Cases such as that of Sun Xidan (1736–84) suggest the profound pain experienced by a scholar father when his own belief collided with that of his daughter. A specialist in classical rituals, Sun did not consider faithful maiden practice appropriate. His sixteen-year-old daughter was, however, determined to pursue faithful maidenhood. When Sun and his wife tried to arrange another marriage for her after her betrothed died, the girl stopped eating and threatened to kill herself.[48] Ostensibly because she was worried that her parents would eventually push her to marry, she became sick. On her deathbed, she asked Sun to send her to the home of her parents-in-law so she could die there. In deep grief, he asked Qian Shixi (1733–95), a friend, to write a biography of her.[49]

Qian Shixi tells us that although Sun loved his daughter very much, he considered her action too extreme. Sun's sadness might have two meanings. He was of course sad to have lost a daughter at such a tender age. He might also have felt disturbed that, despite his love for her, he could not suspend his belief in ancient ritual to praise her action. Writing anything about a daughter's death must be painful, especially when the ideals for which a daughter sacrificed her life are in conflict with one's own.

Fathers who supported the practice might have reacted differently, yet evidence suggests that even men who held favorable views of the faithful maiden practice became ambivalent when a girl they knew personally pursued the faithful maiden ideal. Fang Bao, for instance, had written several faithful maiden biographies. Then it happened that a daughter of a certain friend wanted to become a faithful maiden. When the horrified friend came to Fang, asking him to explain to his daughter that what she had chosen to do was against ritual, Fang accepted the request.[50]

Personal emotion could mediate a father's ideological conviction in complicated ways. Different from Sun Xidan, Zhu Shi changed his position in the controversy later in life. Zhu Shi had betrothed his only daughter to the son of a high official. When she was twenty years old, an auspicious date was chosen for the wedding, but her mother's death postponed the marriage. Two years later, her fiancé became afflicted with a disease and died. According to Zhu, as he was about to arrange another marriage for her a year after her fiancé's death,

> [s]he wept and asked me to let her marry into his family. I said to her: "Have you read the chapter 'Zengzi Asked?' It says if a woman dies before she performs the ritual of becoming a daughter-in-law, her body should be returned to her own family to be buried. Can a woman who has not yet married live in her fiancé's home? [The chapter also says]: 'If the fiancée has died, a man should put on mourning dress and go mourn for her. After the burial, he should remove the mourning garment. A woman should do the same if her fiancé has died.' I have not heard of a ritual that permits an unwed girl to endure widowhood for her fiancé." My daughter did not say a word. However, her will could not be changed. I thereupon agreed to let her do as she wished.[51]

Two biographies of faithful maiden Zhu, written by Lan Dingyuan and Cai Shiyuan respectively, reveal something of what transpired after this conversation. The faithful maiden said little but fasted for three days. Only then did Zhu Shi compromise and give her permission to go live as a widow. Before she left, she asked her father what she should wear to the spiritual wedding in her in-laws' home. Zhu Shi told her: "Nothing is said about it in the ritual. You figure it out according to *yi*. Do not ask me!"[52] Zhu Shi was apparently still unhappy with his daughter's choice.

The two biographies by Lan and Cai were among the most laudatory of all produced in this period: both authors lavished great praise on faithful maiden Zhu's extraordinary virtue. Noticeably, Zhu Shi himself wrote nothing about his daughter until two years after her premature death, when he came across a faithful maiden biography of a young woman named He, also authored by Cai Shiyuan. Like his own daughter, the fifteen-year-old He married into her dead fiancé's home accompanied by her maid. Both girls committed suicide late in the year when He's fiancé's lineage (which coveted his family property) blocked He's wish to adopt an heir. After reading Cai's biography Zhu wrote:

> I feel sorrow for the death of the two girls, and in the meantime remember my own daughter, who died preserving fidelity just as He did. Therefore, I write this essay. In human experience there is nothing more painful than for a betrothed girl to remain faithful to her deceased fiancé, and then to die for her conviction. She treats bitterness as if tasting sweets, and does not falter despite myriad hardships . . . Some people say that what these girls did was perverse and a violation of ritual. They even compare it with heterodox beliefs and say that it is harmful to social customs. How absurd this view is!

Zhu Shi, a ritual expert, then begins his long rebuttal, arguing that what faithful maidens do is not contradictory to ritual. Rather, the misunderstanding comes from the people "who stick to the words [of the classics] and do not seek to understand their meanings in context."[53] Zhu Shi now refuted the position he had long held—even at the time of his own daughter's ordeal.

There is no direct evidence to explain Zhu Shi's change of position. Could it be due to his daughter's death and the emotional distress it inevitably generated? One thing is clear: the thought that his daughter never enjoyed a normal marital life and died at a young age was deeply painful for Zhu Shi. His grief again illustrates the irony integral to the faithful maiden act. Young women like Zhu's daughter chose to be faithful maidens in part because they wanted to bring honor to their parents. Yet it was not the honor but the pain that their families felt most keenly.

Zhu Shi's essay is ultimately less a public discussion of faithful maiden practice than a personal defense of his daughter and the ideas she stood for. It might also be a father's apology for having opposed his daughter. The key difference between this piece and other faithful maiden biographies is that Zhu Shi wrote not simply as a Confucian scholar but as the father of a faithful maiden. His love for his daughter permeates his arguments and prevents him from arguing objectively. His changed position and sentiment bring to light an intimate dimension of the faithful maiden debate. Behind the discordant voices of condemnation and acclamation was painful personal experience. While Zhu Shi and Sun Xidan shared their grief, this grief did not have the same impact. Zhu Shi ultimately abandoned his earlier position, Sun Xidan did not.

Scholars have demonstrated that elite participation in biography writing, as in the construction of memorial shrines for virtuous women, could serve multiple public and personal agendas.[54] Similar observations can be made about the motivation to write faithful maiden biographies. But faithful maiden biographies were ultimately unique. They were, arguably, among the most metaphorical of their genre. Because of her power as the preeminent moral symbol and the extraordinary nature of her deed, the faithful maiden figured prominently in social and cultural debate.

Faithful maiden biographies were far from a uniform site where the Confucian elite articulated their shared moral values or expressed common emotions. On the contrary, profound discord marked these narratives, yielding rare insights into entrenched disagreements over the definition of female virtue and the relationship between ancient rituals and contemporary practice. These texts expose tensions in the evidential intellectual movement. The widely divergent positions various late imperial elites took on this controversy highlight both a deep ideological rift and profound emotional complexity that we seldom observe in other female biographies.

6. Exemplary Time and Secular Times

Wei Xiyuan's Illustrated Biographies of Exceptional Women *and the Late Qing Moment*

Joan Judge

One of the last *Lienü zhuan*-style collections of women's biographies of the kind described by Harriet Zurndorfer and Nanxiu Qian in chapters 3 and 4 was Wei Xiyuan's (Chengbo, Lianshang fl. 1908) *Xiuxiang gujin xiannü zhuan* (Illustrated biographies of exceptional women, past and present). Published some five years before China's last dynasty fell in 1911, this text provides valuable insights into a neglected but historically significant strain of late Qing ideology, "meliorism."[1] Meliorists like Wei were both committed to historical continuity and open to limited historical change. They brought exemplary time, or the paradigmatic in historical time, to bear on the everyday historicity of their own secular times, merging Confucian ethical-ritual principles (*lijiao*) with turn-of-the-twentieth-century reform imperatives.[2]

The range of conceptual registers Wei invokes in the *Illustrated Biographies* conveys the historical complexity of the meliorist position. He writes of Heaven as the source of the myriad things and the nation as the foundation of political strength. He combines support for the formal institutionalization of the new female education with an emphasis on age-old feminine virtues and the relevance of ancient exemplars. He makes reference to the divine sages (*shensheng*) of the legendary Three Dynasties (Sandai) and to the advancement of the citizens (*guomin*), to the ritual classics and to challenges posed by the "white race." He declaims on the unity of the Six Realms (*liuhe*) and the threat of national division. Most paradoxically, his eloquent disquisitions on these various themes are embedded in a text aesthetically indebted to late imperial courtesan albums.

Cognizant of what appear to an early-twenty-first century reader as profound disjunctions, I, nonetheless, do not focus on the apparent hybridity of Wei's stance. Rather than consider him to be a man who straddled a number of cultural universes or lived in a time of "transition," I approach him as an individual who lived in one singular, albeit complex, world: that of the late Qing meliorist. I seek access to his world by reading the *Illustrated Biographies* in two modes. First, intertextually, with references to both Wei Xiyuan's own highly diverse oeuvre and to the *Lienü zhuan* lineage from which it emerged. Second, paratextually by examining Wei's own prefaces to and commentaries on the biographies in his collection. This analysis demonstrates that a compilation of women's biographies can serve as a particularly revealing prism onto otherwise overlooked political and cultural preoccupations of an era. It can also provide an oblique window onto the life-world of a now obscure individual who was, nonetheless, passionately engaged with the pressing issues of his own day.

TEXTUAL CONTEXT: PALACE POETRY AND LEGAL REFORM

Little is known about Wei Xiyuan. He is not featured in any of the major compendia for the Qing period nor in any extant local gazetteers, and he merits only a single (and incomplete) entry in a biographical dictionary.[3] Editors of his works each seem to know only a piece of his story. These various fragments reveal that Wei (*hao*, Xiyuan; *ming*, Chengbo; *zi*, Lianshang) was from Xiangxiang in Hunan province. In addition to having compiled the *Illustrated Biographies*, he was a poet fascinated with the inner workings of the Qing court, and a low-level official with reformist aspirations.

Wei wrote poetry in at least two styles. The first is *gongci*, or palace poetry, which describes palace life, often focusing on the women's quarters (*gongwei*).[4] Wei's 101 palace poems collected in *Wei Xiyuan Qing gongci* (Wei Xiyuan's Qing palace poems) in 1915 depict the society of palace ladies at the Qing court.[5] They note the arrival and dismissal of consorts and include numerous references to the Empress Dowager Cixi (1835–1908, Xiaoqin). One poem describes how a portrait of the Empress Dowager painted by the American Katherine A. Karl (Kegu) could "move the gods."[6] After 1911 when there was effectively no longer any palace life to comment on, Wei began writing *xianglian ge* (poems in "lady's dressing case style"), also known as *yanti* (amorous style).[7] His poems in this sensual and mildly erotic mode were collected in *Pingyetai yanci* (Exquisite words from the open field terrace). Their often trivial subject matter included discussions of dreams (*qimeng*) and cosmetics (*zhifen*).[8]

While Wei's poetry conveys the image of a playful aesthete, he also wrote a legal text somewhat in the genre of fiction on legal matters (*gong'an xiaoshuo*), *Buyong xing shenpan shu gushi xuan* (Selected stories of trials that did not resort to the use of torture). This text reveals Wei to be a conscientious Qing official. He managed state monopolies (*quewu*) in Suqian County, northern Jiangsu Province, some time around the turn of the twentieth century and he was passionately committed to late Qing legal reform.[9] He notes in his preface to the *Selected Stories* that he wrote the book to aid the government in implementing its 1901 Xinzheng, or New Policies. Among New Policies guidelines submitted by influential officials was a proposal for increased leniency in the punishment of criminals including, for example, the replacement of bamboo beatings with periods of imprisonment.[10] Such domestic proposals, together with foreign diplomatic pressure, forced the Qing government to become increasingly attentive to legal reform in general, and to the elimination of long-standing forms of torture (*kuxing*) in particular.[11]

Wei's commitment to just and humane legal process was formulated in this context. Reflecting his meliorist ideals, Wei's concern was to ameliorate rather than challenge the existing political-legal system. He lamented that in current practice, the criminal code (*xingfa*) no longer served as the sovereign's instrument for regulating the people, but as officialdom's instrument for abusing them. Those responsible for carrying out justice at the local level, he was convinced, were often men of mediocre ability while the common people were themselves becoming ever more devious in their efforts to evade the law. He, therefore, compiled his collection to aid those responsible for meting out justice in his own day. The collection offers numerous examples of historical cases that were resolved not through torture but through investigative research, logical reasoning, and inspired methods of eliciting confessions.[12]

The collection of cases presents radically different protagonists from those celebrated in the *Illustrated Biographies*. Whereas the latter are diligent and chaste women of virtue, the former are often wily and depraved commoners. These commoners include a betrothed young woman who plots with her wealthy lover to kill her scholarly but penniless fiancé, a mother who has illicit sexual relations with a monk, and a young widow who engages in adultery with her cousin, a hired laborer.[13] The texts, nonetheless, share two important similarities. Both are collections of historical materials compiled by Wei to influence current behavior and practice.[14] He directly states this objective in the prefaces to the two collections and in his commentaries on individual cases or biographies.[15] Fully aware of the challenges China faced at the turn of the twentieth century, Wei was, nonetheless, convinced that contemporary problems could best be addressed through existing genres and appeals to past exemplars— whether skillful magistrates or virtuous women.

A second similarity lies in the underlying moral message of the two texts. While there are many dissolute women in the *Selected Stories,* there are also upright figures like those more self-consciously celebrated in the biographical collection. In a case entitled "Ziwu" (To falsely accuse one- self), for example, a commoner mother-in-law who is having an affair kills herself once she realizes that her dutiful daughter-in-law has discovered her impropriety. When the daughter-in-law is then accused of causing the suicide, she refuses to deny the charges, preferring to sacrifice herself rather than publicly disgrace her husband's lineage.[16]

TEXTUAL FILIATIONS: *LIENÜ ZHUAN* EXPANSIONS AND HUNDRED BEAUTIES ALBUMS

The dichotomy between moral seriousness and playful aestheticism in Wei's legal and poetic writings is further evident in the *Illustrated Biog- raphies.* The collection is a *"lienü zhuan* expansion," a genre that emerged in the Ming dynasty.[17] Texts in this genre comprise a number of biographies from Liu Xiang's (79–8 BCE) original 34 BCE *Lienü zhuan* (Biographies of women) together with later life-story narratives drawn from local gazet- teers, dynastic histories, and literati writings. While Jie Jin's (1369–1415) *Gujin lienü zhuan* (Biographies of women, past and present) was one of the first expansions, the most widely reprinted were Lü Kun's (1536–1618) *Gui fan* (Exemplars of the inner quarters; 1590) and Wang Geng's (fl. 1600) *Huitu lienü zhuan* (Illustrated biographies of women; 1610–20, 1779).[18] Perhaps the last expansion to appear before Wei Xiyuan's compilation was Liu Kai's (1781–1821) *Guang lienü zhuan* (Expanded biographies of women).[19]

Wei's *Illustrated Biographies* displays the basic characteristics of this genre. Approximately 11 percent (12 of 106 total) of the biographies featured in his collection are from the original *Lienü zhuan.* Wei then added biographies drawn from texts that postdated Liu Xiang's. Eleven, or approximately 10 percent, were from the Qing dynasty.[20] Like all preced- ing compilers of expansions, Wei eliminated Liu Xiang's section on evil women and reconfigured the categories of virtuous women. He replaced Liu's original seven groupings (discussed by Harriet Zurndorfer in chapter 3) with the following nine categories: "Xiao fumu" (Filiality to parents),

"Youai" (Fraternal love), "Xiangfu" (Assisting one's husband), "Shi jiugu" (Serving parents-in-law), "He disi" (Harmony with sisters-in-law), "Jiaozi" (Educating sons), "Qinjian" (Hard work and frugality), "Cihui" (Kindness and benevolence), and "Zhenjie" (Virtue). Finally, as noted above, Wei followed earlier compilers in appending his own commentary—prefaced with the statement "Xiyuan waishi yue" (the unofficial scribe, Xiyuan, says)—to every biography in his collection.[21] In some instances, these two- to fifteen-line encomiums replaced existing commentaries, as in the biographies drawn from the *Lienü zhuan*. In all cases, Wei's commentaries added a new semantic layer to the biographies, resignifying the life-story narrative for the early-twentieth-century reader.

Firmly within the *Lienü zhuan* lineage, Wei's collection nonetheless also reflected the late imperial aestheticization of the *lienü* genre.[22] While expansions like the *Guifan* and the *Huitu lienü zhuan* continued to convey normative principles of female behavior and social order, they also served to varying degrees as objects of conspicuous consumption and artifacts in the connoisseurship of women.[23]

Each life-story narrative in Wei's collection was surrounded by four parabiographical elements that heightened the reader's aesthetic experience of the biography. They include a four-character descriptive title written in the calligraphic style known as clerical script (*lishu*), a poem of four lines, a visual representation of the woman who is the subject of the biography, and what appear to be ink drawings—most likely lithographs—usually of foliage or flowers. These drawings include inscriptions of varying length often penned by Wei himself and signed "Xiyuan tiju" (inscribed by Xiyuan).[24]

These aesthetic parabiographical features of Wei's text reflect the merging in the late imperial period of the genre of *lienü* expansion, which celebrated upright moral exemplars, with the genre of courtesan catalogues, which celebrated sensuous *meiren* (beauties) or *baimei* (hundred beauties).[25] In addition to being closely filiated with the *Lienü zhuan*, Wei's *Illustrated Biographies* was intimately linked to the *Baimei xin yongtu zhuan* (One hundred beauties in new poems and pictures; earliest preface 1787). This High Qing collection included women of the pleasure quarters together with empresses, court ladies, literary or musical talents, goddesses, and immortals.[26] Wei Xiyuan's indebtedness to this text is suggested by his style name, which is homophonous—including tones—with the given name of the *One Hundred Beauties*'s compiler, Yan Xiyuan. His *Illustrated Biographies* features a number of women who appear in the *One Hundred Beauties* and often reproduces elements of its biographical narratives verbatim.[27]

FIGURE 6.1 (*left*).   "Mulan," Yan Xiyuan, 66.
FIGURE 6.2 (*right*).   "Mulan," Wei Xiyuan, *Xiuxiang* I.3.

The clearest evidence of a textual relationship between the *Illustrated Biographies* and the *One Hundred Beauties* lies, however, in the visual representation of the featured women. Illustrations in *lienü zhuan* expansions, including the *Exemplars of the Inner Quarters* and the *Illustrated Biographies of Women,* were generally in the active narrative style, which depicts a dramatic moment in the woman's story.[28] In contrast, Wei Xiyuan chose to have his subjects presented in the static *meiren* style of *baimei* collections, which focused on a woman's adornments and pose. A number of the illustrations in Wei's text were directly taken from Yan's hundred beauties album. Two examples representing very different feminine types are the intrepid woman warrior Hua Mulan (ca. 500)[29] (figures 6.1, 6.2) and the fragile late Ming teenage poet Ye Xiaoluan (1616–32) (figures 6.3, 6.4).

The blurring of the *lienü* and *baimei* genres is most evident, however, when Wei uses images of *meiren* of dubious moral stature to represent women of virtue. In one example, the image of a singing courtesan, Pang Jie (figure 6.5), taken directly from the *One Hundred Beauties* is used to represent a paragon of filiality, Ms. Lu (figure 6.6), wife of Zheng Yizong of the Tang Dynasty, who deftly wielded a knife in order to save her mother-in-law from robbers.

FIGURE 6.3 (*left*). "Ye Xiaoluan," Yan Xiyuan, 79.
FIGURE 6.4 (*right*). "Ye Xiaoluan," Wei Xiyuan, *Xiuxiang* VI.25.

FIGURE 6.5 (*left*). "Pang Jie," Yan Xiyuan, 58.
FIGURE 6.6 (*right*). Lady Lu, Wei Xiyuan, *Xiuxiang*, IV.5.

PARATEXT: DIGNITY AND CHASTITY

Despite these *baimei*-like features that are resonant of Wei's poetic oeuvre, the *Illustrated Biographies* is ultimately animated by the same sense of moral purpose as the *Selected Stories*. In his introduction to the biographical compilation, his prefaces to each of its nine sections, and his commentaries on individual biographies, Wei conveys his vision of a coherent moral universe in which women play a crucial and active role. Their kindness is the source of the life process, their virtue a manifestation of the righteous justice of Heaven and earth, their sagely instruction the foundation of a stable political order.[30]

This comprehensive vision is reflected in Wei's conceptualization of the compilation. "The source of the myriad things lies in Heaven," he writes in his introduction.

The provenance of human beings lies in their ancestors: they are whence I come. The first [section of the collection] is therefore devoted to "Filiality to Parents" (Xiao fumu). All infants know to love their kin and as they grow older, all know to love their older brothers. The next section is, thus, on "Fraternal Love" (Youai). As recorded in the "Taoyao" (Marriage) poem in the "Zhounan" section of the *Shijing* (Book of odes), a woman [marries out], her husband becomes her family and she forms a couple with him. The next section is, therefore, on "Assisting One's Husband" (Xiangfu). In aiding one's husband, nothing is more important than caring for his parents and so the next [section] is on "Serving Parents-in-Law" (Shi jiugu). In serving parents-in-law, compliance is most essential. Therefore the next [section] is on Harmony with Sisters-in-Law (He disi). If [a woman] is acquiescent toward her sisters-in-law and her parents-in-law she is also serving her husband and the way of the family is established. It is the son, however, who is ultimately responsible for continuing the family line. Therefore the next [section] is on "Educating Sons" (Jiaozi). Nurturing is prior to education: while education can only be the product of propriety and righteousness (*liyi*), nurturing can only be accomplished through "Hard Work and Frugality" (Qinjian). This is the next [section]. Those who are hard-working can, however, be narrow-minded, and those who are frugal can be stingy. Narrow-mindedness can lead to fretfulness, stinginess can result in lowliness. The most effective way to eliminate narrow-mindedness and stinginess is through kindness. Therefore "Kindness and Benevolence" (Cihui) is next. Nurtured with kindness, the nature of the child is amiable; cultivated with benevolence the nature of the child is conciliatory. Amiability can, however, result in timidity. Conciliatoriness can produce weakness. In balancing conciliatoriness and tenderness "Virtue" (Zhenjie) is of prime importance.[31]

Wei suggests in this passage that female personhood lies in service to various members of her family. Elsewhere in the compilation he directly states that "women first establish themselves through caring for their kin."[32] At the same time, however, he assumes the importance of gender parity and female dignity. In the preface to the *juan* on "Assisting One's Husband," he asserts that husband and wife are equal (*qi*) in intelligence (*xinsi*) and determination (*zhili*). He further promotes a marital ideal based on compatibility and mutuality, likening husband and wife to the two outside horses of a team of three (*liangcan*) who move, as described in a passage from the *Shijing*, like dancers with a regular and harmonious step.[33]

Wei also elevates female domestic labor by linking it to broader sociopolitical developments. In his preface to the *juan* on educating sons, he ties the role of the mother-instructress to national strengthening. Articulating widely held turn-of-the-twentieth-century anxieties about the "white race" and the specter of China's partition, he asserts the need for China to "majestically raise itself up to join the great powers." The most effective means of reaching this global prominence, he argues, is women's education.[34] In order to establish itself as a world power, he explains, China's sovereignty has to be secure and the nation strong. In order for its sovereignty to be secure and the nation strong, the Chinese people have to be loyal to their ruler and patriotic to their country. In order for the Chinese people to be loyal to their ruler and patriotic to their country these values have to be inculcated—not by government officials, enfeoffed imperial princes (*zongfan*), or unemployed scholars who engage in high rhetoric (*caoye youtan*)—but by wise mothers (*xianmu*). Female education was, therefore, an imperial and national imperative.[35]

Wei uses an extended metaphor of industrial production to describe the process of educating the wise mothers who would, in turn, educate their sons. Young Chinese women are, he explains, the raw metal (*tong*) out of which wise mothers would be cast (*zhuzao*). New schools are the ovens where these metals would be smelted, and their various course offerings the coal that would fuel the fires. Finally, and most important, wise mothers of the distant and recent past would serve as the molds (*mu*) according to which contemporary mothers would be formed.[36]

Elsewhere in the compilation Wei highlights the lessons his contemporaries should learn from the tales of historical heroines. In his commentary on a story originally from the *Lienü zhuan* in which Tian Jizi's mother successfully admonishes her son against political corruption, Wei laments the lack of such moral uprightness in his native Xiang county.[37] He uses the example of the mother of Li Jingrang sagely advising her son, a general of the Tang Dynasty, to assert the need for competent and honorable military leaders in the post-1894–95 war and post-Boxer era.[38] And he announces that the Tang courtesan Guan Panpan exhibited less debauchery than the powerful families he sees around him.[39] Finally, he uses the well-known tale of Hua Mulan to express his support for the contemporary anti-footbinding movement.[40]

Wei's most incisive contemporary commentary was reserved, however, for his measured critique of the late imperial chastity cult described in the introduction to this volume and by Weijing Lu in chapter 5. The title of Wei's text reflects his desire to shift attention away from chastity as the defining female virtue. He uses the term *xiannü* (resourceful, wise, and worthy women of talent and virtue, closely related to the figure of *xianyuan*, the focus of Nanxiu Qian's chapter) to describe the women he celebrates, rather than *lienü* or *lienü* (with fire radical under the *lie*), which most commonly appear in the titles of late imperial expansions.[41] By the late Ming, the more dramatic *lie* (with the fire radical) had overshadowed the more prosaic *lie* and come to signify heroic chastity martyrs. Wei's collection featured fewer women of this heroic martyr type than did most *lienü zhuan* expansions, including recent Qing examples. In Wang Xian's (*jinshi* 1745) *Lienü zhuan*, for example, 55 percent of the women were celebrated for their chastity and 41 percent for being "Heroically chaste" (Zhenlie), a category that denotes suicide.[42] The promotion of female virtue is of central importance to Wei: the *Illustrated Biographies'* final *juan* on "Zhenjie" is the lengthiest (twenty-five biographies) and represents the culmination of his collection. He, nonetheless, refuses to glorify self-destructive acts of female chastity. Only approximately 11 percent of the women included in his entire collection follow their husbands in death.

More important than percentages, however, is Wei's complex engagement with the chastity issue. While he commends widows who remain faithful to their deceased husbands and courageously live on to raise their sons, he does not celebrate widows who took their own lives or mutilated themselves in order to avoid remarriage.[43] I will focus here on Wei's view of the specific category of chaste women featured in Weijing Lu's chapter, faithful maidens (*zhennü*)—young women willing to sacrifice their lives for their sick or deceased fiancés.[44] I have chosen to analyze the three faithful maiden biographies in Wei's collection for two reasons. First, they reveal his nuanced assessment of chaste practices: in the first case he praises the faithful maiden's actions, in the second he implicitly criticizes the *zhennü* cult, and in the third he explicitly decries its tragic consequences. Second, all three faithful maidens are from the Qing dynasty—the third lived just

FIGURE 6.7.   Lady Jin, Wei Xiyuan,
Xiuxiang, VI.17.

decades before Wei's writing. Their tales thus highlight tensions between distant exemplary ideals and immediate experience.

The first of the three biographies is the story of a Miss Jin (see figure 6.7) whose betrothed, a certain Zhang Wenbao, died before their marriage could take place. The young woman then devoted her life to raising the son of a concubine Zhang had impregnated shortly before his death.[45] Miss Jin's story contains one of the dominant tropes in faithful maiden lore, which was popularized in a widely performed play from the sixteenth through the early twentieth centuries: a young woman dedicates her life to a "husband" she had never known by raising a son she had not borne to bring honor to her betrothed's lineage. The heroine of the popular drama, a faithful maiden named Qin Xuemei, may have been the source of inspiration for Miss Jin's actions and/or her biography.[46]

In his commentary, Wei praises Miss Jin for ensuring that her husband's descent line would not be broken and for properly raising his son. He also applauds her emotional investment in preserving her husband's memory. Unlike some critics of the faithful maiden phenomenon who claimed that a young woman bore neither an affective nor a material debt to her dead fiancé, Wei considers Miss Jin's actions a proper expression of the gratitude she owed her "husband."[47] Ultimately, however, Wei's encomium is more a reaffirmation of the importance of patrilineal continuity than an endorse-

FIGURE 6.8. Yuan Suwen, Wei Xiyuan, *Xiuxiang*, IX.21.

ment of the faithful maiden cult: Miss Jin was honorable in his eyes for selflessly securing the future of the Zhang line, not for denying herself sexual and emotional fulfillment.

The second account of a faithful maiden in Wei's compilation is altogether different in tone. It is the well-known story of Yuan Ji (Suwen, fl. 1730) (figure 6.8), the third younger sister of the poet, scholar, and promoter of women writers, Yuan Mei (1716–98). According to the account in Wei's collection, Yuan Ji was betrothed to the son of a man named Gao at a young age. As the time of the marriage approached, the Gao family tried to annul the engagement, claiming that the young man was ill. Yuan Ji refused, making the classic *zhennü* declaration: "Women follow only one man in life, if he is sick I will care for him, if he dies I will remain faithful to him." The marriage rites were thus completed as Yuan Ji alone had wished. She soon learned, however, that her husband was not physically but mentally ill. Irritable and cruel, he abused her and spent the money from her dowry in brothels. When he made plans to sell her, she finally returned to her natal family, heartbroken. Gao died shortly thereafter. Yuan Ji lived in great sorrow for another year before dying herself.[48]

Wei's commentary on the biography expresses sympathy for Yuan Ji without explicitly criticizing the faithful maiden cult. It also conveys respect for Yuan Ji's choice without defending *zhennü* practice. Wei faults

Gao's violence rather than Yuan Ji's conviction for the tragedy, representing the incident as a misfortune for the Yuan family that had otherwise
known happiness and longevity. He neither acknowledges nor echoes the
views of critics of the faithful maiden cult like Wang Zhong (1744–94),
who saw Yuan Ji's fate as the outcome of her own "stupidity." Nor did he
follow Yuan Mei himself in blaming Yuan Ji's desire to sacrifice herself
on her knowledge of historical exemplars and feminine norms. While the
account of Yuan Ji's story that Wei included in his collection notes the
three *juan* of the *Lienü zhuan* and one of the *Shi jing* that she carried with
her, and features an illustration of her holding a book, Wei drew no link
between her learning and her tragic fate.[49]

In sharp contrast to Wei's commentary on the Yuan Ji story, his response to the third faithful maiden selection, the story of Wei Jingqing
(figure 6.9), is not neutral. The parabiograhical elements that precede the
biography and the biographical narrative itself do not foreshadow Wei's
criticism of the young woman's actions that follows in his commentary.
The poem preceding the narrative concludes with the pronouncement that
Jingqing's "virtue was complete, her chastity preserved." The account itself
expresses admiration for the classical education she had received from her
mother, and extols her poetic gifts. Jingqing's talents had been recognized
by a lower-level degree holder, Zeng Shufan, who became her fiancé. They
were a perfect couple: she beautiful and he refined. When Zeng died tragically before the wedding, Jingqing's parents felt it inappropriate for her to
rush to the funeral. Locking herself in her room in desperation, Jingqing
hanged herself at age twenty-six.[50]

Wei began his commentary by stating that Jingqing was only engaged,
not married, and that it would have been appropriate for her to wed after
Zeng's death. He uses an historical analogy to support his argument,
comparing Jingqing to Boyi and Shuqi, Shang loyalists (a comparison others had made to faithful maidens, as Weijing Lu notes in chapter 5) who
chose—wrongly in Wei's view—to starve to death in the mountains rather
than serve the Zhou conquerors in 1200 BCE. He argues that it would not
have been against propriety for Boyi and Shuqi to "eat the grain of the
Zhou" or, by extension, for Jingqing to marry another. As Wei must have
been aware, Wang Wan, a participant in the early Qing debate on the
moral and ritual appropriateness of the *zhennü* cult, had already used this
allusion to defend rather than condemn faithful maidens. Wang declared
that Confucius had not deemed Boyi and Shuqi's actions excessive because
they had served as powerful exemplars of loyalty at a time of social disarray. He analogously asserted that the extreme behavior of faithful maidens

FIGURE 6.9.   Wei Jingqing, Wei Xiyuan, *Xiuxiang*, IX.23.

should be commended as a source of inspiration for those of lesser moral mettle.[51]

Wei ends his commentary by disclosing what may have been the principal reason for his criticism of the faithful maiden ideal in this particular instance. He had familial ties to Jingqing's native Hengyang in Hunan province, and her father, Wei Zhaoting, was one of his paternal uncles. This kinship bond most probably provided Wei with access to privileged sources on Jingqing's life, and it is possible that he personally composed the version of her biography in his compilation. At the same time, Wei did not rely on an existing account in the 1872 Hengyang county gazetteer that he presumably would have had access to. While the gazetteer entry is typically laconic, the biography in Wei's compilation is more personal and sentimental. It goes beyond the formulaic statement in the gazetteer that Jingqing demonstrated cleverness from a young age and was poetically gifted, by describing her literary skills in detail and even quoting a line from one of her own poems. It also waxes more eloquently on the perfect match between Jingqing and Zeng. While the gazetteer merely records that they were engaged, Wei's account describes their first meeting and emphasizes their close compatibility.

What is ultimately most striking in comparing the two sources, however, is not Wei's embellishment of the gazetteer account but his omission of elements that appear in the local source. These include minor details such as Jingqing's given name, Quansheng (Jingqing is her style name), but also a significant new fold in her story. According to the gazetteer, Jingqing lived on after Zeng's death and only committed suicide when her parents attempted to arrange a second engagement for her.[52] Assuming the gazetteer account was correct and that Wei had seen it, the reasons for this omission are unclear. Perhaps Wei was unwilling to publicly blame Jingqing's parents—his blood relations—in print for suggesting a second marriage. Perhaps he believed his readers would more keenly sense the futility of Jingqing's suicide if it was presented as an immediate response to Zeng's death rather than a later reaction to a second proposal.

These questions aside, it is certain that Wei's personal relationship to Jingqing colored his reaction to her death. He is like the "scholarly fathers" of the Qing whom Weijing Lu discusses, men whose intellectual position as either defenders or opponents of the faithful maiden cult was determined by their subjective experience as brothers, fathers, or uncles of *zhennü*. Wei sanctions the practice of faithful maidens who lived on to raise adopted sons in his commentary on the story of Miss Jin. He is pained by Yuan Ji's tragedy but does not question her steadfast devotion to Gao. It is only when confronted with the meaningless death of his own poetically gifted cousin that he articulates a heartfelt critique of *zhennü* practice.

THE ILLUSTRATED BIOGRAPHIES AND THE LATE QING MOMENT

Wei Xiyuan's commentary on Jingqing's tragedy and his overall response to the chastity phenomenon could be summed up by his statement that "the teachings of the sages did not include practices difficult for the human emotions to bear."[53] This position was directly in line with the late imperial critique of the faithful maiden cult that asserted ritual propriety had to express rather than distort authentic human feelings. It also resonated with the views of later May Fourth–period writers who denounced the chastity imperative for not being in accordance with natural emotion.[54]

Wei's passionate concern with an issue that had preoccupied Confucian scholars for some 300 years and would continue to engage New Culture polemicists in the following decade provides important insights into his intellectual and political persona. Together with his pleas to end government corruption and bolster social morality, it demonstrates that this author of a highly aesthetic collection of exemplary female biographies was deeply engaged with the pressing social issues of his day. More than a mere object in the connoisseurship of women or an artifact of an unchanging *lienü zhuan* tradition, Wei's *Illustrated Biographies* is a signifier of temporal and ideological flux. The apparently similar collections in the *lienü zhuan* expansion genre, like the superficially homogenous late imperial editions of the five classics and four books that Cynthia Brokaw has examined, masked tremendous diversity.[55] While their compilers all owed a formal debt to Liu Xiang and all sought to convey a Confucian message in visually-appealing ways, each reshaped the repertoire of exemplars and extended the *lienü* ideal in accordance with his own personal and historical concerns.

Each of these compilers was attentive to the expectations of his projected audience(s). While Wei Xiyuan created a collection with the voyeuristic appeal of a hundred beauties album, he ultimately conceived of the *Illustrated Biographies* as a textbook to be used in the new government-approved schools for girls and women. His compilation was published by a company that specialized in pedagogical materials, the Jicheng tushu gongsi (Great accomplishments book company), in 1908, the year after public female schools were belatedly added to the Qing court's wide-ranging reforms, which Wei so ardently supported.[56] At various points in the collection, Wei articulates his support for the new women's education, extolling the value of girls' schools, praising women who founded educational institutions, and, as discussed above, underscoring the need to educate mothers who could successfully instruct their children.[57]

The print market that Wei's text entered had, however, recently been inundated by new-style texts, including Western-influenced women's textbooks, which used simple language and often dramatic illustrations to promote such values as patriotism, internationalism, and even free marriage and female professionalization.[58] Within this new cultural context, Wei's more erudite and historically resonant collection did not command the audience he anticipated. An advertisement for what seems to have been Wei's text appeared in a 1910 issue of *Shibao* (The Eastern Times), a newspaper that avidly promoted new-style textbooks.[59] While the advertisement declared that the collection was an "unrivaled textbook for girls' schools," it further announced that the compilation could be most effectively used not as an ethics textbook as Wei clearly intended it, but as a copybook for classes on calligraphy or drawing. Its current cultural value was reflected in its market value: the collection was being sold at half price (1 *yuan*, 2 *jiao* per volume, instead of 2 *yuan*, 4 *jiao*).[60]

Remaindered in its own day, Wei's compilation has, nonetheless, been considered worthy of republication in ours.[61] Printed in sharp blue ink and gracefully bound in silk, this new edition is more antiquarian object than site of cultural contestation, its meliorist message trumped by its exotic aestheticism. For readers attentive to the *Illustrated Biographies'* intertextual history and paratextual complexity, however, it continues to serve as a prism refracting a universe of late Qing social and gender concerns distinct both from those heralded in the new print organs of the day or in retrospective narratives of China's revolutionary modernity. It also provides a glimpse into the preoccupations of an otherwise obscure lower official and poet, a man committed to reconciling a historically transcendent exemplary time with the more turbulent secular times that were his own.

7. Gender and Modern Martyrology

Qiu Jin as Lienü, Lieshi *or* Nülieshi

Hu Ying

> QIU JIN: I can't leave! I'm responsible for the failure of this uprising. In any case, self-sacrifice is the natural end of a revolutionary . . .
>
> CHENG: Would death lessen your responsibility?
>
> WANG: This is dumb! This is dumb! Don't do this! Let's get moving, now! Haven't you heard of the old saying: "As long as the green mountain remains, there's no worry for lack of firewood"?!
>
> QIU JIN: A lot of blood has been shed for this failure. Where others bravely died for the cause, how can I run away? . . .
>
> WANG: I didn't know you are so block-headed. Those books on virtue and righteousness that you were brought up on— they ruined you.
>
> CHENG: For one last time, Commander, consider this: Suicide means that you have given up your fight against the Qing government! It means that you admit failure.

I begin with a lengthy quote from *The Spirit of Freedom* (*Ziyou hun*), a play by Xia Yan about the woman revolutionary Qiu Jin (1875?–1907), because it dramatically highlights the usually submerged connection between modern martyrdom and traditional "books on virtue and righteousness."[1] A major subgenre in twentieth-century Chinese history is martyrology, of which commemorative writings about Qiu Jin are a good example. This chapter focuses on the intersection between women, martyrdom, and modernity. It is motivated by the following questions: In what ways does modern martyrology reject, repackage, or reproduce the premodern tradition? More specifically, what happens to the distinctly gendered aspect of late imperial martyrs? In other words, what are the precise historical meanings of *nü* (woman/female) in the prominent category *nü lieshi* (woman martyr)? How is she different from the long tradition of *lienü* (heroic/chaste women) examined by Weijing Lu and others in this volume?

121

The scene above enacts a last-minute confrontation between Qiu Jin and two comrades who are trying to persuade her to flee. It was common knowledge that the historical Qiu Jin had ample time to slip away before the arrival of the Qing soldiers. In other words, it was her determination to die—regardless of who actually wielded the axe, as he was only the instrument of her will—that makes her death a martyrdom or suicide, depending on the interpretation. Qiu Jin's stated intent is "self sacrifice as the natural end of a revolutionary,"[2] that is to say, martyrdom, an exulted death that bears witness to one's beliefs. Yet this self-interpretation is immediately challenged in the play. Cheng Yi deflates the high rhetoric of "self-sacrifice" by equating it with suicide. He then points to its defeatist meaninglessness, which is consistent with his sharp query on moral responsibility. Coming from a different angle, the character of Wang Jinfa undermines the worth of martyrdom by drawing a causal and critical link between Qiu Jin's revolutionary intent and "those books on virtue and righteousness." In comparison with Wang's radical critique of traditional moral teachings, Qiu Jin appears conventional in her ideological positioning.

Despite the widespread critique of traditional morality associated with the May Fourth generation, the playwright Xia Yan would be forced to make repeated self-criticisms over the years for implying that Qiu Jin's death was a suicide rather than a sacrosanct act of revolutionary martyrdom. Xia Yan was in political trouble because he resisted what I will call the eulogistic imperative. And he was the rare exception. For ultimately, under the powerful prerogative of the eulogistic imperative and through the sanctity of revolutionary martyrs, a good deal of the same traditional morality was recuperated.

THE *LIESHI* TRADITION AND
THE EULOGISTIC IMPERATIVE

The exultation of martyrs has a long tradition and is central in orthodox Chinese philosophy. Thus Confucius says: "The determined scholar and the man of virtue will not seek to live at the expense of injuring their virtue (*ren*). They will even sacrifice their lives to preserve their virtue complete (*shashen chengren*)."[3] Likewise Mencius: "I like life, and I also like righteousness (*yi*). If I cannot keep the two together, I will let life go, and choose righteousness (*sheshen quyi*)."[4] These very words were repeatedly cited by generations of martyrs, including Qiu Jin. On the other side, there have always been skeptics and critics. Thus Han Fei (d. 233 BCE) attacked the *lieshi* for his excessive attachment to moral principles, an attachment that he argues is motivated by an extraordinary vanity that seeks singular prominence by rejecting conventional values.[5] In linking the adherence to *yi* with a love of *ming* (name or public recognition), Han Fei points to the *lieshi*'s demand for an audience and thus undermines his purity of intent.[6] The audience need not be immediately present but can be and in fact is often conceived of as coming well after the heroic act, a posthumous audience years or even generations later; thus *ming* is often synonymous with "a place in history," or *qingshi liuming*. Much as the specific principle/cause may change over the centuries, the concept of dying for a publicly recognized cause remains a necessary condition for *lieshi* status.

Crucial to the present inquiry is the gendered inflection of traditional moral precepts, for that determines whether female martyrs were by definition different from male martyrs. As many scholars have observed, the original meaning of *lie* and its close synonym *zhen* as "steadfast adherence to a moral principle" applied to men and women alike in classical times; by the twelfth to fourteenth centuries, the definition of women's primary virtue and heroism narrowed significantly so that chastity became the exclusive structural analogue to the male virtue of loyalty and righteousness.[7] Thus female virtue became increasingly defined by control of her body and sexuality.

As Weijing Lu's essay in this book points out, many late imperial literati criticized what they perceived as excessive and inhumane demands on women.[8] Yet even for those critical of the rising tide of female suicide, there was a powerful countervailing tendency: in aesthetic and psychological terms, there is an "allure" in writing eulogy; in moral terms, there is an "obligation to honor" such a death.[9] Indeed, rare is the survivor/witness capable of honoring such a death without glorifying it. When faced with an extraordinarily traumatic death, to which a conventional response appears drastically inadequate, the always present biographical tendency toward eulogy becomes an imperative, a demand for a sublime response commensurate with the intensity of the traumatic death. Such an exultative response then counters the threatening meaninglessness of all death by ascribing enormous significance to one special death. Fulfilling multiple needs that are at once psychological, moral, and political, the eulogistic imperative is most clearly operative when a death is commemorated in terms of martyrdom. Even when the actual causes of this martyrdom may be a combination of economic, legal, and social factors, the necessary glorification is typically accomplished through the citation of conventionally accepted moral precepts. Thus interpretations of suicides that find their way into eulogies do not so much reveal causes or motives but instead *ascribe* them.[10]

Different, even contradictory, motives and meanings were ascribed to Qiu Jin's death. Some contemporaries made a sharp distinction between her and "the countless Han women who died during the early Qing conquest." Whereas the latter were "benighted and weak," their deaths as "light as feathers," Qiu Jin's was "heavy as Mount Tai."[11] A few, like Xia Yan, despite elevating the significance of her death, interpret her intent within the same moral framework of traditional teachings that presumably motivated countless earlier suicides. How, then, is our modern *nü lieshi* (woman martyr) similar to or different from the long tradition of chaste and heroic women? How is she similar to or different from unmarked though male *lieshi* (martyr)? And how do these gender attributes change over time?

For convenience, the following discussion schematizes three rounds of Qiu Jin martyrology: the first published in China soon after her execution; the second written by her comrades-in-arms in either Japan or China after 1912; and the third written by the May Fourth generation.

FROM *YUANNÜ* (WRONGFUL DEAD) TO *NÜXIA* (FEMALE SWORDSMAN)

In the first phase of Qiu Jin commemoration, published in Shanghai and the surrounding area and mostly in the forms of traditional dramatic scripts and poetry, the key term used to describe her death is *yuan*, literally, wrongful death or death as a miscarriage of justice. Several literary works allude to the cosmic or supernatural effects of *yuan* death in terms of "frost in June" and "snow in June."[12] These supernatural elements are part of an established convention that indicates appeals to a higher authority that corrects the injustice of the human world. Because of the real dangers of government persecution, these commemorative works are often ambiguous with regard to her revolutionary activity, either portraying it as "family revolution" (i.e., gender equality), or shadily hinting at anti-Manchu sentiments.

One surprising element at this stage of commemoration is the intimation that the immediate cause of Qiu Jin's death is the death of Xu Xilin (1873–1907), who, though a subsidiary figure in later Qiu Jin commemoration, was key to her story early on. Xu was a close comrade who was executed after his assassination of the Manchu governor En-ming. In the play *Tragedy at Xuanting* (*Xuanting yuan*), for a typical example, Qiu Jin is portrayed as fainting and crying when she first learns of Xu's death.[13] This extreme grief and the accompanying passivity continue until she is captured herself and put to death. Anyone familiar with the biographies of chaste widows since the late Ming cannot fail but recognize the standard motif of "dying of passionate sorrow" (*tung yi xun*). The operative term in the Chinese original is the particle (*yi*), as it implies the cause of death. Contemporary invocations of this motif are frequent enough to indicate that the widow-suicide model was still serviceable in portraying a heroic woman.[14] Such a woman's action is comparable to yet different from the high political dedication of her husband. It is comparable in that both man and wife demonstrate extraordinary bravery in death but different in that hers is inextricably tied to the notion of sexual fidelity. This interpretative frame is compelling because it is familiar—after all, this is how a woman of late imperial times achieves the highest moral standards. Her heroism is evident in her resolve to sacrifice herself; her femininity is fortified by her passionate expression of sexual fidelity. In Qiu Jin's case, this motif is so compelling that it has been a stock feature in commemorative material. Precisely because it hinges on a traditionally defined female virtue, however, it has also been highly problematic.

For Qiu Jin was not Xu Xilin's widow. Their close association in fact presented an ethical problem brought to light by her implication in his treason plot. Indeed, at the time of her death, rumor darkly hinted at sexual impropriety, and it was countered by another explanation of their relationship in media sympathetic to her: that Qiu and Xu were cousins (which they were not). The point here is not so much to support or dispute either claim. It is to note that, despite the tension between a clearly gender-coded moral convention and the revolutionary action of a heroic woman, the figure of the chaste widow was so tenacious that Qiu Jin could be depicted as if she were following Xu Xilin in death. It is as if there were a scripted role a heroic female was compelled to play, even if that role conflicted with her heroic status.

And indeed, in the earlier dramatic representations, Qiu Jin's role is nothing if not scripted. She is by necessity the lead female, the *dan*, a role-type that belongs to a woman of good family and who must act more or less according to the moral precepts for women of such a class.[15] Thus, in the play *Liuyue shuang* (Frost in June), the stage directions state: "When the soldiers see a female figure (Qiu Jin) crouching in the far corner, they all rush toward her, some pushing and others dragging. The poor woman does not say anything but cries silently as she follows the soldiers to the front stage."[16] Again in *Xuanting yuan* (Tragedy at Xuanting), as she is captured by the Qing soldiers, Qiu Jin "cries as she walks," and at court, she "crouches on the ground crying." Before she is to be executed, she comes on stage "with her hair hanging down and shedding torrents of tears" (*pifa huilei*). While later readers react to these stage directions as demeaning to Qiu Jin's heroic stature, these directions are consistent with the generic portrayal of a woman of good family confronting the legal system. According to established convention, when the *dan* is wrongly accused of a crime and literally dragged through the criminal system, her innocence is expressed through her physical suffering and dramatized in her public humiliation. The suffering and humiliation is further feminized through her winning weakness, thus the necessary crying and crouching postures.[17] These stage conventions control the actor's physical movements and, like any social conventions of bodily behavior, are a direct reflection of gender and class demarcations. Thus, Qiu Jin may be heroic in her action and poetry in the rest of the play, but her body must be correctly feminine according to the convention of the time.

Even offstage, in the biographical essays that came out in the same period, similar feminine constraints are at play. Here, the key term is typically *xia*, the swordsman, a much favored stock figure that overlaps with *lie* in the emphasis on bravery and ready self-sacrifice, as well as disregard for wealth and power.[18] As in the case of the *lieshi*, the addition of "woman" complicates matters, and the question is whether conventional trappings of femininity are still operative when one is a heroic swordswoman. The answer is yes. This is evident in what essayists choose to write about: because the formal essay as a public genre is a close kin to history-writing, the essayist must exercise the historiographical tradition of the "crooked brush" (*qubi*), that is to say, she is expected to elaborate on worthy aspects (*yang*) and suppress potentially damaging aspects (*yi*).

Notably, women essayists especially felt the need to fortify Qiu Jin's sexual reputation. In the epitaph written in February 1908 for the stele inscription (*mubiao*), a highly public record, Xu Zihua (1875–1935) defends Qiu Jin's virtue thus:

> In closely examining [Qiu Jin's] conduct, [we see that] she was careless of details, tended to give free expression to her emotions, and loved wine and swords—all as if she were not to be reigned in by convention. Yet, in her true essence, she was exceptionally upright and prudent. . . . Although she loved freedom, in matters concerning propriety, she never transgressed.[19]

With telling conjunctions of "as if," "yet" and "although" (*ruo, ran, sui . . . er*), Xu Zihua is clearly building a case to explain away Qiu Jin's transgressive behavior. Juxtaposed with Qiu Jin's outward disregard for conventionality, Xu argues for a different, "true essence" (*benzhong*) that lies deep in Qiu Jin, an essence that is "upright and prudent" (*duanjin*), standard terms in descriptions of female paragons of virtue.

The femininity of the protagonist is also typically depicted through weakness. In the same epitaph, Xu Zihua describes Qiu Jin's difficulties in running a feminist journal: "for the women of the boudoir are weak (*guige renruo*), thus few contributed funding."[20] In a more personal memorial, "Qiu Nüshi lishi," Xu altered her language: "Few people contributed funding for the periodical—thus we may see the level of awareness of our women compatriots! Her financial situation worsening, Qiu Jin traveled through several provinces to collect funds: a delicate woman on the road (*ruozhi quchi*), weathering wind and frost." Here the weakness (*ruo*) that is publicly attributed to women in general is reattributed to the heroine herself. Thus even when the expressed intent is to stress the heroism of the protagonist, a heroism that sets her apart from other women, the language of the eulogizer appears to be imprisoned in the conventional rhetoric of the weak woman, a linguistic constraint for the essayist much like the bodily constraint for the *dan*.

FROM *XIANÜ* (SWORDSWOMAN) TO *LIESHI* (MARTYR)

The basic theme of wrongful death that runs through these plays and essays was almost immediately challenged by others. In the essays written by her revolutionary colleagues, we no longer find the tragic female heroine humiliated in public and suffering at the hands of a corrupt judicial system. Instead, the biographers explicitly state her involvement in anti-Qing associations and military plots. Her capture by the Qing soldiers, for example, is portrayed as a self-sacrifice so that other comrades may escape to safety. The key term now is not *yuan* but *lie*, martyrdom for an explicitly nationalist cause.

One such writer, Ye Songqing, starts his essay by solemnly declaring: "If the glorious deeds of the Martyr are not widely recognized, it is the fault of those who survived her." If the previous round of commemoration is marked by its tragic rhetoric, this one is in the high heroic mode: "Among those of us who took great pleasure in sacrificing ourselves for the country . . . Qiu Jin alone was able to achieve this goal."[21] For writers like Ye, a nationalist revolutionary martyr does not just sacrifice herself for the cause, but does so gladly without a tinge of sadness. Her death is thus unequivocally "good." In this heroic mode, there is no room for descriptions of suffering, or for a feminine attitude: the heroic is coded masculine.

Qiu Jin is, in this rhetorical context, an honorary male. Lavish details concerning her involvement with secret societies are presented: the many names of co-conspirators, the secret meetings and secret-society rituals, the code titles conferred on the leaders (Qiu Jin was "White Fan"). This tradition is just as well established as that of the tragic female: it is the tradition of the popular bandit/military romance with its singular but necessary "woman general," such as Hu Sannian in *Brothers of the Marsh*, and Sun Furen in *Romance of the Three Kingdoms*. Now Qiu Jin was commemorated in a closely woven web of fellow male revolutionaries from whom Qiu is always distinguished as a woman but from whom she also derives her identity.[22] Occasionally this laudatory masculinization wanes when the presumed masculine qualities acquire a negative connotation.

Zhang Binglin, for a rare example, argues that Qiu Jin was not a good revolutionary because she was not a good woman. He first pays obligatory tribute to her by confirming the purity of her revolutionary intent and her "thoroughly masculine" approach. He then introduces an apparently irrelevant detail: Qiu Jin's birthplace, Shanyin, is the birthplace of Cao E, the most famous filial daughter commemorated in Liu Xiang's *Biographies of Exemplary Women;* it was, therefore, the place where "the way of the feminine was first established." The point is that Qiu Jin had, in his words, "perverted the way of the feminine."[23] The tension here is between the eulogistic imperative (after all, Qiu and Zhang belonged to the same revolutionary association, and were both from Zhejiang Province), and Zhang's discomfort at Qiu Jin's transgression of gender norms. Zhang resolves this tension by suggesting that Qiu Jin is not unfeminine because of her political engagement per se, but because of her love of public speech-making, which he criticizes three times in this short essay.[24] He then concludes: "I heard that in ancient times, those who were good at swordsmanship held true spirit within and exhibited placid appearance without. Few were garrulous." In other words, despite Qiu Jin's aspirations to being a swordswoman/revolutionary, her departure from both the way of the heroic good swordsman and the "the way of the feminine" is what prevents her from truly fulfilling her mission. She may be heroic (*lie* with fire radical), but if she is not exemplary (*lie* without fire radical), she would accomplish nothing.

And a deeper tension remains, which Zhang Bingling does not address: Qiu Jin did pervert the "way of the feminine," not just in speaking publicly but in forsaking her family and seeking her self-identity in terms other than the familial terms of wife and mother. This tension would make her a misfit even in the May Fourth discourse of women's liberation.

NÜLIESHI (WOMAN MARTYR) VERSUS THE NEW WOMAN

With the advent of the May Fourth and the New Culture movement, what in Qiu Jin's times was considered a lesser revolution (and therefore a lesser crime), namely women's liberation (or "family revolution" in the late Qing), became associated with the most radical political position. Beginning in 1916, numerous articles appeared in *New Youth* denouncing the traditional "Three Cardinal Laws" and "Five Constant Virtues" (*san'gang wuchang*), including a critique of chastity suicide.[25] This is followed by the 1917 special issue on Ibsen's *A Doll's House*, whose Nora would instantly become the model of the New Woman, and whose proclamation—"my sacred duty is to myself"—would be echoed in many literary works of the time. Going well beyond Ibsen, "freedom to love" was taken up as the ultimate expression of individual choice, and "love was regarded as a new morality."[26]

In this context of the exultation of "freedom to love," one might imagine that Qiu Jin, having herself left behind the confines of domestic life, would be reclaimed as an obvious Chinese precedent to Nora. The paradox is that she was at once seen as being outside the rubric of the New Woman, or even Woman, and as the true New Woman. Even the most radical critics of "traditional morality" do not celebrate her for pursuing personal happiness or anything remotely associated with sexual freedom. It is as if the eulogistic imperative—the obligation to honor her status as a revolutionary martyr—precludes any consideration of personal liberty.[27] Remarkably, although not everyone fully subscribed to the imperative, the difference between those who did and those who did not does not depend on how radical one's critique of "traditional morality" was, but on how Romantic one's sensibility and rhetoric were. The more Romantic the writer, the more easily he would succumb to the eulogistic imperative, and the more likely he would find himself singing the praise of the very same "traditional morality" that he denounces elsewhere. This is the odd logic of the "allure" of modern eulogy.

Lu Xun was one of the first to voice a critique of traditional moral precepts, but he did not join the chorus in praise of Nora. Instead, he pointed to Nora's economically untenable position after leaving her husband: she could either return home or become a prostitute. With regard to Qiu Jin, Lu Xun clearly felt both obligated to commemorate her and troubled by this very sense of obligation. In his short story "Medicine," he tells of the futile effort of an old couple to cure their only son from tuberculosis by feeding him bread dipped in human blood. The executed revolutionary whose blood supplies the "medicine" is modeled on Qiu Jin. Conspicuously,

Lu Xun changes the revolutionary's sex. In a recent study, Eileen Cheng gives a compelling explanation, arguing that Lu Xun made the change in order to eschew the spectacle and the potentially alluring effect of a woman executed in public. [28] This is consistent with Lu Xun's relentless critique of the crowd; whether its members condemned or embraced the spectacle made no difference. Indeed at times Lu Xun appears to consider the cheering crowd to be more sinister than the "man-eating" crowd, for it demands not just the body but the soul of the victim.[29]

With explicit reference to Qiu Jin, Lu Xun is well known for his caustic one-liner that "she was clapped to death."[30] While this is often taken as a criticism of Qiu Jin's susceptibility to the cheering crowd, the edge of the attack is most sharply directed at the "clappers." The target of attack is very large indeed, for not just the soulless crowd, but every historian, every writer, every commemorator, and every biographer is potentially a "clapper." In order to put as much distance between himself and the "clappers" as possible, Lu Xun's revolutionary in "Medicine" is not a hero; in fact, he is completely offstage. He makes no speeches, not even at the execution—instead there is only an eerie silence. With extreme economy (and therefore without the possibility of sensationalism and drama), the revolutionary's imprisonment and death are described by an unsympathetic bystander and presented as ugly and humiliating, anything but heroic. The indifferent audience learns that the convict was beaten in prison by the thuggish jailer who even took possession of his clothes after the execution. To the same unheroic effect, his grave—"not yet overgrown with grass" and "with ugly patches of soil still showing"—is among those of the criminally executed, marked off even from the very poor and those who died of contagious diseases.[31]

Far from linking Qiu Jin with the New Woman's search for personal and sexual freedom, Lu Xun required that she be made as little of a spectacle as possible, degendered, unheroic, and offstage. More damning still, the line between the "clappers" and the enemy is so blurred that everyone is potentially among those who, in Lu Xun's words, upheld "history without dates," written all over with the words of "virtue and morality."[32] Twenty years later, Xia Yan (whose play is quoted at the beginning of this chapter) would also link traditional books of "virtue and morality" with Qiu Jin's choice of death.

If Lu Xun's aim in 1919 was to mourn the failure of the 1911 Revolution, in 1936 when Xia Yan wrote his play—in the context of the political polarization of writers in Shanghai and the impending war with Japan—a nationalist heroine was very much in demand. And Xia Yan, much more faithful to the revolutionary cause than the deeply skeptical Lu Xun, produces just such a heroine, a woman who is heroic to the last moment with the obligatory speech and posture. Xia Yan attributes his motivation for writing the play in large measure to his 1933 translation of *Women and Socialism* by the German Marxist August Bebel (1840–1913). Bebel's radical critique of "social hindrances and restrictions" that "impeded the laws of nature" was compatible with the May Fourth advocacy of individual liberation through free love. Half of his *Women and Socialism* (originally published in 1884) is devoted to addressing women's presumed sexual frustration as a result of social and gender oppression. Notably, this aspect of Bebel's thought did not inspire Xia Yan to portray Qiu Jin in search of personal happiness and sexual satisfaction. Xu Xilin, for a telling example, whose presence was crucial in early Qiu Jin commemoration, disappears completely in Xia Yan's play. Years later, the playwright still found it necessary to explain: "Not that I would want to deny the revolutionary friendship between her and Xu Xilin. Yet, I do believe the information found in the sketches, plays, and popular novels published earlier is mostly hearsay and exaggeration. Thus I discarded it."[33] Evidently, the close connection between Qiu Jin and Xu Xilin continued to be a point of anxiety.

Although Xia Yan did not go as far as Lu Xun in changing Qiu Jin's sex, he did thus expunge potential expression of her sexuality. Once again, we find the eulogization of the revolutionary martyr requires the elimination of her sexuality, a price not dissimilar to premodern chastity martyrs, whose canonicity also hinged on a denial of their sexuality. The difference is that while late imperial *lienü* are portrayed as women abstaining from or resisting sex, the modern revolutionary is depicted as devoid of sexual desire, her dedication to the cause effectively neutering her.

The only point that may be said to detract from Qiu Jin's exulted status in Xia Yan's play is the accusation voiced by her folksy comrade, Wang Jinfa, that Qiu Jin was "ruined by those books on virtue and morality." This criticism is rather mild, since Wang can be understood as trying to persuade Qiu Jin to save her own life, yet it does directly link her death to "traditional morality." Wang's radical departure from Qiu Jin's high moral stance is driven home by his departing words: "Fine, you go and play the part of the martyr, and I will play my part as the bandit." In sharply contrasting terms, then, the martyr stays within the game of virtue and honorable death, while the bandit renounces the game altogether, along with its promised moral rewards of glorified death and a place in history. In Xia Yan's portrayal of Qiu Jin's last moment, the social hindrances embodied by those "books on righteousness and morality" that

Wang Jinfa (and Bebel in his context) criticize do not dictate acceptable sexual behavior so much as devalue life itself. It was these teachings that led the heroine to an unnecessary death, just as they led countless others to chastity suicides.

Another aspect of Xia Yan's critique that was influenced by Bebel's thinking is the link between gender and class inequality. It is thus not surprising that the person to voice the radical ideological critique is the quasi-proletarian Wang Jinfa. By comparison, Qiu Jin occupies the more conventional upper-class moral position associated with false consciousness. Given the strong strain of (self-) identification with the rebel/bandit from Qiu Jin's own times through the May Fourth generation to the communists, one might expect approval for Wang Jinfa's radical moral position. This would not turn out to be the case.

One of Xia Yan's most vocal critics was Guo Moruo, the romantic poet–cum–Party propagandist. He was most eloquent in singing the praise of rebels, especially women rebels who transgressed against traditional moral precepts. In poem after poem, play after play, Guo sang the praises of goddesses such as Xiang Furen who transcended human sexual mores, or human females like Zhuo Wenjun who defied their fathers and chose their own husbands. Through their rebellion against the Law of the Father and their exercise of free choice in sexual partners, these women embodied the exulted Romantic spirit of the Rebel. They were the Chinese precursors of the New Woman, much as Ibsen's Nora is her Western inspiration.

The same Guo Moruo waxed poetic on Qiu Jin's voluntary death, however, stressing that "she need not have died and yet serenely chose a death of righteousness." In his essay entitled "The Answer to Nora," Guo is perfectly willing to place Qiu Jin in line with the New Women insofar as she rejected the traditional family, as a Nora who "ran away from the kitchen."[34] But after the door is slammed, Guo's Qiu Jin does not pursue anything remotely linked with personal happiness. More strikingly, she is presented as the real New Woman pitted against the false New Women, whose "heels are high, and whose hair . . . is curled"—contemporary women bound by fashion and the pursuit of personal gratification. It appears that what separates the true from the false New Woman is the absence or presence of a "self." Without a self there is no desire. It is all very well to lament the unhappiness of traditional marriage (part of a long poetic tradition), and by the time Nora came to China, it is also possible to imagine women leaving such a marriage. But if she were merely to seek personal happiness in ways that are not sublimated or ideologically correct, then she has perverted the ideal of the New Woman according to

Guo. What makes Qiu Jin a "true" New Woman is thus her subordination of "women's liberation" to "national liberation."

This privileging of nationalism is not surprising, as scholars have long observed.[35] What is surprising is that Guo's framework for the higher cause of national liberation is couched in the language of "those books on virtue and morality" that he and his generation of radicals so maligned. Thus Guo says that Qiu Jin "was not a victim of her emotions but their master. The expression of her passionate and glorious emotional life is backed up by Reason. Because of this mastery, she was able to 'sacrifice her life to preserve the integrity of her virtue' [*shashen chengren*, Confucius] and to 'choose righteousness over life' [*sheshen quyi*, Mencius]." Remarkably, Guo collapses the Neo-Confucian dichotomy of reasoned principles (*lizhi*) and private feelings (*qinggan*) with the modern dichotomy of Reason versus Emotion. While Guo may allow that the contents of "virtue" and "righteousness" be somewhat different for Qiu Jin than for the chastity martyrs, absolute dedication to those ideals is absolutely required. And this dedication can only be demonstrated through a chaste life and a good death.

Returning to Lu Xun's two answers to the question of Nora's fate after she slammed the door: she could either return home or become a prostitute. In other words, without proper income, she has only one thing to sell: her sexed body. Since a female revolutionary martyr does not have a sexed body, as we have found with the depictions of Qiu Jin by Lu Xun, Xia Yan, and now Guo Moruo, neither of Lu Xun's answers, however bleak, could apply to her—she has to die. Guo's Qiu Jin is the Chinese answer to Nora's problem in high Romantic style, perfectly embodying the social and ideological impasse in its dark implications. With Guo Moruo's Romantic celebration of Qiu Jin's death, we thus come full circle to the logic of the eulogistic imperative and the conventional moral framework that goes with it.

The recuperation of conventional morality is clearly illustrated in the writings of another vocal critic of Xia Yan, the playwright Tian Han. Like Guo Moruo, Tian Han plundered the traditional Chinese repertoire of female exemplars for independent figures who insisted on choosing their own sexual partners against the demands of their parents. Like Guo, again, he applauded Qiu Jin for her good death. How does a writer like Tian, who so persistently criticized "traditional morality," end up exulting in similar morality in a revolutionary hero? In an article written just before the final victory of the anti-Japanese War in 1944, Tian Han tells a personal story that incidentally explains how traditional moral precepts are recuperated in a new interpretive framework.

When he was invited to give a talk at a middle school, he found himself trying to define a new ethical system by finessing the old:

> I said although "chastity" is an old moral precept forced on women for thousands of years, today it could acquire entirely new meaning. For example, . . . I was greatly moved by the five women of the Li family, who drowned themselves when the [Japanese] enemies invaded. I wrote a poem to commemorate them. . . . Indeed, their determination "not to be sullied but to die of resistance" acquires a significance much wider than the narrow definition of chastity martyr: it acquires a glorious patriotic significance.[36]

Just like countless literati of late imperial times, when faced with the burial ground of the five Li women, much as when he faced the legacy of Qiu Jin, Tian Han was moved to honor the martyrs through a familiar poetic eulogy, the convention itself offering a powerful allure because it gives appropriate exultation at a traumatic site. In the case of the Li women, conventional moral precepts were recuperated on two grounds: nation and class. In other words, the difference between old morals and new morals lies in the object of that transitive death, as they died "for" the nation. That these women of the Li family were presumably peasants had the added advantage of transforming moral precepts previously dubbed Confucian into "Chinese" (thus dovetailing nicely with the nation) precepts of "our" proletarian tradition (thus consistent with communist ethos).

READING MARTYROLOGY, THEN AND NOW

To his credit, Tian Han was not unaware of the conflict between this sentiment (call it revolutionary Romanticism) and his erstwhile exultation of the rebel spirit. The story is told in retrospect, as if he was his own audience, reading his own martyrology. His reading experience was uneasy, as evinced in the essay's last paragraph, whose ending conveniently prevents the author from reflecting upon it any further: "After I finished the talk, the white-haired principal shook my hands and thanked me for 'extolling traditional virtues.' This made me a bit embarrassed, a bit fearful. I was greatly discomforted on my way back." As indeed he should be. To explore this discomfort any further would have revealed the deep-seated conflict between the May Fourth critique of traditional moral precepts and the overwhelming demand for nationalist martyrs, a fundamental conflict, we might say, in Chinese modernity.

This study is in part a belated contemplation of this conflict. Having been brought up like most Chinese of my generation on a steady diet of new "books of virtue and righteousness" that celebrate "good deaths" like Qiu Jin's, I found myself pulled by the eulogistic imperative as much as by its opposite, the iconoclastic tendency, especially as encouraged by the theories of poststructuralism. In trying to avoid both reductionist tendencies, I find it useful to investigate the process of martyr production and the cultural mechanisms operative at a given historical moment. For if the primary goal of martyrology is to accord sanctity to a particular death, then the preceding life is necessarily presented in heavily edited form. To read martyrology as it is intended to be read is therefore not getting closer to "the real person." The effect of "the real person" is produced precisely through the reader's participation in the eulogistic imperative. However, to read martyrology "improperly," to read it not as its intended reader but as a historian of religion, so to speak, is to realize that a given martyrology is dictated by prevailing moral precepts at the time of writing in order to serve a particular historical function.

Qiu Jin's case teaches us that the modern martyr is connected to the long tradition of martyrs through deep taproots, some historical, others political, and still others generic. In many ways, the modern nation's need for martyrs echoes the same need from regimes long past. What makes the Republic different is that without an emperor—whose legitimacy, once secured, legitimizes his regime—the nation's need for fortifying its own legitimacy is that much more desperate. For "Nations . . . have no clearly identifiable births because there is no Originator, the nation's biography cannot be written evangelically, 'down time,' through a long procreative chain of begettings. The only alternative is to fashion it 'up time,' . . . through the deaths of martyrs."[37]

In this nationalist frame of the modern martyr, what is the precise meaning of the female gender? In the first phase of commemoration, Qiu Jin was still a close kin to the *lienü*, perhaps unconventional in her dedication to a cause (often unspecified) but conventionally feminine in her morality and frailty. Once exalted onto the altar of nationalism, the constraints of morality appeared even more stringent, and the *nü* of *nülieshi* devoid of any physical specificity or subversive potential, there for color and variety only.

Yet "color and variety" is far from trivial, and "the honorary male" is never a "real man." Instead, the woman martyr is always described as "transcending" her femininity, either by stepping out of the "traditional confines" of the home or in renouncing her sexuality. Thus, ultimately, she is a liminal figure, both inside the male circle of revolutionary martyrs and outside it. As she marks the boundary of this circle, her excess (her extra efforts to overcome her femininity, her extra bravery and heroism, her extra drama, extra color) makes her all the more effective in galvanizing the public to follow her lead. She is thus more effective in fortifying the ethos of the revolutionary martyr and of the nationalist cause. Her extra color is crucial in combating the worst enemy of commemoration— forgetting. For martyrology is nothing if not formulaic, the role of the martyr scripted long ago. The extra color provided by her (transcended) femininity is what makes her name still remembered, against the vast collective and anonymous grave of modern martyrs.

PART III

Alternative "Biographical" Sources

8. Women's Epitaphs in Tang China (618-907)

Ping Yao

Epitaph writing—a form of ancestor worship and obituary practice that reached its height in the Tang dynasty—provides historians with rich insights into Tang women's lives.[1] Among the more than 6,000 extant Tang-period epitaphs, more than 1,500 were dedicated solely to women, 200 were joint-epitaphs (*hezhi*) for married couples, and a majority of those dedicated to men mention female relatives, especially wives.[2] Creating a "memorial culture" that converted dead women into stable female stereotypes, these epitaphs are as much a manifestation of discourses on moral principles, social order, and gender roles as they are records of personal histories.[3] They functioned almost as guidebooks on proper conduct and the articulation of social status for both men and women of the Tang era. Furthermore, the sheer volume of these texts indicates that Tang epitaphs probably reflected an overwhelmingly dominant discourse on gender roles, one not subject to the competing fictional discourses discussed by Katherine Carlitz in chapter 10 in this volume.

Tang epitaphs reveal that while the Confucian four virtues (*side*) were still the principal guideline for women's roles in the family, the content of these virtues was much expanded and the emphases shifted. During the Tang, young girls were cherished not only for their filial nature but also for their sibling love, as well as their talent in reading and writing; wives were often praised for their support and endurance throughout husbands' official careers and for their diligence in keeping a large household functioning and harmonious; and Tang mothers were increasingly credited for their ability to teach their sons literature and classics, and for ultimately guiding the sons to their success in the civil service examinations. In addition, Buddhism apparently played an important role in the configuration of dominant ideology that defined the norms for gender relations.

139

Women's life experiences as seen in Tang epitaphs also mirror social and political changes throughout the Tang dynasty. The dominance of the eminent clans in the early Tang, for example, can be detected through a unique pattern of cousin marriages that are broadly recorded in Tang epitaphs; likewise, the increase in the number of *jinshi* (advanced scholar) authors as well as the elevation of a mother's literary ability reflect the rise to power of civil service examination graduates. Tang epitaphs also allow us to assess more accurately the devastation of the An Lushan rebellion (755–63) as well as the regional wars during the last decades of the dynasty. Statistics based on the epitaphs seem to indicate that the political chaos and economic turbulence of the second half of the Tang had a more adverse effect on elite women than on men.

Although a form of exemplar biography, epitaphs are generically distinct from women's biographies in the *lienü* tradition including those recorded in the *Jiu Tangshu* and *Xin Tangshu*. While life-story narratives in that tradition describe one pivotal moment in a woman's life, epitaphs generally offer a fuller picture of Tang women's roles in various stages of their lives. In addition, with women's epitaphs increasingly authored by family members, they contain a profound emotional content. A modern reader will not have difficulty detecting their aspirations and despair; happiness and worries; concerns about husbands, children, natal family, and parents-in-law; and their ability to make the most of the latitude they possessed for negotiating these relationships.

Before discussing the insights these sources yield into women's intimate and everyday lives, and into Tang social practices, I will describe their format, the social status of the women they celebrated, and the female life course they idealized.

THE EPITAPH AS SOURCE

Form

A typical Tang epitaph consists of the following seven elements: ancestry/ family background; childhood and youth; major events in life; achievements and virtues; immediate family members; funeral arrangements; and eulogy. A representative woman's epitaph of the Tang period is the "Epitaph for the Late Ms. Cui, Wife of Mr. Lu of the Tang Dynasty" of the Dazhong Reign (847–58). The epitaph, commemorating the life of Cui, daughter of Grand Councilor Cui Qun (772–832), was written by her husband Lu Jian.

The first section presents a detailed account of Cui's family background, including the origin and social status of the Cui clan, important official titles held by three generations of Cui's paternal male ancestors and Cui's maternal grandfather, and biographical detail on members of Cui's immediate family. The epitaph then describes Cui's early life as a filial and precocious young woman. Compared to other Tang epitaphs, though, the description of Cui's childhood is relatively brief. In contrast, Lu Jian's account of Cui's life as an adult is quite vivid. We learn that Cui's marriage to Lu, probably her second cousin, was arranged by Cui's father. Cui married late: at the age of twenty-three *sui*, she was nearly six years beyond the typical marriage age for a Tang elite woman.[4] The delay was due to the obligation of observing three mourning years for each of her parents. The epitaph also reveals that after marrying into the Lu household, Cui lost several of her sisters. Furthermore, Lu was constantly transferred among various regional offices and, at one point, was demoted. Disappointed in his political career, he left home to travel, leaving Cui behind. Cui's health deteriorated and she eventually fell victim to pestilence, a plague that savaged Tang China for years between the late 850s and early 860s and took many lives. Cui died in 857 at forty-five *sui*.

In the section summarizing her achievements and virtues, the epitaph praises Cui for her mastery of both Confucian and Buddhist classics. She was also said to be extremely artistic and, most important, well respected by the Lu clan for her wifely virtues. The epitaph then tells us that Cui gave birth to a total of four children, only two of whom reached adulthood. In the section on funeral arrangements, the epitaph reveals that although an elaborate funeral was held for Cui, her burial was temporary, probably due to the ominous result of a divination. The Lu household planned to rebury her later once it received an auspicious sign. Similar to most Tang epitaphs, Cui's eulogy is poetic, informal verses with four or six characters per line. The eulogy summarizes her worthy qualities, mourns the loss of a fine person, and wishes that she will rest in peace.[5]

Demographic Content

Among the 1,560 women commemorated in these epitaphs (representing 26 percent of the total printed epitaphs), nearly 80 percent were reported as married (See table 8.1). Though most epitaphs were for members of the elite, nonelites nevertheless constitute roughly 6 percent of the total.[6] Among the 146 women reported as unmarried, there were 74 Buddhist nuns and 13 Daoist nuns. There were also nine epitaphs dedicated to girls

TABLE 8.1 Women's Marital Status by Epitaph Count

Marital status	Epitaph count	Percent of total
Married	1,230	78.8
Unmarried	146	9.4
Marriage status unknown	47	3.0
Palace women	128	8.2
Courtesans	9	0.6

who died before the age of ten, which provide us with a rare opportunity to explore the Tang perspective on young daughters. The average life span of these 1,560 women was 52.1, the average age for first marriage was 17.6, and the average number of children reported per married woman was 4.8. A characteristic epitaph is shown in figure 8.1.

These demographics should not be taken a priori as characteristic of broad strata of society in Tang China. First, the surviving Tang epitaphs concentrate heavily in the Mangshan area of Luoyang, a burial site for imperial relatives, high-ranking officials, and their family members. Therefore a cross-check with other available sources on Tang demography, such as monographs of the Tang or household and tax records from Dunhuang and Turfan, would be of great benefit. For example, the number of epitaphs for Buddhist nuns (seventy-seven) represents an extremely high ratio (4.94 percent) among women described in the epitaphs. According to the *Xin Tangshu*, the total number of registered Buddhist nuns in a survey conducted during the Kaiyuan Reign (713–41) was 50,576, while the registered population in 732 was 45,431,265.[7] Assuming half the population was female, the ratio of Buddhist nuns among all females was then only 0.22 percent. Second, the numbers indicated in epitaph texts themselves are sometimes questionable. For example, compared to thirty-six women who reportedly married at age nineteen, only fourteen women married at age twenty. Such a sharp drop might indicate that the authors intentionally altered ages to cover the fact that the deceased married late, a sign either of being undesirable or of family hardship (or it might just be a statistical fluctuation). Similarly, epitaph authors might also take the liberty of boosting the deceased's "longevity": while only fourteen women were reported to have died at fifty-nine, the number dying at the age of sixty jumped to thirty-three.

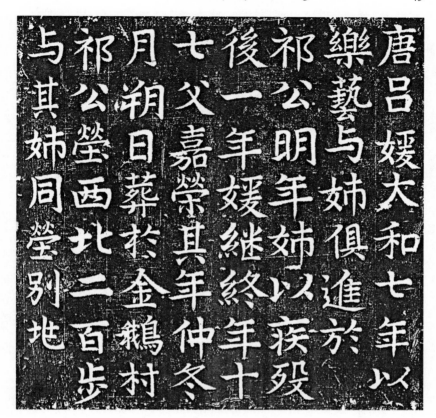

FIGURE 8.1. "Epitaph for Lu Yuan of the Tang Dynasty" (Tang Lu Yuan muzhi), written in 835 by the father of Lu Yuan, who entered a Qi household as a house courtesan. The epitaph reports that she died at the age of seventeen *sui*. 34 cm × 34cm.

TANG EPITAPHS AND WOMEN'S LIVES

The Idealized Female Life Course

In commemorating deceased men and women, Tang epitaphs often portrayed an ideal, if not exaggerated, course of life. An elite man typically came from a prominent family that had already produced generations of high-ranking officials. At a young age he was said to be gifted, brave, filial, and well versed in Confucian classics. He became a government official around his twentieth birthday, either through family connections or through his success in the civil service examinations. Throughout his official career, he was frequently transferred, taking positions both in regional offices and at the central government. His colleagues and subjects would remember him as unusually competent, principled, diligent, decisive, and compassionate. He would marry his first wife, most likely a woman of an eminent clan, around the age of twenty-four, and would probably purchase a concubine from a poor family a few years later. His wives and concubines would give birth to a total of six or seven children.

An ideal life course for elite women centered upon the domestic sphere. Growing up in an elite family, a woman was often said to excel both in needlework and in reading. She was also obedient, gracious, and beautiful. By the time of puberty, many young men had proposed to her family. Her father would select a young man of similar family background, preferably with a civil service examination degree, or possibly a cousin, to be her husband. Upon entering her husband's household, she took over the responsibility of providing offerings to ancestors. Her actions always pleased her parents-in-law, and she was also friendly to her sisters-in-law and benevolent to the servants. As a wife, she was said to be very supportive, sometimes enduring long journeys with her husband, other times staying at home and taking care of her parents-in-law. She had an average of four or five children and treated the children of her husband's concubines as if they were her own. She maintained her dignity as a principal wife and was never jealous when her husband showed affection to other women such as concubines, courtesans, or maids. If her husband passed away, she would choose to remain a widow, raising and educating her children personally. In old age, she took pride in the fact that the household was in harmony under her management, and that her children all grew up to be officials or wives of officials. One of her sons may have even secured her the honorary title of District Lady (*junjun*), conferred by the emperor to reward her son's achievements.

An example of such an idealized life course can be found in the epitaph dedicated to Yuan Zhen's (777–831) mother, Zheng, composed by Yuan's longtime literary friend and eminent poet Bo Juyi (772–846). The epitaph celebrates Yuan's family origin by stressing that "there are five grand clans under the realm, and the Zheng clan of Yingyang is one of them." In describing Zheng's role as a daughter in her natal family, the epitaph praises her filiality and kindness towards her siblings. Once she entered the Yuan household, Zheng took on the responsibility for ancestor worship and other rites with extraordinary diligence.

> In every seasonal sacrifice, Lady (*furen*) would stay up all night, cooking and cleaning by herself. Even in the hottest days of the summer and the coldest days of the winter, Lady always served with her best attitude and offered sacrifices in person. She had never once showed a weary

expression. . . . If people in the two clans [Yuan and Zheng] had any uncertainty about weddings or funerals, they would all consult with Lady. Lady always gave appropriate consideration and her decisions never contradicted the proper procedure of the rites.

Bo Juyi reserved his highest praise for Zheng's role as a mother.

Mr. Yuan died early when Yuan Ji and Yuan Zhen were still young, and the family could not afford a teacher to educate the sons. Thus, Lady held books herself,[8] teaching the brothers tirelessly. Within four to five years, Ji and Zhen acquired offices through their thorough knowledge of the classics.

The most interesting part of this epitaph, however, is Bo Juyi's explanation of why he wrote such a detailed account of Zheng's life. Bo claims that exemplary women in dynastic histories and didactic literature were each known only for a single role, either as daughter, wife, or mother, so that none of them was as deserving as Zheng, who fulfilled every single duty assigned to a woman. Thus, in recounting her life, Bo Juyi purported that the epitaph could serve as a didactic text for women of later generations:

Alas! Women such as Qishi and Tiying of the olden days were righteous daughters, yet they were unknown after they became wives. Bozong and Liang Hong's wives were wise as wives, yet they were unknown after they became mothers. Wenbo and Meng Mu were virtuous mothers, yet they were unknown as well when they were daughters and wives. Meanwhile Lady possessed such daughterly grace, wifely virtue, and motherly presence. She performed all three roles beautifully; she was truly the finest woman in history from the past to the present. . . . Alas! How can my writing of this epitaph be simply a fulfillment of Zhen's request? It is also intended for people of future generations, who learn of Lady's extraordinary example as they pass by the tomb, so that the shrewish wives will become harmonious, bossy mothers will become benevolent, and impertinent daughters will become obedient![9]

Strikingly, this epitaph presents the construction of ideal womanhood quite differently from women's biographies in the *lienü* tradition in general and the *Jiu Tangshu* and *Xin Tangshu* in particular. The *Jiu Tangshu*, for example, listed a total of thirty-one exemplary women. Fifteen are portrayed as chaste, loyal wives who either refused to remarry or died refusing bandits' sexual advances; nine are filial daughters who sacrificed their own happiness to take care of their ailing parents and gave them a decent burial, or avenged their father's wrongful death; and two are mothers who raised their sons properly. In addition, there is a wet nurse who nurtured a sole descendent of a prominent family, a young sister who refused to marry so she could take care of her sick elder sister, and a daughter-in-law who protected her mother-in-law during a home robbery. All except one biography praised these women's single-minded actions in their particular role. Some biographies go so far as to claim that it was impossible for a woman to "perform" two roles or to "shift" roles in her life time.[10] Compared to these biographies, Tang epitaphs, although still reflecting a socially prescribed life course, present a more complete picture of a woman's roles throughout her life.

Intimate Emotions and Everyday Experience

In recounting the life experiences of loved ones, Tang epitaphs, especially those produced during the second half of the dynasty, contain profound emotional content and, sometimes, surprisingly detailed information about the deceased. Thus, they prove to be a great resource in recovering the texture of women's everyday life in specific social and historical locations. An epitaph written by the father of Li Diniang, is a good example. The father's fondness for and pride in his daughter is evident in the epitaph; we also get a glimpse of what Tang people considered attractive in a young girl, aside from the broad perception of filial piety and cleverness. Li Diniang was the eldest daughter of Li Yinzhi, a district magistrate, and was born in the winter of 834 to Li's concubine, Xing. Li Yinzhi named her Diniang to commemorate his success in the civil service examination (*dengdi*) in the spring of that year. Over the twenty years following her birth, Li Yinzhi constantly journeyed from one official position to another, and he "always took her along." The two were "never apart even for one day." The epitaph, written as if the father were talking to the daughter, recounts,

> You went to Guangzhou at the age of three or four. The southern
> region has various mountains and rivers, numerous fruits and herbs,
> strange birds, rare animals, exotic plants and renowned flowers; you
> could already recognize them all and readily pronounce their names.
> In addition, you could recognize clearly what was right and wrong,
> and understand thoroughly what was real and false. Your profundity
> and intuition had no comparison [among your peers].

Li Yinzhi then commented on Diniang's talent in needlework and literature. He recounted how Diniang could memorize everything she overheard from her brothers' lessons on the Chinese classics. She was also said to be affable to her elder brother, younger siblings, and several dozen cousins who all, at one point, lived in a single household. She was said to be quite sensitive to everyone's needs and would make requests on their behalf when she was not yet ten. It seems Li was most pleased with Diniang's carefree personality. Li was often caught up in political conflicts and took comfort that she was not affected by it:

> You were still very young and did not mind it at all. Because of you I felt calm in my heart and completely forgot about the distress caused by my plight. You always saw glory and shame as if they were the same, and did not take to heart the gains and the losses. This is certainly the spirit of a sage, not the mind of a girl. My love to you, thus, intensified everyday.[11]

The intimate emotion reflected in this epitaph is far from an isolated case. Among other Tang epitaphs for daughters, some would record how much thought they put into naming their daughters, others stated how the parents doted on the girls. The "Epitaph for the Young Daughter of the Li Family," for example, explains that the deceased was named Xiuyi, "Embroidered Jacket," by her father because of his career advancement. The epitaph comments that "the depth of love is clearly demonstrated" in such a decision. The epitaph also recounts that Xiuyi's father often had her around to "please his eyes." After the father died, Xiuyi's mother was very distressed and often ill. "When she saw this daughter, she would eat meals for her sake; if she did not see her, she would wail day and night."[12] In another epitaph the deceased, Zhang Chan, was an only daughter and the parents hired several maids just to take care of her. The parents often held her when she was an infant, played with her, and "satisfied all her desires." When Zhang Chan grew older, the parents amassed every conceivable feminine finery for her.[13]

Epitaphs authored by husbands of the deceased often convey marital affection between couples. One epitaph records that the deceased, Zheng, married her cousin, Lu Zhizong, at fourteen *sui*. Ten years into their marriage and one month after giving birth to her fifth child, Zheng fell ill for five months and then passed away. In the epitaph, Lu recounts how he pledged in front of her deathbed not to remarry:

> I will always long for the day we are buried together in one tomb
> and do not dare forget the poet's verses.[14] When Lady was near death,
> I filled up a wine cup in front of her and, with tears, made my vow.
> Lady surely heard it.[15]

Such emotionally charged narratives were quite common among women's epitaphs, as they were increasingly authored by the deceased's immediate families. The epitaph for Cui, for example, depicts an occasionally strained marriage in which both Lu Jian and Cui seemed quite distressed.

Eventually Lu left home and Cui died of illness. The epitaph, written by Lu, thus carries a tone of deep remorse and self-chastisement.[16] Another example was a mid-eighth-century epitaph written by the official Li Gan for his elder sister, who died ten months after her wedding and fewer than ten days after she gave birth to a son. While mourning the loss of a woman of beauty and virtue, this epitaph conveys a quite subtle resentment toward her husband's family, which had excluded her from burial in its clan cemetery.[17]

In addition to emotional content, women's epitaphs would sometimes record remarkably detailed events in the deceased's life, providing modern historians with valuable information on how these women negotiated various relationships and circumstances throughout their lives. An epitaph dedicated to Yu, the granddaughter of the literatus Yang Jingzhi (fl. 827), written by her husband Sun Beiming, recounts that the marriage between Sun and Yu was arranged when Yu's mother was pregnant with her. Sun's mother and Yu's mother, cousins to each other, "caressed their bellies and made a promise to be parents of a married couple." The two families then exchanged formal pledges. Yu's mother died when Yu was just a toddler and her father was demoted. Yu then grew up in the household of Yang Jingzhi, who now "shifted his love" to the granddaughter. It was probably during these years that Yu was exposed to classics and poetry. She eventually left behind four hundred poems and fifty poetic essays. She married into the Sun household in the year 853 when she was eighteen and Sun twenty-two. In the twelve years of their marriage, she gave birth to three sons (ages twelve, five, and four) and three daughters (only one, age ten, survived). Sun suffered repeated setbacks in his official career: even though he passed the civil service examination, for two years his hopes for an official appointment repeatedly came to naught. Yu was distressed over her husband's misfortune and became very ill. A few days before her death, with apparently indomitable will, she got out of her bed, thanked her mother-in-law for her well-being in the Sun household, penned an essay to recount her grandfather's admonitions, and then composed a letter to her uncle, expressing her regret at not being able to help her husband in his official career. She died on the eighth day of the second month of 865 at thirty *sui*.[18]

Women and Buddhism

Because of their idealized representations and ubiquitous presence, Tang epitaphs of women played an important role in shaping gender perceptions, promoting feminine rules of conduct, and, especially, supplying role models. From the above examples, we can see the epitaphs largely conform to the values—if not the form—of the *lienü* tradition. They commemorated women for their familial roles, literary abilities, and moral conduct. However, other prominent themes in women's epitaphs are either absent from or marginal to female biographies in Tang didactic literature or dynastic histories. One such theme is Buddhism.

Considering that the Tang was the golden age of Chinese Buddhism, it is not surprising that it had penetrated every aspect of Tang life. Nevertheless, women's epitaphs reveal that a Buddhist influence on Tang perceptions of gender and on women's life experience might be more profound than historians have previously understood.[19] Indeed, nearly 5 percent of the women's epitaphs were dedicated to Buddhist nuns; in addition, more than 10 percent of the epitaphs of Tang women clearly identified the deceased's Buddhist faith. More importantly, Tang epitaphs credited such faith as either a sign of the deceased's virtue or as her source of moral and ethical inspiration. Overall, Tang society seemed to perceive Buddhism as a positive influence on women's behavior in the roles of daughter, wife, and mother. For example, in an epitaph for a lay Buddhist woman, the deceased was said to be extremely perceptive at six or seven. At the age of nine, she memorized the *Heart Sutra* by listening to other people's recitation. Buddhist learning reportedly instilled in her a sense of right and wrong at a very young age: when she saw her elder brother mistreating household servants, she promptly persuaded him to stop.[20] An epitaph from the Tianbao Reign (742–55) reports that the deceased, Lu Ying, was born into an official family that was known for having produced generations of Confucian scholars. The bright and intuitive Lu Ying followed an alternate Buddhist path, however. From a young age she refused to eat meat or wear silk garments. More striking still, during her girlhood she stopped reading Ban Zhao's *Admonitions for Women* altogether and cultivated a deep interest in Buddhist sutras. Because of her Buddhist faith and conduct, all her relatives looked up to her as a role model, and her compassionate traits were considered especially suited to her role in the household. Surely enough, when her husband was appointed to a regional office, Lu insisted on staying home and fulfilling her duty as a "filial daughter-in-law." Labeling her a "worthy wife," the epitaph proclaims that her "filial deeds were unmatched" throughout Chinese history.[21] Another exemplary filial daughter-in-law was Xue who died in 696. Xue's mother-in-law was once critically ill and no medicine could cure her. Xue, with her pure faith, recited Buddhist sutras ceaselessly. Her mother-in-law soon recovered completely, and all the relatives attributed this restoration of health to Xue's "ultimate filial piety." [22]

Like the virtue of filial piety, Tang epitaphs regularly attributed to Buddhism female virtues such as kindness, benevolence, uprightness, frugality, and understanding; all were associated with Confucianism. In "Epitaph for My Late Wife, Lady Wang of Tai Yuan," Wang, a fervent Buddhist believer, was said to be "respectful" (*gong*) in preparing ancestor worship, "humble" (*qian*) when conducting herself as a daughter-in-law of a large household, and "sincere" (*cheng*) to the servants. She did not display jealousy when her husband repeatedly impregnated a maid, treating the maid's children as her own.[23] Another example of attributing Confucian female virtues to Buddhism occurs in an epitaph for woman Yuan of the Zhenyuan period (785–804).[24] The deceased was reported to become an exemplary woman after twenty years of living as a Buddhist layperson:

> [Yuan] set her heart in Buddhist mediation and did not touch fish
> or meat. In just twenty years, her moral conduct was superior and
> illuminating; her kindness and compassion reached the ultimate depth.
> It is very rare to find comparable ones in ancient books.

Most often, epitaphs especially attributed a woman's determination to stay widowed and raise her children alone to the Buddhist idea of refraining from worldly desires. The epitaph for Buddhist laywoman Zhang of the Tianbao reign reports that after her husband died, Zhang considered herself "to be done with all things sexual and physical" and thus gave up on a mundane life. For thirty years, Zhang "preserved her chastity" and remained widowed until her death at age sixty-eight.[25] Another example is found in an epitaph for Widow Jia of the Jingyun reign (710–11). The epitaph recounts how she "raised her children and managed the household" by herself, and that Buddhism constituted the spiritual resource of her determination to stay chaste. Jia "completely abandoned mundane affairs" and "devoutly followed the Pure Land Sect." Before her death at seventy-four, she had hand-copied more than 500 scrolls of Mahāyāna sutras and commissioned more than 1,000 Buddhist statues.[26]

Tang mothers' Buddhist faith contributed to their children's learning, as well. An epitaph from the Dazhong Reign recounts that Zheng, a mother of four,

> revered Buddhist ideas and read scriptures fervently. Whenever
> she grasped some profound meaning, she would hold the scripture,
> summon all the children, and teach them about it. She educated them
> diligently and always feared that she had not done enough. This is how
> we know that her admonitions were perfect. [27]

The Buddhist influence on motherhood seemed to extend to mothers-to-be, as well. Prior to the Tang Dynasty, *taijiao,* or prenatal education, was strictly centered on Confucian ideals of rites and music. During the Tang Dynasty, however, Buddhism made a major impact on prenatal education. For example, in an epitaph from the Tianbo Reign, the author, Pei Jing, stressed that his mother's "effort of prenatal education" rested completely on her Buddhist faith, and the results of such effort were much more successful than for efforts based on Confucian teaching. The epitaph recounts:

> She often aspired to entrust the power of imperceptible transformation to her efforts in prenatal education. Every time she was pregnant with her sons or during the month each son was born, she would tidy up her room and observe the rules of abstinence. She hand-copied Buddhist sutras and exhausted her effort and money on Buddhist rituals. As a result, each of us has a fine body and appearance. Disasters and illness never afflicted us. She raised us and educated us, and we all grew and matured. Compared to such a marvel, the ancient guidance of sitting and standing gracefully, reading and reciting the *Book of Songs* and the *Book of History* cannot even measure up to one ten-thousandth of it. [28]

Epitaphs for Tang Buddhist laywomen revealed an important aspect of Buddhist Sinification in Chinese history. Clearly the references to Buddhism among female biographies produced in the golden age of Buddhism do not ultimately represent an alternate system of values; rather, they reflect the trend of Buddhist infusion with dominant Confucian ideals: traits of pious Buddhist women were identical to those of virtuous Confucian women. Probably because of such Sinification in the domestic sphere, Buddhism was able to survive the Huichang Persecution in 845 and continued to be a vital influence in Chinese society throughout the post-Tang eras.

Literary Ability

Women's epitaphs of the Tang Dynasty reflected a gradual shift in the discourse on elite women's literary ability. Erudite women had been a consistent theme in the *lienü* tradition since the time of the Han Dynasty; however, such ability was rarely considered crucial to a woman's role in the family as described in *lienü* literature, even in the Tang era. In thirty-one biographies of women in the *Jiu Tangshu,* only two mentioned exemplary women being well versed.[29] Women's epitaphs from the first hundred years of the dynasty portray literary ability in a similar fashion, as a sign of a woman's talent and quality. The descriptions in these epitaphs are usually quite abstract: for example, "she browsed all the books,"[30] or "her learning expanded to nine schools."[31] One exception worth noting is an epitaph for a studious and eloquent woman named Gongsun, who died at age fifty-two in 678. Gongsun, a mother of one son and three daughters and the wife of a regional official, was said to "read extensively the classics and history." At one point Gongsun was devoted to the *Hanshu*, which she loved so much that she could not put it down to do anything else. However, after she read about Wang Mang's (45 BCE–?) usurpation and Yang Xiong's (53 BCE–18 CE) essay "Slash the Qin and Praise the Xin," she was so disgusted by Wang's wickedness and Yang's sycophancy that she could not bring herself to look at the book ever again. Nevertheless, when it came to maternal qualities, the epitaph only briefly mentioned that she possessed the motherly virtue of "cutting the weaving loom" (*duanji*), a reference to Mencius's mother from the *Lienü zhuan*. Whether she taught her sons her literary skills was completely obscured.[32]

From the High Tang on, however, literary ability was increasingly connected to the role of the mother in raising her children. This change paralleled the rising importance of the civil service examinations in recruiting high-ranking officials. In addition, probably because most women's epitaphs were written by educated sons for their mothers, this shift in emphasis on literary ability appeared more prominently in epitaphs than other genres. The epitaph for Yuan Zhen's mother by Bo Juyi (discussed above), for example, claimed that the success of the Yuan brothers was entirely due to the mother's teaching. In the epitaph for his mother, Liu Tui, a *jinshi* degree holder, recounts that his mother taught him the *Book of Filial Piety* (*Xiaojing*) when he was just a toddler. She let him "sit on her lap, held the book in her hands and taught him sentence by sentence."[33]

Epitaph writing also provided examination graduates an opportunity to display their newly gained prominence. This function is indirectly stated in an 841 epitaph dedicated to Zhang, a mother of three sons and five daughters. Zhang's husband died when all the children were still young. The eldest, Miao Yin, was still a child and the youngest fewer than three months old. With no financial help from relatives and no possibility of hiring a teacher, Zhang singlehandedly raised them and taught them. Within fifteen years, all three sons passed the examinations. Among the daughters, three married into prominent families, one died young, and one became a Buddhist nun (Zhang herself was a Buddhist devotee). Miao explains that relatives convinced him to write the epitaph himself:

> Because of [your mother's] instructions and admonishment, all [you]
> three brothers were able to steal the title of examination graduate
> through writings. Will it be a filial act if you use someone else's
> words to glorify her fine virtues?[34]

Indeed, among 4,871 epitaphs from *Tangdai muzhi huibian* and *Tangdai muzhi huibian xuji* that recorded year of death, the rate of authors who were *jinshi* or *xianggong jinshi* (prefectural nominee for advanced scholar) increased dramatically throughout the dynasty along with the new elite's political prominence. During the first century of the dynasty, 184 out of 2,358 epitaphs recorded the author; among them only nine were identified as *jinshi* or *xianggong jinshi*. During the last century, 138 out of 963 epitaphs (750 of them identified the author) were authored by such scholars.

Household Management

Tang epitaphs also provide substantial material on how women ran their households. Compared to the dramatic actions of women recorded in dynastic histories and instructional literature, female exemplarity in the epitaphs was paradoxically often associated with a woman's capability as a household manager and her resourcefulness. The epitaph for Li who died in 794 at sixty-eight *sui*, for example, depicted her as an extremely capable manager of a large household. Li's husband was the direct descendent of a main line of the Cui clan and inherited the responsibility of presiding over clan ancestor worship. Li managed seasonal ceremonies with great care and won respect from every single branch of the clan. During the An Lushan rebellion (755–63), Cui was the magistrate of Linyou and could not take a leave. Li took the whole family to seek shelter at Cui's uncles' household in Hongzhou. She managed a household of 108 people, and all the tasks were performed perfectly under her command. Because of her, the household "thrived in harmony." After the chaos, during which her husband died without having a chance to reunite with the family, Li led the family back to their Luoyang home. Soon, the family again took to the road to flee from bandits in the Eastern Capital, seeking shelter in nearby Jiyuan, where Cui's nephew lived. Shortly thereafter, the nephew died of illness; Li again safely moved the entire family to back to Luoyang.[35]

Marriage

Women's epitaphs from the Tang period provide historians with abundant information for reconstructing Tang gender institutions and also for assessing how these institutions evolved over the 300 years of the dynasty's history.[36] Regarding marriage practices, for instance, we learn that cousin marriage was a widespread practice during the Tang. In addition, unlike later eras, when it was favored for a man to marry his mother's sister's daughter (*yibiaohun*), the dominant pattern of cousin marriage during the Tang was a man marrying his mother's brother's daughter (*gubiaohun*), and a man marrying his father's brother's daughter. This was probably due to the distinctive phenomenon of exclusive intermarriage among the seventeen eminent clans. In addition, the trend toward exclusive intermarriage among these clans and the sense of pride in being a member of such a prestigious group proved to be intransigent. During the early Tang, when the powerful central government distrusted and eventually forbade such practices, the eminent clans were less overt in flaunting their kin ties and often omitted the origin of their clan in the titles listed on epitaphs.[37] But such restraint soon disappeared. Even with the court's adoption of the civil service examination system to counter these powerful clans, the practice of exclusive intermarriage and the display of superiority of birth continued to the very end of the dynasty.

Tang epitaphs also show that finding an appropriate wife demanded so much effort that men from eminent clans often would start a family before officially marrying a woman of equal social status. Thus, it was not uncommon for a young elite woman entering her husband's family to become his principal wife and the legal mother of his children at the same time. Furthermore, since she was the legal mother to all her husband's children, inheritance rights seem also to have applied to children who were born to concubines, maids, and outside mistresses. Such practices signified the decline of the patriarchal clan system (*zongfa tixi*), in which the distinction between sons born to a wife (*di*) and sons born to a concubine (*shu*), as well as the distinction between the direct line (*dazong*) and branches (*xiaozong*), were crucial. Furthermore, quite a few epitaphs reveal that it was not unusual for an elite man to marry into his wife's household, especially when his parents were no longer living or in cases of cousin marriage.

The Effects of Dynastic Decline

Broadly speaking, Tang epitaphs substantiate the descriptions of the dynasty's political evolution found in other sources. The Tang was a golden age in Chinese history that was abruptly devastated by the An Lushan rebellion. The dynasty was able to recover briefly during Dezong's reign (780–804) but could not halt the decline. By Zhaozong's reign (888–903), wars, natural disasters, and plagues completely engulfed society, so much so that the practice of epitaph writing itself nearly ceased. Tang epitaphs also show that political chaos and economic turbulence had an even more adverse effect on elite women than men. While the average life span for elite men remained relatively stable throughout the Tang, the life expectancy for elite women declined sharply after the An Lushan rebellion,

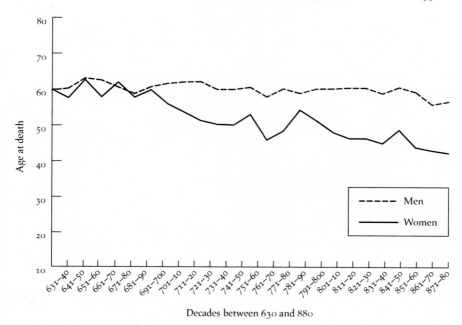

FIGURE 8.2.   Lifespans of men versus women, 630–880.

recovered during Dezong's reign, and then declined to its lowest level at the end of the Tang (see figure 8.2).[38]

The detailed accounts presented in women's epitaphs seem to indicate that elite women often died of illnesses caused by constant traveling and plagues, distress caused by the political mishaps or deaths of family members, and complication during childbirth. The "Epitaph for Daoist Master Zhi" probably best illustrates the political turbulence of the late Tang, as well as what an elite woman's life was like under such circumstances; it thus merits a close reading. The epitaph for Zhi was written in 861 by a Tang official named Zhi Mo for his elder sister, Zhi Xin. Zhi Xin had a Buddhist title name, Zhijian, which she received after converting to Buddhism. However, Zhi died a Daoist Master, having been forced to abandon Buddhism in the middle of her life.

Zhi Xin was born in 812 to a very prestigious family: her grandfather and father were ranking officials at the Tang court and all of her nine brothers held provincial offices. Zhi Xin's father married twice, both times to women from eminent clans. Zhi Xin was born to the first wife. A severe illness determined the course of her life at a very early age. The epitaph indicates that, due to this illness, she became a Buddhist at the young age of nine. Zhi Xin was said to be a "stay-home nun" (*zhujiani*), which required her to recite Buddhist sutras daily, avoid sexual contact, and keep a vegetarian diet. She was never married.

The Huichang Persecution of Buddhism forever changed the life course of Zhi Xin and her fellow Buddhist converts. There are few records that contain information about the lives of monks and nuns after the forced laicization. Presumably they became secular people and moved on with their lives, but female devotees forced to leave the monastery would have had far fewer options in the lay world than their male counterparts. At thirty-three, Zhi Xin had long passed marriageable age. She thus chose the easiest route, resuming her monastic identity under the guise of a different faith: Daoism.

Zhi Xin's later life, between her conversion to Daoism in 845 and her death in 861, mirrored the social turmoil of late Tang China. The first major incident in this period occurred in 853, when her closest brother, Zhi Xiang, died after the "fall of his career" (he was very likely executed). Zhi Xin then took care of Xiang's widow and daughter for eight years. In 861, her younger brother, Zhi Na, was promoted to be the governor of Teng, a relatively rich region in southeastern China. Zhi Na thus invited Zhi Xin to live with him. However, within a month after Zhi Na took office, local bandits started harassing the area. Unable to control the situation, Zhi Na was then transferred to Fuyang of eastern China, a much poorer area. Constant journeys apparently weakened Zhi Xin's health. Furthermore, Zhi Na was completely caught up by his official duties and neglected his sister's well-being. Zhi Xin soon developed ulcers and died at the age of fifty.[39] Even so, she outlived the average woman of her generation by nearly seven years. Among sixty women's epitaphs dated between 861 and 870 that recorded the age at death, the average was forty-three (compared to fifty-six for men, based on eighty-nine epitaphs). Among these contemporaries of Zhi Xin, half would die between the ages of six and thirty-six (sixteen died of illness, two of childbirth, and one during a long journey).[40]

Although Tang dynasty epitaphs represent a highly selective and sometimes less than accurate demography, the intensity of their emotional content and the detailed accounts they provide of everyday life make them valuable sources for understanding the historical experience of Tang women. In addition, epitaphs of Tang women served as model representations of the female life course, thus broadening our understanding of Tang perceptions of gender. Buddhist influence, we learn, was an important element in the idealization of Tang woman. The epitaphs also document a shift in depictions of literary talent, with emphasis being gradually placed on mothers' ability as teachers of sons. Furthermore, compared to the women in *lienü* biographies, who were known for acting under extraordinary circumstances, and to princesses in dynastic biographies, who were often depicted as self-indulgent, Tang elite women in epitaphs were praised for their energy, capability, and wisdom in their day-to-day lives. Finally, women's epitaphs enrich our knowledge of Tang marriage practices, kinship organizations, and most important the overall dynamics of the 300 years of Tang history. Epitaphs from the second half of the Tang vividly retell stories about harsh journeys, postponed weddings and funerals, unattended clan cemeteries, financial crises, and family tragedies due to plagues, political conflicts, regional wars, and bandit attacks, reflecting the extent of the dynasty's deterioration.

9. Fantasies of Fidelity

Loyal Courtesans to Faithful Wives

Beverly Bossler

Scholars have long recognized that one of the most significant developments in the history of Chinese women was the emergence of what is often called "the chastity cult."[1] Visible especially in Ming and Qing dynasty monuments to "chaste" women—both widows who refused to remarry and martyrs who chose death rather than submit to rape or other forms of sexual violation—the cult was defined by the valorization of sexual fidelity over all other values for women. Indeed, as a result of the cult, the word "integrity" or "fidelity" (*jie*), once commonly applied to both men and women, came to be understood almost exclusively in terms of female sexual fidelity.[2]

A critical feature in both the emergence and perpetuation of the chastity cult was the copious production of biographies of faithful women. As I have discussed elsewhere, the most dramatic shift in biographical writing about women took place in the Yuan dynasty, when quite suddenly, literati began to produce hundreds of texts—biographies, prefaces, colophons, and so forth—celebrating the faithful widowhood of women they knew. Most notably, for the first time in Chinese history, literati collected volumes of poetry in honor of faithful wives (often their own mothers or other relatives), prefacing these poetry volumes with a biography of the subject—ideally a biography composed by an eminent political or literary figure.[3]

While the Yuan proliferation of biographies for exemplars is a fascinating phenomenon in its own right, in this essay I focus on earlier precursors of the Yuan fidelity craze, especially the emergence of new conventions of writing about women. Specifically, I attempt to show how both the form and content of the fictive biographies of courtesans that circulated in the late Tang and early Song influenced the ways biographies of faithful exemplars were written in later eras.

GENDER AND TRADITIONS OF BIOGRAPHICAL WRITING

To see the ways that biographical writing about women began to change in the Northern Song, it will be useful first to examine the gendered conventions of biographical writing prior to the Song dynasty.

Clear differences in forms of Chinese biographical writing for men and women were established as early as the Han dynasty (206 BCE–220 CE). In his foundational historical work, the *Records of the Grand Historian* (*Shiji*), Sima Qian (145?–89? BCE) established the individual *zhuan* biography as the most basic genre of biographical writing for men.[4] Such biographies became an essential element of all later standard histories. Yet neither Sima Qian's *Shiji* nor the later standard histories modeled thereon included individual *zhuan* biographies of women. Sima Qian did devote an exclusive chapter to the annals of the reign of Empress Lü and she received the same distinction in the later *History of the Former Han* (*Han shu*), but she was the only Han empress who merited such individualized attention. Other Han empresses and court women appear only as secondary figures in the biographies of emperors and officials.

It is tempting to see Liu Xiang (79–8 BCE), in compiling his famous *Biographies of Exemplary Women* (*Lienü zhuan*) in the first century BCE, as endeavoring to rectify the imbalance between male and female biography in the *Shiji*. Certainly his text provides a set of lively *zhuan* biographies of individual women. But, significantly, unlike most men's biographies in the *Shiji*, Liu's text was organized into chapters devoted to specific virtues, and its subjects—however lively and individualized they are—were expressly included as exemplars of those virtues.[5] Liu Xiang's text apparently did influence the standard histories of later eras, beginning with the fifth-century *History of the Latter Han* (*Hou Hanshu*), for while otherwise adopting a format closely based on Sima Qian's *Shiji*, these later histories added a chapter or two of biographies extolling female exemplars. They also provided capsule biographies for the most eminent "Empresses and Consorts" (*hou fei*) of each reign. Attention to women in the standard histories further expanded with the *New Tang History* (*Xin Tangshu*), compiled by Ouyang Xiu (1007–72) in the Northern Song (960–1126), for in this and later histories imperial princesses were also dignified with their own specialized chapter.[6]

From very early times, then, publicly produced biographies of women tended to focus on well-defined categories of women rather than on individuals. Moreover, women who were not members of the imperial family appear almost exclusively as exemplars of specific virtues. Admittedly, biographies of men in the standard histories also tend to portray their subjects in terms of certain roles or set personae, but the range of roles available, and the potential for individual variation within those roles, was far greater for men than for women.[7]

We do see more individualized biographies of women, however, in various genres of privately compiled biographies. For biographies of upper-class women, by far the most important of these genres was that of funerary inscriptions. Several chapters in this volume provide an excellent sense of the stereotyped but nonetheless diverse content of funerary inscriptions for women during the imperial period.[8] Beginning in the late Southern Song and after, as interest in female fidelity increased, the genre of funerary inscriptions was occasionally deployed for the purpose of celebrating female fidelity. Thus beginning in Southern Song we sometimes see the words "faithful wife" appearing the titles of funerary inscriptions for women.[9] But, perhaps because the families commissioning funerary inscriptions for women saw their deceased loved ones as exemplars of more than a single virtue, funerary inscriptions did not become the main genre of biographical writing about faithful wives or chaste martyrs. Rather, the biographers of faithful exemplars in later imperial China tended to appropriate other genres of private biographical writing—genres that, before the late Northern Song, were not generally used for writing about women, especially not upper-class women. One of these genres was the privately compiled *zhuan*.

From early in the imperial period, literati authors borrowed the conventions of the *zhuan* form seen in the standard histories to compose *zhuan* biographies on their own initiative. Many of these survive in literati collected works.[10] In general, these privately compiled *zhuan* were composed to chronicle the lives of individuals whom the authors found interesting or noteworthy, or in service of a particular argument or point that the author wanted to make. They were often also used to publicize individuals whose exemplary behavior (due to low status or other factors) would otherwise have gone unremarked. Before the Yuan dynasty, however, only a tiny percentage of privately composed *zhuan* record the lives of women. Those that do present a wide variety of subjects. In the Northern Song, for example, Sima Guang (1019–86) wrote a remarkable account of a Buddhist laywoman surnamed Zhang who, sold at age seven by her stepmother in collusion with a monk, ended up as a serving maid in the house of a high court official, was later reunited with her family, and eventually took up residence in a temple.[11] Sima Guang decries Laywoman Zhang's Buddhist practice, but he admires her "loyalty, filiality, honesty, and forbearance" and concludes that, had she been born in an earlier age, Liu Xiang would have transmitted her story. The scholar Wang Ling (1032–59) wrote about a very different kind of woman in his "Biography of Heroic wife Ni" (Liefu Nishi zhuan). Ni was a commoner woman who drowned herself to protest her husband's poor treatment of his brothers. Wang Ling reports that she died in a pond that was no more than three feet deep and stresses that she must have been truly determined. He explains that he has recorded her biography out of pity.[12] Another Northern Song biography tells the story of a filial daughter surnamed Cao, whose father, an upright official, died suddenly while in exile. The author, Cai Xiang (1012–67), praises Cao because, despite the family's poverty and her own unmarried state, she steadfastly refused to accept the contributions of the local clerks to help with her father's funeral, claiming that to use such funds would besmirch her father's pure reputation.[13]

Two general points can be made about these biographies and others like them: first, while they tend to celebrate exemplary behavior, the types of behavior they celebrate are quite diverse (and notably they do *not* emphasize wifely fidelity). Second, they mainly describe women of the lower classes, and/or women not known personally to the author. In the Northern Song, literati men did not commonly write *zhuan* biographies for their own friends and relatives.[14]

In fact, not all *zhuan* biographies were even for human beings. From at least the late Tang, the *zhuan* form accommodated frankly fictional as well as (at least putatively) nonfictional accounts.[15] Literary masters like Han Yu (768–824) of the Tang dynasty (618–907) and Su Shi (1036–1101) of the Song parodied the genre by creating biographies, replete with conventional phrasing and clichéd praises, for inanimate objects like ink stones and fruits. Most such objects were anthropomorphized into male figures, but Zhang Lei (1054–1114) wrote a biography for "Lady Bamboo" (Zhu fu ren), playing on the fact that "Bamboo Lady" (also *zhu fu ren*) was the popular Song term for the bamboo mats that were placed over chairs or beds to help keep the occupant cool in hot, humid weather. Zhang sets his biography of "Lady Bamboo" in the Han dynasty, describing how her family originally "lived in the Southern mountains," until they were wiped out by the Carpenter clan. He notes that she was recommended to court because the emperor was seeking someone "with restraint/faithfulness but not shady" (*you jie er bu yin*—punning on the multiple meanings of *jie* as restraint/fidelity/the sections of bamboo branches). Zhang continues in this tongue-in-cheek vein for some pages, finally describing Lady Bamboo's fall from favor with the cooling of the weather in autumn.[16]

Satirical biographies like these poked fun at the frequently sanctimonious nature of the genre, but the subjects of fictive biographies were not limited to anthropomorphized objects. Fictive *zhuan* were also created as a means to comment (ironically or otherwise) on contemporary social or political issues. Qin Guan (1049–1100), for example, wrote a "Biography of a One-Eyed Courtesan" (Miao chang zhuan) describing how a young man became so infatuated with the subject that he was led to exclaim, "ever since I've met her, other women all look as if they have an extra eye. If an eye is beautiful, one is sufficient; why should anyone need any more?" In his concluding remarks, Qin frames the story as a general comment on the unfortunate human tendency to let benighted passions interfere with reasoned judgment. But his final observation, "A tiny rice husk blinds the eye, and Heaven, earth, and the four quarters all change places," suggests that the story was meant as a critique of Emperor Shenzong's blind faith in the controversial reformer Wang Anshi.[17]

As famous literary masters were playing with *zhuan* in these ways, other authors were experimenting with new literary forms. Of these, the *chuan qi* (or fictive tale) borrowed heavily from the conventions of *zhuan* biographies (along with other literary forms, such as the *zhi guai* anecdote), to create a new genre of extended narrative fiction. These *chuan qi* stories, sometimes matched with narrative poems on the same subject, circulated as entertainment. *Chuan qi* romances represented a new and important development in Chinese literature, and the stories they told served as the basis for much later fiction and drama.[18] More significantly for our purposes, many of these tales took the form of biographies of women, especially women from the demimonde such as the famous courtesans Li Wa and Huo Xiaoyu.[19] These texts, I would suggest, provided new models for writing about women—models that came to have an important impact on the forms and even the content of biographical writing about faithful wives.

BIOGRAPHIES OF COURTESANS

The presence of courtesans as popular subjects of short stories during the late Tang was a reflection of their importance in the social life of the period. That presence only increased during the Song, and Song short stories and anecdotal literature are likewise full of references to literati interaction with courtesans of various types.[20] As objects of romance and members of a despised profession, the women of the demimonde could be written about in ways that upper-class women could not. Their biographies circulated publicly and became the object of commentaries in ways that would have been considered inappropriate and degrading to upper-class women. Yet courtesans were also companions for literati men, and, not surprisingly, in many respects the ideals that men formulated for their fictional courtesan heroines overlapped with those they admired in women of their own class. This slippage was an important factor in the influence of courtesan biographies on later writings for upper-class exemplars.

As we might expect, courtesan biographies almost always begin by praising their subjects for their beauty and entertainment skills. The young courtesan Tan Yige is described as having "translucent skin, elegant bones, lustrous hair and wide eyes; her hands are like delicate shoots; her slender waist a mere handful."[21] Wang Youyu and her sisters surpassed all those of their cohort in their looks, singing, and dancing, and "none of the other courtesans dared compete with them."[22] In this respect, courtesans were portrayed very differently from wives, who (in the Song at least) were rarely described physically, and who were never depicted as singing or dancing.

Courtesans were also valorized for literary talent, however, and here they begin to look rather more like upper-class women. Growing up in the home of her mother's sister, Wen Wan dresses as a boy and studies the classics; as an adolescent, "her heart was drunk on the Odes and Histories, and she deeply understood their fascination, to the point that day and night she silently recited them to herself without ever stopping." Even after she is forced to become a courtesan Wen Wan eschews singing and dancing: when she attends at banquets she is accompanied by a single servant who carries her book cases, brushes, and ink stone. Ultimately she becomes famous for her calligraphy and poetry.[23] In like fashion, Tan Yige matches wits with the local officials in a series of brilliant poetic exchanges (all lovingly quoted in the story) that leave her interlocutors sighing with admiration. Literary talent in courtesans was especially associated with poetry: in the context of banquets, extempore poetry was frequently composed in praise of the entertainers, and poetry contests served as a form of flirtation.[24] Poetry was also the preferred vehicle for exchange of romantic sentiments: at climactic romantic moments courtesan biographies almost always feature poignant exchanges of verse between the heroine and her lover. For this reason, a few Song moralists discouraged upper-class women from flaunting their poetic skills.[25] Yet in practice many upper-class women were trained in poetry, and we shall see below that poetic expression also came to be associated with exemplars of fidelity.

Courtesans look even more like upper-class women in their attitudes toward their own profession. A virtuous courtesan (and virtually all of the romantic heroines in these stories—at least those who are human—are virtuous) inevitably despises her profession. When the ten-year-old orphan

Tan Yige is first brought to the courtesan house where she is to become an apprentice, she wails, "I've been an orphan all my life, wandering over 10,000 *li;* I am powerless and young in years. There is no one who will take pity and save me, and I will be unable to marry a respectable man." Everyone who hears her "exclaims in regret." Wen Wan, on realizing that she is not fated to "entrust myself to a respectable family, and there live out my life," weeps and is "unable to overcome her anguish."[26] Wang Youyu, though celebrated as the most beautiful courtesan in Hengzhou, laments,

> Today, whether it be artisans, merchants, farmers, traders, Daoists, or Buddhist monks, all are able to support themselves. Only our kind plaster on lotion and pat ourselves with powder, using witty words and seductive glances to get others' money. When I think of it I am ashamed beyond measure, but forced by my parents and siblings there is no way for me to escape. If I could marry a respectable man, I could serve my in-laws and manage the sacrifices, so that people would point their fingers and say, "She's someone's wife." When I died there would be a place to bury my bones.[27]

In the imaginations of Northern Song authors, then, courtesans wanted nothing more than to marry and become respectable (*liang*) women. The most virtuous among them, such as Wen Wan, accepts her degraded position only out of filial piety: "How can I be concerned whether my reputation is glorious or disgraced, and make my mother end up starving and with no place to die?"[28] The courtesan's disdain for her own profession, and for the superficial beauty and extravagance it entailed, likewise suggested that she shared other values admired in upper-class women, who were routinely praised for simplicity and frugality in daily life.[29] And accordingly, when courtesans are lucky enough to enter the inner quarters of literati men, they behave like any gently bred daughter-in-law. When she was finally able to marry her lover, the courtesan Tan Yige "managed the inner quarters with ritual and regulations; in dealing with family and kinsmen she was always gracious. Inner and outer were amiable and harmonious, and the *Dao* of the family was fulfilled."

Most significantly, courtesans shared with the ideal upper-class woman a commitment to fidelity: when the heroines of courtesan biographies manage to find men to love, they are unfailingly loyal. Wen Wan has a liaison with a man named Wang who dies in battle: she weeps in grief when she hears the news, and then calls in Buddhist monks to chant sutras for several days for the repose of Wang's soul.[30] When Wang Youyu's lover Liu Fu is forced by his parents to marry a woman of his own class, she dies of grief and leaves her hair and fingernails for him as a memento of their attachment.[31] Tan Yige's paramour Zhang at first abandoned her for a respectable marriage: she shut herself away and received no one, though she continued to send Zhang a stream of poignant letters and poems (again lovingly quoted). Tan's patience and fidelity were rewarded when, after three years, Zhang's wife died and he sought her out. Still, she refused to receive him until he engaged a go-between and married her with full ritual honors. While faithfulness and loyalty were admired in courtesans and upper-class women alike, however, we should note that courtesan biographies present a strikingly new model of fidelity, quite different from that typically seen in the biographies of upper-class women.[32] In courtesan biographies, undying fidelity served to underscore—indeed to make possible—the element of romance.[33] A courtesan's fidelity to her lover was based not on a ritual marriage vow uniting two families, but on her emotional commitment to her lover, and the sincerity of her dedication to him was demonstrated with dramatic gestures—seclusion, illness, even suicide. These elements, too, become common features of later texts celebrating the fidelity of upper-class women.[34]

Finally, if the content of courtesan biographies thus provided some models for later writing about faithful women, the *format* in which courtesan biographies (and perhaps other entertainment texts) were written seems to have been equally important in creating new templates for biographies of female exemplars. Many courtesan biographies feature the mixed use of prose and poetry, and in some, the biography itself functions as a preface to a poem or set of poems.[35] This format in turn seems to have been associated with the circulation of texts, with later authors adding additional commentary. Both the format of prose and poetry and the circulation of texts were to be central features in the proliferation of texts honoring exemplars.[36]

We see signs of the influence of entertainment literature beginning in the late Northern and early Southern Song, as elements of courtesan romances begin to appear in the collected works of literati men. The shift is visible both thematically, with new emphases on personal fidelity and scenes of dramatic self-sacrifice, and in generic format, with novel uses of poetry and commentary thereon as a vehicle for extolling women.

TRANSITIONAL WRITINGS IN LATE NORTHERN AND EARLY SOUTHERN SONG

One early hint of the influence of courtesan biographies on the writings of literati appears in a preface to a volume of poetry, found in the collected works of the scholar-official Liu Yan (1048–1102).[37] Certainly prefaces to poetry collections were a very familiar form of literati writing from well before the Song; and in the Yuan, such prefaces were to become one of the most common genres of text used to celebrate faithful wives.[38] But Liu Yan's "Zhang Wenrou shi xu" is unusual—indeed unique—in Song collected works because it is a preface for a volume of poetry extolling a woman.[39] Significantly, and in striking contrast to Yuan works for upper-class widows, Liu Yan's subject was a courtesan, a local entertainer named Zhang Wanwan.

Like most other examples of the genre, Liu's preface explains how both the poetry collection and the preface itself came into being, while also providing a cursory biography of the subject of the collection. In this case, we are told, a retainer (*ke*) of the author sent him a letter describing a local girl of such beauty that she seemed to be not of this world: her voice was pure and round, her dances fluttering and light. The retainer explained that, having failed to capture the young woman's affections, he had instead devoted himself to writing poems and songs about her. His friends had likewise joined in, until their poetry filled several large scrolls. The retainer begs Liu to provide a preface for the collection, suggesting that only then will others be able to take pleasure in it. Liu Yan modestly expresses some doubt on the last point, but he does compose an elaborate preface. Therein he implicitly compares the courtesan to other rare and beautiful objects (such as pearls, jade, and gold) that are created by Heaven but require human effort to make them known to the world.

In format Liu Yan's preface echoes the conceits of the fictional biographies of courtesans, in which extended prefaces and postfaces describe how the story was passed from hand to hand. Yet his preface is not (or at least is not presented as) fiction: it describes a real individual and appears in the formal collected works (*wen ji*) of a scholar-official of some renown. It reveals a literary milieu in which writings about women (albeit women of the demimonde) were circulating and generating new texts. In addition, although the preface itself tells us almost nothing about Wanwan's activities or behavior (which presumably were described in the attendant poetry), Liu concludes his work by suggesting that poetry is the means by which Wanwan's reputation can become known to the four quarters. In other words, the circulation of the text was expressly intended to publicize its subject. It is hardly surprising, then, that this format would be appropriated by men who wanted to publicize other types of women. One of the earliest to do so was the idiosyncratic figure Xu Ji (1028–1103), in his odd, even bizarre, collected works, the *Faithful and Filial Collection* (*Jie xiao ji*).

XU JI'S *FAITHFUL AND FILIAL COLLECTION*

Although Xu Ji's *Faithful and Filial Collection* contains numerous biographies of faithful and filial individuals, the title of the text does not refer to its contents, but to its author: Xu Ji had once been acclaimed by the Song state as an exemplar of filial piety, and "Faithful and Filial" was the title posthumously awarded to him in a later act of state appreciation.[40]

According to a biography composed shortly after his death, Xu Ji was born the son of a minor official who died when Ji was only three. Ji was reared in his maternal grandfather's family, and was known even as a child for his attention to ritual.[41] He studied with the famous Northern Song teacher Hu Yuan (933–1059) and passed the highest rank (*jinshi*) in the examinations. He became famous for various types of filial behavior: he opposed his uncles' decision to divide the family, and when he could not stop them, let them take what they wanted. He led his family in children's games to amuse his mother, and since he couldn't bear to leave her to take the examinations, took her with him. Since his father had been named "Rock" (*shi*), he avoided stepping on stones his entire life. When his mother died he mourned bitterly, and Heaven responded to his filial sincerity with various supernatural manifestations. In 1086 these manifestations were reported to the court by local officials, and he received an award of silk and rice in honor of his filiality.[42] Xu Ji was something of a celebrity in his own day: although he held only very minor, local offices, he received the homage of some of the most eminent officials of the period, and exchanged poetry with such literary luminaries as Su Shi and Qin Guan. Xu Ji's writings circulated widely in the late Northern and Southern Song periods, as evidenced by numerous celebratory colophons that appear in surviving versions of his collected works. But Xu Ji's writings are unconventional in many respects. The eighteenth-century editors of the Qing imperial library catalog *Siku quanshu zongmu* note that Su Shi was reputed to have called Xu's writing style "strange and uninhibited." They concede that in their view, too, it is "wild, abandoned, self-assured, unrestrained by rules and models," and "mixes the elegant and the vulgar"—though they insist that overall "it does not stray from the words of a Confucian." Xu Ji's collected works are significant for our purposes because they are full of lurid biographies of women—faithful wives as well as pitiful courtesans and concubines—that read far more like fiction than like the sober didactic accounts we are accustomed to seeing in literati collected works. Moreover, many of Xu Ji's most dramatic stories take the form of prefaces to poetry. In this he provides some of the earliest extant examples of biographical poetry and poetry prefaces for exemplary women.

One such piece is Xu Ji's "Song of Ai'ai" (Ai'ai ge), which—significantly—celebrates the fidelity of a courtesan. The long preface opens by explaining that Xu is hoping to improve on an "Ai'ai ge" that was once written by "Zimei" (probably the Northern Song writer Su Shunqin) but had been lost. In any case, Xu says disapprovingly, the language of the original was licentious, "did not get at Ai'ai's true nature, and contained nothing that could be shown to later students." Xu indicates that he is writing his version to "relieve the confusion of scholars." The preface then explains that Ai'ai was an orphaned girl from Wu, who, although reared in a courtesan's household, was unwilling to become a courtesan. She contrived to run away. She came to the capital with a wealthy patron to whom Xu refers as "that person" (*qi ren*). After several years, "that person" returned to Jiangnan and died there. Ai'ai lived on in the capital, considering herself "the one who hasn't died" (*wei wang ren*), and even the best plans of the wealthy and noble could not move her heart.[43] She remained faithful until her death. Xu Ji concludes, "This can certainly not be called minor fidelity; this was an extraordinary girl. [With regard to] what the ancients called a righteous and heroic girl, her heart was the same though her path was different." Xu adds a few lines excoriating the wealthy man with whom Ai'ai had run away, explaining that since he was unfilial and not worthy of being counted as a human being, Xu has chosen to focus exclusively on Ai'ai. The poem that follows, written in simple seven-character lines, describes the beautiful Ai'ai: "Dancing and singing, number one in Wu; just fifteen years old, paired chignons black-blue" (*gewu Wuzhong di yi ren, lü fa shuang huan cai shiwu*). It stresses her vow of fidelity: "the mountains can disintegrate, ah, the oceans dry up; in life there is only one, ah, in death not two" (*shan ke mo xi, hai ke ku; sheng wei yi xi, si wu er*). And it describes her feelings after her lover's death: "this year, this day, all has come to an end; fine gauzes and precious jade I regard as mud" (*jinnian, jinri, wanshi yi; jiaoxiao feicui kan ru ni*).[44]

In the "Song of Ai'ai," then, Xu Ji took a circulating courtesan romance and reconfigured it into the story of a faithful wife. But he used the same format of biographical preface and poetry to tell the stories of other, noncourtesan exemplars, as well. In the preface to another entry, entitled "Poem for the Righteous Wife of Huaiyin" (Huaiyin yifu shi), Xu Ji explains that there was once a wealthy merchant whose wife, née Li, was beautiful. A fellow merchant saw her and admired her, and killed her husband while they were traveling together. Telling Li that her husband had drowned, the murderer spared no expense to bring the body home for burial. He selflessly turned all the husband's earnings over to Li, and waited for the mourning to be over. Making a point of how well he had treated her husband, the merchant persuaded Li to marry him. Then,

> One day there was a great flood, and bubbles formed in the water. Her [new] husband laughed, and the righteous wife asked why. When at first he didn't answer, she persisted. Relying on the fact that she had already borne him two sons, he expected that she would bear him no enmity, so he told her the truth, saying, "Your husband's drowning was my doing. After he was already under water, he re-emerged, as if he were going to save himself. I stabbed him with the boat pole, and he went back under. The place where I stabbed him bubbled up just like what we saw today." The righteous wife was silent, suddenly understanding his plot, and enmity was born in her heart.

Xu relates that Li took the first opportunity to report her husband's murderer to the authorities. Then, realizing that her own beauty had been responsible for her husband's death, and that her sons were the sons of her husband's enemy, she tied the two boys up and threw them in the river, and threw herself in after them. Having concluded the story, Xu turns to a philosophical defense of his decision to call her a "righteous wife." He stresses that although she had served two husbands, she married the second man only because she was moved by his righteousness to her first husband. Once she knew the truth, "the intimacy of the marital bed did not weigh in her heart in the slightest," thus she was able to hate and kill her sons. He ends his disquisition by suggesting that she can serve as a model for men, and bewailing the fact that she has not been recognized by the state as an exemplar. The fairly short poem that follows this long preface slips in and out of the righteous wife's own voice, and is once again in simple, even trite language. For example: "The woman of Huaiyin, how determined and heroic! Her face like a flower, her heart like iron" (*Huaiyin furen he juelie; mao hao ru hua xin si tie*).[45]

There is some evidence that, like "The Song of Ai'ai," Xu's "Poem for the Righteous Wife of Huaiyin" was an attempt to provide a morally improved version of an existing story.[46] Xu also reiterated many of the same themes—and the same format—in his "Poem for the Heroic Wife of Beishen" (Beishen liefu shi). Here a long preface describes the beautiful wife traveling with her husband, a petty trader. He dies en route; a wealthy merchant lends her money for the burial, but then on that basis begins to "regard her as his own property" (*gu qi qi yi wei ji wu*). After she completes the mourning for her husband and returns from the gravesite, the merchant pressures her even more, so she ties her infant to her chest and jumps into the river, where both drown. This time Xu devotes his commentary to exclaiming about how extraordinary she was, especially because, unlike the virtuous women celebrated by poets of old, she came from a poor family where one would not expect to find righteousness. The final poem is short enough to translate in full in all its hackneyed glory:[47]

海水猶可泛, 君身不可犯   Hai shui you ke fan, jun shen bu ke fan,
淮水猶可瀦,君名不可汙   Huai shui you ke zhu, jun ming bu ke wu.
鸞鳳猶可馴,氷霜猶可親   Luan feng you ke xun, bing shuang you ke qin,
不是雲間月,即是月邊雲   Bushi yun jian yue, ji shi yue bian yun.

[The waters of the sea can still swell, but milord's body cannot be betrayed.
The waters of the Huai can still be pooled, but milord's name cannot be polluted.
The paired phoenixes can still be tamed, the icy frost can be embraced
If it is not a moon in the clouds, then it is clouds beside the moon.]

These are not the sorts of writings we are accustomed to finding in the collected works of scholar-officials. Like Liu Yan's use of the poetry preface to describe a beautiful courtesan, Xu Ji's use of biography-with-poetry for the depiction of exemplary women was an innovation: although earlier men had occasionally written poetry in honor of exemplars, and had in very rare instances even composed biographical prefaces thereto, Xu Ji was the first to provide a series of such texts promoting an assortment of exemplary figures.[48] Moreover, both the tone and the structure of Xu Ji's pieces are strikingly reminiscent of entertainment literature: they are full of gory and salacious detail and are amply ornamented with clichéd romantic poetry. They also share with the courtesan biographies an emphasis on fidelity as the most important female virtue. Finally, Xu Ji seems to have expected that his writings would circulate: he wants to reduce the "confusion" caused by licentious writings, and explain his own understanding of virtue. All of these features were to be exhibited by Southern Song and later writings celebrating faithful women, with the important difference that the latter focused not on lower-class women, but on the wives and daughters of literati families.

In focusing on lower-class women, Xu Ji's stories shared the general aesthetic of *zhuan* biographies, which generally did not publicize upper-class women. But about the same time that Xu Ji was writing, we also see an early and novel use of the *zhuan* form to describe a woman of the upper class. The "Biography of Elder Sister Wu," (Wushi zi zhuan) was written in the early twelfth century by the eminent official Zhao Dingchen (1070–after 1122), for his senior female cousin.[49] From the beginning, this text signals its difference from typical biographies of upper-class people by revealing rather unflattering details about the subject's family. Zhao explains that his uncle was a hard-drinking, stubborn man, too unbending to be successful in office. Instead he retreated to his estates, amusing himself with his wealth. Although he had five sons, the uncle's favorite child was his only daughter, and he determined that he would marry her only to someone who would be willing to take up residence with her family. In rather colloquial language, Zhao recounts how his uncle was approached by a go-between, who proposed a match with an orphaned youth surnamed Wu. "The old man was honest and forthright, and was unsuspecting. Delighted, he said, 'Where is he? Bring him around right away!'" The betrothal was duly arranged, and only when it was too late did Zhao's aunt and uncle discover that the man who had become their uxorilocal son-in-law was not only ugly but crude and unmannerly. At this, Zhao tells us, his uncle was so angry he did not eat for days, while his wife, afraid of what the relatives would think, tried secretly to advise and instruct the new son-in-law. Through all this, Zhao's cousin treated her husband respectfully, but over time his behavior only worsened, especially after the father-in-law's death. Eventually Wu's gambling and drinking caused him to be publicly flogged by the county magistrate. At that point, the cousin's mother refused to let the husband see her daughter. The matriarch of the family (the cousin's grandmother) called a family meeting at which she and others, including Zhao himself, attempted to persuade his cousin to abandon her husband. The cousin responded to Zhao's invocation of classical texts by crying, "What are you saying? I do not read books and don't understand your words. I only know that my father married me to Wu. What else is there to say?" In the face of her determination, the family had no choice but to let her go back to her husband. They set the couple up in a separate residence where the cousin worked assiduously while her husband continued his dissolute ways.

Zhao Dingchen concludes the biography of his cousin by recounting how he defended her from public opinion that she was unfilial (in disobeying her elders' wishes), unrighteous (in privately loving her husband), unwise (in subjecting herself to hardship and humiliation) and cowardly (in resigning herself to such degradation). Although he had been among those who attempted to separate her from her husband, here Zhao praises her for her fidelity, asserting that she was more faithful even than the exemplars of the classics. While those exemplars demonstrated their fidelity by dying, she had remained loyal in spite of an unrighteous husband, against parental directive, and in the face of continuing misery.[50]

Here again we have a text that seems to introduce elements of entertainment literature into a story of exemplary fidelity. It valorizes female fidelity maintained even in the face of hardship and ill-treatment (and in this case, even against the dictates of filial piety). It tells its story in an informal, almost colloquial, register. But unlike earlier texts, it publicizes—even at the cost of revealing embarrassing family difficulties—a woman of the literati class, a member of author's own family.

Over the course of the Southern Song, texts like these, highlighting the fidelity of upper-class women in often dramatic and entertaining style—became more numerous. Most were inspired by the traumatic fall of the Northern Song in 1126, which both rendered the issue of loyalty one of the most pressing concerns of the day, and provided numerous instances of heroic deaths by women who refused to submit to the invaders. These Southern Song exemplar texts are interesting for a number of reasons, but here I would like to highlight the ways in which they resonate with the entertainment literature of the Northern Song.[51]

A number of Southern Song biographies for upper-class heroines appear in *zhuan* form, and like courtesan biographies, a number of these highlight attractive and nubile women. Maiden Gui, who protected her father from bandits and then died rather than submit to rape by them, was just at "hairpin age."[52] Chen Liang describes how one of "Two Heroic Maidens" bathed, dusted herself with pearl powder, and applied makeup: she then hanged herself rather than be turned over to brigands.[53] Wives are portrayed as romantically faithful to their husbands, as when Wu Yongnian's wife cried to her husband, "I will not turn my back on you" (*wo bu fu jun*) then threw herself into a river to avoid the invaders.[54] Like the biographies of courtesans, biographies of faithful women circulated, accruing commentary by a number of literati authors. Thus both Wang Zhiwang and a contemporary, Cheng Ju, wrote commentaries on a preexisting biography for a faithful wife surnamed Rong. In language that echoes that of Xu Ji, Cheng's "tribute" (*zan*) compares Rong's purity to jade and iron; Wang's postface stresses that she preserved her integrity even at the cost of sacrificing her children.[55] Xu Ji's poetry and courtesan biographies alike are evoked in a set of poems, complete with biographical preface, composed by Zhou Zizhi (1082–1155). Zhou's text—itself a commentary on an existing account—commemorates the suicides of the wife and concubines of a friend's uncle: all three women drowned themselves rather than be "polluted" by bandits. Zhou's preface stresses the musical talents and beauty of the serving maids; the faintly erotic poems highlight their "jade countenances" (*yu yan*) and the dancing of their red sleeves in the water.[56]

All of these texts were novel in the Song context in featuring upper-class women in publically circulating texts. Nonetheless, these texts still contrasted with those of later eras in several respects. Most of the subjects were not directly related to the authors, and all of the subjects were women who died heroically. Although there was in the thirteenth century some new attention to the fidelity of women who did not remarry after their husband's deaths, in the Southern Song accounts of such faithful widows continued to be confined to funerary inscriptions.[57] This was to change dramatically in the Yuan, when celebration of upper-class faithful widows overwhelmingly took the form of poetry collections, duly accompanied by biographical prefaces that depicted fidelity as the preeminent female virtue.

By the end of the Southern Song, the number of texts honoring female fidelity was still quite small in comparison with later eras. Yet they represent a sea change from earlier biographies of exemplary women in several respects: in their overwhelming emphasis on female bodily integrity, especially in the service of wifely fidelity; in the fact that they commemorate women of literati households, in many cases women known to the authors of the texts; and in their active circulation, evident in the increasing importance of genres like poetry prefaces, commentaries, and poetry as vehicles for female biography. We have seen that many aspects of the new forms appeared first in fictional writings about courtesans that were popular in the same era.

Katherine Carlitz long ago noted the overlap between didactic stories of female virtue and stories for entertainment—with their emphasis on emotion, desire, and women's bodies—in the Late Ming.[58] We have seen here that these elements were part of the intensifying discourse on female fidelity as early as the twelfth century. This in turn alerts us to the possibility that the origins of this discourse lay at least partly *in* entertainment—that it was connected with the flourishing entertainment culture of Song cities, and with the interactions between Song men and the denizens of the entertainment districts. In a society where it was becoming increasingly common for upper-class men to take entertainers into their own homes as "household courtesans" (*jia ji*), and where such women often became the romantic partners of their masters and the mothers of the household's heirs, courtesans became a natural foil for upper-class wives. Song men's anxieties to keep the two classes of women distinct—as when upper-class women were enjoined not to write romantic poetry, or when moralists decried the presence of wives at banquets or the adoption of courtesan fashions by upper-class women—only highlight the ease with which the two groups could be conflated.[59] In this context, female bodily integrity became charged with multiple meanings, all the more powerful for their ambiguity. On the one hand, bodily integrity distinguished upper-class women from courtesans, whose bodies were for sale; on the other, courtesans were imagined as expressing romantic love through bodily integrity (and sometimes even as becoming upper-class wives by doing so!). These meanings easily blurred, so that wifely fidelity took on romantic overtones, and the romantic attachments of courtesans like Ai'ai could be understood as righteous. This was all the more the case when biographies of both courtesans and faithful women were circulated to be read, savored, and commented on.

I certainly do not mean to suggest that entertainment literature was the only, or even the most important, factor contributing to the development of the fidelity discourse in the late Song and Yuan. On the contrary, as I have argued elsewhere, that development grew out of a much larger complex of social and political changes.[60] But I do believe that the popular circulation of writings about courtesans in the Northern Song both helped to normalize a tradition of circulation and commentary on texts specifically about women, and also introduced new images of fidelity that were later easily incorporated into texts about upper-class wives. In this manner, the fantasies of fidelity expressed in courtesan biographies helped shape the ways that wifely fidelity came to be understood and described.

10. Lovers, Talkers, Monsters, and Good Women

Competing Images in Mid-Ming Epitaphs and Fiction

Katherine Carlitz

The preceding chapters by Ping Yao and Beverly Bossler show us how the notion of women's "ideal life course" evolved through the Tang and Song dynasties. This chapter follows that evolution into the Ming, concentrating on the sixteenth century. Following Bossler's lead, I will juxtapose fiction with epitaphs that convey the norms of women's ideal life course, but I will concentrate on fiction that seems to contravene those norms. My aim is to convey a sense of the larger Ming imaginary, in which epitaphs played only one part. We will get a sense of the Tang and Song imaginary as well, since I discuss durable stories whose roots go back centuries before the Ming. This should sharpen our reading of epitaphs, since the larger context can help us discern their social purpose. It will also highlight the complexity of fiction, with its ambiguous relation to conventional morality, and enhance our understanding of Ming dynasty women, subjects of the epitaphs and consumers of the fiction.

Yao's chapter defines the genre of *muzhiming* (epitaphs) that I will focus on here. Ming dynasty *muzhiming*, more conventionalized and normative than the biographies, or *zhuan*, that Bossler discusses, display striking continuities with the Tang epitaphs that Yao analyzes. Social organization changed from Tang to Ming, with clan domination giving way to bureaucratic hegemony, but *muzhiming*, reflecting the ever-increasing influence of the civil-service examination system, continued to help families articulate social status by means of proper conduct. Epitaphs reinforced the norms for an imagined community of governing-class families, whose aspirations were largely shaped by the examination system. As in the Tang and Song, Ming epitaphs for women praise values that could help a family enter this community or rise within it: frugality and restrained demeanor, wise household management, devoted service to one's husband and his parents. These aspirational norms had a major impact on the rest of the society as well.[1]

But epitaphs are a very narrow window onto what women actually thought and felt. As far back as the Tang, depending on available sources or media, women saw plays, read books, heard tales, or participated in religious activities that featured images wildly at odds with the ideals of the epitaphs. In these texts and tales, young people had love affairs, daughters talked back to their parents, concubines stole the babies of legitimate wives, and female monsters devoured unsuspecting young men. How did girls and women—and men, for that matter—integrate these competing images into their lives?

We may be tempted to see this as orthodoxy (the epitaphs) versus a steady current of heterodoxy (popular stories about ungovernable women), but such a model leads us away from actual complexities. The Ming stories discussed here were collected and published by men not vastly different from the educated authors of the epitaphs. Local histories compiled by these educated authors contain anecdotes, presented as verifiable fact, that look much like what we see in Tang, Song, and Ming fiction. Tales of passionate love are echoed in the extravagant sorrow with which Ming literati mourned their wives. We need to explore these epitaphs and stories as elements in dynamic equilibrium, the epitaphs filled with categories of praise that women were doubtless happy to receive, even as the stories served as vehicles for fantasies and terrors, opened up new emotional possibilities, or reinscribed the dominant values in new ways.

The Ming dynasty Chenghua (1465–88) through Jiajing (1522–67) eras, on which I focus, form an understudied but important period. The Ming dynasty commercial boom was gaining strength; the bureaucracy, which employed all of my epitaph writers at different moments, was assuming its mature shape; and crusading magistrates were standardizing virtue by tearing down local temples and putting up shrines to Confucian worthies and martyrs.[2] I will look primarily at epitaphs by Li Mengyang (1473–1529), who made his home in Kaifeng (Henan Province) for much of his life, but I will also touch on epitaphs by his contemporaries and near-contemporaries in other parts of China to show that they spoke a common language when they wrote about women. As others have pointed out, examination education had an enormously homogenizing effect on China's governing class.[3]

To avoid anachronism, I will consider only fiction that could have impacted the subjects of my epitaphs: love stories circulating in the late fifteenth or early sixteenth centuries, prose-verse narratives (*shuochang cihua*) found in Jiading County (Jiangsu Province) at the end of the fifteenth century, and the vernacular short stories in the collection *Qingping shantang huaben,* originally published by Hong Pian of Hangzhou in 1550, though many were written decades earlier. (Following Patrick Hanan, I will refer to Hong's collection as *Sixty Stories*).[4] This stuff-material does not, however, belong to the Ming dynasty alone. The tales examined here all have precursors in earlier dynasties, and thus what we learn from sixteenth-century publication is that the old stories were still vigorously alive, to be taken up by the new media of their day. For some of this material, we also have concrete evidence about readership, which can help us evaluate the likelihood of a specifically female audience.

EPITAPHS

An epitaph by He Jingming (1483–1581), a friend of Li Mengyang's, shows us the typical formulae that were used to praise elite Ming women:

EPITAPH FOR MME REN, TITLED LADY OF VIRTUE (*SHUREN*)

The Honorable Bao Deming, the Assistant Regional Military Commander for my province, lost his first wife. Prior to her burial, he came to me, saying: "My first wife attended to me most diligently. Now that she has died and left me, I wish to request her epitaph from you." My epitaph is as follows: Mme Ren was the daughter of Wei Qing, of the Xinyang Guard Battalion. When she married the Assistant Commander, she was honored with the title Lady of Virtue. This Lady of Virtue exemplified womanly virtues in her person, and wifely deportment in her household. In managing the concubines, she was not jealous. In her treatment of the servants, she was not cruel. Indeed, she was a woman who behaved as a gentleman (*junzi*) would do. When the Honorable Bao became Assistant Commander, the Lady of Virtue was very supportive, and kept her household domain perfectly in order. She did not regard household matters, large or small, as requiring Bao's attention. Bao managed his official domain, and the Lady of Virtue managed her domestic realm. In this way, Bao was able to devote his entire attention to the public realm, with no worries at all about domestic matters."[5]

In this and other epitaphs, He Jingming focuses exclusively on his subject's married life. Earlier, in the Tang dynasty, as Yao demonstrates in chapter 8, epitaph writers (often family members) dwelled lovingly on the childhood and literary accomplishments of their female subjects.[6] But by He's day, epitaphs reflected new attitudes about families, women, and men. Song dynasty Neo-Confucian teachings emphasized the family as a model for the state, and the Ming founder had elevated this model to the level of state policy. The model family was the woman's family of marriage, and her fidelity to her husband was constantly eulogized as the domestic analogue of loyalty to the empire. Tang epitaphs had already emphasized motifs that we will see in the Ming: women's devotion to the welfare of their husbands' families, their lack of jealousy, the likelihood that widows would remain unmarried, and—in a very significant motif to be treated below—legitimate wives raising concubines' children as their own. By the sixteenth century, these motifs tended to exclude all others. Ming epitaphs for governing-class women differ from *lienü* accounts, in that they are accounts of productivity rather than martyrdom. Nevertheless, they share the core values of the *lienü* accounts, and are equally focused on those values.

To obtain epitaphs for the newly deceased, families assembled biographical data, and then, as with Bao Deming and He Jingming above, paid for the best writers they could afford. In addition to their use as funerary objects, the texts of *muzhiming* were also published in the collected works of their authors, and we can probably assume that families were aware of and valued this public aspect. The epitaphs are thus hybrids: their emphases and anecdotes show us what families wanted known, but the personalities that come through in the documents are those of the writers themselves. In Li Mengyang's case, we meet a particularly exuberant personality.

Li Mengyang's turbulent life saw him alternately in high official positions or in jail, for offending first the Hongzhi-era empress; next, the powerful eunuch Liu Jin (d. 1510); third, the officials of Nanchang, where he had been sent to report on the state of education; and one final time after an accusation that he had joined a rebellious clique. From his earliest stay in the capital, after earning the *jinshi* degree at the age of twenty, he was recognized as a leading literary light.[7] This luster never dimmed, and families must have vied for the honor of an epitaph for one of their members. In epitaphs for women in his own family, he happily chronicled his own success. He quotes his wife's mother, moved to tears by her daughter's finery after Li gained office, saying: "As a student Li was insignificant and poor, but now look at this!"[8]

His epitaph for his own wife takes the values he shares with He Jingming to an almost operatic level:

Weeping, I said to someone: "Only now when my wife has died do I know my wife!" This person asked how that might be? I replied: "Previously I studied and took office, and paid no attention to household matters. Now, nobody pays attention to things, and they don't get done. When I had guests, food and drink suitable to their needs were supplied. Now no more guests come, or if they do, nothing is suitable. Previously, I used things without any attention to where they belonged. Now, everything gets thrown about and nobody puts anything away, but everyone's good at breaking things! Previously, we never lacked for pickles and sauces and salted beans, but now, it's not like before! Chickens, ducks, sheep, and pigs were all fed at the proper time—now, they're not fed at the proper time and they're all too thin! When my wife was alive, there was no whispering and giggling inside. If I went out, the door was not barred when I came back at night. Now the door is barred, and inside I hear that giggling! Before, I had no idea of what dirty clothes were. Now, if I don't order them washed, they don't get washed. My wife's hands were constantly busy with sewing, cutting, drawing, and embroidering; now, no hands are busy. Formerly, when I wanted to groan about past and present but did not want to talk with friends, I could talk to my wife. But now when I come home, I have no one to talk to. That's why I say: only now that my wife is dead do I know my wife![9]

Gui Youguang (1507–71) of Jiangsu Province eulogized many similarly competent women: Mao *ruren* (Child Nurturess, a title frequently given to the wives of officials) "brought harmony to the other household wives;"[10] Tang *ruren* saw to the feeding of 100 laborers and the expenses connected with sacrifices, while her husband was off on official journeys;[11] and Zhang *ruren's* husband traveled to famous mountains and rivers, leaving household management and the education of their sons to the care of his wife— as she herself thought proper.[12]

This competent household management was understood to include significant autonomy in managing the family finances, as we can see from Li Mengyang's epitaphs for the women in Subprefectural Magistrate Bian Jie's family. The matriarch, Bian's mother, foiled her sons' efforts to realize cash from her daughter-in-law's jewelry; the daughter-in-law herself, Dong *ruren,* shielded her husband's stepbrother Cheng when he chose to leave the family and take his private savings with him. This earned her the undying gratitude of her sister-in-law: "When Dong *ruren* died, Cheng's wife came from Li City [Cheng's original home] to prostrate herself at Dong *ruren's* grave."[13] Here the family itself has told Li Mengyang about Dong *ruren's* strategic secrets, making clear that they not only allowed her independent judgment but prized it. But at the same time, this paragon of a wife was supposed to be silent, sequestered, and self-effacing. The ideal wife of these epitaphs knew by heart the Han dynasty classic

Nüjie (Precepts for my daughters), by Ban Zhao, with its instruction to be submissive to authority and sparing of speech: "To choose her words with care; to avoid vulgar language; to speak at appropriate times; and not to weary others with much conversation, may be called the characteristics of womanly words." Li Mengyang echoes this in a passage about his mother-in-law: "To the end of her days, she wore plain clothing and ate vegetarian food. Anger did not lead to vituperation; smiles did not show her teeth, and she did not step over her threshold to see visitors."[14] Li Kaixian (1502–68), of Shandong Province, says much the same kind of thing about his youngest sister: she was "reserved in demeanor and dress," and "never went to the kitchen except to cook, nor out of the house except to visit her own parents."[15]

Furthermore, a wife's judgment was to be exercised on behalf of the family as a whole, rather than for her own benefit or that of her own unit within the family. An extraordinary example is that of Mme Hou, who, to preserve her husband's family, sought clemency for the murderer of her own son:

> Mme Hou was the daughter of Hou Yan. She served her mother-in-law just as her husband served his mother, and she served her two elder sisters-in-law just as her husband served his elder brothers. When her sister-in-law's son murdered her son Lu, Mme Hou considered the matter and said to her husband, "Fortunately we still have our son Jun. But your brother [if executed] will have no posterity!" Thereupon she paid 100 *jin* to have [the murderer] released from jail. When he visited her husband, Gao Jin, to make restitution, Gao Jin refused to accept the money, and when he visited Mme Hou she refused as well, saying: "Did I pay to have you released in order to reap benefit for myself?"[16]

Such model wives put their husbands' needs above their own, but they were praised for being stern taskmistresses. Service to the men in her life, for such a wife, required her to demand high performance from them, if she was to fulfill her responsibilities. When Lady Zhang, the mother of Revenue Secretary Pei, was married to Pei's father, her parents-in-law were impressed by her womanly virtue and happily predicted that she would "cause our household to rise." Therefore, instead of rejoicing when her husband passed the provincial examination and became a county magistrate, with fine clothes and food, she wept and reminded him that: "Your parents said I would cause the family to rise! But this is only a small rise!" Her husband felt the force of her words and burst into tears himself, answering that she was correct, since he had risen no higher than his forbears. Shortly thereafter, he died. She then transferred her attentions to her son, weeping and reminding him that his father had not added to the family's accomplishments, and died without having accomplished a "great rise." "All that kept him from despair was his hope for you!" Pei took her words to heart, and gained the *jinshi* degree, resulting in his rank and her title. Thereupon she burst into tears again, saying: "Your father put his hopes in you, but didn't live to see you in office!" Her tears fell in streams, and thereupon Pei was moved to such great efforts that soon his name was known everywhere.[17]

No family harmony, however, could withstand the greatest danger, understood as jealousy between wives and concubines. Statutes and substatutes in the *Ming Code* show that the quarrelsome wife was perceived as a significant threat.[18] The model wife was one who made it easy for her new family to absorb her, and whose loyalty to the family led her to accept other necessary women as well.

A primary imperative shaping these epitaphs was the need to produce sons, bolster the network of marriage alliances by preserving the fiction that sons were always the issue of the legitimate wives, and advertise the families involved as worthy of those alliances. Concubines are presented in these epitaphs as a necessity, and the need for progeny trumps any emotional anguish one or another of the women may have felt. As Li Mengyang presents her, Shen *yiren* (Lady of Suitability, a title for Rank 5 wives) was the occasion of great jealousy on the part of the secondary wife (*fushi*) whom she displaced. In the full story of Shen *yiren*'s gradual conquest of the household, however, Li Mengyang eventually erases the secondary wife's voice, feelings, and even her service to the family:

> Originally, Dong had taken a wife from the Li family, but as Mme Li was sickly and had no sons, he took another wife from the Chen family. Shortly thereafter Mme Li died, and Dong took Shen as the wife who would succeed her. Chen felt greatly wronged by this, and she protested vigorously, saying: "I am the daughter of a scholarly family! My father and brother only let me become your secondary wife because they knew that Mme Li was sick, and had no sons. Day and night they repeated that if Mme Li happened by some misfortune to die, I would succeed her. And now you're marrying Shen, are you?" When Dong's relatives and members of the community heard this, they worried on Dong's behalf, saying that when Shen entered the household the two women were bound to compete.

Still, Shen's wifely competence won the whole family over, and soon, says Li Mengyang, Chen herself began to pay Shen the deference due to a principal wife. The two became like sisters, and the relatives and community members were all delighted, saying to each other that Dong was a happy man to have obtained two such sage and virtuous wives. Shortly, however, the process of Chen's erasure began:

> After about a year, Chen bore a son Lan. Shen held him in her arms, and treated him as though he were her own. Chen bore another son Run, and then a daughter. Shen treated them all as her own, and none of them knew that Shen was not their mother. Someone teased them, saying: "You are not really Shen's children!" The children did not believe it, and when finally they did learn the truth, they felt all the more strongly that Shen was their real mother.

"Even I," marveled Li Mengyang, who had been a close friend of the family, "had no idea that these were not Shen's children."[19] Similarly, Li Kaixian tells us that his own wife, all of whose children had died, was not jealous of his concubines,[20] and like Li Mengyang, he too marvels upon learning that the children of a neighbor are actually the children of a concubine.[21]

Family responsibilities were not restricted to women; they are also a frequent motif in epitaphs for men. The father of Prince Xishun of Fengqiu, for example, reached the age of forty without a son. Sorrowfully, he turned to his tutor for advice. "The virtuous inevitably have posterity," replied the tutor, whereupon the prince mended his ways, ceased to drink wine, curbed his desires—and produced four sons.[22] But whatever the virtues of the husband, the family needed to find a woman with the appropriate qualities to bear or mother these sons. When Mme Jia, wife of one of the Bulwarks-General of the State (*fuguo jiangjun*, a title given to direct descendants of the Ming founder) has a son who is incorrupt, frugal, filial, respectful, and clever, Li Mengyang sees this as her transmission of her own qualities to him, and calls her a "female gentleman."[23]

This conventional epitaph language could be used to express profound and painful emotion, as we see in an epitaph by Wang Jiusi (1468–1551) of Shaanxi Province, briefly Li Mengyang's colleague at the capital. Wang pours into his epitaph for his daughter not only his pain at losing her but also the pain he felt at disappointing his closest friend, the poet Kang Hai, to whose son she was married. She died shortly after her stillborn son, and Wang sees her as having died of despair at disappointing her father-in-law: "My daughter wept in angry frustration, and after three days the pains of regret and remorse attacked her stomach." Here again the language of household competence is used to signal the perfection of her human spirit: "My daughter dreamed of restoring the house to what it had been under her deceased mother-in-law. With her husband she discussed all the details of food offerings and sacrifices, of spinning and weaving, of what to feed the pigs and chickens. Vegetables, fruits, pickles and sauces—with none of these was she unconcerned. Who thought she would die now!" Clearly, this conventional language allows Wang to express real grief, over both the loss of his daughter and the loss of the grandson his dear friend had so longed for. "People say that you were like me," he writes to her, and to him, the clearest evidence of this is her concern with the pickles and the pigs. Whatever other qualities he may have prized in her, in this epitaph he treasures the way her perfect wifely competence deepened his connection to his friend.[24]

The language above is consistent across regions. All four writers praise women's household management, seclusion, modesty, and lack of jealousy. Where we see regional variation is in their treatment of women's literacy. Neither Li Mengyang nor Wang Jiusi mentions women's reading and writing at all. Shandong-based Li Kaixian writes conventionally of his sister's having "learned something of the classics by listening to me study,"[25] but also prefaces a friend's mother's collection of poetry by observing that her own father had praised her as being "in no way inferior to her brothers."[26] Gui Youguang, from book-rich Jiangsu Province, goes farthest: he lists in his epitaphs the books his subjects read (Buddhist sutras, *lienü zhuan*, and historical fiction), and describes one wife who had "had tutors in her youth" and "understood all affairs ancient and modern." She and her husband consoled themselves with books when he failed to advance in the civil-service examinations, much like the couple described by Wilt Idema in chapter 13 of this volume.[27]

FICTION

In another context, I noted that Ming dynasty *lienü* accounts, with their pathetic or horrific details, are products of the great age of Ming fiction.[28] The same can be said even of highly ritualized Ming *muzhiming*. He Jingming's language may be bland and formulaic, but Li Mengyang paints a vivid picture of household and community ferment in his epitaph for Shen *yiren* and her concubine rival. Such fiction-worthy accounts place *muzhiming* in a continuum with the tales of love, sex, resentment, and danger that make up the larger universe of Ming fiction, even as the epitaphs seek to prove that their subjects are untouched by those dangers.

Ming moralists recognized the perils of this fiction universe. Ye Sheng (1420–74), from Kunshan (Jiangsu Province), was distressed that with the recent proliferation of books, everyone, including peasants and "foolish, ignorant women," was learning history and morality from fiction rather than classical teachings.[29] Lü Kun (1536–1618) of Henan Province, a cosmopolitan official who spent much of his life in the capital and at various official posts, focused on dangerous trends in the education of girls, warning against teaching them to write songs, read "low tales" (*bi li zhi yan*), and hear "voluptuous music" (*yan yue*).[30] What matters for us is that these two men, a century apart, perceived that women *were* reading. Even if we treat their assertions as hyperbole (Ye Sheng claims that "every household" has a collection of popular books), we are reminded of the sea of popular culture surrounding women at all social levels. What were they reading, or hearing recited, or watching onstage?

The stories with the most complex relation to the epitaph ideals are those of romantic love. Fiction had been blurring the line between married and unmarried love for some time. From the seventh through the seventeenth centuries, young people from good families were increasingly depicted in literature as having sexual relationships, enjoying them, and getting married only afterward.[31] Hong Pian's *Sixty Stories* includes the tale of the strong-willed Han dynasty heroine Zhuo Wenjun, who ignored her father's wishes and eloped with the poet Sima Xiangru.[32] In the twelfth-century storyteller's version of the famous *Xixiang ji* (Romance of the Western Chamber), where the maid Hongniang brings hero and heroine together for nights of clandestine love, the descriptions of sex are cheerfully explicit, and the story as transformed for the stage remained immensely popular in the Ming and Qing.[33] In the extraordinary thirteenth-century novella *Jiao hong zhuan*, the lovers settle in to a comfortable quasi-marriage under the noses of the girl's unobservant parents, before her misguided father drives them to suicide.[34]

This ideal of romantic attraction did not lead to the dissolution of society that Lü Kun feared. ("If young men and women, in their immaturity, let loose their desires and indecently contravene the Rites, how can the Way of the superior man be carried out?")[35] In the *Sixty Stories* version, it is Zhuo Wenjun's conventional wise management that enables the couple to survive until her husband can get ahead: when Sima Xiangru worries that he has no business skills, Zhuo Wenjun—always referring to herself as *jian qie*, "your unworthy concubine"—competently sells her ornaments so that they can open the wine shop that will see them through hard times. By unanimous consent, Chinese culture transformed *Yingying zhuan*, Yuan Zhen's ninth-century story of shamefaced and bittersweet clandestine love, into *The Romance of the Western Chamber*, which retains the illicit lovemaking but ends with happy marriage and success in the civil-service examinations.[36] Love stories seem to have enriched the entire culture's emotional palette. Sex outside of ritual bounds was something that could never be admitted for governing-class women, but as Anne McLaren points out, a deluxe edition of *Romance of the Western Chamber,* which only the wealthy could have afforded, was published in Beijing at the same time as *chantefables* that are discussed below.[37] As Kathryn Lowry has shown, Ming manuals even recommended phrases from *Western Chamber* as the appropriate language for letters between husbands and wives.[38]

This ideal of married love had a great impact on the way men wrote about their deceased wives. It became conventional to say that grief for one's wife was so great that it overstepped ritual bounds. (This enabled widowers to understand themselves as men of deep feeling, an important literati value in the middle to late Ming.) The irrepressible Li Mengyang was convinced that in his grief he had been vouchsafed a miracle: "The day following her death," he writes, "we sacrificed in her honor. When the intestines of the sacrificial animal were boiled, they spontaneously coiled in such a way as to weave themselves into the shape of written characters *yin* and *yang,* with tassels hanging down and loops above. When I saw this, my agony redoubled. I cried out to her spirit, and wrote the three poems *Jie chang* [Linked intestines]."[39]

For Ming Chinese, the intestine was the seat of emotion: to be broken-hearted was to *duan chang,* split the intestine. *Yin* and *yang* symbolize the complementary union of the genders. An excerpt from the first poem shows Li weaving both images into a despairing cry to his wife:

> Oh pain! The boar's intestines coiled inside the pot.
> Her spirit was dimly present; our hearts were terrified.
> Coiling into balls of meat, they burst out of the broth,
> Twisting left, coiling right, everywhere flowing yellow,
> Weaving themselves together, to write out *yin* and *yang.*
> Paired characters, miraculous, like a phoenix and his mate,
> Tassels hanging down below, and five-inch loops above.
> Why would you have done this, unless you had some purpose?
> Repeatedly I call to ask, but still your soul escapes.
> Ten times I call unanswered; a hundred times I sob—
> Intestines! Intestines! Paired forevermore.

In the third poem, Li employs phrases standard in lovers' language:

> Dust covers embroidered coverlets, wronging the mandarin ducks,
> And the pendants on the silken curtains clink in the midnight wind.

Li Mengyang's friend Zhao Ze also "gave way to emotion" that "exceeded the rites," and he too was vouchsafed a miracle: a magpie (symbol of fidelity) landed on his wife's coffin, and cried out to him in her voice.[40]

The ideal of married love eroticized even the widow-fidelity motif central to the Ming discourse on women's virtue. In an extant fragment of *Xinbian guafu lienü zhuan shiqu* (Newly edited poems and songs on widows and martyred chaste maidens), a collection published in 1465 by the Lu family of Jintai, it is made quite clear that widow-fidelity derives from the memory of passion:[41]

> Heavens!
> When I remember him as he was in the early days,
> He and I sharing our hearts and striking each others' fancy,
> You'd have thought he was Zhang Chang, painting my eyebrows,
> or He Lang touching up my powder.
> Who would have thought him a short-lived Yan Hui!
> He was my fated lover and I was his—
> How much better if we had managed to die together.[42]

Similar language occurs in Ming dynasty governing-class women's poetry:

> Awakened from daydreaming by twittering birds,
> She leans languidly on a silver screen.
> Her slender brows have not been painted by Scholar Zhang—
> She's too shy to see green willow eyes in the east wind.[43]

But the romantic ideal did not affect men and women identically. Love, for young women, was a double-edged sword. On the one hand, the primary value of wifely fidelity was exalted in the language of romantic love (thus, even *The Romance of the Western Chamber* could be harnessed in the service of marriage). But on the other, sexual promiscuity was a social and legal marker associated with courtesans and bondservants, and, just as Beverly Bossler describes for the Song, women of good family had to make sure that no sexual taint would place them in that debased class. Bossler demonstrates that for Song dynasty literati men, association with an educated courtesan could be a sign of high cultivation and integrity. This was also a major hallmark of male literati sociality in the Ming.[44] But for *liang* (noncourtesan) women, any taint of sexual promiscuity could be devastating: the gazetteer of Gui Youguang's Kunshan County reported the suicide of a county clerk's wife after another functionary made a sexual advance.[45] Nor, despite widespread use of their tropes to reinscribe the value of traditional marriage, did romantic tales guarantee that paradise could be realized on earth: the lovers in *Jiao hong zhuan* can realize union only in death, a sentiment echoed in the widow's song above.[46] Unmarried girls may have been frightened of married sex, given the tales they had probably heard about "teasing the bride," currently promoted on Shaanxi tourism websites as a charming bit of tradition, but in Ming times a frightening ruckus created by the groom's friends as the bride underwent her sexual initiation.

And finally, a young woman may have mistrusted any sexual stirrings of her own, since female sexuality was widely represented as monstrous. In one of the Chenghua-era prose-verse narratives discussed below, a family's only son is seduced by a beautiful maiden, who is actually, once unmasked by the famous Judge Bao, a ravenous tiger. A century later, the 1572 Haizhou County (Jiangsu) gazetteer reported that a tiger was demanding the yearly sacrifice of a young boy, but was temporarily tamed by a man who stole her tiger-skin robes, revealed her as a woman, and married her and had two children before she answered the call of the wild and abandoned the family. (The gazetteer editors note that "all details of this account can be verified.")[47]

Two of Hong Pian's *Sixty Stories* tell an even more frightening tale: in the third story, *Xi hu san ta ji* (The three pagodas at West Lake), a young man is entrapped by an old crone covered in chicken skin, who leads him to the side-chamber of a Daoist monastery, a magical place with jeweled eaves and red-washed walls, where a beautiful woman in white seduces him. Soon, however, another young man is brought in, and the old crone and her daughter extract and eat his heart and liver. After half a month of lovemaking, our young hero's skin is yellow and his body emaciated, and he realizes that he is next in line to be sacrificed. He escapes, and his mother nurses him back to health. The same crone and beauty appear in the eighth story, *Luoyang san guai ji* (The three demons of Luoyang), and once again a Daoist priest manages to destroy them.

These succubi endanger vulnerable young men, but women could also be seen as threatening the whole of society by refusing to follow the rules of traditional marriage. Yenna Wu has analyzed the seventh in Hong Pian's *Sixty Stories, Kuaizui Li Cuilian* (The fast-talking Li Cuilian), whose heroine blithely repudiates all the canons of silence and obedience we have seen in the epitaphs above.[48] Li Cuilian bursts onto the page rejecting the virtues of the ideal husband:

> Everyone says a good son-in-law
> Is well-endowed with jewels and wealth,
> Great and rich, and clever, too,
> Knows how to play chess, and all the Six Arts,
> His poems brilliant, his couplets smart.
> As a businessman, nothing he can't do.
> What do I want with a man like that?
> He's a bitter brew that goes down flat."

Bidding farewell at her natal family altar, she first prays for the prosperity of her husband's family, but then reveals a startling ulterior motive:

> If I have any luck [she informs her ancestors], within three years the entire family will die off, and all their possessions come under my control. After that, I should be able to live for a few happy years.

Her horrified parents implore her to keep her mouth closed when she goes to her new home, lest she turn them into a laughingstock, but by the time her mother visits three days after the wedding, Cuilian has insulted the matchmaker and her husband's entire family. She wants nothing to do with the rituals at his ancestral hall ("Why turn West? And why turn East?"). She lets her terrified young husband into the marriage bed on condition that he keep his mouth shut, and she asks her mother-in-law:

> What's the hurry? What's the rush?
>   when told to start her wifely work the next morning.
> She is as competent as any of the wives praised in the epitaphs above:
> I'm not vain, but since my youth
> I've always known just what to do!
> I can weave gauze, I can spin hemp,
> Embroider silk, or cut and mend.
> Make things coarse, or fix things fine,
> Three teas, six meals, ready on time!

But when her father-in-law reminds her that a daughter-in-law should be "gentle and yielding (*wen rou*)," she retorts that on the contrary, from childhood on her nature has been firm (*gang*). Predictably, she is returned to her parents, and her mother, father, brother, and sister-in-law all berate her for the family's loss of face. She solves the problem by changing into her old clothes, and leaving for a nunnery.

Sixty Stories does not represent Li Cuilian's first appearance in literature. Wu points out a long line of such "Problem Daughter" stories, with antecedents dating back to the Han. Li Cuilian herself can be found in an eighth-century *bianwen* text from Dunhuang, and the prosimetric form of this tale in the sixteenth-century *Sixty Stories* suggests that it spread in both oral and written versions, quite plausibly reaching Li Mengyang's epitaph subjects, or women like them, in Henan Province. Another Li Cuilian storyline, in which her husband rescues her soul from the underworld, has persisted in drama texts from Ming times to the present. This alternate Li Cuilian is quite happy to be reunited with her husband, but her sojourn in Hell has the same cause as her divorce in "The Fast-Talking Li Cuilian," namely her refusal to be an obedient and secluded wife. (She has been using family money to feed Buddhist monks, and when her suspicious husband berates her, she hangs herself.)[49]

"The Fast-Talking Li Cuilian" is remarkable in that our clever heroine is completely unapologetic. The story pokes fun not at Li Cuilian, but at everyone who rebukes her. Does this indicate a subterranean current of anti-patriarchal women's literature? Probably, as I have suggested above, it does not. This atypically unapologetic version of the Problem Daughter story was published—and doubtless written—by a reasonably well-educated man, and if we read the story solely as women's subversion of power, we will miss seeing Li Cuilian's appeal to both women and men. It is far more productive to read it as a tale whose multivalence could elicit positive responses from widely different subject positions: from wives who remembered well the difficulties of being a new daughter-in-law, but also from men who lived in an official culture where individuals who stood up to misguided authority were highly valued (though most of them came to grief). Given Li Cuilian's repudiation of the family model so prized by literati culture, she may have been something of a guilty pleasure for men, but we must remember that the story, with its intrepid heroine and her ready tongue, was male-published.[50]

Nevertheless, this comedy has its darker side. Li Cuilian's prayer for the death of her husband's entire family exposes the inherent strains in the traditional marriage model. The dominant pattern, in which wives came to live with their husbands' families, made each wedding a potential crisis: would new brides be loyal? Would they bear sons? Would they help their mothers-in-law, and get along with the other household women? If not, the family might crumble, and with it (by Ming times) the state. Both Yenna Wu and Keith McMahon have analyzed the recurring trope of the virago or shrew in Chinese literature, recurrences that endlessly restate the dangers of bringing an outsider into the nest.[51] By telling a tale, we attempt to master its content, and Li Cuilian reminds us that this particular content was difficult, if not impossible, to master.

Equally difficult was the relationship between wives and concubines, as we can intuit from the need felt by all three of our epitaph writers to assure us that wives were "not jealous." A fifteenth-century *chantefable* collection contains a version of the most famous of all bad concubine stories, that of the fourth Song emperor Ren, raised by the evil Empress Liu, who had stolen him as a baby and banished his real mother.[52] The *chantefable* version, *Song Renzong ren mu ji* (Emperor Renzong of the Song acknowledges his mother) frames this as a detective story: the legendary Judge Bao, stopping at a temple en route to court, finds a filthy old woman living in an abandoned kiln. When he ferrets out the truth of her identity, he compels the emperor to recognize her as his mother. In this story, virtue triumphs, but as a monstrous return of the repressed: the emperor's mother is dirty, unkempt, and unruly, smacking Judge Bao when he refuses to believe her at first. Once cleaned up, however, the emperor's mother pardons Empress Liu and saves her from otherwise certain death, "since after all, she cared for my baby," and the two women live out their lives in sisterly harmony.

In this popular tale, the cultural obsession with the wife-concubine relationship has completely rewritten the historical record. John Chaffee has analyzed the career of the actual Empress Liu (969–1033), from her plebeian origins to her apogee as regent for her adopted son, Emperor Ren.[53] (Like Patricia Ebrey in her treatment of the Song Empress Xiang in chapter 11 of this volume, Chaffee has turned to Song dynasty miscellanies and unofficial histories to fill out the spare accounts in the official Song history.) Emperor Ren was born in 1010 to a palace maid surnamed Li, and was "treated as her own" by the childless then-Consort Liu, whom Emperor Zhen, Renzong's father, was already trying to exalt to Empress. Lady Li (promoted to consort and posthumously made an empress) was effectively removed from her maternal role. Empress Liu was exalted in 1012, and she became regent for Ren in 1022 upon Zhenzong's death. Lady Li lived out her obscure days in the imperial harem until her death sometime before 1033, when Empress Liu died and Emperor Ren learned the truth of his parentage. Emperor Ren thus never met or acknowledged his mother during her lifetime, Lady Li was sequestered but never exiled (and certainly not cast into poverty), and, needless to say, no Judge Bao ever brought the protagonists together.

But the fictional Judge Bao had long served as a symbol of cosmic justice, and it was cosmic resolution that audiences sought in "Emperor Ren Acknowledges His Mother."[54] Significantly, though retribution is meted out in the *chantefable* (Lady Li takes a stick to the emperor, and the emperor threatens Empress Liu with strangulation), the plot resolves matters by displacing actual criminality onto the underlings who perpetuated the deception, and the final message is one of reconciliation. Cosmic intervention accomplishes what actual families apparently found endlessly difficult.

Who consumed this story? Here, too, the sixteenth-century version is not the earliest. Records exist of a late Yuan play with the same title from Jiangxi Province,[55] and we can infer the likely currency of this tale in Li Mengyang's Henan Province from the fact that Emperor Ren is buried there. Ann McLaren's meticulous account shows that the *chantefable* version was printed in Beijing but discovered in the late-fifteenth-century tomb of a Jiading County bureaucrat and his wife.[56] This temporal and geographical range, and evidence that similar *chantefables* were purchased in cheap editions and memorized for recitation in private homes, gives us every reason to assume that the story was known to women like the subjects of Li Mengyang's epitaphs, as indeed it is known to opera fans—including YouTube watchers—today.[57]

On its surface, this tale resolves just as happily as the conflict between Li Mengyang's Shen *yiren* and concubine Chen, but like the Li Cuilian story, its appeal is multivalent, and not all of the appeal is to virtuous impulses. Legitimate wives might secretly wish the concubine-mothers of their adopted sons out of the way, but for concubines, the story could serve as a fantasy of revenge on the women who stole their children. Husbands stuck in lower levels of the bureaucracy, or unable to enter it at all, might enjoy the detective prowess of Judge Bao, able to command even the emperor. Like all successful fiction, this story refuses to oversimplify: it reinscribes the traditional value of wife-concubine harmony, but validates the audience's awareness that such harmony might be purchased at great price.

Here, too, however, there is a darker note. As fictional protagonists, Li Cuilian and Lady Li could tap into general fears about vengeance by women scorned. Gazetteers show us a long line of women mistreated by their communities who were thought to come back as vengeful spirits, causing pestilence and drought. Well into the Ming, shrines in Yangzhou placated a Han dynasty daughter-in-law unjustly accused of murder,[58] and Gui Youguang notes that a three-year drought in Jiading County was only broken by the conviction of a woman's murderer and the erection of a shrine to his victim.[59] These well-attested fears can help explain the continuing appeal of stories acknowledging the difficulties facing women, and offering imaginative resolution of those difficulties.

Though the epitaphs above are constrained by convention, there is no reason to think that they were insincere. Wise management and devoted service were understood as the ways women realized moral personhood, and successful families were very grateful to the women who helped them prosper socially and economically. *Muzhiming* writers expressed society's gratitude by creating epitaphs that were fictional in their own way, omitting all negative details, and assimilating women's "lives" to an easily discernible template. The template is evidence of values deeply held, and it shows us that exemplary wives could expect sincere admiration and intense grief when they died.

We can imagine that young women's relief at earning acceptance in their new homes, and the feeling that they had lived up to their parents' hopes, made the ideals of the epitaphs seem much the safest life choice, however much a rule-breaking story told in the kitchen may have helped them sublimate anger at the difficulties of marriage. The rules themselves survived these assaults because the stories offered ways to break the rules and still return to the fold: illicit love could end in marriage or union after death, and Buddhism offered a safe and culturally acceptable haven to those whom marriage did not suit.

Did the women for whom Li Mengyang wrote epitaphs read these particular stories? We have good reason to think that this kind of material was known to elite women. Sixteenth-century literati enthusiasm for *Romance of the Western Chamber* assures us that bureaucrats as well as well-to-do merchants were among the purchasers—and once a book entered the household, it is folly to assume that no women saw it. The fifteenth-century *chantefables* were found in the tomb of a local elite, and the *chantefables* typically address themselves to an audience of "good men and women."[60]

We can in fact see the stories as strengthening the society of good men and women, including both the governors and the governed. Transgressive as they seem at first glance, these tales survived in Chinese culture for centuries. By appealing to a variety of subject positions, they offered both women and men a range of ways to think about the self. Comedic for the most part (even *Jiao hong zhuan* ends with union after death, and even the young men endangered by succubi are restored to health by their mothers), the stories offer cosmic resolution of problems that bedeviled generation after generation.

By admitting that problems existed (concubines continually lost their children to legitimate wives, and the image of the harsh mother-in-law haunts even the epitaph literature), and by framing the problems in such a way as to afford pleasure to readers (who does not enjoy Li Cuilian's quick tongue?), fiction opened the closed loop of the epitaph prescriptions, allowing one to safely think dangerous thoughts. The social order in which these epitaphs and stories served as foils for each other would break down only later, under pressures as yet foreign to these fifteenth and sixteenth-century women.

11. Empress Xiang (1046-1101) and Biographical Sources beyond Formal Biographies

Patricia Ebrey

The dynastic histories regularly included biographies of empresses, including consorts promoted to empress after their sons gained the throne. These biographies share problems of stereotyping and convention common to other women's biographies, such as the *lienü* biographies discussed by Harriet Zurndorfer, Nanxiu Qian, and other contributors to this volume. In the case of empresses, however, other historical sources often let us reconstruct fuller accounts of their lives. For the Song period, enough information is included in standard sources to reconstruct what was undoubtedly a central part of their lives—the birth, death, or marriage out of the emperor's children, whether their own or their "legal" children born to other consorts. In the cases of empresses who served as regents, either temporarily or for long stretches of time, we have in addition all the sources on the political history of the court, which for the Song and later periods are generally very rich. Of course, the standard political narratives have their own limitations, as very few texts concerned with court politics escaped rewriting motivated by factional politics, but modern historiographical research has done much to teach us how to read these sources.[1]

During the Northern Song period (960–1126), four widowed empresses played major political roles. When Zhenzong (r. 997–1022) died in 1022, his widow Empress Dowager Liu presided over the succession of her stepson, Renzong (r. 1022–63), then only thirteen *sui*, and served as regent until her death in 1032.[2] After Shenzong (r. 1067–85) died in 1085, his mother, Grand Empress Dowager Gao, presided over the succession of her grandson Zhezong (r. 1085–1100), then ten *sui*. She served as regent until her death eight years later. Gao proved a forceful ruler who rescinded most of the New Policies introduced by Shenzong and Wang Anshi (1021–86), making her a hero to the conservative or antireformist faction. Zhezong, when he got the opportunity to rule on his own, did his best to reverse everything she had done and reintroduced his father's policies. When Zhezong died without an heir in 1100, his legal mother and Shenzong's widow, Empress Dowager Xiang, presided over the succession and for half a year co-ruled with the new ruler, Huizong (r. 1100–1125). In 1127, after Qinzong (r. 1125–27), his sons, and his abdicated father, Huizong, were all taken captive by the Jurchens, Empress Meng, the empress that Zhezong had deposed in 1096 and who had been living in a Daoist nunnery for most of the intervening thirty years, was called on to play the role of kingmaker and name the only one of Huizong's sons to escape captivity as the next emperor (Gaozong, r. 1127–62).[3]

In this chapter I examine the biographical sources for the third of these women, Empress Xiang. After translating her biography in the *History of the Song Dynasty*, I show that much of what it omits can be found in other sources, ones that could be used for any Song empress. However, what makes Xiang's case particularly attractive to me is the chance survival of the diary of Zeng Bu (1035–1107), one of the members of the Council of State during the time she participated in the government.[4] This highly detailed diary records conversations among the councilors both in and outside of the imperial presence, and was meant to serve as a type of minute-taking. The three chapters that survived by being copied into the *Yongle dadian* cover the last nine months of Zhezong's reign and the first six of Huizong's. This diary records many conversations between Empress Dowager Xiang and either the group of councilors or Zeng Bu alone, making it possible to discern more of her take on her situation than any other source.

EMPRESS XIANG'S *SONG HISTORY* BIOGRAPHY

Empress Xiang's biography in the *History of the Song* is short enough to translate in full:

> Shenzong's Qinsheng Xiansu Empress Xiang was a native of Henei and the great-granddaughter of the past grand councilor, Xiang Minzhong (948–1019). In 1066 she married the Prince of Ying and was given the title of Lady of Anguo. When [her husband] Shenzong took the throne [the next year], she was promoted to empress.
>
> When Shenzong became ill, Empress Xiang participated with Empress Dowager Gao in settling the decision on the succession. When Zhezong took the throne, she was promoted to Empress Dowager. When Empress Dowager Gao ordered the renovation of the old Blessings Longevity [Qingshou] Hall for her to live in, she demurred, saying, "How can I let

my mother-in-law live to the west and I as daughter-in-law live to the east? This violates hierarchical order." Since she wouldn't move, she lived in a rear hall of Blessings Longevity Hall called Abundant Protection [Longyou] Hall.

When the emperor was going to divine for an empress for himself and wives for [his younger brothers] the princes, Empress Xiang ruled that no girls from the Xiang clan should be included in the group for selection. When among her patrilineal kin there were men who wanted to make use of the precedent to change to a job in the Office of Audience Ceremonies, or when one of them with the rank of a selected man wanted capital rank, even when there were special orders allowing this, the empress would say, "My clan has never used this precedent. What use is there in letting your private feelings disturb rules for the common good?" Not in one case did she let the request be granted. When Zhezong unexpectedly died, she alone decided to welcome Prince Duan [to take the throne].[5] Zhang Dun argued against the plan but was not able to block it.

When Huizong took the throne, he asked her to share governing the country and the armies with him, but she demurred on the grounds that he was an adult ruler. The emperor begged her with tears until she relented. The worthy scholar-officials whom Zhang Dun had had banished in the Shaosheng (1094–97) and Yuanfu periods (1098–1100) began a few at a time to be employed [at court] again. She did not institute any of the practices [of former empress dowagers who participated in government] such as holding court in the main halls, observing her natal family's taboo names, or establishing a holiday for her birthday. Joy would show on her face whenever she heard of good deeds, like entertaining elders, lessening labor service, giving rest to troops, generosity to the common people, or promoting frugality. In less than six months she returned the government [to Huizong].

In the first month of the next year she passed away at age fifty-six. The emperor continually thought of her and several times added to the favors bestowed on his two maternal uncles, Xiang Zongliang and Xiang Zonghui, who both received the title Kaifu yitong sansi and were enfeoffed as princes. In addition, in an unprecedented act, Xiang Minzhong's three generations of ancestors were posthumously given the rank of princes.[6]

This biography shares many of the conventions of biographies of empresses in the *History of the Song*. We learn that Xiang had impeccable family origins. With a highly admired grand councilor among her forbears, she came from the civil elite, not the military elite that had supplied many of the empresses.[7] We are given evidence of her character through carefully selected incidents that show her interacting with her mother-in-law Gao and her legal son Huizong. With Gao, she is shown as continuing to treat herself as the daughter-in-law even after she was a widow herself and her legal son Zhezong was on the throne. Her relationship with Huizong is less fully sketched. She defended his interests against the opposition of the grand councilor Zhang Dun, but made no effort to run the government the way her mother-in-law had done, "turning back" the government to Huizong within six months. The historian also strongly implies that her participation in Huizong's government had something to do with the return to court of conservatives who had been banished by Zhezong.

This biography acknowledges the stereotype of the powerful empress who helps her own relatives by taking pains to disassociate Xiang with such empresses. Thus a substantial proportion of the biography is taken up with relating that she refused requests from her relatives and would not allow girls from her family to be considered as wives of the next generation of imperial sons. By stressing that she promptly returned the government to Huizong, the biographer is acknowledging that his readers were aware that both Liu and Gao did not relinquish power when their charges were old enough to take over themselves, but rather kept it until their own deaths.

Some of what this biography leaves out is easy to recognize. It says nothing about Xiang's relationship with her husband, Shenzong. It mentions no children she bore. It says nothing of her relationships with her husband's other consorts, including the mothers of Zhezong and Huizong. Nor does it say anything about her relations with her daughters-in-law. Let me now turn to other sources that allow us to probe more deeply into these other relationships.

RECONSTRUCTING THE WOMEN AND CHILDREN AMONG WHOM EMPRESS XIANG LIVED

Standard sources contain enough vital data to figure out the principal residents in the palace during any particular year. These data include when consorts received titles and when they died, when sons were born and died, when daughters received titles and died or married out, and the identity of each child's mother.[8] Figure 8.1 gives a simplified genealogy based on these sources. Here, let me summarize what we can infer about Empress Xiang's thirty-five years in the palace (1066–1101) in these regards.

In 1066, when Xiang was twenty-one *sui*, she became the wife of the eldest son of Emperor Yingzong (r. 1063–67). Her husband Shenzong was

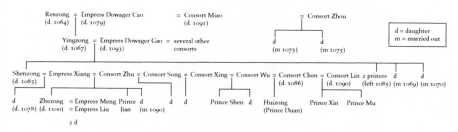

FIGURE 11.1. A simplified genealogy of the imperial family while Empress Xiang lived in the palace (1066–1101). Children who had left by 1066, or who did not survive to age five, are omitted.

nineteen *sui*, his father's eldest son, and before the end of that year would be formally appointed heir apparent. Early in the next year, Yingzong died and Shenzong ascended the throne. Xiang then was appointed empress.

The women attached to former emperors did not leave the palace when the occupant of the throne changed, so Xiang was not the senior woman in the palace. Her grandmother-in-law, Renzong's last empress, Grand Empress Dowager Cao, was still alive at fifty-two *sui*. Three of the daughters born to Renzong and given titles in 1060 and 1061 were living in the palace, then probably seven and eight *sui*. There were also two higher-ranked widowed consorts of Renzong: Miss Miao, who received her first rank in 1038 and in the 1060s held the third-rank title of Defei, and Miss Zhou, who had entered the palace at age four to be with her aunt, received her first title in 1059, bore two daughters, and was given titles in 1060 and 1061. Miss Miao was undoubtedly in her late forties, but Miss Zhou may have been less than ten years older than Empress Xiang.

Empress Xiang's contacts would have been closer with her husband's immediate family. Her mother-in-law, Empress Dowager Gao, at thirty-five *sui* was just fourteen years older than she was. Besides Shenzong, four of Gao's younger children were still living at home, including two daughters probably in their mid-teens (as they would leave to marry in 1069 and 1070) and two sons, one seventeen *sui*, the other eleven *sui*. These two brothers-in-law would continue to live in the palace after marrying, an exceptional arrangement based on Empress Gao's desire to keep them close.[9] Gao had co-widows, as Yingzong had taken other consorts. None of them, however, had born any children. Still, at least three continued to receive promotions in rank for the next two decades.

The families of the former emperors naturally began to recede in prominence as the children grew older and moved out and the new emperor acquired both additional consorts and children of his own. In 1069 and 1070 Shenzong's two remaining sisters married out. Empress Xiang was the first of Shenzong's consorts to bear a child, a girl who received her first title in 1067 and seems to have been born before he ascended the throne. In 1069 three women received titles as Shenzong's consorts. Miss Song gave birth to Shenzong's first son in 1069, but the baby did not survive the year. In 1070 Miss Zhang gave birth to the second daughter, and in 1071 Miss Xing gave birth to the second son, who did not survive a month. Both Miss Xing and Miss Zhang started as ordinary palace ladies (palace servants) and were promoted to the ranks of consorts after Shenzong took an interest in them (or perhaps not until he had gotten them pregnant). Empress Xiang never bore another child after the daughter she bore in 1067, so it is quite possible that Shenzong was more attracted to the palace ladies than to his formal wife.

By 1075, when Shenzong had been on the throne eight years, two more children had been born. In 1073 Miss Song bore the third son, and the next year an unidentified woman the fourth, though that baby died within two days. Both Empress Xiang's and Consort Zhang's daughters were growing up, however, and another palace lady, Miss Zhu, had been promoted to consort. The next year, in 1076, she gave birth to the sixth son. Since four of the first five sons had lived less than two years, the new baby had only one elder brother when he was born, and that brother (son three) would die in 1077 at age five *sui*. By this point, almost all of the children in the palace were Shenzong's, as two of Renzong's daughters left to be married in 1075, leaving only one.

Renzong's empress, Grand Empress Dowager Cao, died in 1079, making Xiang's mother-in-law Empress Dowager Gao the highest-ranking woman in the palace. Now that Gao no longer had to wait on Cao as her daughter-in-law, Xiang probably spent more time attending to Gao. She no longer had any children of her own to look after, as her only child, the first girl, had died in 1078 at age twelve *sui*. In fact, in 1080 Shenzong had only two living children, a son born in 1076 and another in 1078. In 1081 the younger of these two boys died, placing all hopes for orderly succession on a single boy. Probably in response to this precarious situation, Shenzong began favoring other palace women. In 1082 the palace ladies Guo, Chen, Wu, and Lin all received titles as consorts and all bore children that year or the next. Four of the children born in these two years were boys, three born in 1082 and two in 1083. By the end of 1084 there were seven living children, two girls and five boys. Moreover, several of the consorts were pregnant.

In the third month of 1085, Empress Xiang's life took a dramatic turn when her husband Shenzong died of illness at thirty-eight *sui*. His eldest son, Consort Zhu's son Zhezong, then ten *sui*, was placed on the throne. Xiang's mother-in-law acted as regent and proved a strong-willed ruler. Consort Zhu was promoted because of her son's accession, but not to empress dowager, as Xiang was still living. Zhu did, however, move to her own palace complex, known as Sagely Good Omen Palace.

Once the consorts who were pregnant when Shenzong died gave birth, there were naturally no births in the palace for some years, but the composition of those living in the palace changed in other ways. Grand Empress Dowager Gao's two younger sons finally moved out with their families (her youngest daughter also left to marry in 1085). In 1090 Zhezong's elder sister married out and Grand Empress Dowager Gao and Empress Dowager Xiang began making plans for Zhezong's own marriage and the less crucial marriages of his younger siblings.

Even after he had married at seventeen *sui* in 1092, Zhezong was not treated as a full adult, and his grandmother continued to sit next to him behind a screen at court audiences. The next year, however, Grand Empress Dowager Gao died, and Zhezong began to rule on his own. At that point, twenty-seven years after she entered the palace, Xiang became the highest ranking woman there.

By the late 1090s, Zhezong's younger brothers and sisters were leaving the palace. Mansions were built for the five younger brothers, who moved out one by one between 1095 and 1099. Occasionally, Zhezong would go to visit them, sometimes taking Empress Dowager Xiang and the princes' mothers with him. It was at just this time that Zhezong started to have children of his own. Their survival rate was not any better than that of his own siblings; of the five children born from 1096 to 1099, only two survived infancy, and they both were girls.

Late in 1099, Zhezong, then twenty-four *sui*, became gravely ill, and he died in the first month of 1100. Empress Dowager Xiang, as the senior empress, chose Huizong, the second oldest of the surviving brothers of Zhezong, to succeed.

THE AFFAIR OF EMPRESS MENG AND CONSORT LIU

The standard historical sources provide not only vital data but also narratives of events that would have been important to Empress Xiang, even though her own biography is silent on them. A good example is the rivalry that developed between her daughters-in-law. Their conflicts eventually led to accusations of witchcraft against Empress Meng, a secret investigation run by palace eunuchs, the deposing of Empress Meng, the death of several people connected to her, and the eventual promotion of Consort Liu to empress.[10]

While Grand Empress Dowager Gao was still alive, she discussed with the councilors the need to find an empress for Zhezong. The officials supported the tradition of selecting from "meritorious families," which generally meant families that had played a part in the establishment of the dynasty more than a century earlier. The Gao and Xiang families were mentioned as particularly suitable, but both families reported that they did not have girls of the appropriate ages. Empress Dowager Gao agreed that virtue was the most important attribute of a prospective empress, but asked rhetorically how it could be determined when the girl lived at home in seclusion.[11] Perhaps answering her own question, she had more than a hundred girls brought to the palace in order to select an appropriate empress for Zhezong.[12]

In less than half a year, Empress Dowager Gao had narrowed the selection down to ten girls from nine families, and reported to her councilors that a Miss Meng was the best, despite the fact that she was three years older than preferred. She argued that it was best that the family not be too eminent because of the danger that its daughter would then be arrogant, and the officials agreed to have the Meng family closely investigated.[13] Late in 1092 the marriage took place.

After Empress Dowager Gao died, Zhezong was free to show his resentment for the way she had dominated him. He turned against the wife she had picked for him, perhaps in large part because he associated her with Gao. He tolerated, perhaps even encouraged, his favorite, Consort Liu, to act rudely to his young empress. Then when Liu accused Meng of consorting with occult practitioners, he ordered one of the chief eunuchs to conduct a judicial investigation into alleged conspiracies in the women's quarters. After thirty of the palace women and eunuchs were tortured, some ending up with broken bones or their tongues cut out, all sorts of accusations came into the open. For instance, Meng was accused of having had a picture of Liu drawn and then driving a nail through her heart in the picture, hoping in this way to kill her. She was also accused of writing "happiness" on a piece of paper, burning it, and putting the ashes into tea to be served to Zhezong as a way to get him to shift his affections.[14]

After receiving the report on the investigation, Zhezong told his councilors that the "two palaces," (that is, his legal mother Xiang and his actual mother Zhu) had instructed him in writing to depose Meng. His officials discussed the issue with him at length, clearly recognizing that interrogations under torture, especially of weak women, did not necessarily uncover the truth, but they also recognized that Zhezong believed himself to be in danger. In the end they acquiesced to his decision to depose Meng and send her to a Daoist temple.[15]

SELECTING HUIZONG TO SUCCEED

The next event important in Xiang's life, her role in selecting Huizong to succeed to the throne, is recorded most fully in Zeng Bu's diary.

When Zhezong lay dying, the Council of State had four members, Zeng Bu, Zhang Dun, Cai Bian, and Xu Jiang. Although all four can be classed as supporters of Wang Anshi's New Policies (usually called the reformers), they competed among themselves and Zeng Bu saw Zhang Dun as his chief adversary. On the morning of 1100/1/12, when Zeng and the other councilors arrived at the palace, the eunuch manager sent them to a hall where Empress Dowager Xiang received them from behind a screen. She told them that Zhezong had died, and since he had no sons, a decision had to be made concerning the succession. According to Zeng Bu:

> Before the others could answer Zhang Dun in a harsh voice said, "According to the rites and the statutes, Prince Jian should be installed, since as a brother with the same mother, he is the closest." I was surprised and had not yet responded when the empress dowager said, "All of them from Prince Shen on down are all Shenzong's sons. It would be difficult to distinguish among them. Prince Shen has sick eyes. The next is Prince Duan, so he should be established. Moreover, the late emperor once said that Prince Duan would have a long and prosperous life. [Prince Duan] once said, 'For some reason the emperor is unhappy. What has happened?'"[16]
> I quickly responded, "Zhang Dun has not talked this over with the rest of us. Your Majesty's instructions are extremely appropriate." Cai Bian also said, "It is up to Your Majesty," and Xu Jiang concurred, which silenced Zhang Dun.[17]

During this exchange, Zeng Bu records, more than a hundred palace eunuchs were standing in line outside the screen listening to the conversation. Zeng Bu called to one of them to summon Zhezong's five younger brothers. The eunuch astutely pointed out, "Before the five princes are brought in, we should summon Prince Duan to take the throne. After he has taken the throne, we can bring the other princes in." Later it was learned that Prince Duan had asked for the day off and was not in the palace, so someone was sent to find him.[18] While they were waiting for Huizong to arrive, Zeng Bu told the eunuchs that the councilors needed to see Zhezong's body. Once Xiang gave permission, they were ushered in and the cloth over Zhezong's face was lifted so that they could confirm that he was dead.[19] Soon the councilors heard that Huizong had arrived.

> When we got to the chamber with the screen, the empress dowager sitting behind the screen said to the prince, "The emperor has abandoned the world and has no son. You, Prince Duan, should be established." The prince, shaking, strongly declined, saying, "Prince Shen is the eldest. I don't dare accept." The empress dowager said, "Prince Shen has sick eyes. The next should be established. You should not decline." I also said that for the sake of the dynasty he should not decline. The manager and others rolled up the screen curtain and took Prince Duan behind [the screen]. He was still strongly protesting. The empress dowager told him to stop. I also parted the curtains and said, "for the sake of the country, you should not decline." We heard from behind the screen the eunuch managers and the others transmitting the message to take the hat. Then we left and stood below in the courtyard for a while. When the curtain was raised, he was wearing the hat, a yellow jacket, and seated on the throne.[20]

The councilors retreated to work on the final testament to be issued in Zhezong's name, calling on the drafting official Cai Jing to compose it. Before the testament could be read to the court officials, Huizong summoned the councilors. Zeng Bu recounted it this way:

> The emperor was sitting on the throne and our names were announced. We said "ten thousand blessings," then ascended the hall. The emperor said something confidentially to Zhang Dun in so low a voice that the others in line could not hear. I said, "We could not hear the emperor's words." Dun said, "He asks that the empress dowager temporarily govern with him."
>
> The emperor also turned to look at us and said, "Just now I repeatedly asked Mom to govern with me." I said, "Your Majesty is virtuous and humble and thus wishes to proceed in this way. However, there is no precedent for doing this when the ruler is full grown. I don't know what the empress dowager thinks about this."
>
> The emperor said, "The empress dowager has already agreed. I just thanked her. That is why I presumed to order you here. Since the final testament has not yet been issued, this provision can be added to it."[21]

The councilors called back Cai Jing and had the final testament revised. That done, the other officials were informed of Zhezong's death and Huizong's accession. Next the councilors went to offer condolences to Empress Dowager Xiang.

Afterward we again ascended the hall and in front of the screen lined up with the princes and memorialized to the empress dowager that on the order of the emperor we had added a passage to the final testament that she would temporarily rule with him. The empress dowager said, "The emperor is full grown and intelligent. Why should I manage his affairs?" We said, "The emperor informed us that you had already agreed." She replied, "Only because he asked two or three times." I said, "We have already issued the final testament. We would like it if, for the sake of the country, you could force yourself to do what the emperor requests." Then we left.[22]

From Zeng Bu's testimony, Empress Dowager Xiang was quite definite that she wanted Huizong to succeed Zhezong. In other quoted conversations she repeatedly said how intelligent he was, and in one she explicitly said that none of the other princes could compare with him.[23] Once she described him as compassionate by nature, reportedly because he had cried when he heard that a palace woman had died during the investigation into allegations about Empress Meng.[24] There is no reason to doubt that she both liked Huizong and considered him the most capable of Shenzong's surviving sons. Moreover, since he was only three months younger than Prince Shen, the age difference between them had little more than symbolic significance. If the eldest had an eye disease or even just poor eyesight, he would have made a poor candidate for emperor, since emperors had to read through piles of memorials and other documents.

PARTICIPATING IN THE GOVERNMENT IN 1100

Immediately after Huizong told the councilors that he wanted Empress Xiang to govern with him, they retreated to discuss among themselves how this would be arranged. They saw two established alternatives. In the case of two previous child emperors, Renzong and Zhezong, the empress came to the audience hall where a screen was erected and she and the boy emperor both sat behind it. The councilors spoke to both of them at the same time, but in effect were discussing matters with the empress dowager. Moreover, the empress dowager was treated ritually as the ruler in that her birthday was given a name and celebrated and her rule was announced to the Song's principal diplomatic partner, the state of Liao. The alternative precedent that the councilors brought up was the period of Yingzong's illness, when the councilors would first call on Yingzong in the audience hall, then go to call on Empress Dowager Cao in a rear hall, telling her what had been discussed with Yingzong and letting her have the final say. This measure was treated as a temporary expedient and the empress dowager was not treated ritually as the ruler. Zeng Bu contended that the Yingzong precedent was the most applicable, since both Huizong and Yingzong were adults and had been the ones to request help. His fellow councilors offered some objections but eventually were persuaded.[25]

Zeng Bu next tried to convince Huizong. "When Empress Liu ruled, Renzong was only thirteen *sui,* and when Empress Gao ruled, the late emperor was just ten *sui.* How could Your Majesty sit behind a screen [like they did]?"[26] The councilors then went to see Empress Xiang. After they explained to her the Yingzong period precedent, she said, "You ministers decide." Zhang Dun and Zeng Bu then insisted that they needed her view. She said, "Don't bring this up with me. Get a directive from the emperor." Zeng Bu assured her that they had talked to him: "Just now the emperor told us repeatedly to request your views. Moreover, this matter concerns your status, so it is really difficult for the emperor to decide on his own." Zhang Dun added, "This concerns your face." Empress Dowager Xiang then answered: "The emperor is grown up, and there was never a need to manage things this way. It was just that the emperor kept strongly begging, so reluctantly I complied. It will not be long before I return the government fully back to him. Just do it according to the precedent of Empress Dowager Cao."[27]

After the councilors praised her wisdom, the details were settled, including the fact that she would not go to the forward or rear audience halls, nor would she receive the full range of memorials. The members of the Council of State would go to the inner eastern gate to report to her after they had reported to the emperor. Moreover, nothing would be done about her birthday, nor would her participation be announced to Liao.[28]

Over the next couple of days, Empress Xiang was active in bringing up issues concerning the palace women, such as honors for Huizong's deceased mother and living arrangements and titles for Zhezong's widowed consorts. Two days after the accession she wrote out in her own hand an edict saying that before long she would give up participating in the government and that she would not hold audiences.[29] When the councilors showed her edict to Huizong, they remarked that virtue such as hers had rarely been seen in ancient or modern times. When Huizong concurred, Zeng Bu also praised her writing style, saying it was very beautiful, and even the officials of the outer court would not be able to copy it. Huizong responded by saying, "The Empress Dowager is intelligent. During Shenzong's lifetime, she discussed political affairs with him."[30] Since Huizong was only a toddler when Shenzong died, he must have learned this from palace ladies or eunuchs who remembered those days.

Within a few days of the succession, Empress Dowager Xiang ceased taking much initiative, rarely doing more than express approval of what the councilors and Huizong had decided. Occasionally, however, she discussed political matters when the councilors called on her. On 1100/3/9 the councilors started by describing some appointments that had been proposed and speaking of the importance of the ruler distinguishing clearly between the upright and the unworthy.

> After a long sigh she said, "You councilors are often wrong about the former emperor." She also said, "Shenzong was wise and brilliant, without peer among modern rulers. It is just that in his late years he didn't escape some mistakes in employing people, nor escape the whole realm discussing it."
>
> I said, "Shenzong was heroic and sagacious, which no other ruler can match. His employment of talent was also based on getting the best of his day. But even the ancients only hit the mark five times out of ten. No one can avoid all mistakes. Your words say it all. Zhezong's intelligence was also way beyond others, but for a young person to lead, he needs the right people. When I was first serving in his government, much of what I heard him say was praiseworthy. Later, he was swayed by the jeering of the general discussion and became suspicious. Recently because of the astral phenomenon he issued an amnesty and seemed alarmed. In appearance and speech he seemed frightened." Xiang said, "He was frightened."[31]

Later in their conversation Empress Dowager Xiang sighed and said that Zhezong was often deceived by people. Zeng Bu went on to discuss one of the nastier factional controversies that occurred after Zhezong began ruling on his own, the accusation that Gao had plotted to depose him and that Gao was not in fact Shenzong's mother. Xiang responded: "Empress Gao was the adopted daughter of [Renzong's] Empress Cao. When she married Yingzong, it was quite something. Also, Empress Gao was truly jealous. When she was just sixteen or seventeen *sui*, how would she have let another person bear a son for him? The [charges] about deposing [Zhezong] were to get other people in trouble. How would Mom have had an idea like that?"[32]

Zeng Bu, despite seeming to get along well with Empress Dowager Xiang, warned Huizong to be wary of her. Not only did he push for a relatively limited form of regency, but he warned Huizong to make sure that Xiang withdrew in the way she had promised she would. On 5/9 Zeng

Bu brought up the empress dowager to Huizong: "Your Majesty already has a son. There is no reason for an empress dowager with a grandson to continue as regent." Huizong repeated that the regency had never been her idea and that she had put in writing that she would give it up when Zhezong's tablet was installed in the ancestral temple, which was only another month or two away. Zeng Bu, however, pointed out the possibility that she might change her mind, as Empress Gao had done, and warned him that those around her might not want her to lose influence. Huizong should be prepared for them to create some sort of incident, he advised. Huizong did not believe his legal mother could so easily be deceived, but agreed to be on his guard. Zeng Bu then urged Huizong to decide in advance exactly which issues would be brought to the empress's attention after her retirement. To Zeng Bu's relief, Huizong replied that other than issues concerning the princes and princesses, no external matters would have to be reported to her.[33]

After the end of this conversation, Zeng Bu begged Huizong to make sure that no one learned what they had said. "If [this conversation] is not kept secret, the ruler loses his minister, but the minister loses his life."[34] Zeng Bu clearly did not trust some of those around the empress dowager and perhaps the empress dowager herself.

The one political issue that Empress Dowager Xiang intervened in was the effort by Zeng Bu and the new councilor Han Zhongyan to get Cai Jing posted out of the capital. She wanted him to stay and work on revising the history of Shenzong's reign, apparently believing that the coverage of her husband was still too biased by the antireformer court historians appointed during Gao's regency.[35]

On 4/2 when Huizong met with Zeng Bu, he warned Zeng that Empress Xiang wanted to keep Cai Jing, and when Zeng later went to see her, she in fact would not budge. Zeng warned her that he might resign if she did not give in, but she responded, "What does this have to do with the Bureau of Military Affairs?" (Zeng's position on the Council of State was in his capacity as head of the Bureau of Military Affairs). When Zeng Bu said, "Gentlemen and inferior men cannot abide in the same place," she countered, "During the late emperor's reign you were together." Because Zeng Bu kept obstinately returning to this issue, the empress finally had to tell him it was time for him to leave.[36]

At the end of the seventh month Zhezong's funeral rituals were completed and his tablet placed in the Imperial Ancestral Hall. Empress Dowager Xiang formally withdrew from participating in the government and Huizong was freer to change the ministers he had inherited from his brother. Thus, in 1100/9/8 Huizong finally accepted Zhang Dun's request to retire.

With Xiang no longer officially involved in the government, officials were once again free to criticize Cai Jing. Chen Guan, one of the most outspoken of the conservative censors appointed early in Huizong's reign, submitted a memorial on 1100/9/16 criticizing Empress Xiang's relatives and also charging that she had not in fact given up participating in the government. She became extremely upset and would not eat. Huizong tried to console her by saying he would banish Chen Guan. Her companions suggested that the way to calm her down would be to appoint Cai Jing to a councilor position. Huizong did not go that far, but the next day he had Chen Guan assigned a post out of the capital.[37] Chen Guan, for his part, kept submitting memorials that portrayed Xiang as holding on to power.[38]

In the tenth month of 1100 Cai Jing was finally sent away. Zeng Bu told Huizong that the whole realm had been hoping for Cai Jing's dismissal, but he had been afraid to open his mouth about it ever since Empress Xiang had gotten angry at him for his earlier attempt.[39]

Historians have often assumed that Empress Xiang was the one most eager to bring back the conservatives and that only because she died in early 1101 was Huizong able to change course. Huizong discussed many conservatives with his councilors and personally proposed bringing quite a few of them back to court. Xiang, by contrast, was most concerned with keeping the reformer Cai Jing in the government.

CONVERSATIONS WITH ZENG BU ON INTERPERSONAL DYNAMICS IN THE PALACE

A new emperor meant not only changes in the power relations of the outer court of high officials; it invariably also entailed realignments in the inner court as well. At Zhezong's death, three women had particularly strong claims to honor: Empress Dowager Xiang, who was Shenzong's widow and the legal mother of Zhezong and Huizong; Consort Dowager Zhu, who was a senior consort of Shenzong and Zhezong's actual mother; and Empress Liu, Zhezong's widow. Each had her own establishment, with eunuchs and palace ladies assigned to her. For instance, in 1100 there were 700 people living in Sagely Good Omen Hall with Consort Zhu.[40] Empress Xiang's position was if anything enhanced with Huizong's accession, as she was the only one with status as Huizong's mother. Consort Zhu and Empress Liu, by contrast, were no longer closely tied to the main line of succession, and they could probably anticipate that some of those who had sought their favor in the past would now turn their attention to more promising patrons, such as Huizong's young wife, the new empress, or whichever of Huizong's new consorts gained favor. Huizong's wife, now Empress Wang, quickly succeeded in the matter that had eluded Zhezong's first empress. On 1100/4/13 she gave birth to Huizong's first son.

Occasionally, Zeng Bu recorded long conversations with Empress Xiang on palace affairs. On 2/2 she talked about Zhezong's final days and his medical treatment. That day she also complained that her reading ability was not up to handling government paperwork. She did not know the character *xia* (blind) until she saw it as part of a name on a border affairs memorial. Zhang Dun assured her that she was intelligent enough to handle matters and to remember that the Sixth Patriarch of Chan Buddhism had been illiterate.[41]

In the conversations recorded by Zeng Bu, Empress Xiang shows little warmth or empathy for Consort Zhu, with whom she had been living in close proximity for nearly thirty years. She regularly referred to Zhu as "the one who lives in Sagely Good Omen Hall," or even just as "Sagely Good Omen." She and Huizong were both concerned that her surviving son harbored resentment at not being made emperor and needed to be closely watched.[42] On 2/12 Zeng Bu talked to her about Zhang Dun and his behavior the day Zhezong died. She offered the theory that Zhezong's mother, Grand Consort Zhu, was behind Zhang Dun's proposal that her son Prince Jian should succeed. Xiang thought Zhu had had a eunuch tell Zhang Dun that he should repay her for getting him his original appointment as grand councilor, and to do that he should spread the word that on his deathbed Zhezong had said that only his twelfth brother was from his mother's womb and so for stability should be chosen to succeed. Empress Xiang concurred with Zeng Bu that spreading a story like that deserved death.[43] About a month later, Zeng Bu and Empress Xiang exchanged similar stories implicating Consort Zhu and another eunuch, this time saying the eunuch had brought her things to the hall where Zhezong lay ill, apparently because she wanted to be present when he died to see that the succession went her way.[44]

Empress Xiang's lack of affection for her daughter-in-law Empress Liu was manifested above all in her efforts to get her deposed and Meng reinstalled as Empress. Xiang viewed the deposing of Meng as a grave miscarriage of justice. She told the councilors that she had never supported deposing Meng and denied that she had even seen, much less written, the so-called hand-drafted edict authorizing Meng's demotion.[45] Not long afterward, early in the fifth month, Huizong instructed the councilors to deliberate on restoring Empress Meng. Zeng Bu told him that the only precedent for such an act concerned granting posthumous restoration of rank. Moreover, having two empresses would be awkward. On 5/7 Huizong told Zeng Bu that Empress Xiang wanted to depose Liu and reinstate Meng. Zeng Bu insisted that that would not work because it would publicize Zhezong's mistake and, moreover, a younger brother could not change the status of his elder brother's wife. Huizong asked that someone explain this to Empress Xiang. When they brought the matter up with her, she insisted that the long-established principle was one emperor, one empress. Zhang Dun supported her, but the others remained silent. When Zeng Bu had a second chance to talk to her, he tried to redefine the situation to make Zhang Dun's bad influence on Zhezong the main issue, and to stress that he was the one who had forged her edict. Thus dual empresses was the best compromise. Xiang reluctantly consented.[46] On 6/23 an announcement was made at the suburban altar that Empress Meng had been reinstated.[47]

During conversations about the rituals to be followed when Meng was brought back to the palace, Empress Dowager Xiang did not conceal her preference for Meng in many ways. She decided that Liu should bow first to Meng and Meng return her bow, and that Meng should be the one to follow the funeral carriage, with Liu waiting at the palace for the return of the spirit tablet. Then she digressed a little:

> [The eunuch] Hao Sui once took Empress Dowager Gao's robes and put them on Empress Liu. When Zhezong saw this he was startled and asked with a smile if they fit . . . Empress Meng came from a literati family, which made her different. When first engaged, I constantly taught her wifely decorum, for instance, I personally showed her how to perform walking backwards and walking sideways. She cannot be compared to Empress Liu.[48]

Later in the conversation Zeng Bu brought up a delicate subject:

> Once you became empress, you never gave birth to another child. Shenzong had plenty of female attendants, but I never heard of rivalry [between you and them]. In your honored position, how could you compete with those below for favor?
>
> Xiang said, "I never bothered him with such annoyances. But Shenzong could also be extremely easygoing in husband-wife matters. In twenty years as husband and wife, [neither of us] ever got [angry enough to become] red in the face.[49]

When one of the officials expressed unease about how Meng and Liu would get along once made co-empresses, Xiang told the councilors, "Meng and Liu both have tempers. Now I fear they each want to avoid being lower than the other." When the councilors assured her that she would be able to keep them in line, she responded, "Those two are sisters-in-law to the current emperor, which complicates interaction. From now on, other than major rituals and banquets, which they can attend, on other occasions they should not participate. In this they are different from Huizong's empress."[50]

After reading the biographies of consorts in the *History of the Song*, it is refreshing to have a source like Zeng Bu's diary, with conversations quoted, often in colloquial language. The picture of palace life is not entirely surprising (though I would not have guessed Consort Dowager Zhu's establishment would have had as many as 700 people). That Consort Zhu would have tried her best to get her younger son to succeed to Zhezong is entirely plausible, as is the thought that she would have turned to a high-ranking eunuch for help. That there was tension between Xiang and Zhu also makes sense, given that each would have had a stronger position if only the other were no longer living.

From Zeng Bu's conversations, it is clear that Xiang could be tough when she really cared about an issue, such as retaining Cai Jing or deposing Empress Liu. But her power was far from unlimited. The councilors were willing to let Zhezong posthumously have two empresses but insisted that she and Huizong could not posthumously demote Liu. Within two months of withdrawing from participation in governing, Cai Jing was finally sent out of the capital, a sign that her power was markedly reduced after her formal withdrawal from governing.

Comparing the *History of the Song* biography of Empress Xiang to what can be learned about her from other sources shows that the formal biography is not only thin but also frequently misleading. For instance, the biography praises her for not having any Xiang girls considered for Zhezong's empress, but from the conversations recorded in fuller sources, it seems there were no unmarried girls of the right age. The biography praises her for never granting any favors to her own relatives, but fuller sources show that she was quite concerned about them and very upset when they were criticized. The biography hints that she should be given credit for bringing back conservatives, when in reality she was very active in trying to keep the arch-reformer, Cai Jing. The biography hints that it was her natural modesty that led her not to make her birthday a holiday or use her family taboos, in the way that Empress Dowagers Liu and Gao had done, but we see from Zeng Bu's diary that she was strongly pushed by Zeng Bu and the other councilors in that direction. Just because Xiang served Gao for many years as a daughter-in-law does not mean that she shared all of her political sentiments. Perhaps like Zhezong himself she resented Gao's high-handedness. Given her insistence on having Cai Jing rewrite the history of Shenzong's reign, in all likelihood she also resented the bad light cast on her husband by Gao's wholesale rejection of his policies.

All of the contributors to this volume recognize the power of the conventions of women's biography. Some make the conventions themselves their main subject. Others adopt a variety of strategies to learn more about women's lives despite the limitations of their biographical sources. Ping Yao, for instance, shows how aggregating hundreds or even thousands of epitaphs allows us to draw useful information from them. My strategy here has been to use sources that cannot be classed as biographies to, in a sense, write my own biography of a woman whose dynastic-history biography conceals more than it reveals.

I would like to think that my analysis of Empress Xiang's biography in the *History of the Song* suggests reading strategies for other dynastic history biographies of empresses. Readers clearly need to be alert to what is omitted from these biographies and to the possibility of political motivations lying behind what is included. The best way to do this is to read these biographies against other sources. Even biographies of other consorts whose lives overlapped with theirs can provide clues of what has been left out or distorted.

12. Life and Letters

Reflections on Tanyangzi

Ann Waltner

This essay juxtaposes a biography of Tanyangzi, a young woman religious teacher who lived in the Suzhou area in the sixteenth century, with a collection of her letters. The juxtaposition of these two texts clarifies each of them, and allows us to understand each genre in a more complex way. The letters offer us a chance to hear Tanyangzi's voice, to hear her talk about her life and teachings in her own words. They allow us to think about gender and the ways in which she conceptualized gender in the context of her religious enterprise, as well as the way her biographers conceptualized gender. The letters and the biography looked at together suggest ways in which ideas about gender and gender-specific notions of paths to immortality were different in the late Ming than they were in the Qing dynasty. These texts allow us to see how religious practice is part of a wider gender system and opens up one more dimension along which to track changes in that gender system.

Biographies of women in the Chinese historiographical tradition were typically biographies of exemplary women of the kinds discussed elsewhere in this volume. But biographies can serve as more than one kind of example, and Daoist and Buddhist hagiographic traditions recorded the lives of holy women as exemplars, models, and inspiration. These biographies mirror the texts in the historical record in many formal ways. Short and to the point, they often begin by locating the subject in time (genealogical time, through a discussion of parentage) and space (through notation of place of origin.) After a brief excursion through remarkable childhoods, these short texts typically move to the stories which demonstrate how their subjects are exemplary.[1]

Readers of exemplary lives (and other sorts of biographies) may be prompted to ask questions the texts themselves cannot answer. One of the critical questions lying behind many of the rich essays in this volume is the question of voice. One cannot help but wonder when reading these biographies, "How would the subject of this biography have recounted that episode? How would she have made sense of her life?" Recently discovered letters allow me to begin to answer some of those questions for Tanyangzi.

Tanyangzi (1557–80) was a young woman religious teacher who participated in both the Buddhist and Daoist traditions. She was the daughter of Wang Xijue (1535–1610), who became senior grand secretary in 1585. The centerpiece of her religious activity was her ascending heavenward and attaining immortality on the ninth day of the ninth month of 1580. She is known through a number of texts written by her disciples; the most important text about her is the *Tanyang dashi zhuan*, which was produced as a collaboration between her father and Wang Shizhen (1536–90). We know from letters that her followers wrote about her, and from references in the *Tanyang dashi zhuan*, that she herself wrote letters and short texts. But until very recently she was visible only through the voices of her male disciples and critics of the cult.

I have recently come across a painting of Tanyangzi by You Qiu, held by the Palace Museum (Gugong) in Beijing, an album leaf that has as colophons fifty-one pages of text written by Tanyangzi herself and collected by Wang Shizhen.[2] The album (which I will hereafter refer to as the Gugong album), is divided into three *juan*. Within it there are a number of different kinds of texts, but final instructions and letters to members of her family and to the family of Wang Shizhen (and to Wang Shizhen himself) predominate. No part of the Gugong album has ever been published. In this essay I will introduce the texts in the Gugong album and juxtapose them with the *Tanyang dashi zhuan* and draw some tentative conclusions based on that juxtaposition.

TANYANGZI'S LIFE

Tanyangzi's birth was marked by auspicious signs and, as a very young child, she showed a precocious religious devotion to Guanyin. As an adolescent, she stopped eating when her parents began preparations for her marriage to Xu Jingshao, a fellow townsman from Taicang. When her parents voiced their concern, she told them not to worry, that deities were bringing her food. When Xu, her fiancé, died before the wedding took place, she asked that she be allowed to live as his widow. Her father initially resisted, saying that since she had not been Xu's wife she could not be his widow. This argument resonates with the debate about whether a not-yet married woman ought to devote herself to a dead husband, which Weijing Lu discusses in chapter 5 in this volume. Tanyangzi prevailed and was provided with living quarters in the family compound where she had the leisure and independence to carry out religious study, teaching, and practice.

The deities who visited her tested her with a series of temptations (or, more properly, crises), which made it very clear that the resolution of the issue of marriage did not resolve the issue of sexuality. In the first crisis, a well-dressed woman offers to share with her a book entitled "Mutual Longings," a title with clear erotic implications. She rejects the book as wicked. In the second, a young man attacks her, and a second man places a knife at her throat. The text reads:

> Suddenly, his companion appeared, brandishing a knife and shouting: "How dare you hurt my child? If you take my advice and marry him, you'll live. If you don't I'll cut your throat." The teacher extended her neck to endure the knife. The knife was on the point of coming down when Zhenjun arrived with a smile. Then [my teacher] regained consciousness.[3]

In the third crisis,

> [a] young man, gowned and capped, came before her and presented his calling card, saying: "I am Xu. I know that you have endured bitterness on my account; I have come especially to comfort you." My teacher, without any change of expression said: "I have been constant in my intentions; how could I have preserved my chastity out of passion (*qing*)? Are you someone else's ghost? If you are, then disperse. If you are Xu, return and wait for my soul some other day at your grave." The youth, abashed, begged his leave and went.

In the final crisis, a Daoist appears and tempts her with her own beauty.

> "I lament that your life is as brief as mushrooms and dew, and want to save you. If you start eating again, your elegant skin and lovely hair will exceed all earthly models of beauty. How about it?" My master once again did not answer. The Daoist suddenly vanished and Zhenjun and Teacher Ou were by her side. They clapped their hands and said: "We have repeatedly tested you: you have repeatedly passed."[4]

These temptations clearly demonstrate that Tanyangzi's physical, sensual nature must be transcended in order for her to attain immortality.[5]

As time went on, her practice became more and more refined. She visited both the Bodhisattva Guanyin and the Daoist Queen Mother of the West in her visionary experiences, which are described in great detail in the *Tanyang dashi zhuan*. She gradually began to attract disciples, both male and female. In the course of her meditational practice, she was able to soar above the family dwelling. She acquired a snake, which she named "Guardian Dragon." The key to her teachings are *tian* and *dan,* which can be rendered loosely into English as simplicity and tranquility. Her disciples regarded *tian* and *dan* to be the essence of the *dao.*

As was true of many late Ming religious figures, she was devoted to texts of both Buddhism and Daoism, but her central achievement was attaining Daoist immortality. On the ninth day of the ninth month in 1580, with an audience of 100,000 people present, she ascended heavenward in broad daylight (in the company of her snake) and attained immortality. Several of her followers (including her father and her biographer and their brothers) secluded themselves after her death to follow the *dao.* The pressures and lures of ordinary life proved too strong, however, and they returned to normal life after several years. The cult does not seem to have survived her in any substantial way, though there is a local awareness of her story in Zhitang, the small village in Taicang where Xu's grave was located, up through the present time.[6]

THE *TANYANG DASHI ZHUAN*

The *Tanyang dashi zhuan* is the product of a collaboration between Wang Shizhen and Wang Xijue. The text itself recounts (and justifies) the conditions of its own creation. Wang Xijue had kept a diary of Tanyangzi's religious activities beginning in 1574, when she was sixteen *sui.* When, near the end of her life, he showed it to her, she locked it up and then burned it. After her ascent, she appeared to Wang Shizhen and Wang Xijue in identical dreams. Wang Xijue asks:

> "Although you do not seek fame, how can you let your story vanish without leaving behind anything for people to learn? Moreover, the appetite of people for enticing the hidden and drawing out the strange is inexhaustible. They indulge in their own imaginations and paint with a seven-inch brush. What limits do they have?"
>   The teacher nodded and said: "That is true. What shall we do about it?" The academician said: "I myself want to write your biography but an intimate biographer will not do. I want Wang [Shizhen] to write your biography, but an outsider as a biographer will not do either. An intimate is too close to the subject, while an outsider lacks intimate details. Why not then have Wang [Shizhen] write the biography, using a rough draft that I will write? The teacher [i.e., Tanyangzi] nodded again and said: "Fine."[7]

This brief excerpt hits on a number of the key issues in biographical writing, especially in the writing of a woman's biography, in late Ming dynasty China. Tanyangzi herself authorizes the biography; one suspects that strictures about talking about women in public make her authorization and endorsement all the more important. Wang Xijue is alert to issues of intimacy and writing and solves the problem through proposing a collaboration which Tanyangzi herself approves. It is clear that the purpose of the biography is to enlighten later generations, as well as to gain control of the story. By telling the story in detail, Wang Shizhen and Wang Xijue hoped to master a story that had begun to circulate in variant versions. It is also significant that the two Wangs did not suggest to her that they collect her teachings and publish them; what people of future generations would like to read is about her life—her teachings would be made manifest in her life, and the scandal that arose from the unorthodox teachings would be refuted by biography. Biography is a logical genre in which to transmit embodied practice.

The two men did indeed collaborate on the biography, which was completed, published, and distributed within months of Tanyangzi's ascent into immortality. Wang Shizhen, Wang Xijue, and their brothers Shimou and Dingjue were impeached almost immediately upon publication of the text. One of the officials who wrote a memorial urging impeachment writes that "believers in sorcery are daily increasing,"[8] and another says, "Important officials have fomented rebellion and seduced people's minds, greatly harming local customs and the like."[9] The cult of Tanyangzi represented to these two men a part of a general crisis—growing elite support of heterodox religion.[10] The concern that Wang Xijue has abdicated his position of moral authority among the Suzhou population is clear. Even worse than this abdication was his use of his position of moral authority for heterodox ends. The censor Niu Weibing's first reaction upon hearing that the daughter of a good Confucian family was engaging in occult activities seems to have been sympathy. But when he obtained a copy of the text and read it, his sympathy for Wang Xijue vanished. Instead of a father embarrassed by his daughter's activities, Wang Xijue is a promoter of those activities. After giving a rather extravagant description of Wang Xijue's credentials as a Confucian man of letters, Niu writes, "in the space of a single day, he has become mired in gods and demons—all he has studied he has cast aside."[11] The lure of the divine and the demonic is so potent that even the best of Confucian educations is not sufficient to combat it. It is important that Wang Xijue eschew heterodoxy and return to the correct way because the common people would imitate him in his reform as they had imitated him in his heresy. The same power that made the local elite moral exemplars also made them capable of deluding and hence corrupting the masses. This power of Wang Xijue, and what Niu sees as its corruption, is the chief concern of the memorial.

The public nature of the text was central to the controversy that surrounded it. It circulated quickly, in what were likely numerous editions, not all of which were identical.[12] There are reports that suggest a version of the text had reached the capital within a few months of Tanyangzi's attaining immortality.[13] Memorials of impeachment denouncing the biography were written a mere eight months after her ascent. The rapidity of the transmission of the text was in fact one aspect that particularly alarmed the impeaching officials. The documents of impeachment read, in part, that "those who have just read the story print it and distribute it at the morning markets," and requested that printing blocks for the text be destroyed.[14] Nothing came of the impeachment; in fact, a mere five years after the impeachment, Wang Xijue was appointed senior grand secretary.

THE GUGONG ALBUM

Tangyangzi's letters and instructions to various disciples and admirers are collected by Wang Shizhen and are preserved as colophons in the Gugong album, whose frontispiece is a painting by You Qiu. The followers of Tanyangzi made and revered images of her both during her life and after her death. The images, their crafting and their circulation, as well as the reverence paid them, are the subject of letters written by a number of her disciples.[15] Tanyangzi herself wrote in a letter to a female disciple that she could send an image that the disciples could worship in the confines of the women's quarters. She writes that looking at the image would be very much like seeing her (*shi zhi ru jian wu ye*). She cautions that her disciples must keep the image hidden,[16] suggesting both that the image should be concealed as a woman should be secluded, and that the image had religious power which should be available only to the initiated. Images and texts were both used in worship; it is likely that these images were devotional objects, for private use among followers. It would be clear, even if we had no surviving images, that the worship of Tanyangzi was visually rich.

But we do have two surviving images, both by the painter You Qiu. In addition to the one preserved in the Gugong album, late in 1580, at more or less the same time Wang Shizhen was writing his biography, You Qiu painted a portrait, which is now in the possession of the Shanghai museum and was a part of the "Arts of Taoism" exhibit that Steven Little organized at the Art Institute of Chicago in 2000.[17] You Qiu, the son-in-law of the much more famous Qiu Ying, was a professional painter, active ca. 1564–90, of somewhat modest reputation.[18] As one might expect from a professional painter, he painted a wide variety of subjects—figures in landscape, religious themes, beautiful women with decided erotic tones. James Cahill has talked about his "neat, uninspired figures in landscape scenes."[19]

Wang Shizhen was a patron of You Qiu and, according to Louise Yuhas, You painted at least four paintings for him, none of which has survived.[20] Although You Qiu was labeled a "professional" painter (that is, not a literati painter), he seems to have socialized to some degree with Wang Shizhen. At least on one occasion when literati were exchanging poetry, You Qiu contributed a painting in lieu of words, and on another occasion, Wang Shizhen wrote a poem for You Qiu to present to the assembled scholars.[21] (Wu Hung, in repeating this story, called You Qiu "a popular entertainer in a scholar's robe.")[22]

You Qiu's presence in Wang Shizhen's circle strongly implies that he had direct knowledge either of Tanyangzi herself or of the texts that were produced about her. It is entirely possible that the paintings of Tanyangzi were done at the request of Wang Shizhen. Even if they were not, they were produced in the context of a relationship characterized by patron-client exchanges. I would suggest that these paintings are devotional objects, and the images and their substantial colophons function together. The calligraphy for both paintings is done by the same man—one Zhang Zao. The paintings are quite different from each other. In the Shanghai painting, the image of Tanyangzi is the entirety of the painting. There is no background, only her body, looking directly at the viewer. The frontispiece of the Gugong album features Tanyangzi sitting in a mountain scene, writing at a desk, with two attendants. The painting has been trimmed; the seal and signature of You Qiu have been cut off. The album has a wooden cover, and is bound accordion-style, as are many sutras. The text is approximately 8" × 5". One imagines that the painted scene is of her generating the texts that form the colophon. All of the colophons on the Shanghai museum scroll are also in the Gugong album, but the texts in the Gugong album are much more extensive. The core of the colophons in the Gugong text is a series of letters written by Tanyangzi. All fifty-one pages of the colophon purport to be written by her. A note at the end of the second *juan* informs us that the letters in that *juan* at least were collected by Wang Shizhen.

By the late Ming, it was common practice to collect letters written by men (and even some women, though to the best of my knowledge this is the most extensive extant collection of letters by a sixteenth-century Chinese woman). Often letters ended up published in collected works of their authors. Additionally, collections of model letters were published to serve as letter writing guides. Kathryn Lowry has written about collections of model letters and Ellen Widmer has shown how letters made it possible for elite women to form networks of support that were critical to their creative work and their emotional lives.[23] My point here is simply that collecting the letters of a noted figure made sense in the context of late Ming practices of literary preservation. There is some evidence from library catalogs that a text entitled "Tanyangzi yiyan" (The final words of Tanyangzi) circulated.[24] It is not impossible that the letters were collected and attached to the painting as colophons for use in religious practice. I will return to this point in my conclusion.

Some of the letters in the Gugong colophon are farewell messages that impart instructions about the attainment of immortality. Others are ordinary and show Tanyangzi's connections to the world of mundane emotions—she consoles her uncle when her aunt is ill, she gives her brother advice when he has bad dreams. The letters, no matter what their subject matter, show her profound connections to her family and disciples even as she is on the point of attaining immortality. The *Tanyang dashi zhuan* describes the enthusiasm with which people sought to learn from Tanyangzi near the end of her life and suggests something of the context in which the texts in the Gugong album might have been generated:

> At that time, men and women came in a frenzy, asking for an audience with my teacher. She rejected all of them. As time went by, she could not stop the requests of her female relatives. She started to give audience to the senior ones. Subsequently she sighed and said: "This is not a fair method." She gradually gave audience to poor widows and those who were sincere. But there were people who were not able to hear words of my teacher, and yet occasionally heard only one or two phrases, which revealed their innate weaknesses. Conscience-stricken, they repeatedly made vows, asking her to cleanse them and help them reform. Other people begged for riches and profit, like swarming flies and croaking frogs. She only smiled faintly at them, but did nothing. She would bestow gifts according to the degree of a person's inherent goodness.[25]

As the appointed hour of her ascent into immortality drew near, gentry followers (as opposed to the female relatives in the above quotation) also ask for instruction. Since they ask for the instruction in writing, one assumes that they would have received instruction in written form. The *Tanyang dashi zhuan* describes the scene:

Many gentry who admired her presented written requests to her father, hoping to get a "one–word teaching." He attempted to persuade the teacher [Tanyangzi], but the teacher decided not to grant the requests. If she investigated and found someone worth the words, she gave him her words. They were as concentrated (*jing*) as powdered koumiss made from lioness's milk, and as to the point (*yao*) as an arrow striking the target. Of those who received her words, none left without an admiring heart and a satisfied intention.[26]

In a number of other places, the *Tanyang dashi zhuan* tells us that Tanyangzi wrote a text (or a letter) and there is a letter (or text) in the Gugong album that corresponds to that letter—in terms of recipient, subject matter, and sometimes even timing. The central question, which I will be addressing in the remainder of this chapter, is how reading the letters changes and challenges the information we have about her from the *Tanyang dashi zhuan*. The differences are subtle and have not caused me to rethink my earlier conclusions about Tanyangzi. Rather, they have added nuance and depth to the picture that we have received from the *Tanyang dashi zhuan*.

NEW INSIGHTS YIELDED BY THE GUGONG ALBUM

The Gugong album provides us with a text that helps us understand several aspects of the story of Tanyangzi with greater clarity. For example, one of the most intriguing aspects of her story is the nature of her relationship with Xu Jingshao, her fiancé. The Gugong album contains a text that helps us understand the relationship. We already know from the *Tanyang dashi zhuan* that Xu's death was a critical event for Tanyangzi. Marriage preparations precipitate the crisis in which she stops eating and begins having visions, and in which the young man's untimely death frees her to live as a widow. Her family is at first unwilling to regard her as a widow, but, like the faithful maidens discussed by Weijing Lu in chapter 5 of this volume, she convinces them that betrothal was tantamount to marriage and they eventually permit her to reside separately in the family compound. (This is a slightly unusual arrangement for a widow; more usual would be for her to remain living with her deceased husband's family.) His grave is an important site for her cult, and as she is about to ascend and attain immortality, she cuts a chignon off the left side of her head and asks that it be buried with her fiancé, to stand for her body. After the death of her fiancé she wanted to visit his grave but was afraid her parents would not permit it, so she wrote "a eulogy of more than a hundred words and sent a nurse to make an offering and burn it at the tomb."[27] The Gugong album contains a "Eulogy for Xu" (Chu gui ji Xu lang wen), which is 133 words long, suggesting that this may indeed be the text referred to in the biography. In it Tanyangzi expresses regret that she was herself not able to go to Xu's grave. She articulates a vow of chastity (*shi xin wu er li zhi ru shi*) and tells him that she had originally intended to follow him in death, but obstacles presented themselves—his parents and grandparents were still alive. She writes in the eulogy: "If a woman is already married and had entered her husband's household, then she should follow him in death. If she has not yet married and is still at home, she should serve both families with chastity and filiality." She ends the eulogy by stating that she will stop eating and drinking. She vows to make a sacrifice of her body and avoid all luxury in order to recompense the sages who have led her to salvation.[28]

A text that begins as a lament for a dead fiancé, thus, ends as a statement about her own religious attainments. The eulogy shows the ways in which chaste widowhood, loyalty to her family, and her religious practice all appear to her as a seamless whole. In the *Tanyang dashi zhuan*, her father asks her why she remains connected to Xu. He asks, "You have already completed the *dao*, yet you still confine yourself to the faithfulness of a petty woman. This is a great transgression. Behaving this way, even if you don't call it an impediment, is prompted by an affinity of love. How can you call this the *dao*?" Here Weijing Lu's discussion of the faithful maiden in this volume is instructive: she articulates the potential for widow chastity to appear as a problematic virtue, if what motivates it is sexual passion for the deceased husband. (See also Carlitz's discussion in chapter 10 of this volume of sexual passion for a deceased spouse as a motivation for a widow's chastity.) As these discussions so clearly show, chastity as a virtue can never exist outside of a discourse of sexuality. Tanyangzi responds to her father's challenge by telling him that it was her chaste widowhood that caused the deities to empathize with her and accept her.[29] He is ultimately convinced by her explanation, but his first reaction to her desire to remain a chaste maiden is to demean it, to see it as ordinary virtue. She (and the deities who mentor her) see it as a strong act of will which affirms her virtue and her resolution. The choice to be a chaste maiden in this construction is a powerful statement of virtue. Thus we can see in both of these texts that her chastity—her fulfilling the prescriptions of proper behavior for ordinary women—is a condition for her attaining extraordinary secrets of immortality. Confucian morality, in her religious world, is not separable from Buddhist or Daoist spiritual attainments. The connection to her fiancé thus has a religious as well as a social role, and what may begin as (or look like) the "faithfulness of a petty woman" is central to the religious story.

We know from the *Tanyang dashi zhuan* that women played a central role in the cult of Tanyangzi, but we do not know very much about those women. The Gugong album contains two letters to women who are outside of the immediate circle of both Wang Shizhen and Wang Xijue, which are illuminating in this regard. The *Tanyang dashi zhuan* tells us about an elderly Buddhist woman, referred to as "old lady Xiao," who came to visit Tanyangzi.[30] In the letter preserved in the Gugong album, Tanyangzi begins in a tone respectful to Old Lady Xiao, saying that she is not sure that her own basic nature (*gen xing*) is worthy of receiving the lady's instructions. She inquires after Old Lady Xiao's health, which is not good; she is eighty at the time the letter is written. She reveals something of the conundrum facing a woman with a message in late Ming China when she writes, "I am a woman and originally wanted to keep my body and face hidden. Because I had empathy for people, I wanted to save the wise and the dull alike. I made myself visible and carefully cultivated myself. I could not bear to abandon those who might want to study in the future." At this point, the tone of the letter changes a bit, and she takes the tone of teacher in her address to the older woman. She counsels her, "Fix your mind; reduce your thoughts and your spirit will become calm. Of itself, your kidney water will rise, and your illness will be cured. Do not believe in divination or the worship of deities . . . I have stopped eating grains. Instead I enjoy the benefits of the delicacies of the great *yang*. Thus I am never hungry; I am always satisfied. You too should be like this." A letter that began in a tone of great reverence and respect ends with a lecture to the old woman about practices she should engage in to nourish her body and spirit and improve her health. The letter ends with another sharp shift in tone: "When stupid people (*dun ren*) pass by my dwelling, they all laugh and some of them say evil words. I silently tolerate it. The gossip is not worth my attention."[31] Although we know from the *Tanyang dashi zhuan* that the critics of the cult were vocal during Tanyangzi's lifetime, here we see her own response to their scorn and laughter. The tone of the letter is both lecturing and confiding: she writes about her decision to make herself visible (*xian*) in spite of the (unspoken) strictures against so doing, and she writes about the ridicule to which she is subject (though in a context that suggests she is above being disturbed).

There is in addition a letter to "Lady Teacher Ye," who is not mentioned in the *Tanyang dashi zhuan*. Tanyangzi begins the letter by saying that she had not heard from the lady teacher Ye in several years, but whenever she thought of her she remembered banquets and enjoyable conversations that she and Lady Ye had shared. Lady Ye had two days earlier visited the Wang household, and Tanyangzi says: "I wanted to see you but I am already deep in retreat from worldly emotions. I do not even see my parents any longer. I could hardly ask to see you." She goes on to say that she has heard that the Ye family has fallen on hard times, and regrets that she has no way to repay the benevolence of Lady Teacher Ye's instruction. In a remarkable sequence, she says, "I am nearing my attainment of the *dao*, and have renounced all money; my purse is empty. I have nothing with which to repay my teacher." She provides her friend with a pithy teaching: nourish your *qi*, expel your *yin*, and get rid of your belongings—that will lead to the *dao*. Near the end of the letter, she says that once the *dao* has been achieved, food and clothing appear in and of themselves (*yi shi zi ran*). Presumably she is suggesting that Lady Ye resolve the problem of poverty by reducing her desires.[32] As we saw with the letter to Old Lady Xiao, there is a shift in tone in the course of the letter, beginning with the utmost respect (and a suggestion that the older woman occupies a higher status) but ending with what reads almost like a lecture. The opening of the letter to Lady Ye suggests a lively sociability among female religious teacher and student—one of the things Tanyangzi remembers is banquets and lively conversations. We do not know if this lively sociability is absent from the *Tanyang dashi zhuan* because the male authors of the text are unaware of it—that it took place in the sequestered women's quarters hidden from their view—or that they knew of it and did not approve, or even that they knew of it and did not think it worthy of mention.

The *Tanyang dashi zhuan* does not mention that women in Wang Shizhen's family were followers of Tanyangzi, though it does inform us that Tanyangzi's own mother and grandmother became followers. Letters in the Gugong album make the devotion of women in Wang Shizhen's family clear. The absence of women from his family in the *Tanyang dashi zhuan* is an extremely interesting omission; Wang may be protecting the privacy of women in his own family. (Writing about Tanyangzi was necessary in order to make her teachings clear, but he could leave the women in his own family out of the story.) Apparently the connections between Tanyangzi and the women in Wang Shizhen's family were strong; there are letters in the Gugong album to Lady Shen (the wife of Shizhen's son Shiqi), to Lady Li (Shizhen's concubine), and to the wife of Shimou, Shizhen's brother. Another letter refers to Shizhen's wife, Lady Wei. When Tanyangzi offers to send an image of herself to Lady Shen for women to worship in their private quarters, we can assume that there is in fact a group of women in the Wang family who worship Tanyangzi. This omission on the part of Wang Shizhen is an example—which we see evidence of elsewhere in this volume, particularly in chapter 11, by Patricia Ebrey—of how sources external to formal biography remind us that biographies are incomplete and partial renderings of lives, riven with the prejudices and agendas of their authors.

These letters provide important information on the ways in which Tanyangzi thinks about gender and religion. In a pair of letters, one to Wang Shiqi and one to his wife, Lady Shen, Tanyangzi gives advice about Lady Shen's desire to become a disciple. Tanyangzi writes to Lady Shen:

> You have expressed the desire to leave the world of mundane affairs and pursue the *dao*. But I am afraid that daily affairs are an obstruction and ordinary events tie you down. You are not able to throw them off. You are not able to take a vow of discipleship at this point—wait until your sons are grown and your daughters are married and your household affairs are settled—at that time you can face the empty gates and summon a teacher.[33]

She writes to Shiqi, the husband of Lady Shen:

> I have advised her that she should not sever the relations of husband and wife. Your sons and daughters are not yet grown. If she clings to her original intention and does not take my advice, later she will resent me. You had better take a woman of good family as concubine as soon as you can.[34]

I read the advice to get a concubine as a kind of compromise—Lady Shen should not abandon domestic duties, but Wang Shiqi should get a concubine to relieve some of the burdens of wifehood. It is very clear that Tanyangzi regards domestic duties (such as childrearing) both as obstructions to religious attainment and as critical tasks that cannot and should not be deferred. She does not rail against the obstructions: she simply counsels patience. The obstructions will diminish with time. Family obligations will recede in importance when sons are established in careers and daughters married.

She writes on several other occasions to male disciples about their female relatives' interest in declaring discipleship. In a letter to Wang Shizhen, she says that his wife (*da niangzi*) was so eager to become a disciple that she had seen Tanyangzi in a dream.[35] But she too was tightly connected to family affairs. Tanyangzi reports the conversation, and says she told his wife (who was twenty-seven years her senior), "Because I have few female disciples, when you get old I can teach you."[36]

The letters to (and about) female followers reveal a strongly gendered sense of religious practice. We can see in these letters to female disciples a clear sense that women's obligations formed a qualitatively different sort of obstruction than did men's. Tanyangzi voices concern that her male disciples are not yet ready to attain the *dao*, that they are too entangled with worldly affairs. But she never tells a male disciple to defer his religious practice until his children are grown.[37] She sees different obstacles to religious attainment, but she does not articulate a different religious path for men and women followers. Never do we see an indication that the path she herself has followed is inappropriate for her male followers because of their gender. The obstacles gender produces she sees are social, not biological.

The letters enrich our sense of the way Tanyangzi saw the intersection of the ordinary and the extraordinary, or to put it another way, the intersections of religious and family life. They also show her exerting her authority in ways that differ from the way her authority is presented in the *Tanyang dashi zhuan*. Gender is one dimension of her authority. She writes more about her gender and her youth than do her disciples when they write about her; she sees her youth and gender as phenomena to be explained. They are merely the phenomena of an ephemeral body, but nonetheless the phenomena of ephemeral bodies have a great deal of social and experiential significance. This awareness of gender plays a different role in the two texts. One of the things that is remarkable in the *Tanyang dashi zhuan* is how little a role Tanyangzi's gender plays in the construction of the story. It is not absent, but it is not a dominant theme. It arises in interesting ways in the narrative—and, perhaps not insignificantly, in her own voice, such as when she explains to her father that she must soar because she inhabits a woman's body and the resources available to her to gain followers are limited. And her gender does become a dominant theme for later critics. But in general, when Wang Shizhen and Wang Xijue are telling the story of Tanyangzi, her earthly form (including gender) is not of paramount interest. She is a visionary who has visited the court of the Queen Mother of the West, and obtained the secrets of immortality. That is all that counts.

But Tanyangzi herself tells a different story. In the letters, her consciousness that she is a young woman who is teaching older men, men of not inconsiderable accomplishments, is strong. She writes in her farewell to her disciples, "I am just a weak woman with no particular knowledge who quite by chance has been ranked above you."[38] She writes (as we saw above) to old lady Xiao, "I am a woman and originally wanted to keep my body and face hidden." It is her religious calling that impelled her to make herself visible (*xian*). She sees a conflict between a teaching mission and correct gender roles, though it is abundantly clear that her obligations as a teacher outweigh her obligations to follow these gender roles. Correct gender roles are of less concern to her biographers.

But the *Tanyang dashi zhuan* does deal with sexuality in an extraordinarily interesting way, as we saw with the four temptations I recounted above. The biography makes it clear that her sensual potential (an erotic book, attachment to life, connection to her dead fiancé, and her own beauty) must be transcended for her to progress in her studies. She advises Wang Shiqi to get a concubine right away; the fact that the advice is given in the context of his wife's spiritual development clearly implies that sexual activity is an impediment for women in their religious development. But we do not see the same concern with the erotic in the Gugong text as we do in the biography.

Her authority in the *Tanyang dashi zhuan* comes from her visions and her teaching. She has numinous power (*ling*), which draws her disciples to her. In the letters, we see her issuing threats if they slacken in their devotion. One of the dimensions of the threat occurs in regard to the numinous snake (*ling she*), which Tanyangzi named Guardian Dragon, and which ascended with her as she attained immortality. The *Tanyang dashi zhuan* details the appearance of the snake as follows:

> She brought [the snake] home and set it up in a downstairs room in an empty book case. When members of the family saw it they were startled. The snake was docile; it did not move. To its side, there was a sheet of paper with vermilion characters in seal script. For this reason no one dared kill it.[39]

In a text entitled "Announcing to My Disciples That I Am Keeping a Numinous Snake" preserved in the Gugong album, Tanyangzi writes, "Your life and death is in my hands. If you violate my admonitions or if you waver, I will have my divine serpent wrap himself around your body or I will sever your spirit with my sword of wisdom." We know from the *Tanyang dashi zhuan* that the snake made the family anxious, but this is the first time we see it used to threaten the disciples.

In her farewell to her disciples (*bie zhu dizi*), she writes that she is leaving an outline (*yao lüe*) of her teachings behind to serve as their guide to enlightenment. (Note that she does not say she is leaving behind her biography to lead them; the biographical mode of knowledge is not the only mode operating here. Her biography is transmitted by others; she transmits teachings.) She promises that she will return to help them, suggesting that they will see her body but will be unable to hear her voice. Here, as in other places, she threatens the disciples—if they break their vows and violate the precepts (*panmeng weijie*) she will report them to heavenly officials who will see to it that they are punished appropriately. She further cautions the disciples that they should be careful of whom they teach. If pious men and women come to inquire about the *dao*, the disciples should first examine whether the supplicants have observed the precepts and inquire into their abilities. Once they have verified that supplicants have met these criteria, they may teach them. This is a standard caution in Daoist texts—the secrets of immortality are to be transmitted only to those who are ready to receive them. The threat of death by strangulation or by decapitation and the threat of being reported to heavenly officials should one waver from the teachings of Tanyangzi adds an edge of terror to the cult, an edge we see reflected in letters the disciples wrote one another, but which is largely absent in the *Tanyang dashi zhuan*.

The fear is connected to promises that she will return. We do see suggestions that she might return in the *Tanyang dashi zhuan*. She tells Wang Shizhen in a dream sixteen days after her death:

> My *dao* has nothing of the strange about it. It is tranquil and that is that. In the past I have told you to hold fast to your numinous roots (*ling gen*), dispel lust and attachments, dilute strong flavors, and reduce your speech. If you try for a long time but do not immediately succeed, do not become weary. If you meet with some success, do not immediately feel pleased with yourself and think that you've gotten it, because in fact you have not. I now am going to leave you for a long time. Actually I am not really going to take leave of you. If you and my father help one another pursue the great *dao* and do not abandon me, then I vow not to turn my back on you and my father and attain the *dao* myself alone.[40]

The Gugong text is more explicit. She writes in a letter to Shizhen's son Shiqi (who was more or less her contemporary) that she will return, but counsels him to silence on the subject.

In the Gugong album, no letters to men outside her family or the family of Wang Shizhen are preserved. (It is worthy of note that at several points, members of both Wang families asserted that the two families, especially during the lifetime of Tanyangzi, were as one. This intimacy might well account for the inclusion of letters to the family of Wang Shizhen in the album. There might of course be another, more mundane, reason—Wang Shizhen might have had easier access to those letters.) The final instructions that are preserved in the *Tanyang dashi zhuan* are in general to men who are reasonably famous: her teaching to them formed a part of a public record of her activities. The letters in the Gugong album belong to a more private realm.

The edges of scandal that are intimated in the *Tanyang dashi zhuan* (and elaborated in other, later texts) are more strongly portrayed in the Gugong album. In a letter to her brother Wang Heng, she writes: "I just cultivated myself so I could teach people to extend their lives and minimize disasters. I certainly never dared to entice them with falsehoods."[41] She repeats the denial that she had enticed people with falsehoods in a letter to Wang Shizhen.[42] The letter to the old lady Xiao also has intimations of scandal—stupid people are laughing at her, and there is gossip she feels compelled to record that she is ignoring. We know from the *Tanyang dashi zhuan* that there was some concern that gossip would damage her father's career, and that her grandparents anxiety about gossip led them to bring her back to Taicang from the capital.[43]

The final difference I will discuss is a difference of practice, and like the other differences I have enumerated, it is a difference of tone and nuance. In the *Tanyang dashi zhuan,* eight precepts are presented as key to her teaching. The precepts are: love and respect ruler and parents, prohibit and stop lewdness and killing, pity and cherish orphans and widows, tolerate insult, cherish frugality and be modest in your enjoyment of wealth, honor and respect words, don't discuss people's faults, don't harbor unorthodox books (*chanwei*), and finally, don't follow unorthodox teachers who are outside the *dao* or who advocate sexual (literally yellow and white) practices. Although the Gugong album contains the eight precepts (in *juan* 1) the letters refer more prominently to five precepts, which are fully outlined in the letter to Lady Shen, but which are also referred to elsewhere.[44] The five precepts are: cultivate your mind (*xiuxin*); concentrate your nature (*cunxing*); don't strive for reclusion (*jie lao i*); keep your vows (*shouyue*); and expel desires and worries (*chu siyu*). The five precepts are strategies of meditation and are internalized; the eight are precepts about ways of being in the world.

The letters are a remarkable source, and what is most remarkable about them is that they provide Tanyangzi's own voice. It is a sharp voice— she is not afraid to preach, to scold, to threaten. Letters that begin with professions of great respect often end with very specific instructions to the recipient for self-improvement. Part of this may come from youthful arrogance, but surely in great part it comes from religious certainty and charisma. Tanyangzi has visited the court of the Queen Mother of the

West and there obtained secrets of immortality. She would be remiss if she did not insist that her disciples follow her instructions.

Tanyangzi's voice in the letters is a gendered voice, and we see this perhaps most clearly in her writings to other women. But the ways in which the voice is gendered are not simple. It is worth stressing that we see no indication here of gender-specific practices to immortality that would become so important to female Daoists in the eighteenth and nineteenth centuries. While she talks of the differing social roles of men and women, she does not discuss one practice featured in later texts, "cutting the red thread"—meditational and dietary techniques that cause menstruation to cease, thus alleviating what was often considered the obstacle of "polluting" menstrual blood to a woman's religious attainment. There is no sense in any of her teachings that men and women follow separate paths; there is no sense in which her bodily practices cannot be done on a male body.[45] It bears repeating that small children do represent an impediment to religious attainment in her scheme, but it is because children require care, not because of any innate impurities within the female body. Indeed, we do not even see in her own writing the sense that we see in the *Tanyang dashi zhuan* that her own sensuality must be overcome. Her practices are embodied, but they are practiced on a body that in some ways is not defined by its gender. (It is worth comparing this to Buddhist notions of embodiment, which specify that one of the thirty-two marks of the body of the Buddha is a retractable penis).

The ways in which the two texts resonate with one another suggest that perhaps the letters were compiled by Wang Shizhen as a supplement to the *Tanyang dashi zhuan*, for the edification of a small group of disciples. (I am not suggesting that the letters were written as a complement to the biography, but they may have been collected as a complement.) As I suggested earlier, we know that images were used in worship of Tanyangzi; it is likely that this album was used in worship. The letters might be seen as esoteric texts, texts which should be circulated only within a circle of disciples, not to be published but rather to be read by a select group. The *Tanyang dashi zhuan*, printed and distributed as it was, had as its mission explaining Tanyangzi's teachings to a potentially skeptical public. It provides context; it provides justification. It tells a story of religious teaching as a biography. The genre of biography provides a format for the demonstration of embodied teachings in a concrete, lived way.

13. The Biographical and the Autobiographical in Bo Shaojun's *One Hundred Poems Lamenting My Husband*

Wilt L. Idema

> When Liuxia Hui had died, his disciples wanted to compose an elegy for him, but his wife said: "If you want to compose an elegy and eulogize the master's virtue, you don't know him as well as I do." She thereupon composed an elegy . . . His disciples used this as their elegy and could not change a single character.
>
> LIU XIANG, "The Wife of Liuxia Hui," in *Biographies of Women*

Up to the seventeenth century, women writers in China rarely ventured into funerary and biographical genres. Despite the claim of Liuxia Hui's wife that she was better placed than any of his disciples to know her husband and therefore the most suitable person to write his "elegy" (*lei*), the composition of such highly visible works usually was entrusted to men, preferably men who were themselves highly visible.[1] The only woman writer to be known for her elegies is the poet Zuo Fen of the second part of the third century, but these were command performances on behalf of fellow inmates of the imperial harem.[2] When the elegy lost some of its literary eminence in later centuries, a few women composed sacrificial texts (*jiwen*) for their deceased husbands, the most famous being the one by the sixth-century female poet Liu Lingxian for her husband, Xu Fei.[3] But from later centuries we have only fragments of a sacrificial text by the famous female poet Li Qingzhao (1084–ca. 1151) for her husband, Zhao Mingcheng, and from lady Zhang for her husband, the political martyr Yang Jiaoshan (Jisheng; 1516–55).[4] Biographies (*zhuan*) by women, if we go by Zhou Shouchang's *Gonggui wenxuan* of 1846, are limited to the one questionable case of Song Ruozhao's (fl. 800) biography of Niu Yingzhen.[5]

In the genre of *shi*, the third-century poet Pan Yue had created the subgenre of *daowangshi* ("poems mourning the deceased"), when he had written a series of three poems under that title remembering and lamenting his deceased wife. With its focus on private life and private emotions, one would think that this subgenre also soon would be used by women to lament their loved ones. This happens much later, however, than one might have thought. The first female-authored *daowangshi* I am aware of date only from the Ming dynasty, and tend to be limited to a single poem. An early and often quoted example is provided by Meng Shuqing (ca. 1476), a female poet from Suzhou who lived more than a century before Bo Shaojun:

> All covered with stains: gauze sleeves soaked by tears,
> To my great regret I lack the incense to call back his soul.
> The cardamom flower stays behind but he has disappeared—
> The full moon before the curtain accompanies me at dusk.[6]

In view of this very modest tradition indeed, the set of 100 *daowangshi* composed by the seventeenth-century female poet Bo Shaojun (d. 1626) in the year following her husband's death is completely without precedent— not only in size (81 of the original 100 quatrains survive), but also in style, as she deliberately adopts a "masculine" tone in her poems.

If biographical prose by women is rare, autobiographical prose by women from before the seventeenth century is even rarer. Li Qingzhao's "*Jinshi lu houxu*" (Postface to *Inscriptions on Bronze and Stone*) remained unique. In this work, presented as a postface to her late husband's large collection of epigraphical materials, she describes the growth of his library and its eventual dispersal, and while doing so, provides an intimate and relatively detailed account of their married life and her life as widow.[7] But it is of course a Western conception to see in prose the primary vehicle of auto-biographical expression. Modern studies on autobiography in China all seem to assume that the proper model of the autobiography is provided by the long prose narrative, in which the author, looking back on his or her life, provides a coherent account of his or her development, with a special emphasis on psychological development (and the tensions between outer behavior and "true inner self"). Chinese men and women probably were as much concerned as European men and women to leave behind an account of themselves, but in China, where "poetry was the wording of intent" (*shi yan zhi ye*), the preferred format for doing so obviously was the literary collection—carefully compiled (pruned and revised) by the author, and often chronologically arranged.[8] This applied not only to men, but also to women. Traditional Chinese women were not aware of the issues modern scholars in women's studies are interested in, and we will often find their collections frustratingly uninformative—even though individual collec-tions may be more informative than traditional and modern anthologies, which often have a highly normative program. There can be no doubt, however, that Chinese women authors of the Ming and the Qing, despite their keen awareness of the many restrictions imposed on them by genre and decorum, wanted to be known through their collected poetry.[9] And so Bo Shaojun invites us to remember her through her *One Hundred Poems Lamenting My Husband.*

BO SHAOJUN AND HER HUSBAND

Bo Shaojun hailed from Suzhou, in the early decades of the seventeenth century probably the richest city of the Chinese empire. More precisely, she was from the county of Changzhou, one of the two counties that shared the city of Suzhou between them. She would appear to have spent basically all of her life in Suzhou, even though her husband, Shen Cheng (d. 1625), was from Taicang. If we would rely on the information about her provided in her "biography" in the gazetteer of Suzhou prefecture, we would learn only the following bare facts:

> Bo Shaojun hailed from Changzhou. Sweet and graceful, she displayed a strong moral character. She was married to the student Shen Cheng. Cheng enjoyed quite a reputation, but he died without obtaining a higher degree. Shaojun lamented him in 100 poems, which were mournful and determined in tone. On the anniversary of his death she collapsed overcome by emotion as she poured out a libation of wine.[10]

By the early twenties of the seventeenth century, Suzhou had developed into the center of intellectual opposition to the central court, which during the Tianqi reign (1621–27) was increasingly dominated by the power-hungry eunuch Wei Zhongxian. Bo Shaojun's husband, Shen Cheng, was a good friend of his fellow townsmen Zhang Pu (1602–41) and Zhang Cai (1596–1648). Both of these men would rise to fame and fortune in the early years of the Chongzhen reign (1628–44) because of their strident criticism of Wei Zhongxian's adherents following the eunuch's disgrace and death. Shen Cheng was less fortunate, even though he was equally given to social criticism. At an early age he had passed the prefectural examinations with highest honors, but he was less successful in the provincial examinations. After he had participated in these examinations six times without passing, he traveled to Nanjing in 1625 for a seventh attempt. An attack of dysentery forced him to leave the examination grounds prematurely, to die two months later. The highest rank he achieved within the system would appear to have been that of *linsheng* (subsidized student), in 1623 (even though he would only receive his first subvention in 1625).[11]

Bo Shaojun dates her first meeting with her husband to 1613, which most likely also is the year of their marriage. The couple had at least one daughter, who died at an early age, and was remembered by her father in a long and detailed elegy.[12] Both the prefaces by Zhou Zhong and by Zhang Pu to Shen Cheng's collected writings contain references to the couple's otherwise happy life together. But as these prefaces were written after Bo Shaojun's death, when these authors had been able to read her poems, it is not always clear to what extent their descriptions are based on her sketch of their life together, or on their own observation. Zhou Zhong describes how "Shen Cheng's house was nothing but the bare walls, but his spouse Bo Shaojun supported him in all possible ways with her beautiful talent and noble character. Time and again they evaluated the artistic qualities of poems and songs together, and inquired into the hidden subtleties of esoteric sutras. The joy of their 'singing and harmonizing' could not even be equaled, I'm afraid, by the much vaunted Liang Hong and Meng Guang of antiquity."[13] Zhang Pu describes how "Shen lived in quietude with Bo. She understood the Odes and Documents and had mastered the zither. She also loved to venerate the Buddhist scriptures and did not eat fish or meat. The two of them were the best of friends because of their lofty simplicity."[14]

At the time of Shen Cheng's death Bo Shaojun was pregnant, and a baby boy was born 100 days following the death of his father. Bo Shaojun died exactly one year (and one day) after her husband's death, on the day of the one-year service for his soul. Zhou Zhong claims that she was so "depressed by grief and pain" that she lost the desire to eat and eventually passed away.[15] Zhang Pu provides a slightly different version of the events:

> After Shen Cheng had prematurely left her behind, the lady beat her breast day and night, eager to sink away like ash. She wrote 100 poems mourning the deceased, and her sorrow and grief, sadness and pain surpassed the elegy for Liuxia [Hui]. Eventually this developed into a disease, which brought down her body, exactly one year and one day after Shen Cheng's death.[16]

Other early sources about her life usually state that she "collapsed overcome by emotions" (*yidong er jue*).[17] While some contemporaries described her death as *xun* (to follow someone in the grave), they do not suggest she committed suicide. She was, however, officially recognized as a *liefu* (a faithful wife who commits suicide in order to safeguard her chastity) more than two centuries later in Daoguang 17 (1837).

During the last few years at least of the marriage Bo Shaojun and her husband had lived in direst poverty. Shen Cheng's burial had been financed by a lavish gift to his clansmen from Mao Yilu, his former examiner in the prefectural examinations, who happened to be serving as Grand Coordinator for Jiangsu province at the time. Upon Bo Shaojun's death, however, no one came forward to take care of their baby son. Zhang Pu finally took him in, but the boy would die some ten years later.

Shortly after Shen Cheng's death, his friends had his collected writings printed with another financial contribution by Mao Yilu.[18] This collection, in six *juan* ("scrolls" or chapters) and entitled *Jishan ji,* has been preserved. As an appendix to this collection, the editors also included Bo Shaojun's *Daowang shi,* a selection of 81 of the 100 quatrains she had composed in memory of her husband following his death. In his *Tici* (Introductory comments), the editor of the appendix, Zhang Sanguang, provided the following explanation:

> Shaojun provided a detailed portrait of Shen Cheng's deep mind and proud bones, placid nature and transcendent talents. She was not only his loyal comrade during his lifetime, but also his good friend upon his death. In her understanding of fame and success she was completely free of conventional feelings, and in her exceptional and startling conceptions she completely went beyond established wisdom. She may not yet have captured his assiduous diligence throughout his life, but how could one expect to find this in a woman poet?
>
> When she had finished 100 poems, she passed away herself. Her "song for iron clappers" was truly more painful than "an inner-quarter plaint"! One can only wonder why she followed her husband so hastily in death below the earth—why did she not consider the fate of his posthumous son? . . .
>
> The manuscript consisted of three sheets, and each sheet contained over thirty poems, as if she had written them out together after she had composed them. I am afraid that she had become convinced of her impending death, and wanted to make sure they would be transmitted.
>
> Her earlier compositions had all been written in a regular script, but here she also showed the influence of the cursive style. I had always heard that Shaojun's hand was very much like that of Shen Cheng, and it was true indeed. The copy was riddled with errors. But after I had demanded it from her, I returned it to its original beauty by my corrections in order that the abandoned orphan might be able to read these poems at some later date. . . . Originally there were 100 poems, of which I have recorded 81. I have excised 16 poems, and 3 were missing.[19]

Despite all of Bo Shaojun's praise for her husband's moral qualities and for the literary value of his writings, Shen Cheng's own work has been almost completely forgotten. It cannot have helped his later reputation that his collected writings were printed in late 1626 with a preface by Mao Yilu, who would proceed to earn the eternal opprobrium of the literati community by erecting a shrine in honor of Wei Zhongxian, just before Wei's fall from power in early 1627. The little collection of Bo Shaojun, however, immediately attracted attention, which is not surprising as her work is distinguished by considerable wit and, at times, even a remarkable sarcasm, which sets her poetry apart from the more conventional "feminine poetry." Within a few years the full collection was included as a separate *juan* in the *Mingyuan shigui* (Anthology of poetry by famous ladies), perhaps the most important Ming dynasty anthology of women's poetry.[20] In later seventeenth-century anthologies of women's poetry, such as Wang Duanshu's (1621–before 1685) *Mingyuan shiwei* (Classic of poetry by famous ladies) and Qian Qianyi's *Runji* (Supplementary collections) of his *Liechao shiji* (Poetry collections of the successive reigns [of the Ming Dynasty]), Bo Shaojun is represented with a sizable selection of her poems. Bo Shaojun's poems continued to be read throughout the eighteenth and nineteenth centuries, as their echoes may be encountered in the work of later women poets such as Wu Zao (1799–1862) and Xu Zihua (1873–1935).[21] Bo Shaojun may have wanted to be remembered through her poems, but the primary topic of the poems is her husband and his personality.

In the first, programmatic poem of the series Bo Shaojun announces that she doesn't intend to weep for her husband in "an inner-quarters autumn-plaint," but that she will compose her poems in a more masculine style:

海內風流一瞬傾　　Hainei fengliu yishun qing,
彼蒼難問古今爭　　Bi cang nanwen gujin zheng.
哭君莫作秋閨怨　　Ku jun mozuo qiuguiyuan,
薤露須歌鐵板聲　　Xielu xuge tieban sheng.

[This world's most dashing sophistication—destroyed in a flash:
Blue Heaven responds to no question—a quarrel for all eternity.[22]
Weeping for my husband I write no inner-quarter autumn plaint,
My *Dew on Leeks* requires a song to the beat of iron clappers.]

Dew on Leeks is the title of China's best-known funeral lament, which compares the shortness of human life to the ephemerality of dew. Legend has it that the song was first sung by the (male) retainers of Tian Heng. Tian Heng was a descendant of the royal house of Qi, who, in the wake of the collapse of the Qin dynasty, had resurrected that state, but had had to take refuge on an island in the sea when the area of Qi was conquered by Han Xin, one of Liu Bang's most able generals. Following the establishment of the Han, Liu Bang summoned Tian Heng to his court, but shortly before arriving there, the latter committed suicide. Bo Shaojun may well have seen a parallel between Tian Heng, who had been robbed of his lawful inheritance, and Shen Cheng, who never achieved the rank and position to which he felt morally entitled.

The iron clappers are an allusion to a well-known anecdote concerning the song lyrics of the great Song dynasty author and bureaucrat Su Shi (Su Dongpo; 1036–1101). While in contrast to *shi*, song lyrics (*ci*) were considered a feminine genre in subject matter, tone, and style, Su Shi used the language of *shi* to create a new *ci* style often referred to as "heroic abandon" (*haofang*). According to the anecdote Su Shi once asked an excellent singer among his retainers how his song lyrics compared to those of Liu Yong, a representative of the earlier "feminine" style of song lyrics, known as "delicate restraint" (*wanyue*). The singer replied: "The lyrics of Director Liu are only suitable for a girl of sixteen or seventeen, who with red-ivory clappers in her hand will sing of 'A river-bank with willows, / The morning breeze and setting moon.' The lyrics of Your Excellency require a tough guy from Guanxi, who will sing: 'Eastwards the Great River rolls' to the beat of iron clappers."[23] The contrast with the "inner-quarters autumn-plaint" in the line preceding the invocation of the iron clappers makes clear that Bo Shaojun, even though a woman, does not intend to write in a feminine and suggestive style, but in a more masculine and direct way.

This choice of a more masculine style exposed Bo to criticism, but as a woman writer she was in a double-bind. Traditional critics were inclined to criticize women writing in a feminine style as trivial, and condemn women writing in a more masculine mode as coarse. Even Wang Duanshu, the seventeenth-century woman editor of a massive anthology of contemporary female poetry, *Mingyuan shiwei*, in which she included twenty-one of Bo Shaojun's quatrains, could not completely free herself from this prejudice:

> When we read Bo Shaojun's poems in memory of her deceased husband, we have to treasure her spirit of lofty vision and broad gait, and we have to tolerate her "rough and heroic" (*cuhao*) spots. I especially like her grand and untrammeled attitude.[24]

But Bo Shaojun also had her defenders in the seventeenth century. The *Yujing yangqiu* (Chronicles of the Jade Metropole) writes:

> With her exceptional feeling and her exceptional brush Shaojun writes out her exceptional pain. Now composing words of wisdom, then writing words of sarcasm, she has opened up a strange terrain beyond the *Zhuangzi* and the "Lisao." Why does the world have to measure her by the strictest standards and find fault with her metrics? Don't we make ourselves ridiculous in the eyes of that exceptional woman?[25]

The emphasis in the following discussion will be not so much on the literary qualities of these poems, however, but on their biographical and autobiographical aspects. These poems were written to lament Shen Cheng, and as a result have a strong biographical character as Bo Shaojun, time and again, describes and evaluates her husband (often in such glowing terms that her poems turn into hagiography). But as evocations of her husband during his life and meditations on the manner and meaning of his death and afterlife, the poems also, almost unavoidably, touch upon their married life and her own existence and activities following his death. As such the collection contains many autobiographical details, which may be considered in combination with the act of writing itself: in writing a set of 100 poems as a monument for her late husband, the writer also raises a monument to herself as a devoted wife. In the following section I will consider in more detail the ways in which Bo Shaojun portrays both her husband and herself in her poems.

THE *ONE HUNDRED POEMS LAMENTING MY HUSBAND*

Bo Shaojun's *daowangshi* are commonly referred to as "One Hundred Poems of Weeping for My Husband" (Kufu shi baishou). Many of the 81 surviving quatrains are indeed devoted to an idealized portrait of her deceased husband. The very first quatrain credits him in its very first line as having "This world's most dashing sophistication." It continues to associate him in its second line with the three noble heroes who followed an ancient duke of Qin in death and who "could not be ransomed with a hundred men." (no. 1). Elsewhere she recalls: "Your heart like a lotus-flower, your innards pure as snow, / Your spirit like autumn-waters, your breath like the orchid" (no. 29). In the second quatrain she characterizes Shen Cheng as someone who had "studied the Way." Elsewhere Bo Shaojun notes that her husband devoted himself to "substantial studies" (no. 39), that is to say, those matters that had a direct relevance to society and government. If the quality of the writings of the great historian Sima Qian (145?–89? BCE) was due to his wide travels, Shen Cheng's writings far surpassed it as his mind took the whole cosmos into account (no. 59). The moral and artistic qualities of his writings, she promises her husband, will ensure his eternal fame (nos. 5, 12, 34, 71). In the present world, his uncompromising honesty brought him only trouble, of course (nos. 8, 35, 42, 50, 52, 70), as too many contemporaries only recognized his literary talent and ignored his noble mind (no. 20). Success in the examinations continued to elude him (nos. 10, 18, 27, 28, 64), to his (and her) great frustration (no. 27), but elsewhere Bo Shaojun admits that her husband's character did not really predispose him for a successful bureaucratic career (no. 65).

Because Shen Cheng also found no satisfaction in a career as a ghost writer ("Such a shame to make bridal dresses on behalf of other people!" nos. 74, 79), the couple lived a life of grinding poverty (nos. 9, 19, 25, 38, 60), which Shen Cheng endured cheerfully ("Your eyes did not deign to cast a glance at the yellow gold"; nos. 20, 32, 39, 70), even though he was never able to realize his ambition of visiting the famous mountains (no. 73). Bo Shaojun tries at times to take a humorous view their poverty: at their house sparrows are the party-crashers (no. 51), and the couple's treatment of visitors was so shabby that no return invitation was needed (no. 66). One poem describes Shen Cheng as reading by the light of the moon that shines through the holes of the wall of their dilapidated house (no. 64). Despite this poverty, the house was filled with books, and his readings could occasionally fill Shen Cheng with great enthusiasm for the ancients (no. 77). Other quatrains describe his habits in writing poetry and prose (nos. 7, 19, 26).

If lack of success in the examination (and its attendant poverty) was one of the great disappointments in Shen Cheng's life, the lack of a son must have been the other (no. 14). Bo Shaojun would give birth to a boy following his death, an event she describes in startling lines (no. 13):

悲來結想十分痴   Bei lai jie xiang shifen chi,
每望翻然出槨期   Mei wang fanran chuguo qi,
一滴幸傳身後血   Yidi xingchuan shenhou xie,
今朝真是再生時   Jinzhao zhenshi zaisheng shi.

[When grief assails me, my imagination becomes utterly silly:
Each time I hope you'll all of a sudden emerge from the coffin.
One drop fortunately is transmitted as your posthumous blood:
This morning was in truth the hour that you were born again.]

An earlier infant daughter of the couple had died when it had barely started to learn to speak (nos. 16, 17). Aware that she herself may die very soon, our author urges her son to study his father's writings when he grows up (no. 15). In another poem she imagines that when her grownup son will ask about his father's character, she will only be able to point to his portrait, as it would affect her too much to talk about him (no. 30).

While it would appear that Bo Shaojun describes her husband as a strict Confucian scholar, she also draws attention to his Buddhist piety. The kind of Buddhist piety she describes would appear to be the kind associated with the "ledgers of merit and demerit." This form of piety enjoyed great popularity in these years amongst literati, thanks to the proselytizing activities of Yuan Huang (sixteenth century). Based on his own experiences Yuan Huang promised that one could earn success in the examinations and the birth of sons by the accumulation of merits, and the avoidance of demerits—no sin created more bad karma than the killing of living beings. The ledgers of merit and demerit emphasized retribution within one's lifetime.[26] According to Bo Shaojun, her husband "never spent much effort on transcendental deliverance" (no. 56), and she urges him to look on the tortures of the hells and the joys of heaven as "the performance of a play." But she also emphasizes the inevitability of the process of karma (no. 41), and mentions that her husband kept strictly to the fasts (no. 38) and was very circumspect in considering "causes and conditions" (*yinyuan*) of all his actions (no. 39). Keeping strictly to a vegetarian diet (no. 50), he (and she?) achieved the highest level of meditation: the eggplant starts to taste like meat, and fruits replace steamed fish (no. 61). Even so, the couple could not yet completely escape from killing, as in their poverty they use the shells of oysters as knives to cut their vegetables (no. 66). As a scholar of exceptional qualities unrecognized by his contemporaries, Shen Cheng is often, explicitly or implicitly, compared by Bo Shaojun to Su Shi (nos. 3, 70). Su's contacts with Buddhist monks were well known, and his own Buddhism stressed practical piety and the avoidance of killing living beings, which only made the comparison more suitable.[27] As a highly talented but unsuccessful and short-lived literatus Shen Cheng is also repeatedly compared to the short-lived poet Li He (790–816) of the Tang dynasty (nos. 2, 22, 78).

Bo Shaojun hardly touches upon the social aspects of her husband's life, and his many associations outside the house. To the extent that she describes these activities, she limits herself to those aspects, such as her husband's emotional reactions to his examination failures and his poverty, as she could experience in their private life. In general, her portrayal of her husband during his life focuses on his activities at home, on the life they shared.

In view of the moral qualities Bo Shaojun credits to her husband, she can only experience her husband's lifelong poverty and his relatively early death as an injustice. In the very first poem of the set she accuses Heaven of refusing to answer any questions (no. 1). If in quatrain no. 9 she still blames her husband's death on jealous demons, she later also blames it on Heaven's own jealousy of her husband's talents (no. 12). In a sarcastic quatrain, she describes Shen Cheng's death as his punishment for killing Chaos (no. 50). Reworking a conventional euphemism for death, which describes it as being called away to heaven in order to write a poem or rhapsody for the Supreme God, Bo Shaojun argues that her husband must have been summoned to the purple palaces of heaven in order to become Heaven's chancellor (no. 2).[28]

In her description of her husband's death, Bo Shaojun draws on different groups of images. One is based on the dichotomy of dreaming and awakening from a dream. One moment death will be described as an eternal sleep (no. 41), another moment as awakening from a dream (no. 62).[29] The wittiest adaptation of the theme of life as a dream may well be no. 75:

何人不是夢中人　　He ren bushi mengzhongren,
好夢榮華惡夢貧　　Haomeng ronghua e'meng pin.
君是酒人方夢飲　　Jun shi jiuren fang meng yin,
阿誰呼覺未沾唇　　Ashui hujue wei zhanchun.

[Which living being is not a person living in a dream?
A good dream is riches and glory, a bad dream poverty.
You were a lover of wine who just when dreaming of drinking
Was rudely awakened right then—without ever tasting a drop.]

More somber poems envision the state of death as one of darkness and loneliness in the grave. At one moment Bo Shaojun envisions that her husband's only conversation partners there will be "the stone figures in front of the mount" (no. 69), in another quatrain she hopes that his boredom may be relieved by the innocent chattering of his predeceased infant daughter(s) (no. 16). Another consolation, she imagines, may be that after a thousand years and from a myriad of miles an understanding friend may come and "weep before the ancient stele" (no. 71). This contrast with the next quatrain (no. 72), which ends on the lines:

寢終豈是男兒事　　Qin zhong qishi nan'er shi,
應怪家人聒耳啼　　Ying guai jiaren guo'er ti.

[How could it be a real guy's business to die asleep in his bed?
You must blame your family for making such a ruckus by crying.]

A considerable number of poems by Bo Shaojun place her husband in the Underworld (nos. 21, 25, 65). These poems may well have been inspired partly by the rituals of the "Sevens." The soul of the departed was widely believed to have to appear successively before the first eight courts on the Underworld on the seventh, the fourteenth, twenty-first, twenty-eighth, thirty-fifth, forty-second, forty-ninth, and one-hundredth day following his death, and before the ninth and tenth court after one full year and after twenty-seven months. In order to assist the soul during these ordeals, Buddhist monks would be invited to read suitable Buddhist sutras, and these would often visualize their teachings by the display of graphic paintings of the judicial torture and the horrors of hell.[30] Quantities of paper money would be burned to provide the deceased with cash to repay loans taken out at the time of birth and to grease the hands of Underworld guards and runners. But Shen Cheng leaves for the Underworld without a cent of sacrificial money, but yet is willing to berate the main judge King Yama (no. 21). Bo Shaojun wonders what the use may be of his many writings in the Underworld (no. 25), and warns her husband not to indulge in his passion for writing so as not to anger the irascible authorities of the world of darkness (nos. 45, 49), a sarcastic comment on his fate during his lifetime. Other poems voice her confidence that even the strict Underworld judges will find her husband without any moral flaw (nos. 38, 39). Finally she wonders whether her husband who was temperamentally so unfit for this world would be able to find himself "at ease below the earth" (no. 65). Other poems envision the soul of the deceased fusing with the cosmos and speaking to us—and to Bo—through the sounds of rivers and colors of mountains. Quatrain no. 4 seems to hope for a manifestation of Shen Cheng as a god, but also states: "Your bones became the mountains, your breath the tide." And elsewhere we read "River and alp transmit his spirit through sound and color" no. 43).

The complete set of poems is of course one act of memory, but some poems thematize the act of remembering itself. Bo Shaojun remembers the couple's first meeting (no. 3), and a nightlong discussion with her husband one year ago (no. 19). At other times, she believes she hears his footsteps approaching the window (no. 6), his voice reciting a poem (no. 11), or his sigh as she puts away his brushes (no. 26). At times, she still hopes to see him come home late in the day (no. 54). But as the past turns into a dream (no. 3), remembering becomes only more painful when it is combined with the awareness of a fading memory of her husband's precise features (no. 53). This provokes the fear that she might be unable to recognize her husband if she would meet him again in some future life (no. 32):

痛飲高談讀異文	Tongyin gaotan du yiwen,
回頭往事已如雲	Huitou wangshi yi ruyun.
他生縱有浮萍遇	Tasheng zongyou fuping yu,
政恐相逢不識君	Zheng kong xiangfeng bushi jun.[31]

[Drinking heartily, discoursing freely, and reciting rare texts:
Looking back at the past, these events already resemble a mist.
If in some later life we might by chance run into each other,
I'm really afraid I might pass you by without recognizing you.]

No wonder, therefore, that Bo Shaojun would rather turn into a "husband-gazing rock," forever fixed in her longing (no. 40).

A special form of memory is dreaming of the beloved one (nos. 44, 48). While the dream image may be sharper than any daytime memory, in the end it turns out to be even more frustrating (no. 67):

消宵一夢駭重逢	Xiao xiao yimeng hai chongfeng,
夢裏維愁是夢中	Mengli wei chou shi mengzhong.
急把衣裙牽握住	Ji ba yiju qianwozhu,
醒來依舊手原空	Xinglai yijiu shou yuan kong.

[During the night to our surprise we meet again in a dream,
In that dream my only sorrow is that it might be a dream.
I urgently grab the sleeves of your gown and hold on fast,
But when I wake up I stand empty-handed—just as before.]

No tender memories can deny the irreversibility of death and diminish the pain and sadness of the bereaved (nos. 13, 44, 60, 68). Eventually Bo Shaojun's grief extends to all who have passed away: "How can I make the Long River's water turn into wine, / So I may pour a libation on all graves of past and present?" (no. 68). One of Bo Shaojun's conclusion is that one is better off dying first than being left behind to mourn the loved one (no. 58).

Practical matters claim attention from the one who is left behind. In one quatrain Bo Shaojun describes herself deciding on the location of her husband's grave (no. 46). However, the most pressing duty to attend to would appear to have been the preparation of her husband's manuscripts for publication. But when she goes through his boxes to arrange his writings, her eyes are filled with tears as she tries to read the title slips (no. 6).

檢君笥篋理殘書	Jian jun siqie li canshu,
欲認籤題淚轉霏	Yu ren qianti lei zhuan fei.
忽聽履聲窗外至	Hu ting lüsheng chuangwai zhi,
回頭欲語卻還非	Huitou yuyu que huan fei.

[I go through your boxes to arrange your remnant writings,
But as I want to read the title slips, tears turn into a haze.
When suddenly I hear footsteps approach outside the window,
I turn around and want to ask—but again it isn't you.]

Her husband's literary output is mentioned again in no. 12 and in no. 23. Bo describes herself preparing two clean copies of his oeuvre, one to be used for the preparation of printing blocks, one "to be buried with the emperor in his coffin." Her husband's writings, carefully corrected and carefully stored, will ensure him eternal fame (no. 25), despite the obvious misunderstanding of his work by contemporaries (no. 34) and possible misreadings by later generations (no. 36).

Both Zhou Zhong and Zhang Pu stressed in their preface that the marriage of Shen Cheng and Bo Shaojun was based on a deep mutual understanding. In her own poems, Bo Shaojun avoids any romantic or erotic image in characterizing her relationship to her husband. No single mandarin duck is to be found in these poems, only one lonely honking goose, which fills our poet with sadness (no. 48). However, in one poem already mentioned she remembers a conversation with her husband that lasted through the night (no. 19), and one dream-poem recalls even more intimate moments (no. 44):

带夢思君形影疑　　Daimeng sijun xingying yi,
一燈陰處想欣帷　　Yideng yin chu xiang xin wei.
生前幾許牽懷事　　Shengqian jixu qianhuai shi,
並集清宵不寐時　　Bingji qingxiao bumei shi.

[Longing for you in my dreams I seemed to see your face,
In the shade of a single lamp I imagined our happy couch.
The many worries and cares that occupied you in life
Congregated together in that night while I could not sleep.]

Bo Shaojun suggests that her relation with her husband was that of a "true friend" (no. 8), but elsewhere strongly denies that claim of intellectual parity: "Don't blame me for rarely engaging in debates with you—/ A bronze bell of ten thousand pounds crashing into a gnat!" (no. 47). Very early on in the series, Bo presents herself as her husband's deeply devoted (and highly appreciated) pupil, comparing herself to Qin Guan (1049–1100), one of Su Shi's favorite and most devoted pupils (no. 3).

While the texts of the poems do not elucidate precisely what Bo Shaojun read, it is highly likely she read Su Shi who was a very popular character in the booming vernacular literature of the day. More stories are devoted to Su Shi and his circle in the three forty-story collections published by Feng Menglong at Suzhou in the years 1621–27 than to any other major literary figure. One of these stories focuses on the marriage of Su Shi's sister to Qin Guan, and the many literary tests to which she submits her groom on their wedding night. The legend of Zhang Liang, to which Bo Shaojun refers to in two separate poems (nos. 30, 76), was also very popular in vernacular literature.

As may be expected from a set of poems known by titles such as *Daowangshi* or *Kufushi baishou*, the deceased husband is very much the central character of the series. To the extent that the series is an autobiographical statement, it is so first of all through Bo Shaojun's expression of both her undying admiration for her husband's moral stature and of her own enduring grief upon his death; descriptions of scenes from their married life or from her existence as a widow function within this context. Partly because of the very size of this series of poems and partly because of the outspoken personality of Bo Shaojun, her quatrains still allow us fascinating insights into the life of a poor gentry wife in early-seventeenth-century Suzhou.

For three centuries following Bo Shaojun's death, Chinese women writers continued to write *daowang shi* and *kufu shi*. Perhaps under Bo's influence, an increasing number of these compositions consist of sets of poems or lyrics, even if they rarely numbered 100. The only later woman writer to have written a set of more than 100 *kufu shi* seems to have been the late-eighteenth-century Manchu noblewoman Tongjia. She wrote more than 200 *kufushi*, all quatrains in seven-syllable lines, from which she selected 170 poems, which she printed as *Suiwei lei cao* (Tearful drafts from besides the coffin). Despite the number (for which the author apologizes in her preface), these poems do not show the variety of the quatrains by Bo Shaojun, as the author only focuses on her enduring grief and refers to her husband only in the most respectful terms.[32]

To what extent did literate women cross over from lamentations in verse to the more public forms of prose biography in the seventeenth century and later? While women wrote moral tracts for women, the collections of biographical sketches of virtuous women were still usually compiled by men, Lü Kun being one example from the seventeenth century.[33] Men continued to turn out new works in this genre until well into the early twentieth century, as discussed by Joan Judge in chapter 6 of this volume. Women were poorly placed to write biographies of men, however, as biographies were supposed to focus on the social qualities of the deceased. Most who wrote biographies, therefore, wrote them of women. The early-seventeenth-century woman Shen Yixiu (1590–1635) wrote biographies of her youngest daughter and her cousin, for example.[34] Following the collapse of the Ming dynasty, the former courtesan Liu Shi would collaborate with her husband Qian Qianyi in compiling biographical sketches for the women poets included in the *Liechao shiji*.[35] Wang Duanshu wrote more numerous and often more lengthy biographical sketches of women poets provided in her *Mingyuan shiwei*, usually relying on earlier sources such as biographies and prefaces. Wang also may be the first woman writer to have left biographies of men, but even this independent spirit hastened to inform her contemporary reader that she had compiled her biographical accounts of Ming martyrs at the request of a man, Zhang Dai (1597–1689).[36] Once conditions had stabilized by the last quarter of the seventeenth century, biographies of men by women seem to disappear again. Biographies of women by women continue to be rare, but women would often include biographical information in the prefaces they wrote for each other's collections (as discussed by Ellen Widmer in chapter 14 in this volume). They would also continue to compile biographical notices for women authors in female-authored anthologies of women's poetry. In the final years of the Qing we have Wu Zhiying's biography of Qiu Jin, which Hu Ying analyzes in chapter 7.

From the seventeenth century we do have a few short autobiographical prose documents by women.[37] Similar to autobiographical documents by male authors from this period, which were often produced to provide a moral example, didactic intent probably also lies behind these autobiographical documents by women.[38] Precious as these rare documents are, their value is limited because of their factuality and terseness. They thus indirectly underline the value of poetry as a form of self-expression and a mode of autobiography. With its emphasis on feeling and its attention to matters of detail—restrained however by prevailing notions of decorum— poetry offers us glimpses of a woman's life that more formal biographical and autobiographical sources consistently ignore. Bo Shaojun's *One Hundred Poems* are testimony to this illuminating power.[39]

Women as Biographers in Mid-Qing Jiangnan

Ellen Widmer

To what extent and under what circumstances were traditional Chinese women biographers? To answer this question I focus on a small group of women writers from Jiangnan in the mid-Qing. Between the days of Yuan Mei's (1716–97) controversial tutelage of female students in the late eighteenth century and the disruptions of the Taiping Rebellion in the mid-nineteenth century, a number of women developed considerable reputations. The mores of their writerly world differ somewhat from those of earlier and later periods in Jiangnan,[1] as well as from those in at least one other part of China, Guangdong.

My hypothesis is that women's use of the term *zhuan* (biography) was quite circumscribed. Many male writers thought that this public and formal genre should not be used lightly,[2] and this may be the reason that women employed it so seldom. In looking for women biographers, then, we need to look beyond the term *zhuan*. My hypothesis does not apply to writings in the virtuous woman (*lienü*) tradition. As Harriet Zurndorfer argues in chapter 3 of the current volume, it was an innovative but possible move for Wang Zhaoyuan (1763–1851) to compile a work in this vein in 1812. Elsewhere Susan Mann discusses Yun Zhu's (1771–1833) use of this type of writing in her *Langui baolu* (Precious records) of 1831. I also exclude *zhuan* by those unusual women who were able to publish their prose. Some of their prose collections may include a few *zhuan*, whether of family members or others, whether of men or women, but not a lot of these survive.[3]

My hypothesis is based in the main on evidence drawn from the Ming-Qing Women's Writings Digitization Project (McGill-Harvard), an online initiative launched by Grace Fong that is committed to digitizing all works by (and in some cases for and about) women in the Harvard-Yenching Library.[4] A search for *zhuan* under the *wenji* (prose writings) section of this site brings up 4,927 entries; all but a small handful of these refer to the short, introductory passages on individual writers in large collections.[5] Most of these large collections were compiled by men, such as Zhao Shijie (fl. 1628), Zhong Xing (1574–1624), and Xu Naichang (1862–1936). Exceptions are Yun Zhu's *Guochao guixiu zhengshi ji* and *Langui baolu* of 1831 and Wang Duanshu's *Mingyuan shiwei* (Classics of poetry by famous women) of 1667. In this type of "hit," the biographies in question are very minimal: usually just where a person was from, whom she married, what she wrote, and other basic details. They are usually no more than a few lines in length. When it comes to the more elaborate biographies among the 4,927, virtually all of these were written by male relatives or other associates upon the death of the subject.[6]

To be sure, my search method has its limitations, not least because of the vast number of texts that are not include on the website. If one looks elsewhere one can find more *zhuan* authored by women, for example the series of biographies of male Ming loyalists by the seventeenth-century Jiangnan woman anthologist Wang Duanshu.[7] But it is still striking that there are so few *zhuan* authored by women on this site. My reading so far suggests that it was very rare before the Guangxu era for *zhuan* by women to serve as prefaces for other women's writings.

This is not to say that women never wrote biographically inclined prefaces to women's collections. If one calls up the term preface or *xu* on the same website one finds 253 entries, many by women, many of which are significantly biographical in nature. It appears that women rather frequently wrote biographically informative prefaces to one another's literary collections but that they always or almost always did so under the rubric *xu*.

Whether my hypothesis holds up under closer scrutiny, I propose that poetry collections of women offer at least two opportunities for exploring women's biographical talents. The first is their prefaces to one another's literary collections. These are typically called *xu* rather than *zhuan*. In common usage, a *xu* introduces a piece of writing, as well as the author of that writing[8] whereas a *zhuan* depicts a life, usually of an individual or group of individuals, with no necessary reference to writing. Where the two terms overlap is that both are biographically inclined narratives in prose. My point in this chapter is less to insist on the niceties of generic distinction than to ask whether certain *xu* by women might well have been called *zhuan* but for the convention that limited women's access to the latter term. In other words women's *xu* might sometimes have been called *zhuan* had they been written by men.

Basing my argument on data from the website, then, I tentatively hypothesize that the longer, discursive type of *zhuan* used to preface literary collections were generally not used by women in the late imperial period. When they wrote longer biographies/*zhuan* it was either in the virtuous woman tradition or it was materials used for other purposes.

My second example consists of biographically grounded anthologies by women editors. Here I discuss three of the most famous: Wang Duan's (1793–1838) *Ming sanshi jia shixuan* (Selected poems of thirty Ming writers) of 1822, Yun Zhu's (1771–1833) *Guochao guixiu zhengshi ji* (Correct beginnings) of 1831, and Shen Shanbao's (1808–62) *Mingyuan shihua* (Poetry talks on famous women) of 1845. I spend the most time on Wang Duan. This is because her accounts of historical individuals come closest to what we think of today as biography; yet I do not mean to dismiss the efforts of Yun and Shen, which are significantly anchored in biographical concerns.

My answer to the question posed at the beginning of this chapter will turn out to be that as long as one does not insist on the word *zhuan*, and as long as one does not hold too literally to contemporary notions of biography, one will find that the writing of lives was important to traditional Chinese women, indeed that it was fundamental to some of their most enduring contributions. I do not mean to suggest that my two examples constitute the only loci of women's biographical writing, but they are two important places in which such writing can be found. One could even argue, as I do intermittently in the second section, that a tendency toward biographical interest can be detected in certain women's poems. However, when I use the term *biography* in this chapter I follow tradition in referring specifically to prose. The prose biographies by women I consider in this chapter are always linked in one way or another to poetry, no doubt because of the sources of my data; but this does not detract from their capacity as life stories, as long as one is willing to expand one's view of what *biography* means.

PREFACES BY WOMEN TO WOMEN'S LITERARY COLLECTIONS

I proceed now to develop this hypothesis by taking up my first example, women's *xu* to other women's collections of poems. I present these writings in conjunction with adjacent *xu* and *zhuan* by men. My aim is to set them in their full paratextual context, as well as to open a discussion of what a women's *xu* adds and, when appropriate, whether it is significantly different from *zhuan* by men.

My first example is the set of five prefaces to a collection by Yuan Mei's (1716–98) disciple Jiang Zhu. It is entitled *Xiao weimo shigao* (Draft poems of Little Vimalakirti; 1811). Jiang was from Yangzhou but lived mainly in Suzhou. Her other published collection, *Qinglige ji* (Collection of Green Pigweed Studio; 1789), establishes her as a member of the "Ten Women of Wu" (Wuzhong shizi), a celebrated group of women poets of the late Qianlong era.[9] Judging from these two publication dates, Jiang was an active writer for at least twenty-two years. She was a disciple of Yuan Mei, but her poor health meant that she sometimes (perhaps often) missed gatherings involving Yuan.[10] She was known for her erudition, and she was praised by certain critics for writing like a man.[11] Readers of today might ask whether this was a compliment, but in Jiang's time, it was a sign that she wrote very well and, more likely than not, broke with feminine convention. Apart from her literary skill, Jiang was recognized for two seemingly incompatible interests: in swordsmanship and in Buddhism. She was also known for her skill at music and painting. Her elder brother, Jiang Fan (1761–1831), was a celebrated intellectual and protégé of Ruan Yuan (1764–1849). One of Jiang's detractors once speculated that she borrowed text and ideas from her brother, a contention she hotly denied.[12]

Xiao weimo shigao's five prefaces, three by men and two by women, were all written after her untimely demise at age forty. Jiang's husband, Wu Xuehai, was responsible for the collection in which they appear, although he wrote no preface. The five are quite different in tone. I encapsulate them briefly, in order, here.

The first and longest, by elder brother Jiang Fan, emphasizes her virtue, her talent, her skill at domestic duties, and her learning. It mentions that her works were largely lost, making it difficult for her husband to recover her poems. The second is by Chen Xie, a friend of her husband, who asked him to write the preface. He mentions two or three collections of poems by women and goes on to observe that most of their authors led difficult lives. In contrast, Jiang had a good marriage, and her poems would have passed muster with Zhu Yizun (1629–1700), a much admired anthologist of the early Qing.[13] The third preface is by Xu Huang, presumably another friend of Jiang's husband. It is the most interesting of the three prefaces by men. It strongly resists the idea that "lack of talent in a woman is a virtue." Rather, it makes the case that "lack of talent is a blessing" (*wu cai wei fu*), meaning that women live more fully and happily if they are not talented. The preface struggles over what fortune meant in Jiang's case. It does not exactly blame Jiang's talent for her poor health, but it argues that her life lacked good fortune and that talent was at least partly to blame. However,

Jiang could be regarded as fortunate in that she had a good literary reputation, one that will live on now that she is gone. So in a way Jiang's talent was good fortune of a kind, Xu concludes.

The fourth preface is by a woman, Gui Maoyi (ca. 1762–1832). A descendant of the Ming essayist Gui Youguang (1506–71), she was originally from Changshu (Suzhou) and was married to a man from Shanghai. Gui had ties with women from many areas. Her wide ranging contacts stemmed, in part, from her poverty, which forced her to serve as a "teacher of the inner chambers" and to travel widely. Gui had a longstanding acquaintance with Chen Wenshu (1775–1845), which followed her period as a disciple of Yuan Mei.[14] She was quite well known by the time Jiang died, the likely reason that she was called upon to write this preface. Gui's preface begins by telling how she first heard about Jiang and her failed efforts to meet her personally. She notes the extent of Jiang's reputation outside the family. She praises Jiang as a good homemaker and talks of her erudition. Her husband traveled a lot, Gui observes, and when he was away, Jiang held classes for the sons of the household, and, though she was kindly, she treated them "in the manner of a strict teacher." Her strong interest in reading kept her up at night and made her ill, eventually leading to her death. Gui notes that her own life was "more or less like Jiang's." A line in one of Jiang's poems, "one can live long [only] if one is not poor," struck a particularly sympathetic chord in Gui. This preface concludes with the thought that Jiang was too modest to seek publicity through publishing but that her husband was upset at her early death and wanted her writings to survive. Women readers will celebrate this book as a classic, thus keeping it alive, which will bring comfort to her husband, Gui concludes.

Hou Zhi's (1764–1829) preface comes last in the set. Hou was from Nanjing, and she married a man from Anhui who lived in the Nanjing area. Her chief claim to fame today is her editorial and compositional work on *tanci* (plucking rhymes), a signal contribution. Hou was also known for her poetry and for the success of one of her sons, Mei Zengliang (1786–1856), a *juren* (second-highest degree holder) and essayist who achieved considerable fame. Like many prefaces by women, Hou's is autobiographical as well as biographical. It begins by describing Hou's own progress toward literacy. Her "brother" (actually a cousin) Hou Yunjin (*juren* degree 1798) encouraged her to learn to read, despite her father's belief that lack of talent in a woman is a virtue. But once she married she could not keep up literary activities. Falling ill in 1794, she found that writing helped her recover. Hou Yunjin and her other brothers showed her writing to many people, and through this means she became known to

Jiang. The two entered into correspondence. After a hiatus of some years, a brother presented Hou with Jiang's book of poems, which was how Hou learned that Jiang had died. Hou had already read some sections of the work and now, going over the whole collection, she was impressed anew with Jiang's talent and saddened that she had passed on. Hou continues "Now this woman has returned to paradise (*xian shi*), whereas I am still living. Perhaps my [more meager] talent has not attracted the jealousy of the Creator?" The preface concludes with four poems, one of which situates Jiang on the mythical island of Penglai.

What can we conclude from the two women's prefaces to this collection? First, they are presented last among the five. One would hardly expect otherwise, given the tradition of placing women's writings after men's in most types of literary collection. Second, the two women were asked to contribute because they had achieved a certain measure of fame. Their friendship with Jiang, whether direct, as in Hou's case, or indirect, as in Gui's, was another reason they were asked for prefaces, but it is unlikely that Jiang's brother would have sought them out had they not been relatively well known. Third, one might ask, did the collection really need prefaces by women? Did not the men's prefaces already supply enough information about the author? Here my answer is more speculative. I suspect the brother sought out these two women as a way of establishing Jiang Zhu's currency among other women writers. This can probably be taken as a sign of her pride in belonging to the group of Yuan Mei's disciples, but it may also be a way of situating the collection in a zone of acceptability to proper women. I do not mean to imply that women's voices held equal or higher authority in this type of judgment than those of men, only that they may have carried their own type of credentializing function. Also, it seems, the two prefaces have a rather intimate feeling, even though Gui had never met Jiang. Perhaps this is the reason that both Gui and Hou supply autobiographical as well as biographical data. Anyone researching either woman would want to consult the prefaces they wrote to others' works as well as the prefaces or biographies people wrote about them.

Another set of prefaces I shall consider are to Liang Desheng's only known collection of writings, *Guchun xuan shichao* (Draft poems of Ancient Spring Studio; 1849). Liang Desheng was from Hangzhou. She is best known today for her work on Chen Duansheng's *Zaisheng yuan* (Destiny reborn), the leading *tanci*, written in the late eighteenth century. Her literary circle embraced many of the same people as Jiang's and Qian's, but her life took place on a more elevated plane. Descended from a long line of important officials and accomplished scholars,[15] her marriage to *jinshi* (highest degree holder) Xu Zongyan (1768–1819) was to a man at her own social level. Although he died three decades before she did, she was somehow able to keep her family functioning in the same lofty style. The pair of tributes presented below were both written after her death. One is by a man, the other by a woman.

The first is by Ruan Yuan. A devoted patron of his hometown Yangzhou, Ruan was a major force in the period under review. He was a leader in the movement to absorb Western mathematics and astronomy, and he was successively governor-general of three different provinces over the course of his career.[16] Judging from his several prefaces to works by women, he was also a supporter of women's writings, and several female members of his household were literate.[17] Ruan's biography is entitled "Liang gongren zhuan" (Biography of Respected Madam Liang). Ruan's piece is the first we have considered to bear the rubric *zhuan*. It begins with a description of Xu Zongyan's accomplishments. Xu and Ruan passed *juren* examination in the same year, we are told, and Xu passed the *jinshi* examination thirteen years later. Xu is said to have stepped down from official work fairly early because of his elderly parents. This allowed him to work on classics, history, astronomy, and mathematics, along with Ruan. As Xu worked on these fields, he was often away from home, and Liang ran the household. Ruan had great respect for Liang's abilities along these lines, and one of her daughters married his fifth son. Although she came from the highest social stratum, she was never arrogant or wasteful, Ruan exclaims. Various examples are provided of her fine home management. For example, she masterminded the funerals of her husband's maternal uncle (surnamed Fang) and his wife, and she supervised the friendships of her sons. "Only after she had looked into their moral and intellectual outlook and literary talent did she admit them as [her children's] friends." She also saw to it that able tutors were hired for her own and a concubine's sons, so that "all of her sons would be able to establish themselves." Moreover, "her management of the home was orderly and tolerant. Coming across righteous conduct, there was none that she did not extol." When her fourth son failed repeatedly in the provincial examinations she thought of a way to help him, and when he died in office, she helped his widow and took over the education of her grandchildren. "She had no interest in common pursuits but was addicted to poetry her whole life long," Ruan notes in praise. (He conveniently omits mention of her work on *tanci*.)

After this, Ruan begins to focus on Liang's own life, rather than her life with her husband and children. As a child she followed her father to myriad places, and these experiences informed her poems. When her elder sister, married to a Mr. Wang, died early, she took in her two motherless nieces, among them Wang Duan (1793–1838), whom she taught poetry. Wang Duan collected the poetry of Ming people and elucidated it, and she also commented on Ming history. "Was this not [Liang Desheng's] teaching?" Ruan asks rhetorically. The biography concludes with Liang's birth and death dates (both accurate to the hour), the fact that her husband died thirty years before her, the children she left behind and those that predeceased her, and the number of grandchildren (eighteen) and great-grandchildren (seventeen).

The second preface is by the woman poet Pan Suxin and is called a preface, or *xu*, like all five prefaces to Jiang Zhu's work. This account covers some of the same ground as Ruan's piece. Born in 1764, Pan would have been seven years older than Liang. Like Gui Maoyi, she was one of Yuan Mei's disciples, and both she and Liang were close to Chen Wenshu, himself a disciple of Ruan Yuan.[18] Like Liang, Pan was very well traveled as a girl, thanks to her father's official duties. She married Hanlin member Wang Run and lived for many years in Beijing, where she was in touch with a wide range of literate women. Whenever her husband's career took her to a new locale, she entered into relationships with literate women in the vicinity.[19] Pan was also an avid reader of women's writings, even those published far away.[20] Her last datable publication came out in 1851. She wrote prefaces to several collections, including both the first and the sequel volume of Yun Zhu's *Guochao guixiu zhengshi ji*, in 1831, and *Guochao guixiu zhengshi xuji* (Correct beginnings, a sequel) in 1836.[21]

In contrast to Hou's and Gui's prefaces to Jiang Zhu's, Pan's preface to Liang's collection is only minimally autobiographical. It begins by talking about Liang's father, her precocious intelligence, and the male teachers who admired her. Pan's husband is said to have been impressed by Liang. Like Ruan, Pan notes Liang's familial connection to Mr. Fang. Pan further recalls that she attempted to go and see Liang in her youth but did not succeed. Later, she went to the capital, "cold and frosty" Beijing, where she stayed for twenty years. This put her out of Liang's range. Pan observes that Liang's two [surviving] daughters both married, one to the Sun family of Xiuning, the other to Ruan Yuan's family. As the daughter married to Mr. Ruan lived nearby in Beijing and came to her for a preface, Pan was finally able to read Liang's work. She notes that Liang's many travels with her father, to Guangdong and Guangxi, Fujian, Hubei, and Hunan are reflected in her poems, as is the fact that she revisited Guangdong more than once with her husband and children. Reading the poems makes Pan sorry that she had not encountered them earlier. Pan observes that Hangzhou, where Liang was from, has long been known for its well-educated women, among them an ancestor of the very Fang family to whom her husband was related and whose poems are recited by elite people (*shidafu*) to this day.[22] (This is Fang Fangpei's *Zaiputang yingao*—Draft chantings of Hall of Uncarved Jade; 1751). Liang's husband was a famous *jinshi*, and people all over China longed to study with him. Her sons also enjoyed good fortune at the examinations, rather like that of Fang Fangpei's sons. Liang was obviously a very successful poet. Pan modestly claims to know only a little about poetry and has not done much with it in her old age. "Would that I could have a glass of wine with Liang Desheng and enjoy her company, but I cannot," she notes with sadness. "I am at least glad that I worked on poetry for a while. But Liang Desheng is talented in many areas and was unusually fortunate. How could I really hope to have been her literary friend?"

This juxtaposition allows us to move beyond the points developed in Jiang Zhu's case. Ruan's and Pan's accounts have much in common. Both emphasize Liang's family background and her successful management of her home. Both further observe her early display of talent and comment on how successfully she deployed this talent in the family, whether in teaching Wang Duan (and her sister) or keeping a sharp eye on her sons' educations. They also emphasize her husband's network of relatives. But the two accounts offer this interesting point of divergence: even though Pan never met Liang, it would seem, whereas Ruan knew her well and may even have taught her, Pan's piece has a personal tone that is not found in Ruan's. This is especially noticeable in her longing to sit down with Liang over a glass of wine, a moment that harks back to the similarly intimate tone of the biographies of Jiang Zhu by Hou Zhi and Gui Maoyi.

Let us return now to the three observations we made in connection with the collection by Jiang Zhu. First, once again, as expected, the work by the man precedes that of the woman. On the second point, the author's fame, there is little to distinguish Pan's level of visibility from that of Gui Maoyi or Hou Zhi. Third, when we ask what Pan's preface adds to the collection after Ruan Yuan has covered Liang's life so completely, we can only suggest that in its own way it, too, may affirm Liang's credentials as a member in good standing of the women's community, a follower of the womanly way (*fudao*). If this were not the case, Pan Suxin would never have yearned to sit down over a glass of wine with this never-to-be-encountered friend. But why is Ruan Yuan's work designated a *zhuan* and Pan Suxin's a *xu*? It might be possible to identify generic features that make Ruan's work more *zhuan*-like than Pan's. Its effort to narrate the entire life in order could be deemed a reason that it falls into the category of *zhuan*. But in most other respects it and Pan's account cover very similar ground.

I now consider three other collections, one each by the women who will come up for discussion in the next section. Here I merely list the genders of the authors and whether what they wrote was a *zhuan* or a *xu*. Yun Zhu's *Hongxiang guan shici cao* (Draft poems of Hongxiang Studio) was published in 1814, when the author was still alive. It has three *xu*, all by men: Cai Zhiding, Lin Peihou, and Gao E (ca. 1738–ca. 1815, of *Honglou meng* [Dream of the Red Chamber] fame). Shen Shanbao's *Hongxuelou chuji* (First collection of Red Snow Tower) of 1836, also published during the author's life time, has two prefaces (*xu*) by men (Li Shixia and Dong Jingwen) followed by one by a woman, Ding Pei. The final endorsement, billed neither as a *xu* nor a *zhuan*, is by a man, Funi yang'a, but since he is a Manchu official, the fact that his words follows the woman's does not necessarily break the pattern we have been developing up to now.[23] The edition of Wang Duan's *Ziran haoxue zhai shi* (Poems of natural love of learning studio) that was published by the Wang family in 1839, just after Wang's death, has five *xu* by men: Xu Zongyan in 1812, Liang Tongshu (1723–1815) in 1814, Xiao Lun in 1816, Shi Yunyu (1756–1837) in 1826, and Zhang Yun'ao (1747–1829) in 1826, as well as a biography (*zhuan*) by Hu Jing (1764–1845).[24]

The paratextual materials we have looked at so far more or less conform to the conventions articulated above: (1) no *zhuan* for living people, (2) all *zhuan* are by men, and (3) any *xu* by a woman comes after all *zhuan* and *xu* by men. Whatever the reasons for the few small exceptions that we find,[25] the above discussion appears to support the hypothesis that women's literary culture of early–nineteenth-century Jiangnan, if not in other times and parts of China, made room for a rather active participation by female friends and admirers in one another's literary production. This is true whether or not the woman had died by the time her collection appeared. Often this participation took the form of poems of endorsement, but it could also provide an opportunity for women to write prefaces in a biographical, even an autobiographical, vein.

BIOGRAPHY AND ANTHOLOGIES

In this section I take up three leading anthologies of the period and their compilers. My main emphasis is on Wang Duan, whose use of biography was outstanding among women of the Ming and Qing. I also touch on Yun Zhu and Shen Shanbao. I bring these two writers into the discussion in more summary fashion by way of extending the discussion of biography's importance and of creating a context for Wang.[26]

Wang Duan's work was significantly shaped by biography. It was fundamental to three other of her interests, in history, literary criticism, and fiction. Both as the adopted daughter of her aunt and uncle, Liang Desheng and Xu Zongyan, and as the daughter-in-law of Chen Wenshu, Wang had access throughout her life to excellent private libraries.[27] These resources, combined with strong support from her mentors, not to mention her own brilliance and curiosity, led her freely to pursue her interests from an early age, with Ming history as a special focus.

Biographical interest is everywhere in evidence in *Ziran haoxue zhai shi*, the literary collection which was probably published several times during her lifetime and at least three times after that, in somewhat varied editions.[28] Although many of her biographical efforts might not be called biography in modern parlance, she was consistent in her tendency to write on individuals of past eras, whether men or women, whether in poetry or prose. Poem after poem deals with the issues affecting such leaders as Xiang Yu (232–202 BCE) in his fight against Liu Bang (256–195 BCE) at the beginning of the Han Dynasty, or the sad fate of the Ming loyalist Zhang Huangyan (1620–64) at the beginning of the Qing. [29] These particular individuals are not obscure, and other women wrote poems along similar lines; but Wang extends her pursuit of history and the lives that drove it to much less familiar territory. When the subject is very unfamiliar a note often, although not always, explains who the subject was. Such notes may well be biographical in nature and are often longer than the poems.[30] Few among Wang's female contemporaries could keep up with her in such interests, although Gui Maoyi was learned enough to conduct an exchange of poems on four obscure generals of the Tang.[31] Even when Wang wrote poems on her female contemporaries she often cast them in terms of earlier generations of women writers, as when she described Gui via an analogy to the late-Ming poet Huang Yuanjie (1618–85).[32] Huang Yuanjie, Bian Mengjue (seventeenth century) and other late-Ming women became subjects in their own right in other poems.[33] No other woman writer that I know of was so consistently inclined to overlay the late Ming on contemporary times. Although Wang Duan wrote her share of social and occasional poems, even these can become so heavily annotated that they lose their poetic flow. An example of the latter is a poem mourning Yun Zhu's death. It appears at the end of *Guochao guixiu zhengshi xuji*. It is highly informative about Yun's life, because of its heavy annotations, but not as lyrical as some others in the same series.[34] Had Wang lived in a world in which the writing of narrative by women was more readily permitted she might have reduced the amount of poetry in her corpus and concentrated more on prose.

Wang is especially well known for two works on the late Yuan. Both take up the story of Zhang Shicheng's (1321–67) competition with Zhu Yuanzhang (1328–98) for dynastic transcendence as the Ming was gathering momentum but not yet in place. This story piqued Wang Duan's intense interest, but by a very indirect route, one initially couched in terms of literary criticism rather than history. It was her study of the early Ming poet Gao Qi (1336–74) that sent her along this trajectory. She focused on two points concerning Gao. The first was the valuation of later poets who ranked Gao's writings inferior to those of many other poets. Wang set out to overturn this view. The second was her indignation that Gao had been unfairly put to death by the Ming. This led her to consider what might have occurred had the Ming never come to power. These twin interests propelled her to write two pathbreaking books. The first, *Ming sanshijia shixuan* (Selected poems of thirty Ming poets), was published in 1822, when she was twenty-nine years of age. As far as I know this was the first, indeed the only, edited volume by a woman of the Ming or Qing to deal extensively with the writings of men. The second was her novel, *Yuan Ming yishi* (Lost history of the Yuan and Ming—date of completion unknown, but subsequent to *Ming sanshijia shixuan*). She ended up destroying this work after a personal crisis (the deaths of her husband and son) and a turn to Buddhism for solace. This gave her second thoughts about using fiction to arouse the sleeping dogs of history. If this work had survived it would have been the first known novel (or possibly popular history; we are not quite sure of the genre) by a woman author.

Let us now consider the role of biography in each of the two works, beginning with *Ming sanshijia shixuan*. Biographically speaking, the most interesting feature of this work is that every subject is male. Also noteworthy is the length of the biographies of individual poets. Some of these include long excerpts from other historians, but it is not unusual for Wang Duan's own writing about them to go on for pages. The two main emphases are the moral qualities and talent of those whose work she reviews. These biographies are a far cry from the brief reviews of basic facts in Yun Zhu's work.

Turning now to *Yuan Ming yishi,* although Wang Duan destroyed this work she did allow two sets of writings from it (whether true excerpts or revised sections of the original is not known) to be published in her *Ziran haoxue zhai shi*.[35] These are entitled "Zhang Wu jishi shi "(Poems commemorating the affair of Mr. Zhang of Wu, twenty subjects) and "Yuan yichen shi" (Poems of Yuan loyalists, eleven subjects). In addition, *Ziran haoxue zhai shi* presents separate encomia about these individuals and many other poems about Gao Qi.

Each of these two sets presents biographies of important late Yuan and early Ming figures. These are in prose and vary in length from about twenty lines to several pages. Following the biographies are encomiums in verse. The subjects are predominantly male, but there are also seven about women, for example, a female fortune-teller named Miss Jin, who has her own entry (at eight pages the longest in either set), and one entry on seven of the wives of Zhang Shicheng. At the end of each biography is an encomium celebrating the accomplishment of that person(s).

Here is a translation of one of the shorter biographies, that of Zhang Shide, the younger brother of Zhang Shicheng. It comes first in the set *Zhang Wu jishi shi:*

> Zhang Shide was from Taizhou. He was Zhang Shicheng's younger brother. He was good at strategy. If there was a hostile plot he could gain the loyalty of his men. He followed his brother Shicheng in start-ing the uprising. Jiangnan and Zhexi were all controlled by him. In 1357 he fought the Ming soldiers at Changshu. He was taken prisoner and sent to Jinling. The Ming emperor asked him to surrender, but he wouldn't agree. In the meantime he asked that a letter be given to Shicheng. The letter advised Shicheng to surrender to the Yuan. At this point Shide stopped eating and died. Shicheng having surrendered to the Yuan, the Yuan emperor enfeoffed Shide as the Lord of Chu and ordered that a temple be set up for him at Kunshan.[36]

As one can infer from this isolated life history, in Wang Duan's work no biography stands alone. Taken together the thirty-one entries add up to a coherent story about a valiant effort under Zhang Shicheng that failed to supplant the Yuan.

Wang Duan's work makes an interesting contrast to the role of biogra-phy in two later anthologies, one by Yun Zhu, the other by Shen Shanbao. As noted earlier, Yun does not write about any one person at length. However, by combining thousands of "biographies" and poems in a kind of pointillism, she is able to link the virtue of an individual life to the civi-lizing effect of an entire dynasty.[37] For example, her biography of Wang Duan (written while Wang was still living) reads as follows:

> Wang Duan: courtesy name Yunzhuang. She is from Qiantang (Hangzhou) in Zhejiang. She is the official Chen Peizhi's wife. She wrote *Ziran haoxue shi ji.* Note: Pei's courtesy name is Xiaoyun. He

is good at poetry and is Yun Bo's (Chen Wenshu) son. Wang Duan has a deep knowledge of poetry criticism. She once compiled an anthology on thirty outstanding poets of the Ming in two collections. Her knowledge of the people and her discussions of the times are outstanding.[38]

Yun's anthology is first and foremost about poetry, not about lives. After this introduction come four of Wang's poems (some with rather extensive prose prefaces). This arrangement, in addition to the way the type is set, means that the biographical material occupies far less space than the poems. But in the end, in conjunction with biography, the rather virtue-minded poems serve Yun's higher cause. In contrast to Wang's work on the Yuan-Ming transition, Yun's work makes no claim to be a story, but its way of linking parts to whole gives meaning to every entry in ways reminiscent of Wang Duan.

Shen Shanbao's *Poetry Talks on Famous Women* appears to be somewhat loosely structured after *Correct Beginnings* in the progression from gentlewomen through nuns, humble poets, courtesans, and foreigners, and in the chronological arrangement. The focus on multiple lives is also quite similar. Indeed, many individual subjects are the same and Yun's work is frequently cited. But Shen's tone is altogether different. In the first place she treats fewer individuals and gives most of them longer treatments. Her entry on Wang Duan (written after Wang's death) is considerably longer than Yun Zhu's:

Wang Xiaoyun, literary name Yunzhuang, wrote *Ziran haoxue zhai shichao*. Xiaoyun was deeply learned with an outstanding memory and exceptional understanding. At nine years old (*sui*) already excelled in poetry and her manner of expression surpassed her elders. When she grew up she married Chen Xiaoyun. At the time they were known as an ideal couple. Xiaoyun is Chen Yunbo (Wenshu)'s son. The whole family is very sophisticated. They use discussions to improve themselves. Wang Duan managed to complete her learning with them. Wang Duan's poetic style is very reminiscent of her uncle's. It focuses on formal refinements and tonal discriminations, but she manages to convey deep and delicate feelings. Her intentions were to go along with this. They talked over how Ming poetry criticism [thoughtlessly elevated certain poets and disparaged Gao Qi]. Xiaoyun considered this an error. Expending several years of energy she collected her anthology "Ming Poetry" in two collections, complete with verdicts on these poets. She had vast knowledge of the people and the times. When the book came out, among the people that knew poetry there was not one who was not convinced by her judgment.[39]

Shen goes on to present a few lines from various writings by Wang: her assessment of Gu Yanwu (1613–82) and other Ming poets, poems she wrote as she lay dying, and a long extract from the preface to a historical poem about the Three Kingdoms, followed by a poem on this subject. Shen concludes by noting how convincing Wang is in her moral and poetical judgments, and follows with the thought that Wang has few peers among women.[40]

Virtue may enter Shen's calculations in the sense that her collection would not have excluded women who were not held in high regard by those around them, but her chief aim is not to celebrate virtue, as had been the case with Yun, so much as to chronicle the vitality of women's literary culture—its social aspects as well as the quality of the poetry to which it gives rise. Furthermore its tone is less Olympian than Yun's. From reading *Mingyuan shihua* we can learn as much about Shen as about the subjects on which or whom she comments.[41] Although not exactly autobiographical it uses the author's personal experience as one important lens through which to view a vast range of talented Qing women, living and no longer living.

Whether or not we view these two famous collections through the lens of Wang Duan's writings, we can see how essential biography is to both Yun Zhu's and Shen Shanbao's endeavors. It is clearly a major component of all that both women set out to accomplish, despite the fact that neither is as biographically or historically minded as Wang's work, nor as inclined toward prose.

It appears that the early nineteenth century was generous in allowing and respecting the accomplishments of women who wanted to write in a biographical manner, whether their aim was to promote the civilizing mission of the Qing, the brilliance of women's poetry exchange, a new view of Ming poetry and history, or a newly edited *Lienü zhuan*. However for Wang Duan the novel/unofficial history format began to feel uncomfortable, whereas the biography/encomium format of "Yuan yichen shi" and "Zhang Wu jishi shi" was more acceptable.[42] In view of the hypothesis raised in the first section of this chapter, which suggests a certain inhibition among women in the use of the term biography, it is worth remembering as a counterweight that the more biographically oriented "Yuan yichen shi" and "Zhang Wu jishi shi" were a safe fallback for Wang once anxiety over her novel overwhelmed her. Clearly the taboo here was not against the elaboration of life stories per se, nor did it lie in her focus on men, as both of these traits are found in "Yuan yichen shi" and "Zhang Wu jishi shi." Even the sharp critique of Ming history is found in these later renditions. By a process of elimination we conclude that there were two sources of anxiety for Wang with *Yuan Ming yishi* : its form and its exclusive use of prose.

The beginning of this chapter takes up what appear to be conventions affecting women's use of the term biography in their writings. Although the term was used for biographies of virtuous women and standalone pieces, when women wrote prefaces to one another's writings they did not, as a rule, call them *zhuan*. Instead they wrote *xu* that were often biographical in nature. In the final section, however, we begin to suspect that something more complex than semantics is involved. The fact that Wang Duan destroyed one work may tell us more about her as a person than about the wider conventions affecting women, but other things suggest a more far-reaching taboo. That she was the first to write extensively on men but that no one followed her example would seem to show the strength of the inhibition for women against taking up male subjects in mid-Qing Jiangnan. Furthermore, Wang Duan tried to write biography and history, even a novel, in a world that apparently discouraged pure narrative by women writers. If we are right that Wang Duan's narrative urge yielded to the expectation that women wrote mainly poems, this would be another instance of a substantive taboo. In a different social environment Wang Duan might have more freely written biography, history, or fiction and spent less time on poetry. Rather surprisingly, we can identify a woman who made such a choice in eighteenth-century Guangdong;[43] but in early nineteenth-century Jiangnan Wang Duan felt she would be better off mixing prose and poems.

With their very divergent techniques and purposes, we find, innovative women like Yun Zhu and Shen Shanbao had their own way of employing biography in their edited compositions. The results may look more conventional than Wang's work, in large part because of the greater proportion of poetry and the exclusive focus on female subjects, but biography was a major tool of their endeavor even when their work differed from Wang's. The many *xu* by women to one another's collected poems and the biographical strength of all three anthologists encourage us to propose that biography was coming unto its own among mid-Qing women of Jiangnan but was still inhibited by convention far more than it was for men.

15. Beyond Rewriting Life History

Three Female Interviewees' Personal Experiences of War

Yu Chien-ming

Oral history is valuable for historians. It can serve as an important source when other documents have been concealed or destroyed for political reasons.[1] Whereas biographies, autobiographies, epitaphs, and memoirs are generally limited to the achievements of important figures, oral history can give ordinary people their own voice. Other materials may be uncovered in the interview process, such as diaries, letters, yearbooks, photographs, and articles of everyday use. The method of oral history is particularly valuable in recovering women's experience and reconfiguring women's subjectivity. In highlighting previously ignored women's voices, it often presents a reality that diverges greatly from limited documentary records and the previous views of historians. Women's oral history thus offers historians insights that force them to reconceptualize historical problematics.

Like Gail Hershatter's contribution to this volume, my chapter centers on oral interviews of women to reexamine the existing historical record. In my case, this is the record of the Sino-Japanese War. The essay uses three female interviewees' oral records to examine their wartime experience and analyze how the war transformed women's lives. The conclusion discusses how these narrative histories can overturn or modify accepted versions of the Sino-Japanese War and suggest new avenues of research.

First, let me explain my research and interview methodology.

THE INTERVIEW PROCESS

My colleague Lo Jiu-jung and I conducted our project in 1998. The resulting interviews clearly indicate that the war not only altered the historical trajectories of the Guomindang (GMD) and the Chinese Communist Party (CCP), it also changed the lives of countless Chinese—especially women.[2]

The Sino-Japanese War lasted for eight years from 1937 to 1945, and its effects on different regions and groups differed over the course of the war. Because the threat of violence did not distinguish between rich and poor, we did not attempt to select specifically "representative" subjects but rather conducted extensive interviews of subjects introduced to us by elders, relatives, or clan associations. Among the three women I interviewed, Zhang Wang Mingxin was born into an educated family in Huangpo, Hubei Province, in 1918. She graduated from Second Hubei Normal University with a degree in high-school teaching, and she worked as a teacher, an office worker, and also in the publishing business. Yu Wenxiu was approximately the same age as Zhang Wang. She was born in Su County, Anhui Province, in 1921, graduated from elementary school, and worked as an a elementary school teacher and merchandise inspector. Pei Wang Zhihong was slightly younger, born in Beijing in 1928. She attended a few years of elementary school and took on many jobs over the years, such as running a grocery store and a breakfast house, performing domestic services, and babysitting. Thus the three female interviewees came from different regions with different family and educational backgrounds.

A crucial preliminary task in oral history is to establish a sense of trust and rapport between the interviewer and the interviewee. The interviewer must first adjust to the tone of the interviewee. Pei Wang Zhihong was straightforward in conversation, for example, her language often earthy and lively. Though the interview records are not literal transcriptions, I retain the interviewees' diction in interview manuscripts. In addition, it is also important to create a relaxed ambience. In our case, the three interviewees had never been interviewed before and sometimes saw the interviews as informal chitchats. Although I always informed the interviewee of my motives and the general purpose of the interview, they often digressed during the interviews, so I often needed to guide them through the interviewing process. As Pei Wang Zhihong was not a "docile" old lady, she did not initially follow my lead. Later when she learned that I was sincerely hoping to understand the lives of women at wartime through her memories, however, she became very cooperative. This kind of interview—formal but not excessively strict—helps to prevent the interviewee from rambling on about unrelated subjects while at the same time allowing the interviewee's subjective consciousness to emerge.[3]

It is not easy for people to remember and recount the fullness of past events and thus often necessary to supplement their memories with other sources. Zhang Wang kept her educational credentials and résumé, for example, which could be used to cross-check events she had forgotten or misremembered. In addition, Zhang Wang's daughter provided me with her mother's diary, which gave me another way of verifying parts of her interview. Yu Wenxiu and Pei Wang Zhihong often recalled certain incidents or emotions with the help of their families or objects from the past. Old photographs can often produce remarkable results. In the end, it is not possible to verify every detail. We did, however, ensure is that certain major distorting factors were eliminated: our interviews did not involve money or other gain, and the interviewees understood that our purpose is research.

In the following discussion, I divide the article into two sections: "Marriage and Family" and "Refugee Experiences," for these two phases contain the three interviewees' most unforgettable experiences. It was during these periods that they each experienced the transition from girlhood to womanhood, and then to motherhood. Relatively unencumbered by political issues, their narration has greater credibility, providing the historian with rich material to write women's history and to rewrite history.

MARRIAGE AND FAMILY

If we look at newspapers and magazines of the first half of the twentieth century, we see much space devoted to marriage and the family, with phrases like "monogamy," "free love," "celibacy," "marriage according to one's choice," and "freedom to divorce" appearing frequently. This picture did not represent commonly held marriage values, however, and generally applied only to urbanites and intellectuals. It was not until the Sino-Japanese War that marriage and families underwent real change.

In his study on the history of Sino-Japanese War, Lü Fangshang points out that gender relationships became particularly unstable and complex during wartime, with higher rates of divorces and bigamy as well as cohabitation and remarriage. He argues that this phenomenon was closely linked to societal changes and mass migration in wartime, which attenuated the social and moral authority of the traditional large extended family.[4] Oral interviews allow us to discover in greater depth the underlying reasons behind such family disruptions and the particular contexts in which they arose. I am particularly interested in how the interviewees dealt with marital problems in such turbulent times.

Zhang Wang Mingxin: Not Facing Adversity Alone

Behind her mild manners, Zhang Wang Mingxin is a determined woman. She bobbed her hair when she studied at the normal school in Hubei in

FIGURE 15.1.   Zhang Wang Mingxin (*middle*) with her mother and niece in 1935. Reprinted with permission from Lo Jiu-jung, Yu, and Chiu, 62.

1938, and was dubbed "trendy" by her classmates.[5] Although she did not think of herself as a New Woman, her ideas on marriage were quite modern, as she and her best friends all believed in leading their lives as unmarried women. She explained that she was determined not to get married because she saw her close female relatives continuously giving birth to babies after marriage, as if "women lived just to give birth." Thus, when her family tried to persuade her to marry, she threatened to become a Buddhist nun in protest. As a result, Her family did not persist.[6]

Zhang Wang's refugee experiences during the war led her to abandon her belief in staying single, however. While trying to board a train so densely crowded with people that some clung to the roof, she saw the advantage of being married as some women were heaved onto the train by their husbands. Also, many of her female classmates who once shared her belief also got married, which further prompted Zhang Wang to change her mind. She eventually married a graduate from Dongbei University, a man originally from Shandong province. Since her husband was a Christian like herself and took Zhang Wang's father as his teacher, they got married in Chongqing in 1945 with her parents' approval.[7]

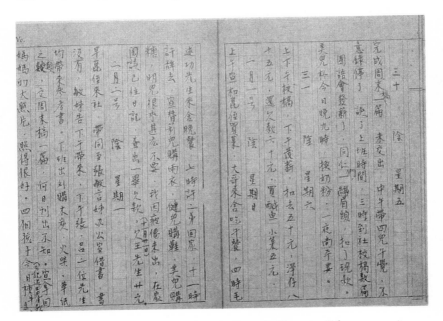

FIGURE 15.2.   The diary of Zhang Wang Mingxin (January–February 1953). Reprinted with permission from Lo Jiu-jung, Yu, and Chiu, 105.

The story should have ended here, but when I delivered the published oral history to Zhang Wang's daughter, she told me that before her parents got married, her father had already been married in Shandong. Unfortunately, Zhang Wang Mingxin herself had died by this point, and I had no way to verify whether she knew of his first marriage. In any case, the original story was the interviewee's reconstruction of her personal history. According to her, her marriage was a happy one. As noted above, bigamy was not unusual during wartime.

What is particularly significant in Zhang Wang's narrative is the change in her view of marriage, and how the once-pampered daughter adjusted to family life after marriage. Before her marriage, she had never performed household chores, which were the responsibility of her sister-in-law and the servants. After her marriage and during the war, the family could not afford a servant. Her husband generally did the cooking—but when he had to work, Zhang Wang had to cook herself. She often wept while she cooked and sometimes burned the dishes or undercooked them. Right after Japan's defeat, her husband got a job in Taiwan, while a pregnant Zhang

Wang was cared for by her mother. She had a difficult labor and gave birth to her daughter after four days and five nights of agony. Although Zhang Wang had meant to stay single so as to avoid giving birth, in the end she was pregnant six times and had four children.[8]

When Zhang Wang's family arrived in Taiwan, her husband got a stable job and she hired a servant. Their financial situation was still precarious, however, and her life remained more strenuous than before war, when she was single. Zhang Wang mentioned that there were times when she had to buy vegetables from the street vendors on credit, and since she didn't have enough breast milk she had to feed her children with rice soup and crackers. Her narrative of this difficult period is corroborated by her diary, written during January and February of 1953, in which she recorded each item she owed.[9] Though her life in Taiwan was difficult, she was mostly content because she had come to appreciate life more fully after the dangers of being a refugee.[10]

Yu Wenxiu: Reinforcing Ties before Marriage

Yu Wenxiu was engaged to her aunt's son around the age of three or four, a case of "reinforcing family ties by marriage." Since she was educated, some people laughed at her acceptance of the early engagement, but Yu believed that "traditional values were ingrained in me from childhood and one must submit to one's fate." After their engagement, the two children spent much time together until they were grown. When her fiancé wanted to have a girlfriend, his family quickly put an end to it.[11] Yu and her fiancé wrote to each other a few times at the beginning of the war, and when her fiancé was preparing to join the army's political education program, their parents decided to let Yu Wenxiu join him. The parents' reasoning was that the training would give them a chance to get to know each other; if they got along, that would be good; if they did not, they could end the engagement. As it turned out, they did like each other. They were married in 1941 after the training and remained happily married.[12] It appears that during wartime, it was not unusual for parents to send unmarried couples together to safe areas.

Yu Wenxiu's economic situation, like Zhang Wang Mingxin's, continuously worsened after her marriage as a result of the war. Two periods stood out in her memory: the first was in 1947, when her husband and father-in-law went to work in Taiwan. Although originally intending to return to the old family home in their village, the war drove them to take refuge in the city, as it did many people in similar circumstances. Their relatives in Su County took them in, but since the house also hosted four other refugee families, there was not enough food. This was Yu's first and only experience of hunger:

> I brought three children with me with the youngest still nursing. By the time I fed the second child, there was no more rice in the pot. My sister-in-law asked me if I had eaten and I lied saying that I had. For that one month, I ate only sometimes, and it was the first time in my life that I went hungry.[13]

Afterward, she moved to a friend's house and stayed there until her husband took the family to Taiwan. In the early days in Taiwan, her husband was unemployed because of the Sun Liren Incident and had to seek work in the north.[14] This was the second difficult period in Yu's life. She had to fight to find food for every meal and even once stealthily picked beans in someone else's garden. During this time, she did get help from her neighbors, who were all originally from the mainland, such as the time when Yu gave birth to a child prematurely and her neighbors helped her find a midwife. This baby ultimately died during their journey to the north. In total, Yu gave birth to three daughters and two sons. Though she did not intend to have so many children, she indicated that there were no contraceptives at the time. Once she took quinine to induce abortion, but it did not work.[15]

In addition to narrating her own marriage and family life, Yu Wenxiu also described the marriage of her fourth brother. This topic was not in my original interview outline, but when I asked Yu about her fourth brother's situation as a Communist after the war, she suddenly shifted to a discussion of his marriage. He was married when he studied at a university in Yanan and became an active Communist. When the GMD army tried to wipe out the Communist army in Henan, he was taken in by a local family, which pretended to the GMD troops that he was their son-in-law. Later, he did in fact become their son-in-law and fathered a son. It was not until the CCP achieved victory that he wrote to his family from Nanjing and informed them of his second marriage. Her mother was outraged and brought the first wife (Yu's sister-in-law) with her to Nanjing. He tried to explain the situation and refused to take in the first wife. When his first wife returned home, she found a job and remarried. To avoid being charged with bigamy, he and his first wife both changed their names. Yu spoke of this incident with emotion: "Fate plays tricks on people, but it was also because of the war."[16]

In telling this story extraneous to the narrative of her own life, Yu Wenxiu provided an important clue to the issue of name changes during

FIGURE 15.3. Yu Wenxiu's five children in 1956. Reprinted with permission from Lo Jiu-jung, Yu, and Chiu, 147.

and after the Sino-Japanese War. In a time of turmoil when the household registration system had essentially collapsed, it was not difficult or unusual for people to change their names, identities, or ages. Unless the person involved later revealed the truth, the secret could remain buried forever. Scholars studying household registration materials should remember this loophole in the system and treat the materials with caution.

Pei Wang Zhihong: Tainted Memories?

Pei Wang Zhihong was different from the other interviewees in that after the formal breakout of war in 1936, she and her family remained in Beijing during the Japanese occupation. Wang's (her maiden name) family was poor. Perhaps the war made their lives a bit worse, but conditions were essentially the same as before the war. Pei Wang grew from a little girl to a young woman during the war, although she did not accept either match-making or any proposals from suitors until the war ended. Through the introduction of a neighbor, she met a soldier from Shanxi who was then stationed in Beijing, and they got married in winter 1945.[17]

This marriage later took an unexpected turn. Before the interview, Pei Wang's daughter-in-law asked me to be particularly careful when asking about her marriage so as not to upset Pei Wang. The daughter-in-law told me that Pei Wang's husband already had a wife before her but that he had lied to Pei Wang and her family. It was not until her husband went back to China to visit relatives many years later that he revealed the truth to Pei Wang. At the time of my interview, Pei Wang's husband had recently died, but she remained upset about it, and her daughter-in-law hoped that I would not bring up the issue. My interviewing ethics dictate that I will not transgress personal boundaries the interviewee has set, especially regarding questions of love and marriage.[18] I kept my promise and, indeed, Pei Wang never directly discussed it. Still, her bitterness showed during the interview. She mentioned, for example, that her second elder brother had tried to persuade her not to marry a stranger, warning her: "You may not suffer for the first two or three years, but you will regret it later."[19] Again, when I asked how she overcame the language barrier in the early stages of their relationship, she told me that Mr. Pei once told her: "I will speak slowly, and then you will understand." Then she added, "He was patient with me, but now when I think of it, he was actually very cunning." Had she not discovered her husband's previous marriage, perhaps she would not have described him as "cunning." This incident also illustrates one of the problems with oral history: the memories of the interviewee may change as new information emerges over time.

It was not uncommon in wartime China for women to choose a soldier from another province as their lifelong partner, as Pei Wang Zhihong did. Some of these marriages did not receive parental permission. On the ship taking military dependents to Taiwan, for example, Pei Wang noticed that some girls had actually eloped with soldiers.[20] Indeed, the war affected not only women's marriage decisions but also men's. When she was liv-

FIGURE 15.4. The wedding of P'ei Wang Zhihong in 1946. Reprinted with permission from Lo Jiu-jung, Yu, and Chiu, 200.

ing in a military community (*juancun*) in Tainan, Pei Wang knew many single soldiers who had come to Taiwan alone and had a hard time finding a wife.[21] Also, the difficult living conditions in military communities often worsened relations between couples. Pei Wang reported incidents she had heard where young wives abandoned their husbands and children to run away with their lovers.[22]

Before her marriage, Pei Wang Zhihong had worked to supplement family income.[23] After her marriage, she and her husband lived in a community of military dependents at Dongbei University and had a fairly stable life. Later in Taiwan, her husband's meager salary was not enough to pay for the children's tuition, so Pei Wang took on various jobs to supplement the family's income.[24] She had a total of three children, which was relatively few in postwar Taiwan, as most women bore more children, regardless of whether they were from China or Taiwan, rich or poor.[25]

REFUGEE EXPERIENCES

As conventional Chinese history narrates it, the Sino-Japanese War unified the Chinese people against the Japanese invaders, and many young people were eager to join the war effort. However, this generalization does not apply to everyone, and people reacted to the war in different ways according to their circumstances and backgrounds. In particular, women and men experienced the war differently. This is evident from the three female interviewees' war stories of their own experience or of others. All three interviewees spoke spontaneously in recounting this part of their life stories, with no need for prompting, demonstrating the deep impression war left on their lives. Their experiences as refugees and of settling in a new land are of great significance for the study of the postwar history of Taiwan, and particularly, of ethnic relations in this period. The interviewees' narratives constitute important historical evidence that challenges the overly politicized language currently used in many studies.

Zhang Wang Mingxin

Zhang Wang Mingxin's family was well-to-do and unconnected to political parties or factions. Whereas other people fled during the war, she and her family rented a boat for "touring." Because she had never been far away from her home before, she enjoyed the scenery as if she were on a leisure trip. She was able to eat well and stay in decent places and quite enjoyed herself.[26] However, a robbery she encountered in Hengyang was an unforgettable life experience. Though many records on the Sino-Japanese War document the atrocities of Japanese soldiers, Zhang Wang Mingxin's family was more afraid of bandits than of Japanese soldiers. She described how one night, on February 27, four bandits dressed in military uniforms broke into their house in Hengyang. Their family escaped calamity only because of her father's wisdom.[27] This personal experience of one family may illuminate the general injury that the war inflicted on the Chinese people as the war brought social disorder that was no less fearsome than the destruction from artillery fire or crimes committed by Japanese troops.

And what of Zhang Wang's experiences of the war itself? Through my persistent questioning, she did eventually recall that she had indeed encountered air raids by enemy planes when living in Chongqing and had often had to hide in the underground air-raid shelters made habitable by the contributions of dozens of local families.[28] Her earlier lapse of memory illustrates the defense mechanisms developed by people living in the GMD regions.

After the war, part of her family returned home while she, shedding her previous fragile persona, accompanied her mother, nephew, and daughter back to Wuhan first. Later she traveled alone with her daughter to reunite with her husband in Taiwan. Because her brother had arranged the trip from Wuhan to Shanghai and then to Taiwan and she had people to help carry their luggage, she described her trip to Taiwan as "very comfortable."[29] Nonetheless, on her way to Taiwan, she encountered several challenges. First, a soldier had occupied her reserved first-class cabin, so she had to muster enough courage to fight for her space by going to his superior. Then, she almost fell into the water, trying to save her daughter's diapers that had blown away.[30] In comparison with other refugees at the time, however, she was very lucky.

After they settled in Taiwan, Zhang Wang's husband had a stable job, although she also took on work in administration, teaching, and proofreading to subsidize her family's income. She often mentioned her relations with the Taiwanese people with whom she had close contact. At the time, many relocated mainlander families hired Taiwanese maids and stories of conflicts were often published in the newspapers of the day.[31] Zhang Wang's case was quite different.[32] In one especially touching instance, Zhang Wang, who apparently looked like the daughter of one of the old Taiwanese women in the neighborhood, became the old woman's goddaughter. For years, Zhang Wang's family maintained a strong relationship with this woman's family. In spring 1947, during what later became known as the February 28th Incident, the old woman's family protected Zhang Wang's family.[33] Another cherished memory was of a Taiwanese nurse who took care of Zhang Wang when she gave birth. They were close in age and became bosom friends.[34] Zhang Wang Mingxin's deep-rooted relationships with these Taiwanese force us to nuance generalizations about ethnic conflicts between the mainlanders and indigenous Taiwanese at this time.

Yu Wenxiu

Yu Wenxiu's refugee experiences were completely different from those of Zhang Wang Mingxin's. The people of her hometown, Linhuan of Su County, Anhui Province, had long been accustomed to instability. Even before the war, local military troops often fought for territory, and whenever the fighting began, people took refuge in relatives' houses, which they simply called "running away" (*paofan*). During the Sino-Japanese war, GMD troops, the CCP's New Fourth Army, and the Japanese army all fought in the area; Yu Wenxiu thus had much direct experience of the war.

Yu described how her family survived a number of calamities. In order to hide from the Japanese army, at the first word of its coming the entire family sought refuge in the remote countryside—even women with bound feet had to run away. People slept in the open air on the muddy slopes of the hills. Since many different armies entered this area, it was difficult for the local people to tell whether they were friend or foe. On one occasion, Yu and other children waved at troops passing by, thinking they were friendly soldiers, while the adults rested on bullock carts with no concern. It was not until later that they discovered they had come face to face with the Japanese army. Yu Wenxiu had heard many stories of Japanese soldiers' sexual violence from neighbors and friends, and she felt very lucky to have escaped unscathed herself.[35]

As mentioned earlier, she and her fiancé received the GMD's basic ideological and military training on Dabie Mountain. During the training, the instructor taught them how to guard against the enemy's attacks and work behind enemy lines. Afterwards, most students were sent to serve at the local level, while Yu was assigned to teach in an elementary school.[36]

Yu's life after marriage was fairly stable until her father-in-law was captured by the Japanese army. The family's political fate was marked by this incident in ways that illuminate the vagaries of politics in this period. Initially, the Japanese seized him because he had worked undercover for Li Zongren, the GMD leader in Guangxi region in the mid-1940s; but rather than hurt him, they made him work in the customs inspection unit.[37] After the war, he was imprisoned for one year by the Chinese government as a traitor. For a while, the family moved to territory controlled by the Communist New Fourth Army, because it was closer to the place where her father-in-law was imprisoned. Later, the GMD refused to accept them on the grounds that they must have become Communists, while the CCP also refused them because they had received GMD training. Having no other recourse, they went into business as wholesalers in Su County until the war was over.[38]

Affiliation with party and state was thus often ambiguous during the war. Yu Wenxiu's story demonstrates the difficulty even when people meant to remain loyal, as some people served the Japanese in order to survive. Thus the war damaged the basis for trust between the state and its people and between the party and party members.

After the war, Yu Wenxiu faced the most difficult days of her life. The journey to Taiwan with her husband, mother-in-law, and three children was extremely dangerous. When they left Su County, the town had been under CCP attack for two months, and they suffered considerable hardships as they fled. The trains did not operate, so they took a truck without cover. It took two days to get to Nanjing, where they transferred to Shanghai. The Tianjin-Pukou railway was seized by the CCP, and the ships to Taiwan were packed with people. They waited for twenty days before

FIGURE 15.5.   Yu Wenxiu (*right*) with her neighbor in 1985. Reprinted with permission from Lo Jiu-jung, Yu, and Chiu,146.

finally finding a ship. Less than a month later, Shanghai was occupied. Nevertheless, Yu Wenxiu still found some opportunity for relaxation on this dangerous journey. As she waited in Shanghai, she visited the Sincere Department Store and took escalator and cable car rides, novel experiences for Yu that remained memorable.

After Yu Wenxiu settled in Taiwan, she did not take formal jobs but mainly stayed at home to take care of her children. Later, she sewed buttons at home for a store. Because this job was well paid and she didn't have to leave home to do it, she worked at it for eight years.[39] The family often moved due to her husband's career. Yu's neighbors, like Zhang Wang Mingxin's, were mostly Taiwanese, from whom she learned to cook Taiwanese dishes; especially in Taoyuan, she made friends with Taiwanese and Hakka women and learned their languages as they learned hers.[40]

Pei Wang Zhihong

When the Japanese army entered Beijing, Pei Wang Zhihong was eight years old and had no fear as she brought her younger brothers and sisters along to watch the crowded, bustling scenes. She recalled also that when the Japanese army first came, they tried to find "pretty girls" (*huaguniang*) in each household. The young girls in the neighborhood had to shave their heads and pretend to be boys in order to hide from them. Chinese people in Beijing were enraged by such incidents, and some Beijing residents retaliated by killing the Japanese. The Japanese themselves eventually began to practice greater restraint, and the situation eased.[41]

According to Pei Wang Zhihong's narration, life in Beijing under the Japanese occupation was marked by less freedom—food and goods were rationed, for example—but it did not fundamentally change. She continued to shop at street markets, watch movies, and enjoy Chinese comic dialogues. After the war was over, however, the civil war had a more direct impact on life in Beijing as inflation skyrocketed. Beijing became even more dangerous in 1948. When her husband's detachment left Beijing, she had to leave as a military dependent as well. Unlike many people during the war, Pei Wang's refugee experiences began well after the victory over Japan.[42]

Members of the army and military dependents went different ways. The young Pei Wang Zhihong and her daughter took the train with other female dependents to Tanggu, then boarded a boat to Shanghai, where they transferred to another ship to Taiwan. The army arranged for a cargo ship to take them to Shanghai, packed full of freight and refugees. She and many other female dependents were not given any space in the cabins and had to stay in the passageways or fight for seats, which she did for herself and her children.[43]

During the three-day voyage from Tanggu to Shanghai, Pei Wang did not have a peaceful time. Chased by Communist ships, many people fell sick, some died, and the babies who had died were thrown into the sea. Once they arrived in Shanghai, some people were able to stroll around the city while they waited for the connecting ship, which allowed for some temporary escape from the tension of being a refugee. However, with a young daughter, it was not possible for Pei Wang to go out for meals, so she had to fight for the coarse food served on the ship and almost died of food poisoning. These memories were so ingrained in her that she was afraid of ever taking another ship again. In 1949, when her husband wanted to return to Shanxi, Pei Wang insisted that unless they take the plane, she would not go back with him.[44] They thus remained in Taiwan, and although Pei Wang had to work unremittingly to subsidize the family's income, she chose to live there for the rest of her life.

Pei Wang Zhihong and a group of military dependents were placed in a military community in Tainan after their arrival in Taiwan. She was not used to life in Taiwan. The way of making a fire was different from in her hometown, for example, and once she almost started a major conflagration.

FIGURE 15.6.   Pei Wang Zhihong (*left*) with her neighbors, in the military community in 1963. Reprinted with permission from Lo Jiu-jung, Yu, and Chiu, 218.

The trauma of this incident was still evident at the time of our interview. Nor did she ever get used to Taiwan's earthquakes and typhoons.[45] Still, once she was settled in Tainan, Pei Wang began working; her circle of friends and acquaintances was mostly made up of people in the military community. She could not speak Taiwanese and rarely came in contact with Taiwanese people.[46] This was not unusual, as the military communities were secluded.

The oral histories above show how war transformed three women's lives, bringing them much suffering but also experiences considerably outside of the ordinary. This observation has important bearing on the debate over whether the extraordinary circumstances of wartime expanded the sphere of female agency.[47] This question can be approached through the examination of three issues: marriage and family, birth rates, and the language of "fate."

It is clear from the above narratives that marriage and family are important topics to consider when discussing how the war affected Chinese women's lives. Zhang Wang Mingxin, for example, abandoned her belief in remaining single; Yu Wenxiu's fourth brother's wife remarried when faced with her husband's bigamy; and Pei Wang Zhihong married a soldier from another province. The question here is not whether their decisions led to happiness, but whether these decisions were made freely or were largely dictated by the war environment.

Birth rate is another fruitful angle for examining women's agency. The high birth rates of Chinese women during the war years were in marked contrast to the promotion of birth control in the 1920s. This birth-control campaign proved ineffective not only among uneducated women but even among women who had received higher education. Though some women tried to induce abortions because of limited access to contraceptives, the majority of women, including two of those interviewed, continued to give birth to a large number of children. I argue that this is a matter at least partly of choice, as the war had brought disease and disasters, and human lives became extremely vulnerable, especially those of babies and children.

A striking similarity among the three interviewees and also among women who lived through the war is that they often attributed their bitter experience to "fate." This is a concept that clearly had currency across class and educational background and beyond the usual "traditional" and "modern" divide. The language of "fate," which belongs to a longstanding repertoire of coping mechanisms, further complicates discussions of women's agency during wartime.

I would like to conclude by outlining a number of areas highlighted in the above oral histories which both help nuance accepted versions of the Sino-Japanese War and suggest new avenues for future research.

First, there are vast regional differences in war experiences, differences that have yet to be fully addressed by historians. Second, during the war the civilian population was threatened not only by Japanese soldiers but by Chinese bandits. Third, national and party loyalty are often compromised during wartime. Fourth, the war produced a long-term refugee problem, which persisted when a segment of the population moved to Taiwan. This phenomenon cannot be subsumed by the term "war." Fifth, we need to pay adequate attention to the importance of the modernization of transportation during the war in assisting the withdrawal, relocation, and migration of large segments of population. Sixth, people who migrated to Taiwan after the war included merchants, cultural elites, government employees, and soldiers and their dependents. They had different degrees of interaction with the Taiwanese people. It is simplistic to reduce this complex social reality to an overly politicized interpretation based solely on provincial origins. Seventh, historians often do not pay adequate attention to the lives of mainlanders in Taiwan after the war and their relationships with relatives who remained in China. While interactions were indeed few before Taiwan residents were allowed to visit relatives in China, historians of the pre-1949 period should not ignore the influence of Taiwan-based mainlanders on China during and after the war.

Ultimately, our understanding of the war is greatly enriched by examining the experience of women and particularly of women of different classes. While these multifaceted historical accounts of or by women have to be treated with the same caution as all historical evidence, they are invaluable in adding nuance to our historical understanding, and at times even in overturning long-cherished assumptions of mainstream history.

16. Epilogue

How to Read Chinese Women's Biography

Joan Judge and Hu Ying

Recall Miss Fa discussed in the first chapter by Susan Mann in this volume, the faithful maiden who lived out her life as a widow in the household of her deceased fiancé. Recorded in history by five cryptic references and one revealing epitaph (not of her but of her forbearing sister-in-law), Miss Fa's story was mostly "shrouded in silence" (in Susan Mann's words). What was her life really like? Suppose we could go back in time and interview her as Gail Hershatter interviewed the labor models of the 1950s. What would she say for herself? Would our conversation reveal an individual distinct from her chosen role as a faithful maiden? What language would she use to talk about her life, the eulogistic language of imperial commendation, the ironic language of literati critique of the faithful maiden cult, or the sentimental language of lyrical poetry?

Perhaps like the labor models, she would turn first to the language of official history, with the glowing words and catchy phrases taught to her by instructors and gleaned from earlier exemplar tales. For the regime of chastity in the late empire, like the collectivization project of the 1950s, was a politically powerful world-making project with systematic state sponsorship, zealous local support, and enthusiastic individual participation. Indeed, so powerful were these projects that an individual's hopes, desires, and even recollections may be fully conditioned by them and could only be articulated through language sanctioned by them.

The premise of this volume is that Chinese women's biography constitutes a major historical tradition. We set out to excavate this rich tradition in order to learn more about Chinese women's history. What we have found is that the widely transmitted and historically enduring women's biographies are almost always implicated in the large and powerful ideological

281

agendas of the day. Even genres that promise access to inner lives, such as private biographical sketches and oral interviews, often narrate those lives by way of the prevailing discourses of the period. Thus the Southern Song loyal courtesans and early-twentieth-century revolutionaries may have been impressive individuals, but the circulation and preservation of their biographies owe themselves to larger cultural and political forces extrinsic to their particular lives. Precisely because the meaning of woman as symbol is unstable, the genre of women's biography was often called upon to serve a normalizing and prescriptive role in times of political and cultural instability such as the Southern Song, the late Ming, and the early communist eras. In such moments, life stories became metaphors, stylized vessels used to transmit urgent lessons. Thus, many of the preceding chapters tell us more about the processes of biographical production, about the transformation, circulation, and transmission of life stories rather than the lives that are allegedly the stuff of these stories. These are, without question, important lessons to learn as they are vital to a critical understanding of the power mechanism in the production of historical knowledge.

But what about the lives? Surely there were real people behind, beneath, or beyond the generic formulas and ideological apparatus?

Naïve as this question may sound, we historians cannot but be haunted by the ghost of the Grand Historian, Sima Qian. His undying passion was to preserve the deeds, speech, and intent of worthy people, even if, as he himself readily concedes, their actions did not necessarily bear fruit and the causes to which they dedicated their lives were at times unworthy of their sacrifice. Add the feminist historian's drive to unearth women's experience, which tends to be buried in the grand historical narrative of past generations, and the question takes on even greater urgency. Where, then, are the Chinese women? Do we find nothing but inarticulate beings "shrouded in silence," or worse, subjects that fully merge with the larger ideological forces that produced them?

This volume demonstrates that the picture need not be so bleak if we ask the right questions and adjust our expectations to historical and cultural specificities appropriate to the materials at hand. For what is at stake in this debate about the subject is epistemology: what we can know and how we know.

It is possible that our imaginary faithful maiden Fa would be more like Tanyangzi, discussed in Ann Waltner's chapter, the extraordinary young woman religious teacher who also claimed the status of a faithful maiden. Operating within the ideological framework of widow chastity so powerful in her time, Tanyangzi nonetheless exercised considerable agency.

She had control over where she lived, a crucial factor in determining the degree of a woman's freedom and her fundamental well-being. And this "room of her own" was significantly located in her parents' house rather than the potentially much less hospitable environment of her parents-in-law (even though the latter choice, taken by the real faithful maiden Fa, was the more orthodox).[1] Tanyangzi also had control over her own words. She used language powerfully in her letters and manipulated a multitude of cultural resources. Forceful and smart in her debates and instructions, she brought Daoist, Buddhist, and Confucian authorities—including the moral authority of the chaste maiden—to bear in justifying her otherwise unorthodox behavior. She also exercised as much control as possible over the telling of her life story as she personally authorized her own first biography.

Or perhaps our faithful maiden Fa could be like Bo Shaojun of Wilt Idema's chapter, the young woman who may be said to follow her husband in death, but not, significantly, until *after* she had composed 100 poems that paint an elaborate portrait of him and of their emotional life together. If Bo's death on the day of her husband's first anniversary could be read as signaling her participation in the heroic-chaste widow cult of the late imperial era, her masterly command of the largely male subgenre of mourning poetry established her reputation in literary history and on her own terms. Even as she followed the footsteps of heroic widows touted in the late imperial *lienü* canon, Bo reached into what Nanxiu Qian calls the *xianyuan* tradition, a tradition that celebrates women for their talent and independent spirit. Similar to Bo, many of the faithful maidens left behind written works, as Weijing Lu's full study of them reveals. These documents are historical traces of their efforts to tell their own life stories, even as they participated in the late imperial cult of faithful maidenhood.

Chinese women's exemplary tales thus challenge us with a conception of biography quite different from the modern Western model that is often the implicit standard for biography. If we take the oft-quoted line from Edmund Gosse as representative, then biography in this model is "the faithful portrait of a soul in its adventures through life."[2] Leaving aside its intimation of the biographer's neutrality and its Romantic emphasis on adventure, the assumption of interiority—of an individuated and unified self with a "soul"—is crucial to the Western conception of the biographical subject and hence to our search for "the real Miss Fa."

In order to understand the life stories of these Chinese women and to appreciate the choices they made, it is thus necessary to remain cognizant of the cultural specificities of the Chinese biographical tradition. Based on a different understanding of the individual life course, this tradition carries a distinct set of assumptions.

According to the longstanding Confucian conception of an ideal life trajectory, early in one's life an individual chooses a role that best reflects his social status and values from among a repertoire of available roles. He performs this role throughout his life by diligently cultivating the moral self and adjusting his role to changes produced by age and political or personal crises.[3] In Confucius's terms, a well-evolved subject should accomplish a fair degree of certainty in selfhood by forty years of age: "At forty, [he] had no doubts" (sishi bu huo), and "at seventy, [he] could follow what [his] heart desired, without transgressing what was right" (qishi er congxinyu bu yuju), such is the degree of perfect accord between his individual needs and social or ritual requirements.[4] The available qualities intrinsic to this ideal subject are conceived as both exterior and interior to him: the subject only comes into being as he gradually cultivates the qualities he aspires to and inhabits the role(s) he chooses. Neither completely free nor totally powerless, he exercises a degree of agency in confronting role choices and role changes.

Not everyone has a full range of choices, however, as most of the studies in this volume reveal. Our use of the pronoun "he" above is meant to indicate that the full subject with the widest range of choices could not have been a woman (nor could he be a lower class man, for that matter). As we noted in the introduction, the model for Chinese men's biography is thus useful to us only to a limited degree. Compared with the spectrum of choices for the aspiring Confucian gentleman, the ideal model of Confucian womanhood has been historically more restricted, especially after the chastity cult gained momentum from the eleventh century. This limited range of choices is further affected by gender-specific life course markers, such as marriage, childbearing capacity, and old age.[5] Ultimately, women who entered the Chinese biographical canon are those considered wise in their choices and accomplished in their life performance, within a certain normative sphere at a given historical moment.

The difference between those who were subsumed by the highly restrictive ideological apparatus of their time and those who were able to exercise some degree of agency lies, in part, in their access to cultural resources. Faithful maiden Fa's silence, to continue with her tragic example, means that her story was exclusively told by others, either those who praised her or those who blamed her (implicitly of course). Despite her existence as a biographical subject in official records, her muteness serves as an index of her abject position in history, a case of psychosis (xinji) of "unspeakable speech," not to be mentioned except at an exceptional moment and only as a means of differentiation from another female exemplar, her forbearing sister-in-law.[6] In contrast, Bo Shaojun and Tanyangzi were able to wrestle some control over the narration of their lives through their poems and letters. For certain, even in their cases they are far from the Romantic conception of autonomous subjects: their agency is limited and fragile, and the languages they employ are not and cannot be fully "their own." They, nonetheless, managed to deploy considerable cultural resources and construct subject positions more conducive to the exercise of their individual agency.

Tanyanzi and Bo Shaojun are perhaps at one end of the spectrum in terms of their degree of agency, and Miss Fa at the other. Most of the biographical subjects discussed in this volume lie somewhere in between. The 1950s labor models, for example, are unique in their relationship to cultural resources: formerly disenfranchised peasant women, they were taught literacy by the "squatting cadres," probably in the cadence of official propaganda. That they would articulate their memory through this powerful discourse remains provocative. Not unlike Bo Shaojun and Tanyangzi (despite clear class differences), even as these communist exemplars made history with their lives and their words, their fragile agency was exercised through the language that produced them.

We can now reframe our earlier question, "Where are the Chinese women?" "Real" Chinese women are not "beneath, behind, or beyond" the larger cultural projects that produced them; they are "within" these projects, participating to different extents in their own production, leaving disparate traces of accommodation, negotiation, and appropriation. This dialectic subject, simultaneously constructed and constructing, allows us to address the question we raised in the introduction to this volume: Could a biographical subject, such as the late imperial faithful maiden who is constituted by the cultural project of female chastity and the prevalent literati discourse, still be a critical subject? As a number of the preceding chapters indicate, she indeed can by resignifying the power discourse with subversive citations from within. No doubt she is not an autonomous subject in the Romantic sense with full agency and total free choice as her "inner self" is as much a part of the cultural projects as her "outer self." Nonetheless, a number of the biographical subjects we have studied were able to contest the process of their production and manipulate the terms of representation, and thus to intervene in the narration of their lives, and ultimately, in the writing of history.

Traditional Chinese Genres
of Biographical Material

Chapters that discuss a particular genre are listed under author's last name in parentheses.

aici 哀辭, *leici* 誄辭, *wanci* 輓詞	rhymed eulogy, mourning verse, funeral oration; *leici* typically reserved for prominent individuals, *aici* for people who died before their time, and *wanci* the more general term (Idema, Mann)
bei 碑	stele erected in front of a tomb; can be conventional and didactic but may also contain a fuller picture of an individual's roles than formal biography (*zhuan*); both a public document for the deceased and her or his family as well as a private demonstration of the personality of the writer (Carlitz, Hu, Yao)
bie zhuan 別傳, *sizhuan* 私傳, *xiaozhuan* 小傳, *zhuanlue* 傳略	unofficial biography, alternative biography, private biography, brief biography; popular genre since at least the Song; typically written by private scholars not appointed by imperial or local government; can be found in the collected works of literati authors; often written to display the author's literary merit, though it can also be commissioned; sometimes written as draft versions to be later submitted as material for official biography and history (Bossler, Mann)
daowang shi 悼亡詩	series of poems commemorating and lamenting a deceased spouse with focus on private life and private emotions; invented in the third century by the poet Pan Yue; initially only written by men to mourn their wives but from the sixteenth century occasionally used by women to mourn their husbands (Idema)

dashi zhuan 大士傳, *dashizhuan* 大師傳, *gaoshi zhuan* 高士傳, *shengzhuan* 聖傳	hagiography; religious biography that records the lives and instructions of Buddhist and Daoist saints (Waltner)
diao wen 弔文, *jiwen* 祭文	sacrificial essay, eulogy, memorial address; essays written to console the deceased; often burned in front of the grave (Idema)
jingbiao 旌表	imperial testimonials of merit for chaste widowhood or martyrdom, or for the receipt of posthumous honorific titles; the subject is usually commemorated with the briefest description of her or his exemplary virtue, which is inscribed on a wooden plaque, a stone arch, a decorated platform or other such structure; beginning from the Han dynasty, imperial recognition usually came with material benefits such as gifts of money and relief from the corvée levies (Lu, Mann)
lienü zhuan 列女傳	biography of exemplary women; first canonized in 32 BCE with Liu Xiang's *Lienü zhuan;* not meant to narrate a life but only the important deeds that demonstrate particular exemplary virtues; dynastic histories and local gazetteers usually contain a section of biographies of women, generally following a section of biographies of men (Bossler, Judge, Mann, Qian, Zurndorfer)
lienü zhuan 烈女傳, *zhennü zhuan* 貞女傳	biography of heroic women (Hu, Lu)
mubiao 墓表, *shibiao* 石表, *taming* 塔銘, *muzhi* 墓誌, *muzhiming* 墓誌銘, *kuangzhi* 壙志, *cuozhi* 厝誌	epitaph or funerary essay written to be carved in stone, and buried in or displayed at the tomb of the deceased; often with a formal poem at the end; presents genealogy and progeny; the texts of *muzhiming* were typically published in the collected works of their authors (Carlitz, Hu, Mann, Yao)
nianpu 年譜	chronological biography; rich in textual evidence of the subject's life at various stages; because of its emphasis on public career and publication, the form is typically reserved for successful men in public office (Zurndorfer)

shiji 詩集, *wenji* 文集, *shujian* 書簡	the tradition of posthumously publishing a person's collected works, usually including the entire corpus of his literary output; typically carries prefaces and postscripts written by notable writers that supply biographical or autobiographical information on the author (Bossler, Ebrey, Idema, Judge, Mann, Widmer)
xinglüe 行略, *xingshi* 行實, *xingshu* 行述, *xingzhuang* 行狀	biographical sketches or "records of deeds," accounts of conduct, truthful accounts, brief accounts of conduct; biography composed by family members or close friends that can range from records of virtuous behavior to intimate anecdotes that would not be recorded in more public biographies (Lu, Mann)
xu 序, *tici* 題辭, *ba* 跋	introductory comments, preface, epilogue; usually appear at the beginning and end of a poetry collection; may be composed by the poet or by another author; often contains biographical information about the poet (Idema, Judge, Mann, Widmer)
yishi 遺事, *yishi* 逸事, *yishi* 軼事	memoir, anecdotal memoir; similar to private biography, usually written by close friends containing intimate or humorous anecdotes inappropriate in more public biographies (Hu, Mann)
zhuan 傳	official biography written by court appointed official; Sima Qian's *Shiji* (Records of the Grand Historian), written from 109 BCE to 91 BCE, is the first and usually understood as the best example; since Sima Qian's time, every dynastic history and local gazetteer contains a substantial section of official biography (Bossler, Idema, Widmer)

APPENDIX B

The *Lienü* Tradition in Dynastic Histories

	Time of compilation	Author
1	Han	Sima Qian (ca. 145–ca. 86 BCE)
2	Later Han	Ban Gu (32–92)
3	Liu-Song	Fan Ye (398–445)
4	Jin	Chen Shou (233–97)
5	Tang	Fang Xuanling (578–648) et al.
6	Liang	Shen Yue (441–513)
7	Liang	Xiao Zixian (489–537)
8	Tang	Yao Silian (557–637)
9	Tang	Yao Silian
10	Northern Qi	Wei Shou (506–72)
11	Tang	Li Baiyao (565–648)
12	Tang	Linghu Defen (583–666) et al.
13	Tang	Wei Zheng (580–643) et al.
14	Tang	Li Yanshou (7th c.)
15	Tang	Li Yanshou
16	Five Dynasties	Liu Xu (887–946) et al.
17	Song	Ouyang Xiu (1007–72), Song Qi (998–1061)
18	Song	Xue Juzheng (912–981)
19	Song	Ouyang Xiu
20	Yuan	Tuotuo (1313–55) et al.
21	Yuan	Tuotuo et al.
22	Yuan	Tuotuo et al.
23	Ming	Song Lian (1310–81) et al.
24	Qing	Zhang Tingyu (1672–1755) et al.
25	Minguo (1922 ed.)	Ke Shaomin (1850–1933)
26	Minguo (1928 ed.)	Zhao Erxun (1844–1927) et al.

NOTE: All editions cited are published by Zhonghua shuju except for Ke Shaomin's *Xin Yuanshi* (published by Yiwen yinshuguan).

Title	Lienü *entries*
Shiji (Records of the Grand Historian), 130 *juan*	No *Lienü* chapter
Hanshu (History of the Han [202 BCE–220]), 100 *juan*	No *Lienü* chapter
Hou Hanshu (History of the Later Han [202 BCE–220]), 120 *juan*	17 *Lienü* entries
Sanguo zhi (History of the Three Kingdoms [220–65]), 65 *juan*	No *Lienü* chapter
Jinshu (History of the Jin [265–420]), 130 *juan*	33 *Lienü* entries
Songshu (History of the Song [420–79]), 100 *juan*	No *Lienü* chapter
Nan Qi shu (History of the Southern Qi [479–502]), 59 *juan*	No *Lienü* chapter
Lian shu (History of the Liang [502–57]), 56 *juan*	No *Lienü* chapter
Chenshu (History of the Chen [557–89]), 36 *juan*	No *Lienü* chapter
We shu (History of the [Northern] Wei [386–534]), 114 *juan*	17 *Lienü* entries
Bei Qi shu (History of the Northern Qi [550–577]), 50 *juan*	No *Lienü* chapter
Zhoushu (History of the Northern Zhou [557–581]), 50 *juan*	No *Lienü* chapter
Suishu (History of the Sui [581–618]), 85 *juan*	15 *Lienü* entries
Beishi (History of the Northern dynasties [386–618]), 100 *juan*	34 *Lienü* entries
Nanshi (History of the Southern dynasties [420–581]), 80 *juan*	No *Lienü* chapter
Jiu Tangshu (Old history of the Tang [618–907]), 200 *juan*	30 *Lienü* entries
Xin Tangshu (New history of the Tang [618–907]), 225 *juan*	47 *Lienü* entries
Jiu Wudai shi (Old history of the Five Dynasties [and the Ten Kingdoms] [907–79]), 150 *juan*	No *Lienü* chapter
Xin Wudai shi (New history of the Five Dynasties [and the Ten Kingdoms] [907–79]), 74 *juan*	No *Lienü* chapter
Songshi (History of the Song [960–1279]), 496 *juan*	38 *Lienü* entries
Liaoshi (History of the Liao [947–1125]), 116 *juan*	5 *Lienü* entries
Jinshi (History of the Jin [1125–1234]), 135 *juan*	22 *Lienü* entries
Yuanshi (History of the Yuan [1260–1368]), 210 *juan*	80 *Lienü* entries
Mingshi (History of the Ming [1368–1644]), 332 *juan*	170 *Lienü* entries
Xin Yuanshi (New history of the Yuan), 257 *juan*	127 *Lienü* entries
Qingshi gao (Draft history of the Qing [1644–1911]), 536 *juan*	412 *Lienü* entries

The *Xianyuan* Tradition in the *Shishuo ti* Works

Time	Author	Title
LIU-SONG		
1	Liu Yiqing (403-44) & staff	*Shishuo xinyu* (A new account of tales of the world)
TANG		
2	Wang Fangqing (d. 702)	*Xu Shishuo xinshu* (Continuation of the *Shishuo xinshu*), 10 *juan*, not extant
3	Feng Yan (*js* ca. 756)	*Fengshi wenjian ji* (Feng's memoirs), 10 *juan*, comp. ca. 800 or later
4	Liu Su (fl. 806–20)	*Da Tang xinyu* (New account of the Great Tang), 13 *juan*, author's preface dated 807
SONG		
5	Kong Pingzhong (fl. 1065–1102, *js* 1065)	*Xu Shishuo* (Continuation of the *Shishuo*), 12 *juan*, earliest extant ed. with Qin Guo's preface dated 1158
6	Wang Dang (fl. 1086–1110)	*Tang yulin* (Tang forest of accounts), 8 *juan*
MING		
7	He Liangjun (1506–73)	Hoshi yulin (He's forest of accounts), 30 juan, Wen Zhengming's preface dated 1551
8	Wang Shizhen (1526–90, *js* 1547)	Shishuo xinyu bu (Supplement to the Shishuo xinyu), 20 juan, abridged from Shishuo xinyu & Hoshi yulin, Wang Shizhen's preface dated 1556, pub. 1585
9	Jiao Hong (1541–1620, *js* 1589)	Jiaoshi leilin (Jiao's taxonomic forest), 8 juan, author's preface dated 1585, other prefaces, 1587
10	Li Zhi (1527–1602, *jr* 1552)	Chutan ji (Writings on the pond), 30 juan, pub. 1588
11	Li Hou, dates unknown	Xu Shishuo (Continuation of the Shishuo), 10 juan, with Yu Anqi's preface dated 1609
12	Li Shaowen (fl. 1600–1623)	Huang Ming Shishuo xinyu (Imperial Ming Shishuo xinyu), 8 juan, with Lu Congping's preface dated 1610
13	Zheng Zhongkui (fl. 1615–34)	Qingyan (Pure talk), or Lanwan ju qingyan (Pure talk from the Orchid-Fields Studio), 10 juan, comp. 1615, 1st ed. 1617
14	Jiao Hong	Yutang congyu (Collected accounts from the Jade Hall), 8 juan, all prefaces, including the author's, dated 1618
15	Zhang Yong (fl. late Ming)	Nianyi shi shiyu (Extracts from twenty-one standard histories), also named Zhuxiang zhai leishu (The Bamboo-Fragrance Studio encyclopedia), 37 juan, not seen
16	Lin Maogui (fl. 1591–1621)	*Nan Bei chao xinyu* (Southern & Northern dynasties [*Shihshuo*] xinyu), 4 *juan*, author's preface dated 1621

Xianyuan *entries and time covered*

32 *XY* entries; late Han & Wei-Jin (ca. 150-420); biographical info in Liu Jun's commentary

Unclear

Tang, no *XY* chapter

Tang, no *XY* chapter

25 *XY* entries; Southern & Northern to Five Dynasties (ca. 420–960)

10 *XY* entries; Tang (618–907)

22 XY entries; Han to Yuan
   (ca. 206 BCE– 1368); bio info in He's own commentary
41 XY entries; Han to Yuan
   (ca. 206 BCE–1368); bio info in original commentaries

No XY chapter; 26 equivalent entries in ch. "Fufu" 夫婦 (Husband & wife); antiquity to Yuan (ca. 3000 BCE–1368)
No XY ch.; 79 equivalent entries in ch. "Fufu"; antiquity to Yuan (ca. 3000 BCE– 1368)
16 XY entries, Southern & Northern dynasties (420–589)

20 XY entries; ea. to mid-Ming (ca. 1368–1572)

9 XY entries; Han to mid-Ming (ca. 206 BCE–1572)

No XY chapter

Unclear

17 *XY* entries; Southern & Northern dynasties (420–589)

Time	Author	Title
17	Yan Congqiao (fl. around 1639)	*Seng Shishuo* (Monks *Shishuo*), 24 *juan*, author's preface, 1639; other prefaces 1640
18	Zhao Yu (fl. Late Ming?)	*Er Shishuo* (Children *Shishuo*), 1 *juan*, publication dates unclear

QING

19	Liang Weishu (1589–1662, late Ming *jr*)	*Yujian zunwen* (Distinguished accounts of the jade sword), 10 *juan*, author's preface dated 1654, other prefaces 1655 or 1657
20	Li Qing (1602–83, *js* 1631)	*Nü Shishuo* (Women *Shishuo*), 4 *juan*, comp. ea. 1650s, pub. ea. 1670s
21	Wang Wan (1624–91, *js* 1655)	*Shuoling* (Bell of tales), 1 *juan*, Wang's preface dated 1659, 1st ed. 1661
22	Wu Sugong (fl. 1662–81)	*Ming yulin* (Ming forest of accounts), 14 *juan*, comp. 1662, 1st ed. 1681
23	Jiang Yourong & Zou Tonglu (both fl. ea. Qing)	*Mingyi bian* (Compilation of Ming anecdotes), 10 *juan*, pub. ea. Qing, not seen
24	Wang Zhuo(b. 1636)	*Jin Shishuo* (Contemporary *Shishuo*), 8 *juan*, author's preface dated 1683
25	Zhang Fukong (fl. ea. Qing)	*Han Shishuo*, 14 *juan*, pub. ea. Qing, not seen
26	Zhang Jiyong (fl. ea. Qing)	*Nan Bei chao Shishuo* (Southern & Northern dynasties *Shishuo*), 20 *juan*, not seen
27	Yan Heng (1826?–54)	*Nü Shishuo* (Women *Shishuo*), 1 *juan*, 1st ed. 1865

MING-GUO

28	Yi Zongkui (b. 1875)	*Xin Shishuo* (New *Shishuo*), 1 *juan*, author's preface dated 1918

JAPAN TOKU-GAWA

29	Hattori Nankaku (1683–1759)	*Daitō seigo* (Account of the Great Eastern World), 5 *juan*, 1st ed. 1750
30	Ōta Nanbo (Ōta Fukashi) (1749–1823) & Imai Kyūsuke (1786–1829)	*Kana Sesetsu* (Tales of the world in Kana), 2 *juan*, preface dated 1824, pub. 1825 under Shokusan sensei & Bunhōtei Sanboku
31	Ōta Nanbo & Imai Kyūsuke	*Kana Sesetsu kōhen* (Tales of the world in Kana, continued edition), not seen.
32	Ōta Nanbo	*Sesetsu shingo cha* (Tea of the *Shishuo xinyu*), ca. 1770, under Yamanote no Bakajin.
33	Tsunoda Ken (Tsunoda Kyūka, 1784-1855)	*Kinsei sōgo* (Accounts of recent times), 8 *juan*, Tsunoda's preface 1816, 1st ed. 1828.
34	Tsunota Ken	*Shoku Kinsei sōgo* (Continued accounts of recent times), 8 *juan*, 1st ed. 1845.

MEIJI (1868-1912)

35	Ōta Saijirō (fl. 1892)	*Shin seigo* (New account of the world), 1892.

NOTE: *js* = *jinshi; jr* = *juren.*

Xianyuan entries and time covered

No *XY* chapter

No *XY* chapter

14 *XY* entries; Ming (1368–44), bio info in Liang's commentary

759 entries; antiquity to Yuan (ca. 3000 BCE–1368)

Not categorized

16 *XY* entries; Ming (1368–44)

Unclear

6 *XY* entries; ea. Qing (ca. 1644–80); bio info in Wang's commentary

Unclear
Unclear

79 entries; ea. Qing to Yan's time (1644-1854)

33 *XY* entries; Qing (1644-1911); bio info in Yi's commentary

15 *XY* entries; Heian (794–1185) & Kamakura (1185–1333); bio info in Hattori's commentary
2 *XY* entries; ea. Tokugawa (1603-1867)

Unclear

No *XY* chapter

18 *XY* entries; ea.—mid-Tokugawa (1603-1788); bio info in Tsunoda's commentary
14 *XY* entries; Tokugawa (1661-1821); bio info in Tsunoda's commentary

Not categorized

Notes

1. The biography of the woman of Qishi is found in the *Lienü zhuan*, 3:13; Liu Xiang, *Lienü*, 121–24; O'Hara, 95–97.

2. Qiu Jin, "The Man," with a minor change to the translation. The original poem, which was composed around 1904–5 in reference to the Russo-Japanese War, can be found in Guo Yanli, ed., *Qiu Jin xuanji*, 94.

3. For the translation, see O'Hara. For scholarship on the *Biographies* see Raphals, *Sharing*; Mou, *Gentlemen's*.

4. Cardinal studies of the standard Chinese biographical genres include those in Wright and Twitchett.

5. As a mark of the prominence of female biography in the Chinese historical tradition, from the seventh century when the four divisions of learning—*jing* (classics), *shi* (history), *zi* (philosophy), and *ji* (belles-lettres)—were established in the *Suishu* (History of the Sui Dynasty, 581–618), through the eighteenth century when the *Siku quanshu zongmu* (Annotated catalogue of the complete library of the four treasuries) was compiled, the *Lienü zhuan* was categorized as history (*shi*). Mou, *Gentlemen's*, 24n21.

6. The field of Chinese women's history has been gaining depth and breadth since the 1990s. Key figures in its establishment have essays in this volume or have otherwise contributed to its genesis. They include the authors of the following landmark studies: Ebrey, *The Inner*; Ko, *Teachers*; and Mann, *Precious*.

7. Raphals develops this concept in *Sharing*, particularly in the introduction and first four chapters.

8. Birge, "Levirate."

9. Ko, *Teachers*.

10. The definitive article on the historical evolution of the chastity cult remains Elvin; see also Mann, "Historical." On Qing dynasty developments, see Theiss, *Disgraceful*; Elliott.

11. See Durrant; Moloughney.

12. Studies of Western women's biographies include Natalie Zemon Davis's reflections on the different purposes collections of "women worthies" have served in Western history from Plutarch to the nineteenth century; see Davis, 79–80. One example of relatively recent feminist scholarship is Margadant, *The New*. While we, like Margadant and the other contributors to *The New Biography* volume, analyze fissures in gender and ideological discourses that open up new spaces for women, the aims of our respective volumes differ significantly. We are, for example, attempting to unravel the biographical practices of historical Chinese authors rather than interrogate those of contemporary academics.

13. There are commonalities in recent approaches to Western biography and our approach, however. The fluidity—and thus the constructedness—of biography that we discuss has, for example, been recognized by Margadant and others as one of the key discoveries in recent studies of constructed identities based on gender, race, and ethnicity. Margadant, "Introduction," 1057.

14. Benhabib et. al., *Feminist*.

15. Butler, "For," 135.

CHAPTER 1

The author gratefully acknowledges comments and criticism by participants in the Conference on Women's Biography and Gender Politics in Chinese History, University of California, Irvine, March 3–6, 2006, with special thanks to the editors of the present volume.

1. Yun Zhu, *Langui*. Selections from the anthology are translated in Mann, "Biographies."

2. Zhang Xuecheng, 16:74b.

3. Wright.

4. See Nomura Ayuko's analysis of "birthday greeting prefaces" written for women in the Ming-Qing period.

5. Bossler, "Funerary." See also Hsiung, 128–55. Hsiung observes that mothers had an abiding interest in making sure their sons preserved these emotionally fraught memories.

6. Bossler, "Shifting." Bossler argues that the figure of the Song courtesan became a "foil *against* which the literatus as moral exemplar could be defined" (36), but she also notes that a virtuous woman served equally well as a foil against which the moral *lapses* of the literatus could be defined.

7. Shen Shanbao, 8:4a. Cailü is an error, although the adult name (*zi*) given is correct. Shen Shanbao is referring to Wanying's first and second daughters. On Wanying and her sisters, see Mann, *Talented Women*.

8. Titles for the poetry collections of the four daughters born to Wanying are listed in several sources, including Hu Wenkai, 234–35. Hu examined only Caipin's collected works; he was unable to locate the others, for which he supplies titles. My own attempts to locate the rest have failed. No poetry by Cailü is mentioned in any source except the mistaken reference in Shen Shanbao's work.

9. In her assessment of Zhang Qieying as a poet, Shi Shuyi (512–13 [orig. ed. 9/2b–3a]) foregrounds this passage from Bao Shichen's collected works. In the original text, Bao uses the Zhang daughters' adult names rather than their given names; I have used given names in my translation.

10. Zhang Yuesun, afterword (*ba*) for the collected poems of his second elder sister, Zhang Guanying. See Zhang Guanying.

11. Robertson, especially 183–85.

12. Zhang Qieying's remembered description of her mother's silk appliqué work, as dictated to Shen Shanbao and recorded in Shen Shanbao, *Mingyuan shihua*, 8/5a–5b.

13. Tang Yaoqing.

14. See remarks about Tang Yaoqing's father in biographies in *Wujin*, 26/40b; and *Guangxu*, 23/37b–38a.

15. Famous quotation, oft-repeated in later biographies of Zhang Lunying, from Zhang Yuesun, "Yishu tu tici" (Encomium for the painting *Practicing Calligraphy*), printed in Zhang Lunying, 4/1b–2a.

16. Ibid., 4:2b–3a.

17. Elegy ("Sun Shuyu ai ci") by Zhang Yuesun, reprinted in Zhang Lunying, 5: 3b–6a, quotation on 5b.

18. Zhang Huiyan, *xia* 21a–b.

19. Ibid., 21b.

20. "Xianbi shilüe," in Zhang Huiyan, *xia* 23a–25a (paraphrased).

21. Ibid., 25a–b.

22. Zhang Qi, "Wang shi Tang ruren xinglüe" (Biographical sketch of my wife the lady Tang Yaoqing); printed as the preface to her collected poems, *Pengshi ouyin*, in *Wanlin shi wen, fujuan*, 1a–5b, quotation on 2a.

23. Zhang Yuesun, "Xian fujun xingshi," printed in Zhang Qi, *Wanlin*, 1a–10a, quotation on 7a.

24. Ibid., 8b.

25. Bao Shichen, 17b–18a. Bao invokes the classical allusion to the mother who "cut off her hair [and sold it] to provide delicacies for a guest [of her son]."

26. Zhang Xuecheng, 20:16a–18b.

27. An allusion to a poem by Zuo Si titled "Funü shi": "*Wujia you jiaonü / Jiaojiao po baixi*" (In our family there is a beautiful young woman / Radiant with dazzling purity).

28. Zhang Xuecheng, 20: 18b.

29. See Weijing Lu, "Uxorilocal." Lu stresses the importance of promising sons-in-law who offered intellectual companionship to both the bride and her father, while enabling the father to keep a cherished daughter at home.

30. Zhang Xuecheng's biography of Lady Xun is translated in Mann and Cheng, 220–27.

31. Mann, "Women."

32. Wei Yuan devotes most of his epitaph for Magistrate Shi to a forceful critique of the imperial government's misplaced administrative priorities before finally settling down to a brief account of his subject's life and death.

How the two are related is pretty much left up to the reader's intuition and prior knowledge. See Kuhn and Fairbank.

33. In writings about women's lives, cavernous silences often surround the anomalous figures called *zhennü*. The subject of a chapter in this volume, and a book, by Weijing Lu, faithful maidens were young women who either committed suicide or pledged lifelong fidelity to the man to whom they were betrothed if he died before the marriage ceremony. See Weijing Lu, *True*.

34. Fang Junmo, "Zhangjun qi Bao ruren cuozhi" (Gravestone inscription for Lady Bao, late wife of Master Zhang), in Zhao Zhen, 12a–b. Fang was a local scholar of some note, but the source of his gossipy knowledge is unclear in written records.

35. Zhang Qi, "Wangshi Tang ruren xinglüe," in *Ming fa*, "Xinglüe," 6a.

36. See *Guangxu*, 9/6a.

37. Sommer; Theiss, *Disgraceful*.

CHAPTER 2

My first and most heartfelt acknowledgements go as always to my companion and teacher in this research, Gao Xiaoxian. I am grateful for research assistance provided by Jin Jiang, Wenqing Kang, Xiaoping Sun, and Yajun Mo[o].

1. Raphals, *Sharing*, passim.

2. "Laodong," 194–198.

3. Li Xiuwa (pseud.), interview with Gao Xiaoxian and Gail Hershatter, 1996.

4. For more detail on this point, see Hershatter, "Local."

5. Liu Zhaofeng (pseud.), interview with Gail Hershatter, 1996.

6. Fulian archives 178-27-023 (1952).

7. Lu Guilan, interview with Gail Hershatter, 1996.

8. For a discussion of this transition, see Gao Xiaoxian, "'Yinhua,'" "'The Silver.'"

9. Li Xiuwa (pseud.), interview with Gao Xiaoxian and Gail Hershatter, 1996.

10. Liu Zhaofeng (pseud.), interview with Gail Hershatter, 1996.

11. Li Xiuwa (pseud.), interview with Gao Xiaoxian and Gail Hershatter, 1996. This account, rendered forty years after the fact, is also a retrospective attempt by a Women's Federation cadre to validate the work of her own youth.

12. Wang Meihua (pseud.), interview with Gao Xiaoxian and Gail Hershatter, 1996.

13. Shaanxi Provincial 194-748 (Nongye ting, July13, 1961), 47–49.

14. Shaanxi Provincial 194-8 (Nongye ting, Oct. 30, 1951), 26–27.

15. *Cao*.

16. Shaanxi Provincial 194-534 (Nongye ting, 3–4, 1956), 81–85.

17. Shaanxi Provincial 194-534 (Nongye ting, 3–4, 1956), 81–85.

18. Shaanxi sheng minzhu, 33–40.

19. Gao Xiaoxian, "'Yinhua.'" One example of such a publication is Shaanxi

sheng nonglin. For another example, with a few more rhetorical flourishes, see Shaanxi sheng nongye.

20. In Shaanxi, the most famous and longest-running labor competition was the "Silver Flowers Contest," run by the Shaanxi Provincial Women's Federation in the cotton-producing districts of Guanzhong from 1956 until the early 1980s. Zhang Qiuxiang was one of the "Silver Flowers." For details on this contest, see Gao Xiaoxian, "'Yinhua,'" "'The Silver'."

21. MacFarquhar, 51 and passim.

22. On Shan Xiuzhen's work in creating Qiuxiang fields in her commune, see *Shan Xiuzhen, guangrong* 178-313-001 (1962).

23. Jiang Xinghan and Cheng Wanli, 6–7. See also *Shaanxi ribao* (June 27, 1958).

24. Zhonggong Weinan xianwei, "*Huangmao;*" Women.

25. *Shaanxi ribao* (July 5, 1958).

26. *Shaanxi ribao* (November 7, 1958).

27. *Shaanxi ribao* (January 1, 1959).

28. Fulian 178-216-002 (January 17, 1960), 9; see also 178-45-006 (July 31, 1961).

29. *Shan Xiuzhen, guangrong* 178-313-001 (1962).

30. Bossler, "Faithful Wives and Heroic Martyrs," 510.

31. Hershatter, "Forget."

32. Lu Guilan, interview with Gail Hershatter, 1996.

33. Shan Xiuzhen, interview with Gao Xiaoxian and Gail Hershatter, 1997.

CHAPTER 3

1. Idema and Grant, 12–13.

2. On men and the *Lienü zhuan*, see Wu Shuping, 143–50; Zhang Tao, 249–57; on women and the *Nü jie*, see Ch'en Yu-shih, 229–32 and 256–57; Ebrey, *The Book of Filial*, 47–48; Martin-Liao, 170–71; and Swann, 82–99. On the *Lienü zhuan*'s relation to the *xianyuan* genre, see Nanxiu Qian's chapter in this volume.

3. Hu and Judge; Mou, *Gentlemen's Prescriptions*, 26–34; Raphals, *Sharing*, 20–22.

4. Mou, *Gentlemen's*, 30.

5. Ban Gu, *Hanshu*, vol. 5 (cl. ed.), *juan* 36:1958. This citation originates from Liu Xiang's biography in the *Hanshu* which may be found in the section *zhuan* (vol. 5, *juan* 36:1928–66).

6. Cutter and Crowell, 41; Hinsch, "Reading," 148–49; Zhou Yiqun, 39–42.

7. Mou, *Gentlemen's*, 29.

8. Ibid., 28–29.

9. Mou, *Gentlemen's*, 29; Robin Wang, "Virtue, " 98.

10. Lo Yuet Keung (Lao Yueqiang),"Zhen," 356–59. For more insight on the significance of the *Shiji*'s impact on the institution of marriage in Han China, see Van Ess, 221–27 and 251–54.

11. Gipoulon, 99–106.
12. Lo Yuet Keung, "Zhen," 356; Hinsch, "Reading," 156–57.
13. Nylan, 17–56.
14. Mou, *Gentlemen's*, 76; Carlitz, "Shrines," 630–33; Mann, "Historical," 69–74.
15. Mou, "Writing," 109–10, 138n3; Sung, "The Chinese," 70.
16. Mou, *Gentlemen's*, 15–16.
17. Wei Zheng, 33:978.
18. Raphals, *Sharing*, 110.
19. Hinsch, "The Textual," 97.
20. Liu Xu, 46:2002; Raphals, *Sharing*, 107–8.
21. Ouyang Xiu, 58:1486.
22. Wang Yaochen, vol. 1, 2:105.
23. Hinsch, "The Textual," 101.
24. Ibid., 102.
25. Hinsch, "The Textual," 102; Raphals, *Sharing*, 114.
26. Raphals, *Sharing*, 110; Hinsch, "The Textual," 102.
27. Song Lian, 24:536. Compare comments about this phenomenon by Nanxiu Qian in chapter 4 of this volume.
28. Chia, 92, 113.
29. Carlitz, "The Social," 120–21; Ko, *Teachers*, 29–68.
30. Carlitz, "The Social," 132.
31. See Zurndorfer, "Old," 161–62.
32. For sample Huizhou-produced *Lienü zhuan* and *Gui fan* illustrations, see Bussotti, 341–43.
33. Raphals, *Sharing*, 116.
34. With regard to filiality, careful reading of Han-Song editions reveals that the category of filial devotion is missing; there is no mention of *xiaonü* (filial daughters) among Liu Xiang's concrete models of womanly virtues. See Lo Yuet Keung, "Filial," 71, 75; Raphals, "Reflections," 219.
35. Raphals, *Sharing*, 120–36.
36. Ibid., 136.
37. Ibid., 137. See Qian's essay in this volume on Ming era alternatives to the *Lienü zhuan* emphasis on chastity and filiality.
38. Ban Gu, *Hanshu*, vol. 4 (cl. ed.), 30:1727.
39. Xu Jian, 25:6b.
40. Bussotti, 132n19.
41. Ibid., 219n3.
42. Hummel, 418.
43. Clunas, 482.
44. Holzwarth, 53.
45. Edgren(162) argues that the text of the *Huitu lienü zhuan* has incorrectly been attributed to the great Huizhou literatus Wang Daokun (1525–93).
46. Bussotti, 73.
47. Cahill, "Paintings," 6–11.

48. Raphals, *Sharing*, 137.

49. Idema and Grant, 349.

50. Epstein, *Competing*, 62–74; Eifring, 11–31.

51. Hsü, 72–76.

52. Brook, *Confusions*, 238–62.

53. Chow, 79–97; Mann, *Precious*, 23–25; Zurndorfer, "Introduction," 8.

54. Raphals, *Sharing*, 138.

55. Hummel, 417–19; Edgren, 163.

56. Xu Weiyu, 187. On Wang Zhaoyuan's life history, see Zurndorfer,"Wang Zhaoyuan," "The 'Constant,'" "How," "Wang Zhaoyuan and the Erasure."

57. Xu Weiyu, 187.

58. Ibid., 191.

59. Ibid., 198.

60. Ibid., 196.

61. Ibid., 198.

62. Ibid., 200.

63. Ibid., 202.

64. Xu Weiyu, 201. See also Kaltenmark, 5–6.

65. Xu Weiyu, 202.

66. Wang Zhaoyuan, *Lienü zhuan buzhu, xu,* 1a–b, *Haoshi yishu* edition (1879). There are two other editions of Wang's *Lienü zhuan* commentary, to be found in *ce* 23–25 in the *Longxi jingshe congshu,* edited by Zheng Guoxun (1857–1920), and printed in 1917; and in a *chuban* edition printed in 1937 by the Shangwu yinshuguan in the *Guoxue jiben congshu* (zhi 1).

67. Wang Zhaoyuan, *Lienü zhuan buzhu, xulu,* 11a–b (*Haoshi yishu* edition).

68. Hinsch, "The Textual," 105, summarizes the extant information about the three women.

69. Wang Zhaoyuan, *Lienü zhuan buzhu,* 192 (*Guoxue jiben congshu* edition); Zhao Erxun, 508:14052.

70. On this methodology, see Elman, *From,* 67–68.

71. Wang Zhaoyuan, *Lienü zhuan buzhu* 2:10b-11a (*Haoshi yishu* edition).

72. *Lienü zhuan buzhu* 1:10b (*Haoshi yishu* edition—hereafter, all citations to this edition of the text).

73. Ibid., 8:11a.

74. Ibid., 1:2a. *Shiji suoyin* was first written by Sima Zhen (ca. 656–720), and later amended by Wang Shizhen (1526–90).

75. Ibid., 1:15b.

76. Ibid., 6:28a.

77. Yoshikawa, 296.

78. Xu Weiyu, 206–7.

79. Widmer, "Considering," 294–95.

80. An and Geng, 73–4.

81. Widmer, "Considering," 295; Widmer, *The Beauty,* 173.

82. Widmer, "Considering," 295.

83. Liu Fengyun, 127–28. A comparison of the *Lienü zhuan* texts by Wang Zhaoyuan and Liang Duan is discussed in Xu Xingwu. Liang Duan's *Lienü zhuan jiaozhu* may be accessed in the modern *Sibu beiyao* edition.

84. Hummel, 822; Widmer, *The Beauty*, 109.

85. Hu Wenkai, 244.

86. See Zurndorfer, "Wang Zhaoyuan and the Erasure."

87. Catherine Yeh, *Shanghai*, 230; Edgren, 170.

88. Hu Wenkai, 768–9; Chan Chi Ming, 243–45.

89. Judge, "Blended," 102–07; Judge, *The Precious*; Nanxiu Qian, "'Borrowing,'" 60–4.

90. Zhu Dongrun, 19–22; Zurndorfer, "Wang Zhaoyuan and the Erasure," 40.

91. Widmer, *The Beauty and the Book*, 3–30; Zurndorfer, "Wang Zhaoyuan and the Erasure."

92. Wen-hsin Yeh, 64–65.

93. On Chen Duansheng, see Sung, "Chen," 16–18.

94. Widmer, "The Rhetoric," 216–19.

CHAPTER 4

A draft of this chapter was originally presented at the conference on "Women's Biography and Gender Politics in China," March 3–5, 2006, at the University of California, Irvine. Thanks to the organizers, Hu Ying and Joan Judge, for involving me in this splendid project. Thanks to the discussants, Michael Nylan and Stephen Durrant, the readers, Beverly Bossler and Yi Jolan, and the anonymous reviewers of this volume for their insightful comments and invaluable input. Thanks to Richard J. Smith for inspiring suggestions and encouragement. Thanks also to David Morasco for editorial help. Unless otherwise stated, all translations are mine.

1. As indicated in Ban (pb. ed.), *juan* 36, 7:1957–58, and Ban (pb. ed.), *juan* 30, 6:1727. See also Raphals, *Sharing*, 105. On debates over the *Lienü zhuan*, see Raphals, *Sharing*, 105–8, and Zurndorfer, chapter 3 in this volume; see also Liu Jingzhen, "Liu," 16.

2. Historians have considered Liu Xiang one of the most important thinkers who helped solidify the Han Confucian moral-political system; see Liu Jingzhen, "Liu," 3, 6.

3. Ban (pb. ed.), *juan* 36, 7:1957.

4. For example, *xian* appears in the *Lunyu* (Analects of Confucius) twenty-five times; see Yang Bojun, 303. *Xian*'s meaning can be found in the *Shangshu* (Book of documents), "Da Yu mo" (The counsels of the Great Yu): "No men of virtue and talents (*xian*) will be ignored by the court; and the myriad States will all enjoy repose," in Ruan, *juan* 4, 1:134, and Legge, *Chinese Classics*, 3:53; see also Yang Bojun, *Lunyu*, IV, 17; VI, 11; XV, 14; etc.

5. Xu Shen, 127. Duan Yucai's commentary quotes Zheng Xuan (127–200): "*Zhen* is defined as 'query,' and a query should be addressed to a righteous person. Only to a person who can rectify him/herself may one present a query"

(ibid.). According to Jia Yi, *Xinshu* [*jiaozhu*] (303) , "Daoshu" (Daoist tactics): "*Zhen* means to conform words to actions."

6. This meaning possibly originated from the explanation of the Second Yin of the Hexagram "Zhun" (Birth Throes) in the *Yijing* (Book of changes): "The girl practices constancy and does not commit herself to marrying [a second time]" (*nüzi zhen bu zi*); *Zhou Yi* [*zhu*], 1:235). Clearly from this source there arose expressions such as "a loyal subject will not serve two rulers, nor will a chaste women marry two husbands" (*zhongchen bushi erjun, zhennü bugeng erfu*), as quoted in Sima Qian (145–ca. 86 BCE), "Tian."

7. Ban (pb. ed.), *juan* 36, 7:1957; Raphals, *Sharing*, 19.

8. According to Shen Yue (441–513), *Songshu* (History of the [Liu-]Song), "Fan Ye zhuan" (Biography of Fan Ye), Fan Ye served on the staff of the Liu-Song prince of Pengcheng, Liu Yikang. In the ninth year of the Yuanjia era (432), he offended Liu Yikang and was banished to be the prefect of Xuancheng. There he compiled the *Hou Hanshu* based on previous historical works on the Later Han (see Shen Yue, *juan* 69, 6:1819–20). The Zhonghua shuju introduction to Fan Ye in *Hou Hanshu* misreports Fan Ye's banishment as in the first year of the Yuanjia era (423); for a detailed discussion of this problem, see the Zhonghua shuju collation notes to Shen Yue, "Fan Ye zhuan," in Shen Yue, *Songshu*, 6:1832.

9. According to Shen Yue, "Lei Cizong zhuan" (Biography of Lei Cizong), in Shen Yue, *Songshu*, *juan* 93, 8:2293–94, in the fifteenth year of the Yuanjia reign (438), Emperor Wen (r. 424–53) decreed to establish four academies: *Ruxue, Xuanxue, Wenxue,* and *Shixue.* These divisions should have reflected the scholastic trends of the time. Whether *Wenxue* meant today's literature is unclear, but it surely stood for a subject apart from the Confucian, Abstruse, and Historiographic learnings.

10. Liu Yiqing served nine-years as the mayor of the capital, and eight years as the governor of Jingzhou, the border state on the upper Yangtze River that possessed half of the court's resources. There Liu maintained peace and prosperity for the west part of the Liu-Song territory. Because of his good service, Liu received high honorific titles such as the Commander Unequalled in Honor (*kaifu yitong sansi*). See Shen Yue, "Liu Yiqing zhuan" (Biography of Liu Yiqing), in Shen Yue, *Songshu*, *juan* 51, 5:1475–77; comments on his personality from ibid., 5:1477.

11. See Zhou Yiliang, 16–22.

12. Shen Yue, "Fan Ye zhuan," in Shen Yue, *Songshu*, *juan* 69, 6:1831. For Fan Ye's political career, see ibid., 6:1819–29.

13. Fan Ye, "Lienü zhuan," commentary by Li Xian (651–84), in Fan Ye, *juan* 84, 10: 2781.

14. Ibid., *juan* 84, 10:2784–92.

15. Ibid., *juan* 84, 10:2800–03. Liu Zhiji (*juan* 8, 1:238), for one, criticized Cai as "excessive in literary talents while short on integrity" (*wenci youyu, jiegai buzu*) .

16. Fan Ye, *juan* 84, 10:2803.

17. For the *Shishuo xinyu* texts, the Chinese original is from Yu Jiaxi's edition, see Liu Yiqing, and the English translation/paraphrase based on Mather. Both Yu and Mather numbered each entry, so references to the *Shishuo xinyu* text will give only the chapter and entry numbers. Yu Jiaxi comments on Nun Ji's comparison of Xie Daoyun with the other woman: "This episode tells us that Lady Wang [Xie Daoyun], though a woman, possesses the style of famous [male] scholars; therefore Lady Gu cannot measure up to her . . . Daoyun, as a woman, has a Bamboo Grove aura; this is enough to prove her an outstanding female scholar. The comment about Lady Gu being a 'flower of the inner chamber' only reveals her to be an outstanding woman, and nothing more. Although [the *Shishuo* author] did not distinguish the superior from the inferior, the difference is self-evident. This is the beauty of the Jin rhetoric" (Liu Yiqing, 2: 698, n1 to 19/30).

18. See Liu Yiqing, "Rendan" (Liu Yiqing, *Shishuo xinyu* 2:725–64), for the accounts of the "Seven Virtuous and Talented Men of the Bamboo Grove"; see also Liu Yiqing, 2:725–64; and Mather, 371–91.

19. A.C. Graham's interpretation of the Wei *Xuanxue* founder Wang Bi's (226–49) definition of *de*; Graham, 13. For a full discussion of the *Xuanxue* redefinition of *Dao*, *de*, and *xian*, see Nanxiu Qian, *Spirit*, 126–28.

20. As termed by Mather (371) on the Seven [Virtuous and Talented Men] of the Bamboo Grove.

21. See *Laozi*, ch. 37, in *Wang Bi ji [jiaoshi]*, 1:91.

22. As exemplified in the *Shishuo xinyu*, "Xianyuan" chapter, episodes 19/1, 19/5, 19/7, 19/8, 19/10, 19/17, 19/18, 19/19, 19/20, and 19/22.

23. As exemplified in the *Shishuo* "Xianyuan" episodes 19/11, 19/12, 19/13, 19/14, 19/16, 19/18, 19/19, 19/24, 19/30, and 19/31.

24. Women's talent in *renlun jianshi* is exemplified in the *Shishuo* "Xianyuan" episodes 19/9, 19/11, 19/12, 19/26, 19/28, 19/30, and 19/31. For a detailed discussion of character appraisal and its connection with Wei-Jin *Xuanxue*, see Nanxiu Qian, *Spirit*, ch. 2.

25. Shan Tao was appointed the head of the Selection Bureau because of his perspicuous "recognition and judgment of human character types"; see Fang Xuanling, *juan* 43, 4:1223; and Liu Yiqing, 18/3.

26. For Wei-Jin women's theoretical contribution to character appraisal, see Nanxiu Qian, *Spirit*, 158–61.

27. Wei Zheng, *Suishu*, "Jingji zhi" (Bibliographic treatise), records the two *juan* collection of Xie Daoyun's literary works (Wei Zheng, *juan* 35, 4:1070). For a detailed discussion of Xie Daoyun's poetic accomplishments in relation to a widespread interest in and respect for women's poetic talents during the Six Dynasties, see Kang-i Sun Chang, "Ming-Qing," 244–45.

28. See, for instance, Zheng Xuan's commentary on the *Yili* (Manner rituals), "Sangfu" (Mourning ritual): "The husband is the wife's Heaven" (*fuzhe, qi zhi tian ye*); *Yili [zhushu]* ([Commentary on the] Manner rituals), "Sangfu," commentary by Zheng Xuan, Jia Gongyan, in Ruan Yuan, *juan* 30, 1:1106.

29. A similar story also tells how Xie An's wife Lady Liu peeps at her hus-

band's guests and then criticizes Xie An for befriending unworthy men. For this reason, she contends, her husband cannot come up to her brother, Liu Tan. On hearing her words, Xie An appears "deeply embarrassed" (Liu Yiqing, 26/17).

30. See Liu Yiqing, 2:663, n1 to the title "Xianyuan."

31. Fan Ye, "Lienü zhuan," in Fan Ye, *juan* 84, 10:2781.

32. Tuotuo (1313–55), *Song*, *juan* 460, 38:13477–78.

33. Wei Zheng, *juan* 80, 6:1811–12.

34. Tuotuo, *Liao*, *juan* 107, 5:1471.

35. For Kong Pingzhong's connections with the Su Shi circle, see Zhou Bida's (1126–1204) preface to Kong, *Qingjiang;* see also Tuotuo, "Kong Wenzhong zhuan" (Biography of Kong Wenzhong), "Kong Wuzhong chuan," and "Kong Pingzhong zhuan," in Tuotuo, *Song*, *juan* 344, 31:10931–34. For Wang Dang's connections with the Su Shi circle, see Zhou Xunchu, 1:i–iv.

36. Bol (2): "The moral philosophers who established *Tao-hsüeh* (the 'Learning of the Way'), Neo-Confucianism in a narrow sense, contended that each individual was innately endowed with the patterns of the integrated processes of heaven-and-earth. It was only necessary, then, that men realize the 'pattern of heaven' (*t'ien-li*) that was in their own nature, for this was the real foundation for a moral world."

37. *Er, juan* 21b, 2a.

38. Ibid., *juan* 25, 6b.

39. Ibid., *juan* 18, 95a–96a.

40. *Han Fei zi*, "Jie Lao" (Interpreting the *Laozi*), in *Han Fei*,1:365. Guo Shaoyu (168) cites this couplet to interpret Su Shi's *Dao*. Su Shi himself never explicitly defines his *Dao*, possibly because he considers the *Dao* an uncertain, indefinable concept. For Su Shi's understanding of the *Dao*, see also Kidder Smith, 72–81.

41. See Su Shi, "Riyu" (On finding an analogy for the sun), in *Su Shi wenji, juan* 64, 5:1981; see also Bol's discussion of "Riyu," 275–76.

42. Although Su Shi did not compose a *Shishuo* imitation, he contributed over a dozen brief essays on the *Shishuo* personalities; see Su Shi, *Su Shi wenji, juan* 65, 5:2021–8.

43. For a detailed discussion of the Tang-Song *Shishuo* imitations, see Nanxiu Qian, *Spirit*, ch. 6.

44. These cases about women's capacity and talents include: "Xin Xianying . . . was intelligent, sunny, and talented in judging [human character types] (*conglang you caijian*)" (*juan* 96, 8:2508); "Yan Xian . . . was profound in her capability of recognizing [human character types] (*you shiliang*)" (8:2509); "Zhong Yan could compose poetry and prose when only a few years old. She grew up intelligent, smart, erudite, and elegant, with a broad reading knowledge. She had a beautiful appearance and bearing, and was well-versed in whistling and chanting. . . . She was also intelligent and farsighted in judging and recognizing [human character types] (*conghui hongya, bowen jiji, mei rongzhi, shan xiaoyong, . . . mingjian Yuan shi*)" (8:2510); "Née Sun . . . was by

nature intelligent and quick-witted. She surpassed the others with her talent in judging and recognizing [human character types] (*xing congmin, shijian guoren*)" (8:2513); "Xie Daoyun . . . was intelligent in recognizing [human character types] and talented in reasoning . . . and deeply imbued with poetic elegance. She had a lofty aura, and her remarks were pure and graceful (*congshi you caibian . . . you yaren shenzhi . . . fengyun gaomai, xuzhi qingya*)" (8:2516–17); "Née Chen . . . was intelligent, smart, and capable of composing poetry and prose (*congbian neng zhuwen*)" (8:2517); "Liu E . . . was intelligent and smart from an early age. She concentrated on women's work during the day, and read books at night. Her nurse frequently stopped her from learning, yet E studied even harder. She often discussed the doctrines of classics with her brothers, and she was so sophisticated and profound (*liqu chaoyuan*) that her brothers deeply admired her. Her elder sister Ying was also intelligent, quick-witted, and learned. She surpassed E in writing, reasoning, and the knowledge of political governing (*wenci jibian, xiaoda zhengshi*)" (8:2519); "Wei Cheng's mother, Née Song, was a woman scholar from a family with a tradition of learning. She received from her father expertise in the study of Zhou ritual (*Zhouguan yinyi*) . . . [The court decreed to] establish a lecture hall at the Song household and enrolled one hundred twenty students. Lady Song taught them behind a scarlet curtain" (8:2522); "Née Zhang . . . was intelligent in reasoning and talented in recognizing [human character types] (*mingbian you caishi*)" (8:2522); "[Su] Hui . . . was well-versed in literary composition . . . She wove a piece of brocade. The eight hundred forty characters on it could be read cyclically into numerous poems of sadness . . . " (8:2523); "Née Murong . . . was talented and smart. She was learned in classics and history, and good at playing the zither" (8:2525).

45. Fang Xuanling, *juan* 96, 8:2516.
46. See Liu Zhiji, *juan* 17, 2:482.
47. Fang Xuanling, *juan* 96, 8:2516.
48. See Kong Pingzhong, *Xu Shishuo*, 134; Liu Xu, *juan* 193, 16:5138.
49. Zhao Erxun, "Lienü I," *juan* 508, 46:14020.
50. Ibid.
51. In chapter 3 of this volume, Zurndorfer notes a similar evolution of the meaning of *xian*.
52. Zhao Erxun, "Lienü I," *juan* 508, 46:14020.
53. Zhang Tingyu, *juan* 301, 25:7689.
54. Song Lian, *juan* 200, 15:4484.
55. Ke, "Lienü A," *juan* 244, 5:2169.
56. Zhang Tingyu, 25:7689.
57. See Li Zhi's prefaces to *Chutan ji*, 1–4.
58. The category of *Fufu* includes the following subcategories: *Hehun* (Marriage), *Youhun* (Ghost marriage), *Sang'ou* (Loss of a spouse), *Dufu* (Jealous women), *Caishi* ([Women's] Talents and knowledge), *Yanyu* ([Women's] Speech and conversation), *Wenxue* ([Women's] Literature and scholarship), *Xianfu* (Talented and virtuous husbands), *Xianfu* (Talented and virtuous wives),

Yongfu (Virile husbands), *Sufu* (Vulgar husbands), *Kuhai zhuao* (Miserable women), and *Bi'an zhuao* (Immortal women). For more detailed information about the *Chutan ji* and its connection with Li's commentary on the *Shishuo xinyu bu*, see Li Zhi, *Chutan* and Wang Zhongmin, *Zhongguo*, 340 and 391.

59. See Li Zhi, *Chutan*, 1. For the *Lixue* contention of the origin of things, see Chan Wing-tsit, 463, 489, 491, and 589–91; Hou, 1:384.

60. See Li Zhi, *Chutan, juan* 2, 26, and *juan* 4, 56.

61. See ibid., *juan* 4, 51–58.

62. As noted by Yongrong, *juan* 131, 1:1120. The publication of the *Li Zhuowu [Li Zhi] pidian Shishuo xinyu bu* (Supplement to the *Shishuo xinyu* with commentary by Li Zhi) in Japan in 1694 also inspired Japanese study and imitations of the *Shishuo xinyu*; see Kawakatsu 2; and Ōyane, 92. At least seven Japanese *Shishuo* imitations appeared in the Tokugawa (1603–1867) and Meiji (1868–1912) period; three contained "Xianyuan" chapters. Hattori Nankaku's (1683–1759) *Daitō seigo* (Account of the Great Eastern World) borrowed the *Shishuo* genre to portray free-spirited Heian aristocrats in order to oppose the Tokugawa state orthodoxy based on Zhu Xi's *Lixue* school. The Heian women comprising its "Xianyuan" chapter exhibited refined aesthetic tastes, excellent artistic and literary talents, and a strong sense of subjectivity. Tsunoda Ken's (1784–1855) *Kinsei sōgo* (Accounts of recent times) and *Shoku Kinsei sōgo* (Continued accounts of recent times) portrayed late Tokugawa personalities under the dominant Zhu Xi *Lixue*. His two "Xianyuan" chapters presented an amalgamation of both talented and chaste women. There were certainly Japanese *lienü* imitations as well; a comparative study of the two traditions in Japan awaits further research.

63. Li Qing's dates are according to Wang Zhongmin, "Li Qing," 333. Yan Heng's dates are given in her husband Chen Yuanlu's postscript to her *Nü Shishuo*, 14a–b. According to Chen, Yen Hang died in 1854, before reaching the age of thirty. Ye Shi Liwan's preface to Yan, *Nü Shishuo*, records that she had Yan's manuscript published in the year *yichou* of the Tongzhi Reign (1865).

64. For a detailed discussion of the two *Nü Shishuo*, see Nanxiu Qian, "Milk," 187–236.

65. See Zhao Erxun, *juan* 508, 46:14020.

66. For a detailed discussion of Xue's establishment of a new moral system for Chinese women, see Nanxiu Qian, "Borrowing," 60–101.

67. Mou, *Gentlemen's*, 191.

68. This paragraph has incorporated an anonymous reviewer's comments.

69. See Chang Qu, 699–831.

70. Ye Shaoyuan (1589–1648), for instance, openly argued in his preface to the *Wumeng tang ji* (Collections from Mid-Day Dream Hall) (1:i.), the collected works of his wife and three daughters that Ye had edited: "Men have three [ways of achieving] immortality—through establishing virtue (*de*), deeds (*gong*), and words (*yan*). Women, too, have three ways—through their virtue (*de*), talents (*cai*), and beauty (*se*). Both [men and women can thus make themselves] so splendid that they can almost stand majestically for a

thousand years to come" (*zhangfu you san buxiu, lide ligong liyan; er furen yiyou san yan, deye, cai yu se ye, ji zhaozhao hu ding qiangu yi*). The earliest work of this genre was perhaps Feng Menglong's (1574–1646) *Meiren baiyun* (One hundred poems about beauties). For a full sample of this genre, see Yan Xiyuan. This genre, along with the traditions of *lienü* and *xianyuan*, might have influenced pictorial portrayals of women's stories in late Qing pictorial journals and monographs. For detailed discussions of late Qing pictorial portrayals of women's lives, see Chen Pingyuan, "Male," 315–48, and chapter 6 in this volume, by Joan Judge. For an ongoing book project on the *lienü* and the *xianyuan* traditions I am conducting further research on these other genres.

CHAPTER 5

1. Qian Yiji, 7224–25.

2. Most cases involved the death of a fiancé. In less common situations, a fiancé was afflicted with a fatal disease, sojourned away from home and never returned, or suffered the decline of his family's status. All this could result in the cessation of a betrothal agreement initiated by the woman's or the man's families.

3. Note that even though some faithful maidens ended up marrying their first betrothed who were alive, they were still addressed as *zhennü* the rest of their lives.

4. In Wang Yuan's case, after futile attempts at dissuasion, her fiancé's father, who had also reasoned with her, gave in to her request. He promised her that as soon as his elder son gave birth to a second boy, he would make the boy (his second grandson) her late fiancé's heir and have her move in with his family. He kept his promise. A few years later, when the boy was born, Wang Yuan married into his family and adopted the boy. Qian Yiji, 7225. In most cases, however, adoption occurred after a faithful maiden had lived with the family for some time.

5. For an account of the history of the faithful maiden cult, see Weijing Lu, *True*.

6. According to Liu Xiang, Lady Weixuan's fiancé, a duke, died when she was traveling to his state to marry him. She refused to return home, and observed three years of mourning for him in the role of a wife. Liu Xiang, *Gu*, 97.

7. The cult declined in the early twentieth century after China ushered in the Republican era. As Joan Judge demonstrates in chapter 6 of this volume, in the late Qing faithful maiden stories, while viewed from slightly different perspectives, remained at the center of intellectuals' social and moral critiques .

8. "Songs" refers to the *Book of Songs*, "History" refers to the *Classic of History*, two of the five Confucian classics. "'Songs' and 'History'" was a common shorthand for a Confucian classical education.

9. Faithful maiden biographies were written with a range of subgenres, including *zhuan, shilu, xiaozhuan, shu, shu . . . shi, ji*, and *muzhiming*, but the majority were *zhuan*. In existing records, they appeared most often in

individual scholars' collected works, but also in formal dynastic history or biographical or composition collections such as *Bei zhuan ji* (Collection of epitaphs and biographies).

10. In comparison with the hundreds of thousands of chaste widows that Ming-Qing society claimed, the number of faithful maidens was much smaller. Though small in number, they occupied a strikingly visible place in female biographical writings. For instance, in the *Collection of Epitaphs and Biographies* compiled by Qian Yiji (1783–1850), ten volumes are on Qing women, of which two are of faithful maiden, or one-fifth of the total, the same proportion as the chaste widow biographies. Faithful maiden biographies also appeared regularly in the individual *wenji*, or collected works of the literati. Often more than one entry can be found by a single author. The neo-Confucian scholar-official Lan Dingyuan (1680–1733), for example, included biographies of seventeen women in his *wenji*, of which eleven were chaste widows and five were faithful maidens. The astonishingly disproportionate representation of faithful maidens in biography attests to the male literati's enduring interest in these women.

11. Sima Qian, *Shiji*, 2457.

12. Sun Qifeng, 559.

13. According to the Ming and Qing court records, *Shilu* (Veritable records), from 1368 to 1850 about 6,000 faithful maidens were recognized by the court with the *jingbiao* honor. The real number of faithful maidens is no doubt higher. As I demonstrate elsewhere, although such an award did not theoretically exclude members of underprivileged classes, in reality, families with no economic means or social and political connections had a much lower chance of receiving one. See Lu, *True*, 85–86.

14. During the Yuan, a petition to honor a faithful maiden who had committed suicide was blocked by a chief councilor, Yu Que (1303–58), who argued that her deed exceeded the mean (*zhongyong*), and should not be made an example for the people. Chen Menglei, 48754.

15. The Ming government expanded its program to honor faithful maidens in the early sixteenth century. One of the earliest Ming debates, which occurred in 1505, involved a case in which a faithful maiden was recommended by her prefecture for a court *jingbiao*. See Lu Shen, 885:51, Chen Hongmo, 64–65, and Chen Menglei, 48754.

16. Chow, 8.

17. Elman, *From*.

18. Gui (1929), 3/5a.

19. Ibid.

20. Mao Qiling used to be a supporter of the faithful maiden cult. He changed his position later in his life.

21. Mao, 1590–91.

22. Wang Zhong, 525.

23. Qian Yiji, 7213.

24. Zhu Yizun, 53/13b.

25. Wang Wan, 35/13a.

26. Ibid., 35/13a–b.

27. This is according to Wang Wan's epitaph of the Song daughter; ibid., 19/3a. In the elegiac essay Ji himself wrote for the girl he stated that the reason he did not agree to her request was his fear that his mother and ailing wife could not withstand the sadness caused by the event of her arrival. Ji, (*jibu* vol. 228) 723.

28. Ibid. (*jibu* vol. 228), 723; and Wang Wan, 19/3a.

29. These are part of the ancient betrothal rituals.

30. Zhu Yizun, 58/12a.

31. Wanyan Yun Zhu's *Guochao guixiu zhengshi ji* and its *xuji*, for example, contain a good number of poems by faithful maidens. Faithful maiden poems can also be found in male-scholar-compiled volumes such as *Liang Zhe youxuan lu* (compiled by Ruan Yuan) and local gazetteers, or cited in their biographies. A sample of these poems are analyzed in Lu, *True*, chs. 5 and 6.

32. Qian Yiji, 7233. The essay from which this excerpt is quoted is also attributed to Jiao Tinfu (see *Congshu jicheng xinbian*, vol. 78). Reading it in conjunction with another of Jiao Xun's essays, "Chao *Yi Gui Cao* xu," it seems reliable to conclude that this piece was by Jiao Xun.

33. Li Ciming, 304.

34. Zhang Xuecheng, 128; Jiao Xun, 85; and Li Wenzao, 357.

35. Gui (1929), 16/15b–16a.

36. For example, commenting on faithful maiden Huang, a little daughter-in-law, Zhang Shiyuan emphasized that Huang had entered the gate of her fiancé. Therefore, her situation was different. Qian Yiji, 7232.

37. See Wu Ding, 2/29a–31a, 8/14a–15b, 11/5a–6a, 11/12a–13a.

38. Ibid., 2/29a–30b.

39. Ibid., 9/18b.

40. Liu Dakui, 464.

41. Qian Daxin, 347.

42. Ibid., 689.

43. Ibid., 348.

44. Fang Bao, 1420:662.

45. Qian Yiji, 7166.

46. Liu Taigong, 8/17a; Wang Zhong, 525.

47. One of the faithful maidens was from his native place, Gaoyou in Jiangsu province; the other was a daughter of a high-ranking official, Peng Yuanrui, under whom Liu passed his examination. Liu Taigong, 8/14b–15b.

48. Qian Yiji, 7234.

49. Ibid., 7235–36.

50. Fang Bao, 1420:535.

51. Zhu Shi, nianpu/12b–13a.

52. Qian Yiji, 7215. Note the tone of Zhi Shi's reply. He is saying, "This is your idea. You must know what the rules are!"

53. Zhu Shi, 2/31b.

54. See, for example, Katherine Carlitz, "The Daughter, ;" Beverly Bossler, "Faithful Wives and Heroic Martyrs;" and T'ien.

CHAPTER 6

1. I examine what I call the meliorist chronotype together with three other late Qing chronotypes in *The Precious.*

2. My concept of exemplary time is similar to Huang Chun-chieh and John B. Hendersen's notion of "supertime." Huang defines "supertime" as the paradigmatic in time which patterns time into the human tapestry called history, which can be discerned only in history and is best exemplified in the work of the historical sages. Huang Chun-chieh and John B. Henderson, introduction to Huang Chun-chieh and Henderson, xii–xiii.

3. Sun Wenguang, 1104.

4. On the *gongci* genre, which was initially associated with Wang Jian of the Tang dynasty, see "Chuban shuoming" in Wu Shijian, 1.

5. It is unclear when the poems were written. They are included in Wu Shijian, 22–41.

6. Wu Shijian, 37. Katherine A. Karl spent ten months painting Cixi in 1903 for the St. Louis Exhibition. In 1905 she wrote *With the Empress Dowager* to dispel rumors about her experience in China.

7. This style of poetry was associated with the late Tang poet Han Wo (844–923) author of the *Xianglian ji.*

8. Sun Wenguang, 1104.

9. Wei Xiyuan, *Buyong,* 128. According to Hucker (199), the *quewu* functioned from the Song-Jin period as the Monopoly Tax Commission and by the Qing dynasty was possibly associated with customs duties. Wang Zhenda, the editor of the 1987 edition of Wei Xiyuan, *Buyong,* describes Wei's position in Suqian as managing monopoly affairs (131).

10. This proposal was included in a series of three joint memorials to the throne submitted by the governor-general of Jiangsu, Anhui, and Jiangxi Provinces, Liu Kunyi (1820–1902), and the governor-general of Hubei and Hunan Provinces, Zhang Zhidong (1837–1909), in July 1901. For details of these proposed reforms, see Reynolds, 129.

11. Zhang Guanfa, "Xu" (Preface).

12. "Xu," 2 in Wei Xiyuan, *Buyong.*

13. Wei Xiyuan, *Buyong,* "Banlang" (Bridegroom's companion), 6–9; "Suilu" (To smash the skull), 132–37; "Pihu" (To tear a household asunder), 148–151.

14. The cases featured in the *Selected Stories* were generally drawn from Ming-Qing materials which were themselves often derived from earlier texts such as Hong Bian of the Song dynasty's *Yiguai zhi,* which was reprinted in Zheng Xuan's *Zuo feiyan rizuan* in the Ming. A number of cases were drawn from Feng Menglong's (1574–1646) *Zengzhi nang bu* (Expanded supplement to gems of Chinese wisdom).

15. While Wei appended commentaries to all entries in the *Illustrated Biographies,* he did so more sporadically in the legal compilation.

16. Wei Xiyuan, *Buyong,* "Ziwu," 178–81. A clever magistrate who suspected the true circumstances of the case ultimately exonerated the daughter-

in-law. His method for proceeding was, however, questionable. He had a local shrew flogged (for no particular reason) and then placed her in the same cell as the daughter-in-law. The latter announced to the complaining shrew (while one of the magistrate's assistants was listening) that it was better to be flogged for no reason than it was to be innocent and have one's reputation destroyed.

17. The English designation for this genre coined by Carlitz ("The Social," 126), corresponds to a number of Chinese terms including *Xu lienü zhuan* (Continuation of the biographies of women), *Lienü zhuan zengguang* (Enlarged biographies of women), and *Guang lienü zhuan*.

18. On the *Gujin Lienü zhuan* see "Retsujo," 8. On the *Guifan*, see Handlin. On the *Huitu*, see Carlitz, "The Social;" and Raphals, *Sharing*, 116.

19. Liu Kai was a member of the Tongcheng school (Tongcheng guwen) and a disciple of Yao Nai (1732–1815), a famous Tongcheng promoter of *guwen* (ancient-style prose writing).

20. Carlitz ("The Social," 133) estimates that 16 percent of the cases in the *Huitu lienü zhuan* date from the Ming while only 3 percent of those in Lü Kun's *Guifan* do.

21. On these basic characteristics of *lienü zhuan* expansions, see Handlin, 16; and Carlitz, "The Social."

22. I am not implying that the genre was not aestheticized before this time—see Zurndorfer's discussion in chapter 3 of this volume of Gu Kaizhi's supposed illustration of an early edition of the *Lienü zhuan*—but there was a prominent late imperial tendency in that direction.

23. This point is brilliantly made by Carlitz in "The Social," especially 139–41.

24. The poems functioned like formal poems found at the end of *mubiao* (grave notices) or *muzhi* (grave records), which praised the virtues of the celebrated individual without adding any new dimensions to the biography. See Nivison, 459.

25. On the *meiren* genre, see Wu Hong, "Beyond," specifically on the emergence of the genre, 323. Catherine Yeh ("Creating," 440) asserts that illustrated courtesan albums were known under the rubric of *baimeitu*. See also Tan, 5; and Mann, "Jiuzhong."

26. The *Baimei xin yongtu zhuan* went through numerous reprintings in the Qing dynasty and through the 1990s. There are at least two recent reprints of this text, from Taipei (Qiantang) and Beijing (Yan). The text is composed of four volumes: two feature prefatory remarks, an index, and poems, and two contain the pictorial biographies of one hundred beauties.

27. Three of the biographies in the final section of Wei's compilation on "Virtue" (Wei Xiyuan, *Xiuxiang*, IX.7, 9, 11) were similar to Yan's, for example.

28. See Raphals, *Sharing*, 114.

29. Yan has himself taken this image of Mulan from Jin Guliang, *Wu shuang pu* (A record of famous personages), an early Qing dynasty work (1690) featuring woodblock prints of eminent personages in Chinese history. Many thanks to Dorothy Ko for pointing this connection out to me.

30. Wei Xiyuan, *Xiuxiang* VII, IX, VI.

31. Wei Xiyuan, *Xiuxiang*, "Xu" (Preface).

32. Ibid., I.

33. Ibid., VI. The *Shi jing* passage is from the "Da Shu yu Tian" (Greater Shu has gone hunting, Mao #78) in the "Zheng feng" section of the "Guo feng" (Airs of the Domains.) I am basing my interpretation on James Legge's exegesis of the passage. Many thanks to Graham Sanders for assistance in tracking down the many translations of this quotation.

34. Ibid., VI.

35. Ibid., VI.

36. Ibid., VI.

37. Ibid., VI.4.

38. Ibid., VI.10.

39. Ibid., IX.11.

40. Ibid., I.3.

41. The term *xiannü* appears in the "Chenfeng," "Dongmen zhi chi, xu" section of the *Shi jing*. In the novel *Honglou meng* (Dream of the Red Chamber) it is used to describe virtuous women of the past featured in such texts as the *Lienü zhuan* and the didactic collection the *Nü sishu* (Four books for women).

42. On the breakdown of categories in Wang Xian's text, see Yamazaki, 48. The other categories included *muyi* (maternal rectitude), comprising 11 percent of the biographies, *xianxiao* (wise and filial), 28 percent, and *caiyi* (talented and skilled), 6 percent.

43. On the widow Tao Ying from the *Lienü zhuan* who Wei declared an exemplar for living on after her husband's death and raising her sons, see Wei Xiyuan, *Xiuxiang* IX.4. On his disapproval of self-mutilation, see commentaries on the story of Lady Huan from the *Hou Han shu*, Wei Xiyuan, *Xiuxiang*, IX.5; and Lady Xiahou, of the Han dynasty, Wei Xiyuan, *Xiuxiang*, IX.6.

44. I have benefited tremendously from Weijing Lu's research and from conversations with her in thinking through the meanings of faithful maidenhood in the late Qing and before.

45. Wei Xiyuan, *Xiuxiang*, VI.17.

46. The earliest version of this drama, written in the late fifteenth century by Shen Shouxian, was entitled *Shang Lu sanyuanji*. Part of the story was based on historical fact. Weijing Lu, *True*, 163.

47. Wei Xiyuan, *Xiuxiang*, VI.17. This critique of the *zhennü* was voiced by Yu Zhengxie (1775–1840).

48. Wei Xiyuan, *Xiuxiang*, IX.21.

49. Ibid., IX.21. On Yuan Mei and Yuan Ji, see Weijing Lu, *True*, 242–44, on Wang Zhong's comment and on the connection between Yuan Ji's erudition and her devotion, Weijing Lu, *True*, 244. See also Mann, *Precious*, 84–85.

50. Wei Xiyuan, *Xiuxiang*, IX.23.

51. Boyi and Shuqi were princes of a small kingdom and sons of Guo Zhujun. On Wang Wan, see Weijing Lu, *True*, 220–21. On the story itself, see Sima Qian, II:1–7.

52. Peng Yulian, 1031.

53. Wei Xiyuan, *Xiuxiang*, IV.6.

54. On May Fourth period views on chastity, see Lu Xun, "Wo;" Hu Shi. Wei's critique cannot be construed as a direct lineal antecedent of New Culture views. Lu Xun, Hu Shi, and others made no reference to the ongoing, 300-year-long debate within which Wei's position was firmly grounded. This may have been due to ignorance, to the dismissal of a trend that May Fourth writers considered too entrenched in obsolete values to be of any use to them, or to the willful cultural amnesia necessary to the New Culture project of positing a radical rupture with "tradition."

55. Brokaw, "Reading," 226.

56. On the Jicheng tushu gongsi, see Lufei, 213.

57. Wei Xiyuan, *Xiuxiang*, VI (preface); VI.18; VI.16.

58. On these new-style women's textbooks, see Judge, "Meng;" *The Precious*.

59. *Shibao* had a special contract to print advertisements for textbooks published by the Commercial Press, one of the largest and most innovative publishers of this new genre. Judge, *Print*, 44.

60. *Shibao* (October 1, 1910). The title given for the work advertised, *Huitu daban gujin xiannü zhuan*, is slightly different from Wei's. However, "Huitu daban" (illustrated large edition) could have been used descriptively, replacing the term *xiuxiang* (referring to the illustrations) in Wei's title.

61. Wei Xiyuan, *Xiuxiang*.

CHAPTER 7

1. The opening dialogue is from Xia Yan, 46–47. Qiu Jin was convicted as an anti-Manchu revolutionary and executed on July 15, 1907. For research material, see Guo Yanli, *Qiu Jin yanjiu*. See also Rankin, "The Emergence."

2. This is consistent with the intent expressed in many poems by the historical Qiu Jin. See, for example, "Zhegu tian" and "Untitled," in Chang and Saussy, 656–57.

3. Legge, *The Chinese Classics*, 1:297.

4. Legge, *The Chinese Classics*, 2:411.

5. *Han Feizi*, 2:935–36.

6. Xiong.

7. Meijer; Elvin; and Mann, "Widows."

8. In addition to chapter 5 in this volume, Paul Ropp gives an excellent summary of the critical tradition in his introduction to Ropp, Zamperini, and Zurndorfer, 3–21.

9. For the "allure," see ibid., 3–21; for "obligation," see ibid., 22–46.

10. Recent scholarship approaches the large number of late imperial chastity suicides by close studies of economic, legal, and social conditions. Roughly speaking, there are two related conclusions: (1) women were not victims but also agents; (2) ideological precepts of neo-Confucianism are not the only or primary cause for women's suicide. My point here is that before we reach any

conclusion, we need to remind ourselves of the especially slippery ground between cause and interpretation in martyrology.

11. Guo Yanli, *Qiu Jin yanjiu*, 513. Scholars have observed a steady trend of increasing politicization in women's martyrology. See Grace Fong's observation of the combination of the personal/feminine virtue of chastity with the political virtue of loyalty to empire. Fong, "Signifying," 105–42.

12. The two stock expressions respectively refer to Zou Yan, a historical figure in the Warring States period, and Dou Er, the tragic heroine *par excellence* in Guan Hanqing's play *Dou Er yuan;* both died as the result of a miscarriage of justice.

13. Xiaoshan xianglingzi (pseud.), in A Ying, 108–47. Originally published in *Guohun bao*, 1908.

14. Tan Sitong's wife, Li Run, was said to have committed suicide when she learned of her husband's execution after the failure of the 1898 Reform. See Judge, *The Precious,* introduction and ch. 5. The wife of Wu Yue, who attempted to assassinate the five Qing emissaries to Japan in 1905, is also said to have "followed her husband in death" after learning of his failed suicide attack. Bian and Tang, 90.

15. That Qiu Jin should be cast as *dan* is inevitable if only because of her family's literati-official background.

16. Guyue yingzong jinü (pseud.), in A Ying, 148–76. Originally published by Gailiang xiaoshuo hui in 1907.

17. Notably contemporary criticism of her execution never failed to mention that the executed was a *shi* (literati) and a *nüshi* (female literati) at that, thus consistent with the theatrical portrayal of the upper-class woman, the innocent victim of the legal system.

18. James J. Y. Liu; and Chen Pingyuan, *Qiangu.* Chen Pingyuan argues that earlier depictions of *nüxia* does not require sexual chastity but that in late imperial times, that requirement is added.

19. Guo Yanli, *Qiu Jin yanjiu*, 559.

20. Ibid.

21. Ibid., 81–82.

22. Thus Tao Chengzhang appendixes Cheng Yi's biography after the one on Qiu Jin, ibid., 83–87. Sun Yat-sen commemorates her in a triplet of two other male martyrs. See Wang Qubing and Chen Dehe, *Qiu Jin shiji*, 3–4.

23. Guo Yanli, *Qiu Jin yanjiu*, 341.

24. Rash speech is the opposite of one the four cardinal feminine virtues, "prudence in words," and as such counts as one of the seven classic reasons to warrant expulsion of one's wife. Zhang Binglin, "Qiu Jin ji xu" (Preface to *Qiu Jin's Collected Works*), in Guo Yanli, *Qiu Jin yanjiu*, 341.

25. For historical context, see Furth, 396–400.

26. Lee, 479.

27. The role of a sexually liberated new woman, controversial as it may be, was only open to a small sector of the female population in any case, excluding married woman, especially women who had borne children. For contemporary

reflection on this restriction, see Shi Pingmei, "Lin Nan's Diary," in Dooling and Torgeson, 115. Ironically, while most May Fourth New Women slammed the door on their parents in refusing arranged marriages, Qiu Jin was one of the few who, like Ibsen's Nora, walked out on her marriage.

28. Eileen J. Cheng.

29. At the end of "The True Story of Ah Q," for example, a crowd followed Ah Q as he was driven to the execution ground; as they cheered him on and even demanded an aria, their eyes were "dull yet penetrating, that, having devoured his words, still seemed eager to devour something beyond his flesh and blood."

30. Lu Xun, *Lu Xun quanji* 3:465. This section of my paper is much indebted to Cheng, "Gendered Spectacles."

31. One of Qiu Jin's last wishes was that her clothes not be stripped after the execution. Like Lu Xun's revolutionary, her remains were initially buried in the foothill burial ground used by paupers and executed criminals. Guo Yanli, *Qiu Jin yanjiu*, 571, 573.

32. Lu Xun, "Kuangren," 10.

33. Guo Yanli, *Qiu Jin yanjiu*, 509.

34. "Nala de da'an" (The Answer to Nora), in Guo Yanli, *Qiu Jin yanjiu*, 466–71.

35. Wolf.

36. *Tian*, 18:561. Originally published in *Yunnan ribao*, December 5, 1943.

37. Anderson, 205.

CHAPTER 8

ACKNOWLEDGMENTS: I am grateful to Joan Judge and Hu Ying for including me in the volume, and to Suzanne Cahill, Stephen Durrant, Patricia Ebrey, Susan Mann, Michael Nylan, and Scott Wells for their critical suggestions.

1. "Epitaph" is an approximate translation for *muzhiming*. Unlike the Western tombstone, the *muzhiming* was to be placed on top of a coffin and buried underground. In addition to *muzhiming*, I also include other funeral inscriptions such as *shibiao, mubiao,* and *taming* in this study. For a study on pre-Tang funeral writings, see Ebrey, "Later;" and Brashier. For an overview of epitaph writing in Chinese history, see Zhao Chao.

2. Among the 6,000, 925 epitaphs were collected in Dong Gao et al.'s *Quan Tang wen* (hereafter, *QTW*). Most epitaphs in this collection are eloquent and dedicated to high-ranking officials or prominent figures. Another major source of Tang epitaphs is *Tangdai muzhi huibian* (hereafter, *HB*) and *Tangdai muzhi huibian xuji* (hereafter, *XJ*), both compiled by Zhou Shaoliang and Zhao Chao. They contain 5,119 epitaphs, all from archeological discoveries. Compared to *QTW*, *HB* and *XJ* contain a more representative sampling of Tang epitaphs: the writing style varies widely; the deceased range from servants, courtesans, and monks, to officials and emperors; and the epitaph writers are less well known. At least three epitaphs in *HB* identify the author as female (Zhenguan 181, Kaiyuan 336, and Tianbao 12), and an epitaph dated in 834 was coauthored by

the son and the daughter of a woman named Zheng (*XJ*, Dahe 49). In addition, at least another twenty epitaphs in *HB* and *XJ* were likely penned by women. More recently archaeologists have excavated a Tang epitaph dedicated to an official named Li Quanli and composed by his wife, Zheng Rouci (See Institute of Archaeology, 288). Kegasawa identifies more than 6,800 Tang epitaphs.

3. On the concept of "memorial culture," see Brashier, 27.

4. *Sui* is a Chinese term for reckoning age. A person is one *sui* from birth until the first Chinese New Year, when he or she will be two *sui*. All references to age in this chapter refer to *sui*.

5. *HB*, Dazhong 128. For a complete translation of the epitaph, see Robin Wang, *Images*, 300–304.

6. I define "elite" in this study as someone whose family had at least one male who served at any level of government office.

7. Ouyang, *juan* 48.

8. The phrase "holding books by oneself" (*qin zhi shu*) was often used in Tang literature to stress the person's engaging teaching method.

9. *QTW, juan* 680. A full text translation of the epitaph is included in Robin Wang, *Images*, 304–7.

10. In " Liu Ji qi Xiahoushi," Xiahou requested that her husband dismiss her so she could take care of her ailing father and eventually give him a proper burial. Similar stories appear in the *Xin Tangshu* and the *Jiu Tangshu*. For a discussion of role and performance in Chinese biographies, see Wright.

11. *XJ*, Dazhong 61.

12. *XJ*, Zhenyuan 18.

13. *HB*, Kaicheng 41.

14. "The Poet's verses" implies mourning poems written by Pan Yue (247–300).

15. *HB*, Dazhong 83.

16. Ibid., 128.

17. *HB*, Tianbao 69.

18. *HB*, Xiantong 040. The lid of the epitaph was lost, so we do not know its exact title.

19. For a study of Buddhist influence on Tang women's lives, see Yao, "Good."

20. *HB*, Kaiyuan 468.

21. *HB*, Tianbao 200.

22. *HB*, Wansuitongtian 14.

23. *XJ*, Xiantong 11.

24. *HB*, Zhenyuan 74.

25. *XJ*, Tianbao 84.

26. *XJ*, Jingyun 5.

27. *HB*, Dazhong 91.

28. *XJ*, Tianbao 108.

29. " Song Tingyu qi Weishi" and " Nüdaoshi Li Xuanzhen." Significantly, these are the only two biographies that did not make it to the *lienü* biographies in *Xin Tangshu*.

30. *HB*, Xianheng 33.
31. *HB*, Yonghui 59.
32. *HB*, Yifeng 34. Gongsun's husband's last name is ineligible.
33. *HB*, Dazhong 130.
34. *HB*, Huichang 3.
35. *HB*, Zhenyuan 62.
36. For a study of marriage practice in Tang China, see Ping Yao, *Tangdai*, chs.1–6.
37. Wang Pu, *juan* 36.
38. It is worth noting that the reported life spans for women tend to be inversely correlated with the number of women's epitaphs throughout the Tang dynasty. Therefore, it is possible that the statistical measure of decreased life expectancy for women during and after the An Lushan rebellion is due to the episodic inclusion of additional epitaphs for women who died young. This is obviously a caveat concerning all data reported here, however, there is no evidence suggesting that women who died young were excluded from epitaphs in early Tang periods (or men who died young were excluded from epitaphs in later Tang periods). However, inclusion of a larger spectrum of epitaphs also means that the data pool is larger, and hence more accurate. Additionally, because woman generally live longer than their male counterparts, inclusion of the appropriate number of such hypothesized early deaths would normally result in less gendered life span disparity rather than the reduced women's life spans reported here.
39. *HB*, Xiantong 020. For a full translation of the epitaph, see Robin Wang, *Images*, 310–12.
40. The rest of the eleven epitaphs omitted the cause of death.

CHAPTER 9

ACKNOWLEDGMENTS: I would like to express my appreciation to the participants at the conference at which this volume began, and to two anonymous readers, for helpful comments and suggestions. I would especially like to thank the editors, Joan Judge and Hu Ying, for their tireless efforts to bring the volume to press.

1. There is a large literature on this cult, especially for the Ming and Qing periods. For important studies in English, see Carlitz, "Desire, Danger," "Shrines," and "The Daughter;" as well as Elvin; Weijing Lu, *True*; and Theiss, *Disgraceful*. See also chapters 10 and 5 in this volume, by Carlitz and Lu respectively.
2. In chapter 5 of this volume, Weijing Lu shows that by Ming and Qing times the cult even encompassed "faithful maidens"—betrothed girls who refused to remarry after their fiancés' deaths.
3. I have outlined this phenomenon in Bossler, "Faithful Wives and Heroic Martyrs." The new concern with female fidelity was one aspect of a more general shift in gender roles between the tenth and the fourteenth centuries. That

shift is the subject of my forthcoming book, tentatively titled *Courtesans, Concubines, and the Cult of Wifely Fidelity: Gender and Social Change in China, 1000-1400.* Some of the book's arguments with respect to female fidelity, and especially the importance of the Song political situation in encouraging the production of texts focused on women's loyalty, are also adumbrated in Bossler, "Faithful Wives and Heroic Maidens."

4. The *zhuan* genre typically provided such basic information as a man's name and geographical origins, and details of his political career. It described his career and aspects of his behavior designed to permit judgment about the subject's morality or lack thereof. In contrast to modern Western biographies, the *zhuan* genre did not explore the psychological motivations for a subject's actions.

5. Lisa Raphals points out that from earliest times women's biographies tended to focus on exemplars (both good and bad) and were often used by men to exhort other men. See Raphals, *Sharing*, 6.

6. This latter innovation may reflect the increased importance of descendants and affinal relations in elite Chinese society in the Song and after.

7. Hans H. Frankel (104) stresses the distinction between the biographies included in the chapters devoted to such categories as "literary men" or "loyal and righteous officials" and the unclassified biographies. He notes that the classified biographies "seem to be reserved for those who fall short of the Confucian ideal of a well-rounded gentleman—the biographies of the greatest men of the dynasty are always unclassified." Frankel also points out that the "classifications follow each other on a descending scale which roughly reflects the value system of the historiographers." Here it is notable that biographies of exemplary women in the standard histories tend to come nearly last, prior only to those of barbarians and rebels.

8. In this volume, the chapters by Katherine Carlitz (10), Weijing Lu (5), Susan Mann (1), and Ping Yao (8) brilliantly elucidate the uses and limitations of funerary inscriptions as women's biography. For use of funerary inscriptions to trace the ways values for women's behavior changed over time, see Bossler, *Powerful*, 12–24.

9. Bossler, "Faithful Wives and Heroic Maidens," 765–69. More commonly, funerary inscriptions were titled simply with the name and/or rank of the subject.

10. I discuss the distinctions between public and private *zhuan* biographies in more detail in "Faithful Wives and Heroic Maidens," 751–84; see also chapter 5 in this volume, by Weijing Lu.

11. Sima Guang, 72.883–85. For an extended discussion of this biography and its implications for understanding women's Buddhist practice in the Song, see Halperin.

12. Wang Ling, 22.1–2b.

13. Cai Xiang, 32.583–84. A more detailed version of Cao's biography, attributed to Zhang Wangzhi (n.d., but a near contemporary of Cai Xiang), survives in the Southern Song literary collection *Song wen jian*, compiled by

the famous neo-Confucian Lü Zuqian. Zhang's biography explains that when Cao refused their contribution to the funeral expenses of her father, the clerks suggested that the funds be used for Cao's own wedding expenses. At that point she excoriated them, asking rhetorically how she could bear to benefit from her father's death, and pointing out that ritual would be violated should she think about her wedding while still in mourning, or, as a denizen of the inner chambers, accept tainted money from outside the family. This version of the biography makes explicit much that is only hinted at in Cai's version.

14. This fact sharply distinguishes *zhuan* biographies from funerary inscriptions in this period.

15. Although for convenience I am using the terms "fiction" and "nonfiction" here, the reader should be aware that in imperial China the boundaries between the two were not necessarily self-evident. In particular, a longstanding tradition of "unofficial biography" (*bie zhuan*) acknowledged alternative versions of biographical "truth."

16. Zhang Lei, 43.3a–4b. Many Song, Yuan, and Ming authors played with the anthropomorphized image of "Lady Bamboo" in poetry as well as prose. The Northern Song poet Huang Tingjian (*zheng ji*, 10.246) in particular, was famous for insisting that "supporting a man's legs is not the proper occupation of a lady" and proposing that she be called "Green Slave" (*Qing nu*) instead. Lü Nangong (1047–86) (18.4a–6a) anthropomorphized what appears to be the same object in his "Biography of Lady Flatcool" (Pingliang fu ren zhuan). In the thirteenth century Lin Jingxi (21b–23a) wrote a similarly satirical biography for a "Bathwoman" (Tang po zhuan) .

17. Qin Guan, 25.166.

18. On the implications of these stories for late Tang culture, see Owen, *The End*. The early Song collection *Taiping guang ji* preserves a number of such stories from the late Tang and Five Dynasties; see Li Fang, *juan* 484–91.

19. See Dudbridge. It is impossible to judge the historicity of the heroines in the Song *chuan qi* biographies, but it is worth noting that some, like Wen Wan (discussed below), seem to have been regarded as historical figures by later authors. (Qing) Li E's collection *Notes on Song Poetry* (Song shi ji shi) 97.1–1b quotes Wen Wan's poetry, and in the Republican period Hu Wenkai likewise included her in his *Lidai funü zhuzuo* (Women's writing through the ages), 52. One might add that there is no more or less reason to trust in the historicity of such widely vaunted figures as Song poet Zhu Shuzhen.

20. On the varied roles and social impact of courtesans in Song and Yuan, see Bossler, *Courtesans* and "Shifting." The Northern Song stories of courtesans I examine here are drawn from Liu Fu, which contains a range of materials ranging from short anecdotes and *zhi guai* stories to longer *chuan qi*. Although the collection contains some items drawn from works of earlier provenance, considerable material is based on historical Song individuals and situations. Although the *chuan qi* it contains are considered to be inferior to those of the Tang in literary merit, the collection provides a wealth of information about social practices and attitudes of the Northern Song.

21. Liu Fu, *bie ji*, 2.213.

22. Liu Fu, *qian ji*, 10.95–99.

23. Liu Fu, *hou ji* 7.166–73.

24. Seo Tatsuhiko has identified playfulness in poetry as a central element in the construction of "romance" in the Chinese context.

25. On Song animus against gentlewomen writing poetry, see Ebrey, *The Inner*, 124.

26. Liu Fu, *bie ji*, 2.212; *hou ji*, 7.167.

27. Liu Fu, *qian ji*, 10.96.

28. Liu Fu, *hou ji*, 7.168.

29. On the admiration of literacy and the ability to manage money in upper-class Song women, See Bossler, *Powerful*, 17–19, and Birge, "Chu," passim.

30. Liu Fu, *hou ji*, 7.171.

31. Liu Fu, *qian ji*, 10.99.

32. It should be emphasized that in the Northern Song widow fidelity, though always admired, was not the social norm. Even among the upper class, young widows could remarry without stigma. Likewise, the fidelity of courtesans was recognized even at the time as largely a literary conceit: the authors of courtesan biographies admit that the kind of fidelity they are describing is exceedingly rare among the entertainers of their day. See Liu Fu, *qian ji* 10.99; *hou ji* 7.166.

33. As Stephen Owen (*The End*, 132) has pointed out, the romantic nature of men's relationships with courtesans was always threatened by the financial transactions that underlay those relationships. He argues that in Tang stories about such relationships "negating financial compulsion in the woman's relation to the man is an essential plot element."

34. On the importance of romance in the biographies of faithful women of the Ming and Qing, see chapters 10 (Carlitz) and 5 (Lu) in this volume.

35. Dudbridge (25–26) has suggested that this format was central to the development of early *chuan qi*, which functioned essentially as prose prefaces to pre-existing narrative poems.

36. The interleaving of multiple biographical texts, poems, and commentary is especially striking in the biography of the courtesan Wen Wan, which includes prefaces and postfaces appended to a collection of thirty of "her" poems. See Liu Fu, *hou ji*, 7.166–8.180.

37. "Zhang Wenrou shi xu," in Liu Yan, 24.17–19b.

38. See Bossler, "Faithful Wives and Heroic Martyrs," 528–31, and Bossler, "Gender," 197–223.

39. Literati of the Song and earlier commonly wrote prefaces for poetry collections celebrating the activities of men, but I have found no other Song preface for a poetry collection extolling any type of woman.

40. The political context of Xu Ji's elevation to exemplar status is detailed in Bossler, *Courtesans*. Xu Ji garnered some recognition in later imperial China as he continued to be celebrated as an exemplar long after the Song. Coincidentally, he is also known for providing us with one of the earliest extant refer-

ences to footbinding (another sign of the unconventionality of his writings). See Ko, "In Search," 403.

41. Xu's biography (an "account of conduct," *xing zhuang*) was compiled by one Wang Zishen [1050–1127] (Wang identifies himself as an affine) sometime between 1116 and Wang's death in 1127. See Xu Ji, 32.10b–17b.

42. This was precisely the period of factional conflict in Song government, when exemplars began to be used to serve political ends. Perhaps for this reason, and in spite of (or because of?) Xu Ji's fame, there are some puzzling discrepancies in the historical record concerning him, including different dates for his attainment of the *jinshi* degree (variously 1065 and 1067), and different dates for his first appointment to office (variously 1086 and 1100). Although these discrepancies are quite interesting in the context of late Northern Song factional conflict, they need not concern us here.

43. "The one who hasn't died" was a standard locution by which faithful widows referred to themselves.

44. Xu Ji, 13.8b–11.

45. Xu Ji, 3.5b–7.

46. A very similar story, down to the incident with the bubbles, is preserved in Hong Mai's Southern Song collection the *Yi jian zhi* (*bu*, 5.1590), with the very significant difference that in the version Hong Mai tells, the wife is not virtuous and loyal, but rather has been having an affair with the man who kills her husband.

47. Xu Ji, 3.7b–8.

48. I have found one earlier example of a poem with preface celebrating an exemplary woman: a rhyme-prose (*fu*) poem written by the Li Hua [715–66] of the Tang, describing the daughter of an acquaintance who was captured by bandits but managed to pass her husband's seal of appointment to an old village woman before committing suicide. Li's poem, however, is far more sophisticatedly written and far more elevated in tone than those of Xu Ji. See Li Hua, 1.11a–12a.

49. In Chinese kinship terminology, cousins in the same generation were addressed as "sisters" and "brothers."

50. Zhao Dingchen, 14.1a–4b. It is possible that this biography was in fact meant as political allegory, as a justification for continued loyalty to the feckless emperor Huizong. Yet since Zhao associates himself personally with the subject, I am inclined to take it at face value.

51. For a discussion of other aspects of exemplar text production in the Southern Song, see Bossler, *Courtesans*. I have discussed the dramatic rhetoric of these texts in Bossler, "Faithful Wives and Heroic Maidens."

52. Wang Zhiwang, 15.6–8, "Gui nü zhuan."

53. Chen Liang, 13.160, "Er lie nü zhuan."

54. Chen Zhangfang, 2.8–9, "Er liefu zhuan."

55. Cheng Ju, 17.3b; Wang Zhiwang, 15.5b. Rong's biography survives in the *Song History* (Tuotuo, *Song*, 460.13481).

56. Zhou Zizhi, 10.13, "Du Xu Boyuan shu wai jia yi shi; zuo er jue ju yi ji zhi, bing xu." I have been unable to identify Xu Boyuan.

57. The two late Southern Song examples I have found are Yang Wanli, 131.3b–5b, "Jie fu Liu shi mu ming"; and Liu Kezhuang, 149.10b–11b, "Li Jie fu mu zhi ming." These texts are unique among Song funerary inscriptions in explicitly designating their subjects as faithful wives (*jie fu*) in the title of the texts.

58. Carlitz, "The Social." See also her "Desire." Carlitz's chapter (10) in this volume likewise underscores the importance of fiction in shaping the world and worldviews of late Ming women.

59. Carlitz ("The Daughter") describes a similar conflation in depictions of fidelity suicides by courtesans and faithful wives in the Ming period.

60. Among other factors, political crisis, invasion, government policies, and elite competition were all implicated in this development as well. See Bossler, *Courtesans.*

CHAPTER 10

1. *Muzhiming* were produced by and for the governing class, which limits the degree to which we can draw general conclusions about Chinese women from them. However, by late imperial times certain attributes praised in elite epitaphs are found in such a variety of sources that we can assume they were widespread norms. Ming gazetteers list women at all social levels willing to die rather than remarry, and Theiss (*Disgraceful*) shows that Qing dynasty village women guarded their chastity jealously. Ming and Qing legal case narratives show that harmony between household women was expected at all social levels. See Epstein, "Making;" Theiss, "Explaining;" and Ocko, 268–71.

2. Carlitz, "Desire and Writing," 624–37.

3. Elman, "Political;" Hanan, *The Chinese Vernacular,* 1–16.

4. A trove of printed and illustrated *shuochang cihua* was discovered in Jiading county in 1967 and published in facsimile by the Shanghai Museum in 1973. See *Ming Chenghua.* The collection is analyzed in McLaren. Hong Pian and *Sixty Stories* are discussed in Hanan, *The Chinese Short,* 3; *The Chinese Vernacular,* 56–57.

5. *Gao feng shuren Ren shi muzhiming,* in He Jingming, 36.23b–24b.

6. Ming literati also wrote lovingly about their daughters: see, for example, Wang Jiusi's epitaph for his daughter, quoted below, and Gui Youguang's for two of his young daughters: *Nü Rulan kuang zhi,* in Gui Youguang, *Zhenchuan xiansheng ji,* 1981, 535–36; and *Nü Er-er kuang zhi,* in Gui Youguang, *Zhenchuan xiansheng ji,* 1981, 536. These make up a small percentage of Ming funerary writing for women, however.

7. Goodrich, 841–45.

8. *Feng yiren wang qi Zuo shi muzhiming,* in Li Mengyang, 45.7b–10b. Epitaphs for women in one's own family were a convenient vehicle for autobiography. Li Kaixian, discussed below, writes in an epitaph for his sister about

his family's early poverty, but his epitaph for his wife celebrates the wealth he achieved during a successful career: "We now lived happily without the poverty of my student days, or the anxieties of official life. Our gardens and orchards, pavilions and gazebos, were complete." *Gao feng yiren wang qi Zhang shi muzhiming*, in Li Kaixian, 632.

9. *Feng yiren wang qi Zuo shi muzhiming*, in Li Mengyang, 45.7b–10b.

10. *Mao ruren muzhiming*, in Gui Youguang, *Zhenchuan xiansheng ji*, 1981, 519.

11. *Zhou zi jia shi Tang ruren*, in ibid., 503.

12. *Zhang ruren muzhiming*, in ibid., 506.

13. *Ming gu feng xundafu Dai zhou zhizhou Bian gong he zang zhi ming*, in Li Mengyang, 44.17b.

14. *Yibin Zuo gong he zang muzhiming*, in Li Mengyang, 44.5a–7a.

15. *Wang mei Yuan shi fu muzhiming*, in Li Kaixian, 583.

16. *Gao chushi he zang muzhiming*, Li Mengyang, 45.15b.

17. *Ming gu feng tai an ren Pei mu Zhang shi muzhiming*, ibid., 44.16a.

18. Quarreling with parents-in-law was one of the "Ten Abominations" in the Great Ming Code, and was specifically dealt with in articles 351–54. See Jiang Yonglin, 18, 191–92; and Huang Zhangjian, 846–47, for substatutes and specific cases.

19. *Ming gu Shen yiren muzhiming*, in Li Mengyang, 44.13b.

20. *Gao feng yiren wang qi Zhang shi muzhiming*, in Li Kaixian, 632.

21. *Zeng ruren Li qi Ying shi muzhiming*, in ibid., 634.

22. *Fengqiu Xishun wang muzhiming*, in Li Mengyang, 44.1a.

23. *Furen Jia shi muzhiming*, in Li Mengyang, 44.9b. She also managed her household perfectly so that her husband would be free to travel and study.

24. *Kang shi nü muzhiming*, in Wang Jiusi, 521–24.

25. *Wang mei Yuan shi fu muzhiming*, in Li Kaixian, 583.

26. *Chi zeng anren Xiang mu Zhou shi mu biao*, in Li Kaixian, 690.

27. *Mao ruren muzhiming*, in Gui Youguang, *Zhenchuan xiansheng ji*, 1981, 519.

28. Carlitz, "Desire, Danger."

29. McLaren, 70.

30. Lü Kun, *juan* 1, passim.

31. See the *Qing gan* (Romantic love) section of Li Fang, *juan* 274, for several Tang dynasty tales.

32. *Feng yue rui xian ting* (The lovers' rendezvous), story no. 5 in Hong Pian.

33. For the twelfth-century version, see *Dong jieyuan Xixiang ji*, translated in Ch'en Li-li. West and Idema translate and analyze the dramatic version popular in Ming.

34. Song Meidong, dates unknown, *Jiao hong zhuan*, in Cheng Boquan, 280–323. See Richard G. Wang. This tale was dramatized by Meng Chengshun (1599–ca.1684) as *Jiao hong ji*.

35. Lü Kun, 1.2a.

36. Carlitz, "On *Yingying*."

37. McLaren, 49–50.

38. Lowry, "Duplicating," 258–59.

39. *Jie chang pian*, in Li Mengyang, 22.18b–20a.

40. *Zhao qi Wen shi muzhiming*, in ibid., 44.12a.

41. This same Jintai Lu family publishing house brought out collections of love songs and an edition of *Xi xiang ji*.

42. An official under Han Yuan Di (r. 48–32 BCE), Zhang Chang refused to be discomfited by questions about why he painted his wife's eyebrows; He Lang is He Yan of the third century CE, whose own brilliantly white skin led others to assume (incorrectly) that he was wearing powder; and Yan Hui was the favorite disciple of Confucius, who bitterly lamented Yan's untimely death.

43. Zhu Jing'an (fl. 1450), "Grievance from the Boudoir," in Chang and Saussy, 156.

44. See Blanchard; Carlitz, "Desire and Writing," and Carlitz, "The Daughter."

45. 1539 *Kunshan xianzhi*, 13.18b–19a. Only in 1733 was causing a woman's suicide by sexual innuendo specifically criminalized (see Theiss, "Managing," 66), but this Kunshan gazetteer shows us that such cases were known as early as the Hongwu era (1368–99).

46. The ninth of Hong Pian's *Sixty Stories, Feng yue xiang si* (The lover's Reverie), deeply influenced by *Xi xiang ji,* ends in a similar *liebestod.*

47. *Haizhou*, 8.10b–11a.

48. Yenna Wu, 166–72.

49. See the Ming novel *Xi you ji* (The western journey), chs. 11–12, and later operas (Zeng Bairong, 386).

50. The vastly popular maid Hongniang in *Xi xiang ji*, discussed below, was also celebrated for standing up to authority. Hongniang's, however, is a relatively uncomplicated case, since she stands up to authority easily seen as unjust (the heroine's mother can be understood to have reneged on a promise of marriage).

51. McMahon.

52. *Song Renzong ren mu ji*, 4C of the *Ming Chenghua.* I am grateful to Wilt Idema for pointing out the relevance of this story.

53. Chaffee.

54. See Hanan, "Judge;" St. André; and Youd for the transformation of the historical Song dynasty jurist Bao Zheng into the justice hero of texts and television from the Yuan dynasty to the present.

55. Authored by Wang Yuanxiang, late Yuan, Jiangxi Province. Play is no longer extant.

56. McLaren, 15–76.

57. *Chantefable* recitation in the home, McLaren, 70. Clips from the Cantonese opera *Limao huan Tai zi* (The wildcat exchanges the crown prince) can be found on youtube.com.

58. See Carlitz, "Desire and Writing," 623, 624, for shrines to Filial Daughter-in-Law Dou, and reference to another shrine to her in *Haizhou*, 8.15b–16a.

59. *Zhang zhennü yu shi*, in Gui Youguang, *Zhenchuan xiansheng ji* 1981, 92–94.

60. McLaren, 30.

CHAPTER 11

1. On how factional politics shaped the historical record for the Song period, see the articles by Charles Hartman, especially "The Making" and "A Textual."

2. On her career, see Chaffee.

3. Here, following common English-language practice, I refer to the empresses by their family names. It was more common in Chinese sources to use their titles. Thus Empress Dowager Cao is called Cisheng, Empress Dowager Gao is called Xuanren, and Empress Dowager Xiang is called Qinsheng. Even in translations below I normally make these substitutions to aid clarity. I also make other comparable ones as well, translating former emperor as Shenzong or Zhezong, depending on who is being referred to, and the Yuanyou empress as Empress Meng and the Yuanfu empress as Empress Liu.

4. *Zeng Bu*. On the diaries Song councilors kept, see Yan Yongcheng.

5. Before Huizong became emperor, he was referred to as Prince Duan.

6. Tuotuo, *Song*, 242.8630. An earlier version of this biography survives in Wang Cheng, 14.2b–3a. It includes additional information on her ancestors, but most of the text is identical or very close.

7. On the marriages between the imperial family and the military elite, see Chung; Lorge.

8. The sources used are Tuotuo, *Song*, chs. 242, 243, 246, and 248; Xu Song, *dixi* 1.36a–41a, 8.20b–38b; Li Zhi, *Huang*, 4.124–27, 7.198–99, 8.210–13, 11.263–65, 15.320–26.

9. Tuotuo, *Song*, 246.8720.

10. These narratives are found several places, including Tuotuo, *Song*, 243.8632–38, Chen Bangzhan, 47.459–63; Yang Zhongliang, 113:1a–10a; and *Xu zizhi*, esp. 13.523–28.

11. Yang Zhongliang, 113.1a–b.

12. Tuotuo, *Song*, 243.8632.

13. Yang Zhongliang, 113.2b–3b.

14. *Xu zizhi*, 13.523–25.

15. Ibid., 13.523–26.

16. This last sentence is somewhat obscure. Perhaps the empress is trying to indicate that Prince Duan was perceptive and attentive to Zhezong, though it is possible that here Xiang is referring to Shenzong as the former emperor (she used the term for both Shenzong and Zhezong).

17. Tuotuo, *Song*, 19.357–58, records this conversation in almost identical detail, but the judgment on Huizong at the end of his annals (Tuotuo, *Song*, 22.417–18) asserts that "At Zhezong's death, before Huizong was enthroned, [Zhang] Dun said he should not be ruler of the realm because of his frivolous-

ness." In all likelihood the historians here drew on one of the often embroidered stories that circulated in anecdotal literature. There were, for instance, several stories of fortune tellers or seers who predicted Huizong's accession, which undoubtedly circulated only after he came to the throne.

18. *Zeng Bu,* 9.3a-b.
19. Ibid., 9.3b.
20. Ibid., 9.3b–4a.
21. Ibid., 9.4a–b.
22. Ibid., 9.4b–5a.
23. Ibid., 9.10a.
24. Ibid., 9.10a.
25. Ibid., 9.6a–7a.
26. Ibid., 9.7a–b.
27. Ibid., 9.7b–8a.
28. Ibid., 9.8a.
29. Ibid., 9.8b.
30. Ibid., 9.9a.
31. Ibid., 9.39a–b.
32. Ibid., 9.39b–40a.
33. Ibid., 9.67b–68a.
34. Ibid., 9.68a–b.
35. On the revision of the histories in this period, see Levine.
36. *Zeng Bu,* 9.48a-b. See also *Xu zizhi,* 15.584-85.
37. *Xu zizhi,* 16.606–7. For the full memorial, see Zhao Ruyu, 35.346–49.
38. Zhao Ruyu, 35.350–51..
39. Yang Zhongliang, 120.13b.
40. *Zeng Bu,* 9.59b.
41. Ibid., 9.24a–b.
42. Ibid., 9.70a.
43. Ibid., 9.31b–32a.
44. Ibid., 9.40b–41a.
45. Ibid., 9.56a–b.
46. Ibid., 9.65a–b.
47. Ibid., 9.66a–b.
48. Ibid., 9.69a.
49. Ibid., 9.69a–b.
50. Ibid., 9.69b.

CHAPTER 12

1. For biographies of Buddhist nuns, see Tsai; for Tang Daoist biographies, see Suzanne Cahill.
2. The unpublished album is listed in *Zhongguo* 21.1–1962, 355. The title given is "Wang Xianshi yiyan tu yi kai" (A picture of Immortal Teacher Wang writing her final words, one album).

3. The point here is that her chastity mattered to her more than life itself.

4. Wang Shizhen, *Yanzhou shanren xugao*, 78/6a-b, 3799–3800.

5. For Ming dynasty fears of female sexuality, and the ways in which young women might have internalized them, see Carlitz, ch. 10 of this volume.

6. Waltner, "T'an-yang-tzu."

7. Wang Shizhen, *Tanyang dashi zhuan,* in *Yanzhou shanren xugao, juan* 78.

8. *Wanli,* 117.

9. Ibid., 119.

10. On the general increase in alarm about religion beginning in the Wanli era, see ter Haar, 109. See also the discussion of the growing interest of the late Ming elite in Buddhism, and occasional Confucian criticisms of it in Brook, *Praying,* 92.

11. *Wanli,* 119.

12. The library catalog (*Mowangguan shumu*) of Zhao Qimei, the son of Zhao Yongxian (1535–96), who was a disciple of Tanyangzi, contains an entry for a text entitled *Tanyangzi shi lüe* (A draft essay on the matter of Tanyangzi) with no author indicated; Zhao Qimei, *zi* 39b.) The catalog also contains a notice for a text entitled *Tanyang dashi zhuan* (*zi,* 36b). Evidence that a text other than the *Tanyang dashi zhuan* was circulated is provided by Wu Yuancui, who referred to the fact that in 1580, a friend of his in the capital gave him a text entitled *Tanyang zhuan* (Biography of Tanyang); Wu Yuancui, (shang) *bie ji* 2/5b. The section on Daoism in the library catalog of Xu Qianxue (*Chuanshilou shu mu*) lists two copies of a text entitled *Tanyangzi chuan* (Biography of Tanyangzi) in two *juan,* again with no attribution of authorship (Xu Qianxue, 3/38b, 753). A text with the same title (but in only one *juan*) is listed in the *Qianqing tang shumu,* a catalog of the library of Huang Yuji. The *Qianqingtang* entry lists Wang Shizhen as author. There is concrete evidence for another edition of the text as early as 1581. A modern catalog lists a *Tanyang dashi zhuan* (with no divisions into *juan*), attributed to Wang Shizhen, published by one Zhang Qi in 1581 (Du Xinfu, 4/43). In addition to the three entries with variant titles discussed above, we find a text entitled *Tanyang dashi zhuan* in other library catalogs, including in that of Zhao Yongxian and in that of his son Zhao Qimei mentioned at the outset of this note.

13. Wu Yuancui, shang, *bie ji* 2/5b, 234.

14. *Wanli,* 117–21.

15. Letter to Wang Zhongyan, in Wang Shizhen, *Yanzhou shanren xugao,* 8242. Wang Shizhen refers to images of Tanyangzi in a number of other letters. See Wang Shizhen, *Yanzhou shanren xugao,* 8589, for example. This latter letter discusses the proper rituals and reverence with which to approach the images. See Tu Long's (6/18b, 342) discussion of two images he owned.

16. Wang Xianshi, *juan* 2.

17. Little, 286. The painting is a hanging scroll which measures 118.5 cm × 57.3 cm, and is dated the twelfth month of the year corresponding to 1580.

18. See Siren, 7:274. You Qiu is briefly discussed in Oertling, 187–88. Two

religious paintings by You Qiu are reproduced in Weidner—a painting of Guanyin holding a willow branch is reproduced on p. 13 and a painting entitled "Lohans Crossing the Sea" is reproduced and discussed on pp. 367–72. See also the discussion in Xu Xin, vol. 317, which notes that You Qiu was a painter of beautiful women. Xu's *Ming hua lu* was compiled around 1630.

19. Cahill, *Parting*, 210.

20. See the discussion in Yuhas, 45–46.

21. Wang Shizhen, *Yanzhou shanren sibu gao*, 37/1a–b; vol. 4, 177–78. Cited in Yuhas, 149.

22. Wu Hung, *The Double*, 190.

23. Lowry, "Personal," "Three," and "Editing"; Widmer, "The Epistolatory"; and Pattinson.

24. Xu Qianxue, 3/38b, 753.

25. Wang Shizhen, *Tanyang dashi zhuan*, in *Yanzhou shanren xugao*, *juan* 78:21a.

26. Ibid., 28a.

27. Ibid., 7a.

28. Wang Xianshi, *juan* 3.

29. Wang Shizhen, *Tanyang dashi zhuan*, in *Yanzhou shanren xugao*, *juan* 78:19b.

30. Ibid., 27b–28a.

31. Wang Xianshi, *juan* 3.

32. Ibid.

33. Wang Xianshi, *juan* 2.

34. Ibid.

35. *Da niangzi* almost always means wife; however, I am not completely convinced that this reference is to Wang Shizhen's wife (Lady Wei) rather than his concubine (Lady Li). On Lady Wei and concubine Li, see my "Remembering." We know that concubine Li had religious attainments, and I suspect that Wang Shizhen's discipleship caused a rupture with Lady Wei.

36. Wang Xianshi, *juan* 2.

37. We should, however, not minimize the degree to which male disciples felt conflicted about the tension between religious and familial duty. When Wang Shizhen went into religious retreat at the death of Tanyangzi, he wrote repeatedly about his guilt at abandoning his children, and indeed, the family seems to have suffered from his absence. But Tanyangzi does not express worry about Wang Shizhen's children in her letters to him (though she does in letters to his concubine). It may be that she sees male roles in family responsibilities and dynamics in a more straightforward way than does Wang Shizhen. See my "Remembering."

38. Wang Xianshi, *juan* 1.

39. Wang Shizhen, *Tanyang dashi zhuan*, in *Yanzhou shanren xugao*, *juan* 78:16a.

40. Ibid., 25a.

41. Wang Xianshi, *juan* 1.

42. Ibid., *juan* 2.

43. Wang Shizhen, *Tanyang dashi zhuan*, in *Yanzhou shanren xugao*, *juan* 78:7a, 22a.

44. The text of the precepts is identical in the two versions, except that in the biography the first precept is labeled *shou* and in the Gugong text it is labeled *yi* (both meaning first); the second precept is labeled *ci* (meaning the next and often used for the second in a set of terms) in the biography and in the Gugong text it is labeled *er* (meaning two).

45. For Qing practices that are very clearly differentiated by gender, see Valussi, "Beheading" and "Men." The earliest female alchemy text Valussi has found dates from 1683 and was not published until much later. While earlier texts acknowledge gender difference, they do not prescribe specific techniques for women. See also Despeux and Kohn.

CHAPTER 13

1. See O'Hara, 65–66, for a translation of Liu Xiang's entry on the wife of Liuxia Hui, which includes the text of her elegy.

2. For a brief account of the life of Zuo Fen, including translations of some of her literary works (but none of her elegies), see Idema and Grant, 43–48.

3. For a brief account of the life of Liu Lingxian, including a translation of her sacrificial text, see ibid., 146–53.

4. Among the more than 6,000 epitaphs (*muzhiming*) of the Tang dynasty, fewer than two or three were written by women; see Ping Yao, *Tangdai*, 111–12. We know these epitaphs only from recent archaeological discoveries, however, and none of these texts was preserved in the tradition.

5. For a translation of this text (which is also attributed to Niu Yingzhen's father, Niu Su), see Idema and Grant, 167–73. While "biography" is the established translation of *zhuan* in Sinological scholarship, it cannot be stressed enough that the *zhuan* usually is only a few pages in length at most, and that in premodern China, book-length studies of a single life were practically nonexistent. In style and length a *zhuan* usually is much closer to an obituary or a biographical notice than to a book-length biography, also because the *zhuan* tends to focus on the social career of its subject rather than its inner life. Only *zhuan* of villains would stress the contradiction between their outward actions and their inner emotions.

6. Zhong Xing, 25:4a–5b, 283–84. This poem was widely anthologized in the late Ming, so we may safely assume it was known to Bo Shaojun. The cardamom flower is an image for the young bereaved widow.

7. For a very fine translation and study of this text, see Owen, *Remembrances*, 80–98. Also see Idema and Grant, 207–14. Li Qingzhao's place in the tradition of Chinese autobiographical writing is briefly discussed in Wu Pei-yi, 64–67.

8. In the same way, the compilation of an author's writings as his collected works may well be the closest equivalent of writing his or her biography.

9. See, for instance, the very clear statement on this issue by Bo Shaojun's contemporary Liang Mengzhao, in Idema and Grant, 354.

10. *Suzhou fuzhi*, quoted in Kobayashi, 14–15.

11. The primary sources on the life of Shen Cheng are, apart from his own writings, the various prefaces and other biographical materials in his collected works. See Shen Cheng.

12. Ibid., 2:28b–31a. Kobayashi, 16–24, provides a translation into Japanese.

13. Zhou Zhong, "*Shen Junlie yiji* xu," 6a, in Shen Cheng, 41:553. Liang Hong and Meng Guang lived in the first century CE. Liang Hong was an outspoken critic of corruption in the government of his time. The couple lived in poverty, but Meng Guang never failed in respect toward her husband.

14. Zhang Pu, "*Jishan ji* xu," 2a, in Shen Cheng, 41:556. The "Odes and Documents" refer to two of the Confucian Five Classics.

15. Zhou Zhong, "*Shen Junlie yiji* xu," 6b, in Shen Cheng, 41:553.

16. Zhang Pu, "*Jishan ji* xu," 3a–b, in Shen Cheng, 41:556.

17. Kobayashi, 14–16, collects the early biographical entries on Bo Shaojun in gazetteers and anthologies.

18. Mao Yilu had to spend considerable time in Suzhou in 1626 in connection with the arrest of the highly respected Zhou Shunchang (1584–1626), which had been ordered by Wei Zhongxian and incited widespread popular protests in the city (see Dardess, 108–12). One can only speculate to what extent Mao's largesse towards the deceased Shen Cheng may have been intended as a gesture to placate local gentry sentiment.

19. Kobayashi, 139. According to Kobayashi, this *Tici* precedes the *Fuke* of the *Jishan ji*, but I have been unable to locate this text in the *Jishan ji* as reprinted in *Siku jinhuishu congkan*, which is based on the copy kept in the Beijing University Library. As Bo Shaojun was in very poor health during the last months of her life, the "corrections" may well refer to inadvertent mistakes that had been made in copying. Zhang does not provide any explanation on what ground he excised what kind of poems.

20. The *Mingyuan shigui* is available through HOLLIS, the online catalogue of Harvard University. The poems of Bo Shaojun are found on pp. 1634–64.

21. Bo Shaojun's poems are also well represented in the many anthologies of women's poetry that have come out in recent decades. A small selection of her poems, translated by Shuen-fu Lin, was included in Chang and Saussy, 218–21. In Japanese, Kobayashi devoted a monograph to her work in 2003, providing extensively annotated translations of all of her poems. This work advances the highly questionable thesis that Bo Shaojun's poems are best read as a detailed diary of a year-long preparation for a highly ritualized suicide in order to follow her husband in death. Such a reading would greatly enhance the autobiographical value of Bo Shaojun's collection, but unfortunately it is in my opinion not borne out by a close reading of the poems.

22. "Blue Heaven" is an allusion to the poem "Huangniao" from the Book of Odes (*Shijing*). This poem famously describes the act of *xun* of three fine

young men of the state of Qin, who had promised to follow their duke into his grave. Rather than praising these young men for their bravery, the poem laments their death before their time and decries the injustice of Heaven. As such, the poem is often alluded to in compositions lamenting the death of someone who has passed away in the prime of his life, for instance by Liu Lingxian in her sacrificial text for her husband.

23. Quoted in Su Shi, *Dongpo*, 544.

24. Wang Duanshu, 7:13b–14a.

25. Quoted in Hu Wenkai, 204. *Yujing yanqiu* would appear to have been a major work of literary criticism on seventeenth-century women poets. In Hu's work, excerpts from this work appear in quotes from the *Gonggui shiji yiwen kaolüe*, one of the few preserved sections of the *Ranzhi ji* by Wang Shilu (1626–73).

26. The classic English-language study on this subject is Brokaw, *The Ledgers*.

27. One of the works that may have inspired Bo Shaojun to her exceptional work may well have been the set of fifteen poems by the monk Daoqian (Canliao) in memory of Su Shi, entitled "Dongbo xiansheng wanci" (*Quan*, 10800–802). The first poem in this series ends with an unanswered question to Heaven, a close parallel to the second line of Bo Shaojun's first poem. Daoqian refers at least three times to Su Shi's unique "dashing sophistication" (*fengliu*), the very same quality that is also credited her husband by Bo Shaojun in the very first line of her first poem. Bo Shaojun's poem no. 43 and poem no. 55 develop allusions also used by Daoqian in the last poem of his series. For a more detailed discussion of Daoqian's set of poems, see Egan, 355–57.

28. The Tang poet Li He was said to have been called to Heaven to compose a record of a newly completed palace. Shen Cheng's male friends, who may have seen this poem, continue to describe his death in such a way, but Bo Shaojun overturns this image.

29. Almost unavoidably we encounter a reworking of the famous anecdote from the *Zhuangzi* about the Daoist philosopher Zhuang Zhou, who dreamt he was a butterfly, and upon awakening wondered whether he now was perhaps a butterfly dreaming to be Zhuang Zhou (no. 73).

30. Teiser.

31. The last two lines of this poem may have been inspired by a well-known lyric by Su Shi, to the tune of *Jiangchengzi*, written in memory of his wife, in which he expresses the fear that even if they would meet she may not recognize him anymore because his looks have changed so much in the ten years since her death (Wang Shuizhao, 256–57).

32. A copy of the original edition may be found in Beijing Library. The Harvard-Yenching Library houses a Xerox copy.

33. Handlin.

34. For a translation of Shen Yixiu's moving biography of her youngest daughter, Ye Xiaoluan (1616–32), see Idema and Grant, 400–406.

35. For examples of Liu Shi's biographical notices in English translation,

see Idema and Grant, 359–61; 364–65; 366–67; 368–69; 370–71; 384–85; and 514–15. From the middle of the seventeenth century we also have some biographies of Buddhist nuns by Buddhist nuns. These texts, and the other writings by these nuns, are studied by Beata Grant.

36. "Selected Short Works by Wang Duanshu (1621–after 1701)," in Mann and Cheng, 178–94; and Idema and Grant, 439–45.

37. For a rare example of autobiographical prose from the seventeenth century, see "Record of Past Karma" by Ji Xian (1614–83)," translated by Grace Fong, in Mann and Cheng, 134–46. Some of the seventeenth-century Buddhist nuns studied by Beata Grant also wrote brief autobiographies for the edification of their disciples. For a translation of one of these, see Idema and Grant, 457–59. Also see Barr, which discusses a brief prose memoir by Lu Xinxing (1652–after 1707).

38. On didacticism in male autobiography, see Bauer, 680. Bauer detects this didactic tendency also in the autobiography of Mao Zedong as told by him to Edgar Snow.

39. Wedding laments and funeral laments allowed peasant woman a ritualized space to air their grievances, and even to curse their relatives. The literature in women's script from Jiangyong in southernmost Hunan comprises as one of its subgenres long autobiographical ballads in which women relate the personal injustices they have endured. A few of these ballads are translated in Idema and Grant, 553–57.

CHAPTER 14

1. One contrast with earlier eras is that the term biography/*zhuan* could sometimes be used for living writers in the late Ming and early Qing. See, for example, "Wang Duanshu zhuan" and "Ding furen zhuan" in Wang Duanshu. After the period I am considering women's literary networks suffered terribly from the ravages of the Taiping rebellion. Still later, the conditions of women's publishing began to change. Starting in 1872, literary magazines put out by *Shenbao* began accepting contributions from women. Although some of the authors identified as women in such journals may actually have been men, some can be identified as women through their listing in Hu Wenkai.

2. See Hu Ying, 126n29.

3. For example, Lu Qingzi of the late Ming's "Zhang Ruren xiaozhuan" (Small biography of Madam Zhang) and Yun Zhu's biography of her male ancestor Yun Richu (1602–79), "Yun Richu xiansheng jiazhuan"(Family biography of Mr. Yun Richu), in Wang Xiuqin and Hu Wenkai, *shang*, 65–66 and *xia*, 81–82. Note how few *zhuan* there are in this collection, compared with prefaces (*xu*) and other genres.

4. *Ming Qing*. By now some works from other libraries have been added, though that was not the case initially. Altogether about ninety works have been digitized, of which several are anthologies. In all they draw from approximately 5,000 authors and 20,000 titles.

5. In most cases the term was added by the compilers of the website and appears in brackets.

6. A very few *zhuan* on the website are by women, such as one by the mid-eighteenth-century writer Shen Cai. Shen's *Chu Xiansheng zhuan* (Biography of Mr. Chu) and Cao Zhenxiu's (fl. 1815) *Huang Furen jia zhuan* (Family Biography of Madam Huang) are the only fully elaborated *zhuan* by women that I have found on this site from before the Guangxu era (1871–1908); however, neither of these was written as a preface to an extant woman's poetry collection. (Indeed, Shen Cai's biography is of a man.) It is possible I have under-counted. When I could not ascertain the gender of an author, as happened in a very few cases, I counted that writer as male. It is also possible that some *zhuan* were not indexed on the website, for example two by Shen Yixiu (1590–1635), on which see Wang Xiuqin and Hu, *shang*, 67–72.

7. For these, see Wang Duanshu's *Yinhong ji*, section 20.

8. There is a whole second usage of the term *xu*. It is used as a sendoff for someone going on a trip. I do not discuss that kind of *xu* in this chapter.

9. For more on this group, see Robertson; Idema and Grant; and Chang and Saussy, among others. For Jiang's titles see Hu Wenkai, 287.

10. Goyama, "En," see especially 129–30.

11. According to Gui Maoyi's preface, discussed below, critic Kang Kai praised Jiang in these terms.

12. Ko, "A Man," 65–93.

13. On Zhu's prominence in the era, see Polachek, 49.

14. Gui was Yuan's disciple. Chen Wenshu has an entry on her in his *Xiling guiyong* 14:1, a series of sketches and encomiums on celebrated women. For more on Gui, see Widmer, "Border."

15. Hummel, 505–6.

16. Elman, *On Their*, 265–70. See also Hummel, 399–402; and Meyer-Fong, 114–27.

17. See Hu Wenkai, 219, 328, 356, 376, 712, 721, 945. Meyer-Fong, 122, notes that his mother educated him in his early years.

18. Chen Wenshu's *Xiling guiyong* has entries on both women. 13:12a and 15:1a.

19. See, for example, Hu Wenkai, 937, 938.

20. She had read Shen Shanbao's writings even before Shen arrived in Bei-jing from Hangzhou. See Shen Shanbao, *Mingyuan*, 7:4b.

21. For Pan's birth date, see Goyama, "En,"129; for 1851, see Hu Wenkai, 605. See also Ann Waltner's entry on Pan in Ho, 166–69.

22. For the special connotation of *"shidafu"* in this period, see Polachek, 11.

23. The edition described by Hu Wenkai (366–67) does not mention the untitled words by Funi yang'a. It is found in Shen Shanbao, *Mingyuan*.

24. Later editions change the title slightly and mix these in with other prefaces. See Hu Wenkai, 357. Hu lists four versions of this text under the title *Ziran haoxue zhai shi*. Copies in the National Library of China are entitled *Ziran haoxue zhai ji, Ziran haoxue zhai shi, Ziran haoxue zhai shiji*, and

Ziran haoxue zhai shichao. The edition I cite in this study is not any of the ones just described but the one edited by Mao Jun in the collection *Linxia ya yin ji* (Collected elegant sounds of women) of 1884 in the Harvard-Yenching Library. It is entitled *Ziran haoxue zhai shichao*, and it includes a biography by the man Chen Wenshu and a preface by the woman Guan Yun. It also adds other paratextual materials.

25. Among them the placement of the words by the Manchu Funi yang'a in Shen Shanbao's *Mingyuan shihua* in such a way that it comes after Ding Pei's *xu*. It is possible, even likely, that had he been Chinese his preface would have preceded Ding Pei's. The other is in the edition of Wang Duan's *Ziran haoxuezhai shi* by Mao Jun. It includes a preface by the man Zhang Yun'ao after one by the woman Guan Yun. Perhaps the fact that this edition came out in 1884 during the Guangxu era, and hence late in the Qing, is the reason for this unusual arrangement. Or it may only be because the paratextual materials in this edition are quite sloppily arranged.

26. For other treatments of these writers in English, see Widmer, *The Beauty* and "Ming;" Fong; Idema and Grant; and Hummel.

27. The catalogue of Xu Zongyan's library is available. See Xu Zongyan.

28. Early editions appear to have come out in 1821, 1839, and 1844. Xu Zongyan (565, 569) lists two separate titles, *Ziran haoxue zhai shichao* and *Ziran haoxue zhai shi*.

29. Wang Duan, *Ziran haoxue zhai shi*, 1:12b, Xiang Yu, 1:16b, Zhang Huangyan.

30. Wang Duan, *Ziran haoxue zhai shi*, 9:7b–8a.

31. For example, Wang Duan, *Ziran haoxue zhai shi*, 2:1b–2a.

32. Ibid., 3:11a.

33. Ibid., 4:6b–7a.

34. See Yun Zhu, *Guochao*, 4a–5b.

35. The relationship between these two series and the novel are discussed in the two biographies of Wang Duan in *Ziran haoxue zhai shi*.

36. Wang Duan, *Ziran haoxuezhai shichao* 6:1b–2a.

37. For more on the "civilizing mission," see Mann, *Precious*, 215–16.

38. Yun, *Guochao*, 20:5b.

39. Shen Shanbao, *Mingyuan shihua*, 6:4b–6b. With appreciation to Wai-yee Li for help with this and other translations.

40. She appears not to have had a copy of *Ming Sanshi jia shixuan*, as she does not cite it.

41. For example, in one typical entry on Shen, Wu Zao talks about a going away party for Shen that Wu held and reprints the poem Shen wrote on that occasion.

42. Many men, too, stayed away from fiction, or if they wrote it used assumed names.

43. On Li Wanfang (eighteenth century) and her *Dushi guanjian* (My humble opinion on the study of history), published in 1787, see Hu Wenkai,

337. *Dushi guanjian* is Li's edition of Sima Qian's(145–90 BCE) *Shiji* (Historical records) with her own annotations.

CHAPTER 15

I would like to thank all those who commented on earlier drafts of this chapter. Special thanks to Han Ling for translating this essay, and to Joan Judge, Hu Ying, and Peter Zarrow for correcting it attentively.

1. Wang Ming-ke, 179.
2. Lo Jiu-jung, Yu, and Chiu. Li Xiaojiang's edited volume, *Rong nüren ziji shuohua,* is also based on oral history. Li and her collaborators' methodology differs somewhat from ours in that their interview subjects include women who participated in the CCP's land reform and whose lives remained tied to the mainland. In contrast, our interview subjects are women who migrated from China to Taiwan after the war, when wartime experiences continued to be refracted in the context of postwar Taiwan. While Li's interviews focus on the experiences of her subjects as witnesses or direct participants in war, we are primarily interested in women's personal experiences of war as well as their postwar lives.
3. Yu Chien-ming, *Qingting,* 37; and Yu Chien-ming, *Tamen,* 53–54.
4. Lü Fang-shang, 120.
5. Yu Chien-ming and Huang, 67–68.
6. Ibid., 78–79.
7. Ibid., 78–81.
8. Ibid., 82, 84, 102.
9. Ibid., 103–5.
10. Ibid., 113.
11. Yu Chien-ming and Chen, 122–23.
12. Ibid., 128–31.
13. Ibid., 135.
14. Sun Liren was trained at the Virginia Military Institute and served under General Joseph Stilwell in the Burma campaign during World War II. He then became commander-in-chief of the Chinese Nationalist ground forces. In 1955, one of Sun's subordinates, Major Guo Tingliang, was involved in a Communist spy incident. Chiang Kai-shek then put Sun under house arrest where Sun remained until his release in 1988 after Chiang Ching-kuo's death.
15. Yu Chien-ming and Chen, 142–43.
16. Ibid., 126–28.
17. Yu Chien-ming and Chu, 198–201.
18. Yu Chien-ming, *Qingting,* 47.
19. Yu Chien-ming and Chu, 201.
20. Ibid., 199–200, 203.
21. "Military communities" (*juancun*) were group housing for mainlander soldiers and their dependents provided by the Taiwan Ministry of Defense.

Originally, the infrastructure of military communities was quite poor, a hodge-podge of housing with virtually no privacy.

22. Yu Chien-ming and Chu, 215–16, 220.

23. In poor Chinese families or villages it was common for young girls like P'ei Wang Zhihong to share the financial burdens of the family.

24. Yu Chien-ming and Chu, 212.

25. Ibid., 222–23.

26. Yu Chien-ming and Huang, 72–77.

27. Ibid., 77–78.

28. Ibid., 83.

29. Ibid., 86–88.

30. Ibid., 88–89.

31. Yu Chien-ming, "Dang," 197–206.

32. Yu Chien-ming and Huang, 91–92.

33. Ibid., 99–101. On February 27, 1947, officers from the Monopoly Bureau, a government office that controlled the sales of cigarettes and liquor, man-handled a private cigarette saleswoman, and in the process the police shot and killed a bystander. The incident led to large-scale protests and general mayhem that soon enveloped Taiwanese society. By March 8, it escalated to military clashes between the protestors and GMD troops. An estimated 10,000 to 20,000 died in the next five days. This incident was later represented as "ethnic conflict" between mainlanders and the indigenous Taiwanese. In the 1980s, the GMD modified its own discourses on "ethnic conflict" and tried to redress the grievances of the victims. In recent years, each political party in Taiwan has sought legitimacy via its own version of the incident. See Wang Hsiao-po; and also Lai Zehan; Zhang Yanxian.

34. Yu Chien-ming and Huang, 102–5.

35. Yu Chien-ming and Chen, 123–26.

36. Ibid., 128–31.

37. Li Zongren was elected as the vice-president of the Republic of China in spring 1947.

38. Yu Chien-ming and Chen, 132–34.

39. Ibid., 144–45.

40. Ibid.

41. Yu Chien-ming and Chu, 188–89.

42. Ibid., 190–98, 201–3.

43. Ibid., 203–4.

44. Ibid., 205–7, 213–14.

45. Ibid., 216–18.

46. Ibid., 220.

47. Some studies of women during times of war suggest that women had greater opportunities for the exercise of their subjectivity during war. See Marwick, *War* and Marwick, *Total War*, x–xxi; see also Harold L. Smith, 61–62; and Summerfield.

EPILOGUE

1. The quotation is from Virginia Woolf's famous 1929 essay (Woolf), in which she recognizes, as does Tanyangzi, the importance of physical location for a woman's personal liberty and her ability to write. For more reflections on Miss Fa's difficult situation, see Waltner, review of Mann, 39.

2. *Encyclopaedia Britanica*, 11th ed.

3. Wright, "Values."

4. *Analects* 11.4; Legge, *Confucius*, 146–47.

5. Mann, *Precious*, ch. 3.

6. Regarding Miss Fa's mental illness, see Mann, *The Talented*, 172. On the abject and psychosis, see Butler, "For," 139; *Bodies*.

Character List

"Ai jiefu fu"	哀節婦賦
"Ai'ai ge"	愛愛歌
aici	哀辭
An Lushan	安祿山
Anhui	安徽
ba	跋
Bai [née]	白氏
baimei	百美
Baimei tu	百美圖
baixi	白晰
Ban Zhao [Cao Dagu]	班昭
Banlang	伴郎
Bao (Judge Bao)	包
Bao Mengyi	包孟儀
Bao Tingbo	鮑廷博
bao zhu chengqin	抱主成親
Bei Qi shu	北齊書
Beishi	北史
benzhong	本衷

Bi Daoyuan 畢道遠
bi li zhi yan 鄙俚之言
Bi Yuan 畢沅
Bian Mengjue 卞夢珏
"Biantong zhuan" 辯通傳
bie zhu dizi 別諸弟子
bie zhuan 別傳
Bo Juyi 白居易
Bo Shaojun 薄少君
boxue gaocai 博學高才
boxue you caibian 博學有才辯
Boyi 伯夷
Bozong 伯宗
Bunhōtei Sanboku 文寶堂散木
bushi yu yu 不失於愚

cai 才
Cai Bian 蔡卞
Cai Jing 蔡京
Cai Shiyuan 蔡世遠
Cai Yan 蔡琰
Cai Zhiding 蔡之定
cainü 才女
caishi 才識
caixing gaoxiu 才行高秀
caiyi 才藝
canliao 參了
Cao Dagu [Ban Zhao] 曹大家
Cao E 曹娥
Cao 曹
[Empress Dowager (Cisheng 慈聖)]

Cao Zhenxiu 曹貞秀
Cao Zhi 曹植
Cao Zhuxiang 曹竹香
caoye youtan 草野游談
Chang Qu 常璩
chanmian feice 纏綿悱惻
chanwei 讒緯
Chen [consort] 陳
Chen Duansheng 陳端生

Chen Guan	陳瓘
Chen Qubing	陳去病
Chen Shou	陳壽
Chen shu	陳書
Chen Xie	陳燮
Chen Yan	陳衍
Chen Yinke	陳寅恪
Chen Yuanlu	陳元祿
Chen Yunbo	陳雲伯
cheng	誠
Cheng Yi	程毅
Cheng Yi	程頤
Chenghua	成化
"Chi zeng anren Xiang mu Zhou shi mu biao"	敕贈安人項母周氏墓表
Chiang Kai-shek	蔣介石
chizhang	笞杖
Chongqing	重慶
Chongwen zongmu	崇文總目
"Chu gui ji Xu lang wen"	初歸祭徐郎文
chu siyu	除思虞
"Chu Xiansheng zhuan"	楮先生傳
chuan qi	傳奇
Chûgoku no dentô shakai to kazoku	中國の傳統社會と家族
chunxiao	純孝
Chutan ji	初潭集
Chuxue ji	初學記
ci [tender loving, mother]	慈
ci [place in sequence]	次
ci [lyric]	詞
Cihui	慈惠
Cixi 慈禧	[Xiaoqin 孝欽]
Ciyuan	辭源
congbian neng zhuwen	聰辯能屬文
conghui hongya, bowen jiji, mei rongzhi, shan xiaoyong, . . . mingjian yuanshi	聰慧弘雅,博覽記籍,美容止,善嘯詠 . . . 明鑒遠識
conglang you caijian	聰朗有才鑒
congshi you caibian . . . you yaren shenzhi . . . fengyun gaomai, xuzhi qingya	聰識有才辯 . . . 有雅人深致 . . . 風韻高邁,敍致清雅

cuhao	粗豪
Cui	崔
Cui Qun	崔群
cunxing	存性
cuozhi	厝誌
da niangzi	大娘子
Da Shu yu Tian	大叔于田
Dabie	大別
dafu	大夫
Daitō seigo	大東世語
dan [female opera role]	旦
dan [tranquil]	澹
Daoqian	道潛
Daoshu	道術
daowangshi	悼亡詩
Daoxue	道學
dashi zhuan [biography of the enlightened one]	大士傳
dashi zhuan [biography of the enlightened teacher]	大師傳
dazong	大宗
de	德
Defei	德妃
dengdi	登第
Dengzhou	登州
di	嫡
dian zhi cheng dai yi cun ji	典質稱貸以存濟
"Ding Furen zhuan"	丁夫人傳
Ding Lingwei	丁令威
Ding Pei	丁佩
diyige nongmin chushen de yanjiuyuan	第一个农民出身的研究员
Dong jieyuan Xixiang ji	董解元西廂記
Dong Jingwen	佟景文
Dongbei	東北
"Dongpo xiansheng wanci"	東坡先生挽詞
"Dou E yuan"	竇娥冤
"Du Xu Boyuan shu waijia yishi; zuo er jueju yi ji zhi bing xu"	讀徐伯遠書外家遺事; 作二絶句以紀之并序

duan chang	斷腸
Duan, Prince	端王
duanji	斷機
duanjin	端謹
dundian	蹲点
dunren	鈍人
Dushi guanjian	讀史管見
"Edo jidai ni okeru *Sesetsu* kenkyū no ichimen"	江戶時代におけろ世說研究の一面
er	二
"Er lie fu zhuan"	二烈婦傳
"Er lie nü zhuan"	二列女傳
Er Shishuo	兒世說
Erya	爾雅
Fa (née)	法氏
Fang Junmo	方駿謨
fei furen shi	非婦人事
Feng Menglong	馮夢龍
Feng Yan	封演
"Feng yiren wang qi Zuo shi mu zhi ming"	封宜人亡妻左氏墓志銘
Feng yue rui xian ting	風月瑞仙亭
Feng yue xiang si	風月相思
fengliu	風流
"Fengqiu Xishun wang mu zhi ming"	封丘僖順王墓誌銘
"Fengshi wenjian ji"	封氏聞見記
fu	賦
"Fu gui pian, da Li ling"	富貴篇, 答李令
fudao	婦道
fufu	夫婦
fuguo jiangjun	輔國將軍
Funi yang'a	富呢揚啊
Funü daochu nao jingsai	妇女到处闹竞赛
"Funü shi"	婦女詩
furen	夫人
"Furen Jia shi muzhiming"	夫人賈氏墓誌銘
furen zhi mei	婦人之美
Fushan (*xian*)	福 山(縣)

fusheng	附生
fushi	副室
fuze	婦則
fuzhe, qi zhi tian ye	夫者,妻之天也
fuzi	父子
Gai Qi	改琦
gang	剛
Gao	高
	[Empress Dowager (Xuanren宣 仁)]
Gao	高 [氏]
"Gao chushi he zang muzhiming"	高處士合葬墓誌銘
Gao E	高鶚
"Gao feng shuren Ren shi mu zhi ming"	誥封淑人任氏墓誌銘
"Gao feng yiren wang qi Zhang shi mu zhi ming"	誥封宜人亡妻張氏墓誌銘
Gao Qi	高啟
gaoqing	高情
gaoshi	高士
gaoshi zhuan	高士傳
Gaoyou Wang fuzi, Qixia Hao fufu	高郵王父子, 棲霞郝夫婦
Gaozong	高宗
Gemensi	閤門司
gen xing	根性
gewu Wuzhong di yi ren, lü fa shuang huan cai shiwu	歌舞吳中第一人,綠髮雙鬟繞十五
gong	恭
gong'an xiaoshuo	公案小說
gongci	宮詞
Gonggui shiji yiwen kaolüe	宮閨氏籍藝文考略
Gonggui wenxuan	宮閨文選
gongjian	恭儉
Gongsun	公孫
gongwei	宮闈
Gongyang zhuan	公羊傳
Gu	顧
Gu Congyi	顧從義
Gu Guangqi	顧廣圻
Gu Kaizhi	顧愷之

Gu Lienü zhuan fu kaozheng	古列女傳 附考證
gu qi qi yiwei ji wu	顧其妻以為己物
gu quan daju, ying nan er jin	顾全大局, 迎难而进
Gu Taiqing	顧太清
Gu Yanwu	顧炎武
Guan Panpan	關盼盼
Guan Yun	管筠
Guang lienü zhuan	廣列女傳
gubiaohun	姑表婚
Guchun xuan shichao	古春軒詩鈔
Gui fan	閨範
Gui Maoyi	歸懋儀
Gui nü zhuan	桂女傳
guifang zhi xiu	閨房之秀
guige renruo	閨閣荏弱
guiyou	歸友
Gujin lienü zhuan	古今列女傳
Gujin Lienüzhuan yanyi	古今列女傳 演義
Guliang zhuan	穀梁傳
Guo feng	國風
Guo Moruo	郭沫若
Guo Tingliang	郭廷亮
guo zhong	過中
Guochao guixiu zhengshi ji	國朝閨秀正始集
Guochao guixiu zhengshi xuji	國朝閨秀正始續集
guomin	國民
Guomindang	國民黨
Guoyu	國語
Haizhou zhi	海州志
Hakka	客家
Han	漢
Han Fei	韓非
Han Shishuo	漢世說
Han Wo	韓偓
Han Yu	韓愈
Hanshu	漢書
hao	號
Hao Yixing	郝懿行
haofang	豪放

Hattori Nankaku	服部南郭
He disi	和娣姒
He Lang	何郎
He Wei	何褘
He Yan	何晏
Henan	河南
Hengyang	衡陽
Hengzhou	衡州
heya	和雅
hezhi	合誌
Hong Bian	洪邊
Hong Mai	洪迈 [洪邁]
Hong Yixuan	洪頤煊
Honglou meng	紅樓夢
Hongniang	紅娘
Hongxiang guan shici cao	紅香館詩詞草
Hongxuelou chuji	鴻雪樓初集
Hongzhi	弘治
hou fei	后妃
Hou Hanshu	後漢書
Hou Yunjin	侯雲錦
Hou Zhi	侯芝
Hu Chenggong	胡承珙
Hu Jing	胡敬
Hu Sannian	扈三娘
Hu Yuan	胡瑗
Hua Mulan	花木蘭
huaguniang	花姑娘
Huaiyin furen he juelie; mao hao ru hua xin si tie	淮陰婦人何決烈, 貌好如花心似鐵
"Huaiyin yifu shi"	淮陰義婦詩
Huakai shili xiang wanjia	花开十里香万家
"Huang Furen jia zhuan"	黃夫人家傳
Huang Ming Shishuo xinyu	皇明世說新語
"Huang niao"	黃鳥
Huang Yuanjie	黃媛介
"Huangchi feng ruren Shandong Guantao xian zhixian Zhangjun qi Tangshi muzhiming"	皇敕 封孺人山東館陶縣知縣張君妻 湯氏墓誌銘
Huangfu Mi	皇甫謐

Huangpo	黄陂
Huayang guozhi	華陽國志
Huayang guozhi [*jiaozhu*]	華陽國志[校註]
Hubei	湖北
huilie	徽烈
Huitu daban gujin xiannü zhuan	繪圖大版古今賢女傳
Huitu Lienü zhuan	繪圖列女傳
Huizhou	徽州
Huizong	徽宗
Huo Xiaoyu	霍小玉
huwen	互文
Imai Kyūsuke	今井久助
Ji	濟
ji	記
ji [belles-lettres]	集
Ji Kang	嵇康
Ji Yun	紀昀
Jia	賈
jia ji	家妓
Jiajing	嘉靖
jian qie	賤妾
Jian, Prince	簡王
Jian'an	建安
Jiang (née)	姜氏
Jiang Fan	江藩
Jiang Shiquan	蔣士銓
Jiang Yourong	江有溶
Jiangchengzi	江城子
Jianhu nüxia	鑒湖女俠
Jianning	建寧
jiansheng	監生
Jianyang	建陽
Jianyang Yu [family]	建陽余
Jianzhi shuizhai cang shumu si juan	鑑止水齋藏書目四卷
Jianzhi shuizhai ji	鑑止水齋集
jiao	角
jiao [to exchange]	交
Jiao hong ji	嬌紅記

Jiao hong zhuan	嬌紅傳
Jiao Hong	焦竑
Jiaoshi leilin	焦氏類林
jiaozi	教子
jiaxue	家學
jiazhuan	家傳
Jicheng tushu gongsi	集成圖書公司
jie	節
"Jie chang pian"	結腸篇
jie fu	節婦
"Jie fu Liu shi mu ming"	節婦劉氏墓銘
Jie Jin	解晉
jie lao yi	戒勞逸
Jie xiao ji	節孝集
jiefa limian	截髮剺面
jiefu	介婦
jielie	節烈
"Jieyi zhuan"	節義傳
jin	金
Jin (née)	金氏
Jin Song shugu	晉宋書故
jing	精
jing [classics]	經
jingbiao	旌表
Jinghua yuan	鏡花緣
"Jingji zhi"	經籍志
Jingying xiaosheng chuji	鏡影簫聲初集
Jingzhou	荊州
jinnian, jinri, wanshi yi; jiaoxiao feicui kan ru ni	今年今日萬事已; 鮫綃翡翠看如泥
Jinnian youle zong luxian	今年有了总路线
jinshi [degree]	進士
Jinshi	金史
"*Jinshi lu* houxu"	金石錄後序
Jinshu	晉書
Jintai	金臺
jinyan	謹言
Jishan ji	即山集
jiu mo ze gu lao, zhongfu suo jisi binke, mei shi bi qingyu gu, jiefu qingyu zhongfu	舅沒則姑老,冢婦所祭祀賓客,每事必請於姑,介婦請於冢婦

Jiu Tangshu	舊唐書
jiwen	祭文
jiya	羈押
ju	鞠
juan	卷
juancun	眷村
Juanjing lou congke	娟鏡樓叢刻
junchen	君臣
junjie	峻節
junjun	郡君
junzi	君子
juren	舉人
kaifu yitong sansi	開府儀同三司
Kana Sesetsu	假名世說
Kana Sesetsu kōhen	假名世說後編
Kang Hai	康海
Kang Kai	康愷
"Kang shi nü mu zhi ming"	康氏女墓誌銘
kaozheng	考證
ke	客
kegu	克姑
Kinsei sōgo	近世叢語
"Kuaizui Li Cuilian"	快嘴李翠蓮
kuangzhi	壙志
kufu	哭夫
kufu shi	哭夫詩
Kufushi baishou	哭夫詩百首
"Kuhai zhu'ao"	苦海諸熳
kujie	苦節
Kunshan xianzhi	崑山縣志
kuxing	酷刑
Langui bao lu	蘭閨寶錄
Lanwan ju qingyan	蘭畹居清言
Laozi	老子
lei	誄
"Lei Cizong zhuan"	雷次宗傳
Leilin	類林
Li [Lady, promoted to Consort and posthumously made Empress]	李

li [principle]	理
li [measurement unit]	里
li [clerk]	隸
Li Baiyao	李百藥
Li Diniang	李第娘
Li Gan	李旰
Li He	李賀
Li Hou	李垕
"Li jie fu mu zhi ming."	李節婦墓誌銘
Li Jingrang	李景讓
"Li Qing zhushu kao"	李清著述考
Li Qingzhao	李清照
Li Quanli	李全禮
Li Ruzhen	李汝珍
Li Shaowen	李紹文
Li Shixia	李世冾
Li Wa	李娃
Li Wanfang	李晚芳
Li Xian	李賢
Li Yanshou	李延壽
Li Yinzhi	李胤之
Li Zhi	李贄
Li Zhuowu [Li Zhi] pidian Shishuo xinyu bu	李卓吾[李贄]批點世說新語補
Li Zongren	李宗仁
liang	良
Liang Duan	梁端
"Liang gongren zhuan"	梁恭人傳
Liang Hong	梁鴻
Liang Mengzhao	梁孟昭
Liang Qichao	梁啟超
Liang shu	梁書
Liang Tongshu	梁同書
Liang Weishu	梁維樞
Liang Zhe youxuan lu	兩浙輶軒錄
liangcan	兩驂
Lianshang	蓮裳
"Lianyin ji xu"	蓮因集序
Lianyin	蓮因
Liaoshi	遼史

Lidai funü zhuzuo kao	歷代婦女著作考
Lidai mingyuan wenyuan jianbian	歷代名媛文苑簡編
lie	烈
liecao	列操
Liechao shiji	列朝詩集
liefu	烈婦
"Liefu Nishi zhuan"	烈婦倪氏傳
lienü [exemplary woman]	列女
lienü [heroic woman]	烈女
Lienü hou zhuan	列女後傳
lienü zhuan [biography of exemplary women]	列女傳
lienü zhuan [biography of heroic women]	烈女傳
Lienü zhuan buzhu	列女傳補注
Lienü zhuan buzhu zheng'e	列女傳補注正訛
Lienü zhuan buzhu zhengwei	列女傳補注正譌
Lienü zhuan jiaozhu	列女傳校注
Lienü zhuan jiaozhu duben	列女傳校注讀本
"Lienü zhuan song"	列女傳頌
Lienü zhuan songtu	列女傳頌圖
Lienü zhuan songyi	列女傳頌義
Lienü zhuan yaolu	列女傳要錄
"Lienü zhuan zan"	列女傳讚
Lienü zhuan zengguang	列女傳增廣
lieshi	烈士
Liexian jiaozheng	列仙校正
Liexian zhuan	列仙傳
liezhuan	列傳
Liji	禮記
lijiao	禮教
Limao huan Tai zi	狸貓換太子
Lin [consort]	林
Lin Maogui	林茂桂
Lin Peihou	林培厚
ling	靈
ling gen	靈根
ling she	靈蛇
Linghu Defen	令狐德棻
Linhuan	臨渙

linsheng	廩生
linxia fengqi	林下風氣
liqu chaoyuan	理趣超遠
lishu	隸書
Liu [consort, empress]	劉
Liu Bang	劉邦
Liu E	劉娥
Liu Fu [of Song Dynasty]	劉斧
Liu Fu [character in Ming fiction]	柳富
Liu Ji qi Xiahoushi	劉寂妻夏侯氏
Liu Jin	劉瑾
Liu Jun	劉峻
Liu Kai	劉開
Liu Kunyi	劉坤一
Liu Lin	劉琳
Liu Lingxian	劉令嫻
Liu Rushi biezhuan	柳如是別傳
Liu Shi	柳是
Liu Tui	劉蛻
"Liu Xiang zhuan"	劉向傳
Liu Xin	劉歆
Liu Xu	劉煦 [昫]
Liu Yikang	劉義康
Liu Ying	劉英
"Liu Yiqing zhuan"	劉義慶傳
Liu Yong	柳永
liuhe	六合
Liu-Song	劉宋
Liuxia Hui	柳下惠
liuxu yinfeng qi	柳絮因風起
Liuyue shuang chuanqi	六月霜傳奇
Lixue	理學
liyi	禮義
Longyou	隆祐
Lu [family of Jintai]	魯
Lu Congping	陸從平
Lu Guilan	魯桂兰
Lu Jian	盧緘
Lü Jinshu	呂繒叔
Lu [née, wife of Zheng Yizong]	鄭義宗妻盧氏

Lu Tanwei	陸探微
Lu Qingzi	陸卿子
Lu Tui	陸退
Lu Ying	陸英
Lu Yinpu	卢荫溥
Lu Zhizong	盧知宗
Lü Zuqian	呂祖謙
Lunyu	論語
Lunyu yizhu	論語譯註
Luo Qilan	駱綺蘭
Luo Zhenyu	羅振玉
Luoyang san guai ji	洛陽三怪記
lüshi	律詩
Ma Ruichen	馬瑞辰
Mangshan	邙山
Mao Jun	冒俊
"Mao ruren muzhiming"	毛孺人墓誌銘
Mao Yilu	毛一鷺
Mao Zedong	毛澤東
Mei Zengliang	梅曾亮
Meiji	明治
meiren	美人
Meiren baiyun	美人百韻
Meng [empress]	孟
Meng Chengshun	孟稱舜
Meng Guang	孟光
Meng Mu	孟母
Meng Shuqing	孟淑卿
Mengshu	夢書
Miao [consort]	苗
"Miao chang zhuan"	眇倡傳
Miao Xi	繆襲
Miao Yin	苗愔
miaojian	廟見
Min Shin jidai no josei to bungaku	明清時代の女性と文學
ming [name, reputation]	名
ming [fate, destiny]	命
"Ming gu feng tai an ren Pei mu Zhang shi mu zhi ming"	明故奉太安人裴母張氏墓誌銘

"Ming gu feng xundafu Dai zhou zhizhou Bian gong he zang mu zhi ming"　明故奉訓大夫代州知州邊公合葬墓誌銘

"Ming gu Shen yiren mu zhi ming"　明故申宜人墓誌銘

Ming sanshijia shixuan　明三十家詩選

Mingshi　明史

Ming yulin　明語林

mingbian you caishi　明辯有才識

mingshi　明識

mingshi yuantu　明識遠圖

Mingyi bian　明逸編

mingyuan shigui　名媛詩歸

Mingyuan shihua　名媛詩話

Mingyuan shiwei　名媛詩緯

Mou Ting　牟庭

muzhi　墓誌

muzhiming　墓誌銘

mu　模

mubiao　墓表

Murong　慕容

muyi　母儀

"Muyi zhuan"　母儀傳

Nan Bei chao Shishuo　南北朝世說

Nan Bei chao xinyu　南北朝新語

Nan Qi shu　南齊書

Nanshi　南史

Nanshu fang　南書房

nazheng　納徵

Nei ze　內則

nianpu　年譜

Nianyi shi shiyu　廿一史識餘

niebi luanwang zhe　孽嬖亂亡者

"Niebi zhuan"　孽嬖傳

Niu Su　牛肅

Niu Yingzhen　牛應貞

Niu Weibing　牛惟炳

Nü Er-er kuang zhi　女二二壙志

nü lieshi　女烈士

"Nü Rulan kuang zhi"　女如蘭壙志

Nü Shishuo	女世說
Nüdaoshi Li Xuanzhen	女道士李玄真
Nüjie	女誡
Nüshi xiufolou shi	女士繡佛樓詩
Nüshi zhentu	女史箴圖
nüzi zhen bu zi	女子貞不字
Ōta Nanbo	太田南畝 [Ōta Fukashi 太田覃]
Ōta Saijirō	太田才次郎
Ou	欧
Ōyane Bunjirō	大矢根文次郎
pai'ao	排㟸
Pan Suxin	潘素心
Pan Yue	潘岳
Pang Jie	龐姐
panmeng weijie	叛盟違戒
paofan	跑反
Pei Jing	裴儆
Pei Wang Zhihong	裴王志宏
Pei Yuxian	裴羽仙
Peng Duanshu	彭端淑
Peng Yuanrui	彭元瑞
pifa huilei	披髮揮淚
Pihu	劈戶
"Pingliang fu ren zhuan"	平涼夫人傳
Pingyetai yanci	平野台艷詞
Pu Qilong	浦起龍
qi [vital force]	氣
qi [equal]	齊
qi ren	其人
Qi Wusui	綦毋邃
qian	謙
Qian Qianyi	錢謙益
Qian Shixi	錢世錫
"Qianfu lun"	潛夫論
"Qie bo ming"	妾薄命
qimeng	綺夢
Qin Guo	秦果

"Qin Xianglian" 秦香蓮
Qin Xuemei 秦雪梅
qin zhi shu 親執書
qing 情
Qing nu 青奴
qinggan 情感
Qinglige ji 青藜閣集
Qingpingshantang huaben 清平山堂話本
Qingshi gao 清史稿
Qingshi leilüe 情史類略
qingshi liuming 青史留名
Qingshou 慶壽
Qingyan 清言
qinjian 勤儉
qinken laoshi, jianku pusu 勤恳老实,艰苦朴素
Qinyou tang 勤有堂
Qinzong 欽宗
qishi er congxinyu bu yuju 七十而從心欲不踰矩
Qishi 漆室
"Qiu Nüshi lishi" 秋女士歷史
Qiu Ying 仇英
qiuren 求仁
Qiuxiang hongqi biandi cha 秋香紅旗遍地插
Qixia (*xian*) 棲霞(縣)
Quansheng 泉生
qubi 曲筆
quewu 権務

Ranzhi ji 然酯集
rendan 任誕
renlun jianshi 人倫鑒識
Renmin gongshe yizhi hua 人民公社一枝花
renyi lizhi 仁義禮智
"Renzhi zhuan" 仁智傳
Rong 榮
roushun 柔順
ru 乳
Ruan Ji 阮籍
ruozhi quchi 弱質驅馳
ruren 孺人
Ruxue 儒學

Sandai	三代
Sangfu	喪服
san'gang wuchang	三綱五常
Sanguo zhi	三國志
sanjiazhu	三家注
se	色
Seng Shishuo	僧世說
Sesetsu shingo cha	世說新語茶
Sesetsu shingo to rikuchō bungaku	世說新語と六朝文學
Shaanxi	陝西
Shaishu tang waiji	曬書堂外集
shan ke mo xi, hai ke ku; sheng wei yi xi, si wu er	山可磨兮海可枯;生唯一兮死無二
Shan Tao	山濤
Shan Xiuzhen	山秀珍
Shandong	山東
Shanhai jing	山海經
Shangshu	尚書
shangtu xiawen	上圖下文
Shanxi	陝西
Shaosheng	紹聖
shashen chengren	殺身成仁
Shen [prince]	申
Shen Cai	沈彩
Shen Dacheng	沈大成
Shen Feng	沈鳳
Shen Fu	沈復
Shen Yixiu	沈宜修
Shen Yue	沈約
Shenbao	申報
Shengrui gong	聖瑞宮
shengyuan	生員
shengzhuan	聖傳
shense bu bian	神色不變
shensheng	神聖
shenshi gaoxing	深識高行
Shenzong	神宗
sheshen quyi	捨身取義
shi [stone]	石
shi [history]	史
shi [affair]	事

Shi jiugu	事舅姑
shi xin wu er li zhi ru shi	失心無二立志如石
shi yan zhi ye	詩言志也
shi zhi ru jian wu ye	視之如見吾也
Shibao	時報
shibiao	石表
shidafu	士大夫
shihua	詩話
Shiji	史記
shiji	詩集
Shiji suoyin	史記索引
shijie	誓節
Shijing	詩經
shilu	實錄
shilüe	事略
Shin seigo	新世語
Shipu	詩譜
Shisan jing zhushu	十三經註疏
Shishuo	詩說
Shishuo xinyu	世說新語
Shishuo xinyu bu	世說新語補
Shishuo xinyu jianshu	世說新語箋疏
Shitong [tongshi]	史通[通釋]
Shiwu bao	時務報
Shixue	史學
shiyou	師友
Shoku Kinsei sōgo	續近世叢語
Shokusan sensei	杏花園蜀山
shou	首
shou yue	守約
shoujie	守節
shu [commoners]	庶
shu [writing about]	書
shu . . . shi . . .	書 . . . 事
shujian	書簡
Shuo yuan	說苑
shuochang cihua	說唱詞話
Shuoling	說鈴
Shuowen chongwen guanjian	說文重文管見
Shuowen jiezi	說文解字

Shuowen jiezi [zhu]	說文解字[注]
Shuqi	叔齊
shuren	淑人
Sibu beiyao	四部備要
side	四德
Siku quanshu zongmu	四庫全書總目
Sima Xiangru	司馬相如
Simei ju	四美聚
sishi buhuo	四十不惑
sixiao	死孝
sizhuan	私傳
Song	宋
Song [consort]	宋
Song Renzong ren mu ji	宋仁宗認母記
Song Ruozhao	宋若昭
Songshi	宋史
Song Shiying	宋實穎 [Jiting 既庭]
Song suoyu	宋瑣語
Song Tingyu qi Weishi	宋庭瑜妻魏氏
Song-Ming lixue shi	宋明理學史
Songshu	宋書
Su	宿
Su Hui	蘇蕙
Su Shunqin	蘇舜欽
Su Song	蘇頌
sui	歲
suilu	碎顱
Suishu	隋書
Suiwei lei cao	總帷淚草
Sun Beiming	孫備銘
Sun Furen	孫夫人
Sun Jie	孫劼
Sun Liren	孫立人
"Sun Shuyu ai ci"	孫叔獻哀詞
Sun Xidan	孫希旦
suqian	宿遷
Taicang	太倉
taijiao	胎教
Tainan	臺南
Taiping guang ji	太平廣記

Taiwan	臺灣
Taizong	太宗
taming	塔銘
Tan Yige	譚意歌
tanci	彈詞
Tang	唐
"Tang po zhuan"	湯婆傳
Tanggu	塘沽
Tanyang dashi zhuan	曇陽大師傳
Tanyangzi	曇陽子
Tao Chengzhang	陶成章
Taoyao	桃夭
Taoyuan	桃園
tian	恬
Tian Han	田漢
Tian Heng	田橫
Tian Jizi	田稷子
"Tian Dan liezhuan"	田單列傳
Tiandao	天道
Tianli	天理
Tianming	天命
T[t]ici	題辭
Tiying	緹縈
Tōhōgaku	東方學
Tokugawa	德川
tong	銅
tong yi xun	痛以殉
Tongcheng guwen	桐城古文
Tongguan	潼關
Tongjia	佟佳
Tongmeng hui	同盟會
Tongzhi	同治
Tushuguan xue jikan	圖書館學季刊
waifu	外婦
Waiguo lienü zhuan	外國列女傳
wanci	輓詞
Wang [empress]	王
Wang Anshi	王安石
Wang Bi	王弼

Wang Bi ji jiaoshi	王弼集校釋
Wang Caifan	王采繁
Wang Cailü	王采綠
Wang Caipin	王采蘋
Wang Daokun	汪道昆
"Wang Duanshu zhuan"	王端淑傳
Wang Fangqing	王方慶
Wang Fu	王符
Wang Geng	王庚
Wang Hui [of Song Dynasty]	王回
Wang Hui [of Qing Dynasty]	王翬
Wang Jian	王建
Wang Jinfa	王金髮
Wang Kangnian	汪康年
Wang Ling	王令
Wang Mang	王莽
"Wang mei Yuan shi fu mu zhi ming"	亡妹袁氏婦墓誌銘
Wang Niansun	王念孫
Wang Qiong	王瓊
Wang Run	汪潤
Wang Shaolan	王紹蘭
"Wang shi Tang ruren xinglüe"	亡室湯孺人行略
Wang Shilu	王士祿
Wang Shimou	王世懋
Wang Shiqi	王士騏
Wang Xian	汪憲
Wang Xianzhi	王獻之
Wang Xijue	王錫爵
Wang Xiwei	王錫瑋
Wang Yinzhi	王引之
Wang Youyu	王幼玉
Wang Yuansun	汪遠孫
Wang Yuanxiang	汪元享
Wang Yun	王筠
Wang Zilan	王子蘭
Wang Zishen	王資深
Wanyan Yun Zhu	完顏惲珠 (cf. Yun Zhu)
wanyue	婉約
wei	為
Wei Cheng	韋逞

Wei Jingqing	魏鏡情
wei wang ren	未亡人
Wei Xiyuan Qing gongci	魏息園清宮詞
Wei Zhaoting	魏召亭
Wei Zhongxian	魏忠賢
weihun shoujie	未婚守節
Wei-Jin	魏晉
Wei-Jin Nan-Bei chao shi lunji xubian	魏晉南北朝史論集續編
Weinan	渭南
Weishu	魏書
weixing jiansu, gua shiyu, aihao wenyi	為性簡素,寡嗜欲,愛好文義
wen rou	溫柔
Wen Wan	溫琬
Wen Yiduo	聞一多
Wen Zhengming	文徵明
Wenbo	文伯
wenci jibian, xiaoda zhengshi	文詞機辯,曉達政事
wenci youyu, jiegai buzu	文詞有餘,節概不足
wenji	文集
wenxue	文學
wo bu fu jun	我不負君
Wu	吳
Wu [consort]	武
wu cai wei fu	無才為福
Wu Daozi	吳道子
Wu Sugong	吳肅公
Wu Xuehai	吾學海
wu yi ri buzuo shu ruo you suo shi yu ba buneng yi	吾一日不作書若有所失欲罷不能矣
Wu Yuancui	伍袁萃
Wu Zao	吳藻
Wu Zetian	武則天
Wuhan	武漢
"Wujia you jiaonü / Jiaojiao po baixi"	吾家有嬌女 皎皎顏白晰"
Wumeng tang ji	午夢堂集
"Wushi zi zhuan"	武氏姊傳
wuwei	無為
Wuzhong shizi	吳中十子

"Xi hu san ta ji"	西湖三塔記
Xi you ji	西遊記
xia [knight-errant]	俠
xia [blind]	瞎
xian [virtuous and talented]	賢
xian [prominent]	顯
xian [visible]	見
"Xian fujun xingshi"	先府君行實
"Xianbi shilüe"	先妣事略
xianfei zhenfu	賢妃貞婦
xianfu	賢婦
xian shi	仙逝
xiang	香
Xiang	向 [Empress, Empress dowager (Qinsheng 欽聖, Xiansu 獻肅)]
Xiang Minzhong	向敏中
Xiang Yuan	項原
Xiang Yu	項羽
Xiang Zonghui	向宗回
Xiang Zongliang	向宗良
xiangfu	相夫
Xiang Furen	湘夫人
xianggong jinshi	鄉貢進士
xianglian ge	香奩格
Xianglian ji	香奩集
Xiangxiang	湘鄉
"Xianming zhuan"	賢明傳
xianmu	賢母
xiannü	賢女
xianü	俠女
"Xianxian shinü zongzan"	先賢士女總讚
xianxiao	賢孝
Xianyuan	賢媛
xiao	孝
Xiao Ao	蕭媼
Xiao Daoguan	蕭道管
xiao fumu	孝父母
Xiao Lun	蕭掄
Xiao weimo shigao	小維摩詩稿
Xiao Zixian	蕭子顯

xiaofu	孝婦
Xiaojing	孝經
xiaonü	孝女
Xiaoyun	小雲
xiaozhuan	小傳
Xiaozong	小宗
Xie An	謝安
Xie Daoyun	謝道韞
Xiling guiyong	西泠閨詠
Xin Tangshu	新唐書
Xin Xianying	辛憲英
Xin xu	新序
Xin Yuanshi	新元史
Xinbian guafu lienü zhuan shiqu	新編寡婦烈女傳詩曲
xing	性
Xing	邢
Xing [consort]	邢
xing congmin, shijian guoren	性聰敏,識鑒過人
xingguo xianjia	興國顯家
xinglüe	行略
xingshi	行實
xingshu	行述
xingzhuang	行狀
xinji	心疾
Xinshu	新書
xinsi	心思
Xinzheng	新政
xiongdi	兄弟
xiu shen	修身
xiuxin	修心
Xiuyi	繡衣
Xixiang ji	西廂記
Xiyuan tiju	息園題句
Xiyuan waishi yue	息園外史曰
xu	序
Xu Fei	徐悱
Xu Huang	徐煌
Xu Ji	徐積
Xu Jiang	許將
Xu Jingshao	徐景韶

Xu lienü zhuan	續列女傳
Xu Naichang	徐乃昌
Xu Po	徐勃
Xu Shishuo xinshu	續世說新書
Xu Shishuo	續世說
Xu Xilin	徐錫麟
Xu Yun	許允
Xu Zihua	徐自華
Xuancheng	宣城
"Xuanting yuan"	軒亭冤
"Xuantingxue chuanqi"	軒亭血傳奇
Xuanxue	玄學
xue	學
Xue	薛
Xue Juzheng	薛居正
Xuetang congke	雪堂叢刻
xun	殉
xunguo	殉國
xunjie	殉節
Yamanote no Bakajin	山ノ手の馬鹿人
Yan Congqiao	顏從喬
Yan Hui	顏回
Yan Xian	嚴憲
yan yue	艷樂
Yan'an	延安
Yanagida Setsuko sensei koki kinen ronshû henshû iinkai	柳田節子先生古稀記念論集編集委員會
yang	揚
Yang Guifei	楊貴妃
Yang Jiaoshan	楊椒山 (Jisheng 繼盛)
Yang Jingzhi	楊敬之
Yang Xiong	楊雄
Yangzhu	楊朱
yanti	艷體
"Yao"	藥
yao	要
yao lüe	要略
Yao mianhua kaifang bi yun da	要棉花开放比云大
Yao Nai	姚鼐

Yao Silian	姚思廉
Ye Nüshi	葉女師
Ye Sheng	葉盛
Ye Shi Liwan	葉石禮紈
Ye Songqing	葉頌清
Ye Xiaoluan	葉小鸞
yi [honor-bound duty]	義
yi [potentially damaging aspects]	抑
Yi li [*zhushu*]	儀禮[註釋]
yi shi zi ran	衣食自然
yibiaohun	姨表婚
"Yibin Zuo gong he zang mu zhi ming"	儀賓左公合葬墓志銘
Yichou	乙丑
yidong er jue	一慟而絕
Yijian zhi	夷堅志
Yijing	易經
yike hongxing xiangzhe dang	一顆紅心向着党
yin	隱
Yingying zhuan	鶯鶯傳
Yingzong	英宗
Yinhong ji	吟紅集
yinyuan	因緣
yinzhi	隱志
yiren	宜人
yishi	遺事 [anecdotal memoir]
yishi	逸事 [anecdotal memoir]
yishu	懿淑
"Yishu tu tici"	肄書圖題辭
"Yiwen zhi"	藝文志
yixing	義行
yong wu shi	詠物詩
Yongjong	永瑢
Yongle dadian	永樂大典
yongxia bianyi bi zi fufu zhi lun shi	用夏變夷必自夫婦之倫始
you jie er bu yin	有節而不隱
You Qiu	尤仇
you shiliang	有識量
youai	友愛
youjun	幽儁

Yu	于
Yu Que	余闕
Yu Wenxiu	余文秀
Yu Zhengxie	俞正燮
Yu Zhenjie	虞貞節
yuan [injustice]	冤
yuan [currency]	圓
Yuan Huang	袁黃
Yuan Ji	袁機 (Suwen 素文)
Yuan Mei	袁枚
Yuan Ming yishi	元明逸史
Yuan Shou	袁綬
Yuan Zhen	元稹
"Yuan yichen shi"	元遺臣詩
Yuanfu	元符
Yuanjia	元嘉
yuannü	冤女
Yuanshi	元史
Yuanyou	元祐
Yue Fei	岳飛
yueli	約禮
Yujian zunwen	玉劍尊聞
Yujing yangqiu	玉京陽秋
Yulin	語林
"Yun Richu xiansheng jiazhuan"	惲日初先生家傳
Yunbo	雲伯
Yunzhuang	允莊
Yutang congyu	玉堂叢語
Zaiputang yingao	在璞堂吟稿
Zaisheng yuan	再生緣
zan	贊
Zang Yong	臧庸
Zeng Gong	曾鞏
"Zeng ruren Li qi Ying shi mu zhi ming"	曾孺人李妻應氏墓誌銘
Zeng Shufan	曾樹蕃
Zengzhi nang bu	增智囊補
Zengzi wen	曾子問
zhancui	斬衰

Zhang [consort]	張
Zhang Bingling	章炳麟
Zhang Cai	張采
Zhang Chang	張廠
Zhang Dai	張岱
Zhang Dun	章惇
Zhang Fugong	章撫功
Zhang Guanying	張絪英
Zhang Huangyan	張煌言
Zhang Jiyong	章繼泳
Zhang Juesun	張珏孫
Zhang Juzheng	張居正
Zhang Liangyu	張良御
Zhang Ping	張憑
Zhang Pu	張溥
Zhang Qi	張麒
Zhang Qieying	張綰英
Zhang Qiuxian	张秋香
"Zhang ruren mu zhi ming"	張孺人墓誌銘
Zhang Sanguang	張三光
Zhang Shicheng	張士誠
Zhang Shide	張士德
Zhang Wang Mingxin	張王銘心
Zhang Wangzhi	章望之
Zhang Wanwan	章婉婉
Zhang Wanying	張紈英
Zhang Wenbao	章文寶
"Zhang Wenrou shi xu"	章文柔詩序
"Zhang Wu jishi shi"	張吳紀事詩
Zhang Yong	張墉
Zhang Yue	張說
Zhang Yuesun	張曜孫
Zhang Yun'ao	張雲璈
Zhang Yunsui	張允隨
Zhang Zhengping	章正 (政)平
Zhang zhennü yu shi	張貞女獄事
Zhang Zhidong	張之洞

zhangfu you san buxiu, lide ligong liyan; er furen yiyou san yan, deye, cai yu se ye, ji zhaozhao hu ding qiangu yi	丈夫有三不朽,立德立功立言;而婦人亦有三焉,德也,才與色也,幾昭昭乎鼎千古矣
"Zhangjun qi Bao ruren cuozhi"	張君妻包孺人厝誌
Zhao Mu	趙母
"Zhao qi Wen shi mu zhi ming"	趙妻溫氏墓誌銘
Zhao Shijie	趙世杰
Zhao wo guantong	昭我管彤
Zhao Yi	趙翼
Zhao Yu	趙瑜
Zhao Ze	趙澤
Zhaode renxin kaile hua	照得人心开了花
zhen	貞
zhen, buwen ye	貞,卜問也
zhenfu	貞婦
Zhenjun	真君
zheng	正
Zheng feng	鄭風
Zheng Sengyu	鄭僧禹
Zheng Xuan	鄭宣
zheng yidai deshi	正一代得失
Zheng Zhongkui	鄭仲夔
zhengqi	正氣
zhenjie	貞節
zhenlie	貞烈
zhennü	貞女
Zhenqi tang	振綺堂
"Zhenshun zhuan"	貞順傳
Zhenzong	真宗
Zhezong	哲宗
zhi guai	志怪
Zhi Mo	支謨
Zhi Na	支訥
Zhi Xi	支欣
Zhibuzu zhai	知不足齋
zhifen	脂粉
zhili	志力
Zhimige	直秘閣
zhiqi gao, ganjin da	志气高,干劲大

Zhitang	直塘
Zhong Xing	鍾惺
Zhong Yan	鍾琰
zhongchen bushi erjun, zhennü bugeng erfu	忠臣不事二君;貞女不更二夫
zhongfu	冢婦
Zhongguo meishujia renming cidian	中國美術家人名詞典
Zhongguo shanben shu tiyao	中國善本書提要
Zhongguo zhexue shi yanjiu	中國哲學史研究
Zhonghua shuju	中華書局
zhongyi qingsheng	重義輕生
zhongzhuang	忠壯
Zhou [consort]	周
Zhou Shunchang	周順昌
Zhou Yi [*zhu*]	周易[註]
Zhou Zhong	周鍾
"Zhou zi jia shi Tang ruren mu zhi ming"	周子嘉室唐孺人墓誌銘
Zhouguan yinyi	周官音義
Zhounan	周南
Zhoushu	周書
Zhu [consort]	朱
Zhu Dongrun	朱東潤
Zhu *fu ren*	竹夫人
Zhu Jian	朱琰
Zhu Shuzhen	朱淑真
Zhu Yuanzhang	朱元璋
zhuan	傳
zhuanlüe	傳略
zhuci bishi	屬詞比事
zhujiani	住家尼
Zhulin qixian	竹林七賢
Zhuo Wenjun	卓文君
Zhuxiang zhai leishu	竹香齋類書
zhuzao	鑄造
zi [courtesy name]	字
zi [philosophy]	子
zicui	齊衰
Zimei	子美
Ziran haoxue zhai ji	自然好學齋集

Ziran haoxue zhai shi	自然好學齋詩
Ziran haoxue zhai shichao	自然好學齋詩鈔
Ziran haoxue zhai shiji	自然好學齋詩集
ziwu	自誣
Ziyou hun	自由魂
Zong luxian shi dengta	总路线是灯塔
zongfa	宗法
zongfan	宗藩
Zou Tonglu	鄒統魯
zui	罪
Zuo feiyan rizuan	昨非魘日纂
Zuo Fen	左芬
Zuo Si	左思
Zuo zhuan	左傳
zuofeng wenti	作风问题
zuowen hai Dao	作文害道

Bibliography

NOTE: Various editions of and collections within the *Siku quanshu* 四庫全書 (The complete collection of the Four Treasuries [1,500 vols.]) are cited by the author and title of each text and the edition consulted.

A Ying 阿英 (錢杏邨), ed. *Wanqing wenxue congchao: Chuanqi zaju juan* 晚清文學叢鈔:傳奇雜劇卷. (A compendium of late Qing literature: Volume on dramatic literature). Shanghai: Zhonghua shuju, 1960.

An Zuozhang 安作璋 and Geng Tianqin 耿天勤. "Hao Yixing he ta de *Saishutang ji*" 郝懿行和他的《曬書堂集》 (Hao Yixing and his *Collected works of the Studio for Airing Books in the Sun'*). *Shixue shi yanjiu* 史學史研究 2 (1989): 73–80.

Anderson, Benedict. *Imagined Communities: Reflections on the Origin and Spread of Nationalism*. London and New York: Verso, 2003 [1983].

Ban Gu 班固. *Hanshu* 漢書 (History of the Former Han). 8 vols. cl. ed. (pb. ed.: 12 vols.). Beijing: Zhonghua shuju, 1962.

Bao Shichen 包世臣. "Huangchi feng ruren Shandong Guantao xian zhixian Zhangjun qi Tangshi muzhiming" 皇敕封孺人山東館陶縣知縣張君妻湯氏墓誌銘 (Epitaph for the Imperially Commended Wife (née Tang) of Zhang Jun, Magistrate of Guantao County, Shangdong Province). In *Beizhuan ji bu* 碑傳集補 (Collected eulogies from stele inscriptions, supplement) vol. 1000, *juan* 59.17a–18b. 1931. Rpt. Taibei: Wenhai chubanshe, 1973.

Barr, Allan H. "The *Ming History* Inquisition in Personal Memoir and Public Memory." *Chinese Literature: Essays, Articles, Reviews (CLEAR)* 27 (2005): 5–32.

Bauer, Wolfgang. *Das Antlitz Chinas. Die autobiographische Selbstdarstellung in der Chinesischen Literatur von ihren Anfängen bis Heute*. Munich: Carl Hanser, 1990.

Benhabib, Seyla. "Subjectivity, Historiography, and Politics: Reflections on the 'Feminism/Postmodernism Exchange.'" In Benhabib et al., *Feminist Contentions*, 105–25.

Benhabib, Seyla, Judith Butler, Drucilla Cornell, and Nancy Fraser. *Feminist Contentions: A Philosophical Debate*. New York: Routledge, 1995.

Bian Xiaoxuan 卞孝萱 and Tang Wenquan 唐文权, eds. *Xinhai renwu beizhuan ji* 辛亥人物碑传集 (Collected epitaphs and biographies of notable figures in the 1911 Revolution). Beijing: Tuanjie, 1991.

Birge, Bettine. "Chu Hsi and Women's Education." In *Neo-Confucian Education, the Formative Stage*, ed. William Theodore de Bary and John Chaffee, 325–67. Berkeley and Los Angeles: University of California Press, 1989.

———. "Levirate Marriage and the Revival of Widow Chastity in Yuan China." *Asia Major* 8.2 (1995): 107–46.

Blanchard, Lara C. W. "A Scholar in the Company of Female Entertainers: Changing Notions of Integrity in Song to Ming Dynasty Painting." *Nan Nü: Men, Women and Gender in China* 9.2 (2007): 189–246.

Bloch, Maurice, and Jonathan Parry, eds. *Death and Regeneration of Life*. Cambridge: Cambridge University Press, 1982.

Bol, Peter. *This Culture of Ours: Intellectual Transitions in T'ang and Sung China*. Stanford, CA: Stanford University Press, 1992.

Bossler, Beverly. *Courtesans, Concubines, and the Cult of Wifely Fidelity: Gender and Social Change in China, 1000-1400*. Cambridge, MA: Harvard University Asia Center, forthcoming.

———. "Faithful Wives and Heroic Maidens: Politics, Virtue, and Gender in Song China." In *Tang Song nüxing yu shehui* 唐宋女性與社會 (Tang-Song women and society), ed. Deng Xiaonan 鄧小南, 751–84. Shanghai: Shanghai cishu chubanshe, 2003.

———. "Faithful Wives and Heroic Martyrs: State, Society and Discourse in the Song and Yuan." In *Chūgoku no rekishi sekai, tōgō no shisutemu to tagenteki hatten* 中国の歴史世界、統合のシステムと多元的発展 (The world of Chinese history, unified systems and pluralistic developments), ed. Chūgokushi gakkai 中国史学会, 507–56. Tokyo: Tokyo Metropolitan University Press, 2002.

———. "Funerary Writings by Chen Liang (1143–1194)." In *Under Confucian Eyes: Writings on Gender in Chinese History*, ed. Susan Mann and Yu-yin Cheng, 71–85. Berkeley and Los Angeles: University of California Press, 2001.

———. "Gender and Empire: A View from Yuan China." *Journal of Medieval and Early Modern Studies* 34.1 (winter 2004): 197–223.

———. *Powerful Relations: Kinship, Status, and the State in Sung China (960–1279)*. Cambridge, MA: Council on East Asian Studies Publications, Harvard University Press, 1998.

———. "Shifting Identities: Courtesans and Literati in Song China." *Harvard Journal of Asiatic Studies* 62.1 (June 2002): 5–37.

Brashier, K. E. "Text and Ritual in Early Chinese Stelae." In *Text and Ritual in Early China*, ed. Martin Kern, 249–84. Seattle: University of Washington Press, 2005.

Brokaw, Cynthia J. *The Ledgers of Merit and Demerit: Social Change and*

Moral Order in Late Imperial China. Princeton, NJ: Princeton University Press, 1991.

———. "Reading the Best-Sellers of the Nineteenth Century: Commercial Publishing in Sibao." In *Printing and Book Culture in Late Imperial China*, ed. Cynthia J. Brokaw and Kai-wing Chow, 184–231. Berkeley and Los Angeles: University of California Press, 2005.

Brook, Timothy. *The Confusions of Pleasure: Commerce and Culture in Ming China*. Berkeley and Los Angeles: University of California Press, 1998.

———. *Praying for Power: Buddhism and the Formation of Gentry Society in Late-Ming China*. Cambridge, MA: Harvard University Press, 1993.

Bussotti, Michela. *Gravures de Hui: Étude du livre illustré chinois de la fin du XVIe siècle à la première moitié du XVIIe siècle*. Paris: École française d'Extrême-Orient, 2001.

Butler, Judith. *Bodies That Matter: On the Discursive Limits of Sex*. London and New York: Routledge, 1993.

———. "For a Careful Reading." In Benhabib et al., *Feminist Contentions*, 127–44.

Cahill, James. "Paintings Done for Women in Ming Qing China?" *Nan Nü: Men, Women and Gender in China* 8.1 (2006): 1–54.

———. *Parting at the Shore: Chinese Painting of the Early and Middle Ming Dynasty 1368–1580*. New York: Weatherhill, 1978.

Cahill, Suzanne. *Divine Traces of the Daoist Sisterhood: Records of the Assembled Transcendents of the Fortified Walled City*. Honolulu: University of Hawai'i Press, 2006.

Cai Xiang 蔡襄. *Cai Xiang ji* 蔡襄集 (Collected works of Cai Xiang). Shanghai: Shanghai guji chubanshe, 1996.

*Cao Zhuxiang danxing cailiao*曹竹香单行材料 (Materials on Cao Zhuxiang). Shaanxi Provincial Archives 178, unnumbered, n.d. Xi'an.

Carlitz, Katherine. "The Daughter, the Singing-Girl, and the Seduction of Suicide." *Nan Nü: Men, Women and Gender in Early and Imperial China* 3.1 (2001): 22–46. Rpt. in *Passionate Women: Female Suicide in Late Imperial China*, ed. Paul S. Ropp, Paola Zamperini, and Harriet T. Zurndorfer. Leiden: Brill, 2001.

———. "Desire and Writing in the Late Ming Play *Parrot Island*." In *Writing Women in Late Imperial China*, ed. Ellen Widmer and Kang-i Sun Chang, 101–30. Stanford, CA: Stanford University Press, 1997.

———. "Desire, Danger, and the Body: Stories of Women's Virtue in Late Ming China." In *Engendering China*, ed. Christina K. Gilmartin, Gail Hershatter, Lisa Rofel, and Tyrene White, 101–24. Cambridge, MA: Harvard University Press, 1994.

———. "On *Yingying zhuan*, by Yuan Zhen." In *Ways with Words: Writing about Reading Texts from Early China*, ed. Pauline Yu, Peter Bol, Stephen Owen, and Willard Peterson, 192–97. Berkeley and Los Angeles: University of California Press, 2000.

————. "Shrines, Governing-Class Identity, and the Cult of Widow Fidelity in Mid-Ming Jiangnan." *Journal of Asian Studies* 56.3 (August 1997): 612–40.

————. "The Social Uses of Female Virtue in Late Ming Editions of *Lienü zhuan*." *Late Imperial China* 12.2 (1991): 117–52.

Chaffee, John W. "The Rise and Regency of Empress Liu." *Journal of Song-Yuan Studies* 31(2001): 1–25.

Chan Chi Ming. "Xiao Daoguan." In *Biographical Dictionary of Chinese Women: The Qing Period, 1644–1911*, ed. Clara Ho, 243–45. Armonk, NY: M. E. Sharpe, 1998.

Chan Wing-tsit. *A Sourcebook in Chinese Philosophy*. Princeton, NJ: Princeton University Press, 1972.

Chang Jui-te 張瑞德. "Zizhuan yu lishi—dai xu" 自傳與歷史—代序 (Biographies and history—a preface). In *Zhongguo xiandai zizhuan congshu* 中國現代自傳叢書 (Series on autobiographies in contemporary China), ed. Chang Yu-fa 張玉法 and Chang Jui-te 張瑞德, 1–18. Taibei: Longwind Publications, Ltd., 1989.

Chang, Kang-i Sun. "Ming-Qing Women Poets and the Notions of 'Talent' and 'Morality.'" In *Culture and State in Chinese History: Conventions, Accommodations, and Critiques,* ed. Theodore Huters, R. Bin. Wong, and Pauline Yu, 236–58. Stanford, CA: Stanford University Press, 1997.

Chang, Kang-i Sun, and Haun Saussy, eds. *Women Writers of Imperial China: An Anthology of Poetry and Criticism.* Stanford, CA: Stanford University Press, 1999.

Chang Qu 常璩. *Huayang guozhi jiaozhu* 華陽國志校註 (Collation and annotation of the state records of Huayang), coll. and ann. Liu Lin 劉琳. Chengdu: Bashu chubanshe, 1984.

Chen Bangzhan 陳邦瞻. *Songshi jishi benmo* 宋史紀事本末 (Narratives from the *Song History* from beginning to end). Beijing: Zhonghua shuju, 1977.

Chen Hongmo 陳洪謨. *Zhishi yuwen* 治世餘聞 (Anecdotes from an era of peace). Beijing: Zhonghua shuju, 1995.

Chen Liang 陳亮. *Chen Liang ji* 陳亮集 (Collected works of Chen Liang). Beijing: Zhonghua shuju, 1974.

Ch'en Li-li, trans. *Master Tung's Western Chamber Romance: A Chinese Chantefable.* New York: Cambridge University Press, 1976.

Chen Menglei 陳夢雷, comp. *Gujin Tushu jicheng* 古今圖書集成 (Completed collection of graphs and writings of ancient and modern times). 1726. Rpt. Beijing: Zhonghua shuju; Chengdu: Bashu shuju, 1985.

Chen Pingyuan 陈平原. "Male Gaze/Female Students: Late Qing Education for Women as Portrayed in Beijing Pictorials." In *Different Worlds of Discourse: Gender and Genre in Late Qing and Early Republican China,* ed. Nanxiu Qian, Grace S. Fong, and Richard J. Smith, 315–48. Leiden: Brill, 2008.

————. *Qiangu wenren xiakemeng: Wuxia xiaoshuo leixing yanjiu* 千古文人俠客夢:武俠小说类型研究 (The thousand-year long chivalric dream of the literati: A topology of the Chinese chivalric romance). Beijing: Renmin wenxue chubanshe, 1992.

Chen, Shih-Hsiang. "An Innovation in Chinese Biographical Writing." *Far Eastern Quarterly* 13.1 (November 1953): 49–62.

Chen Wenshu 沈文述. *Xiling guiyong* 西泠閨詠 (In praise of Hangzhou women). 1827. Harvard-Yenching Library.

Ch'en Yu-shih. "The Historical Template of Pan Chao's *Nü Chieh*." *T'oung Pao* 72 (1996): 229–57.

Chen Zhangfang 陳長方. *Wei shi ji* 唯室集 (Collected works of Chen Zhangfang). *Siku quanshu* ed., vol. 1139. Taibei: Taiwan shangwu yinshuguan, 1983.

Cheng Bi 程玭. *Ming shui ji* 銘水集 (Collected works of Cheng Bi). *Siku quanshu* ed., vol. 1171. Taibei: Taiwan shangwu yinshuguan, 1983.

Cheng Boquan 成伯泉. *Gudai wenyan duanpian xiaoshuo xuanzhu* 古代文言短篇小说選注 (Selected traditional classical-language short fiction). Shanghai: Shanghai guji chubanshe, 1983–84.

Cheng, Eileen J. "Gendered Spectacles: Lu Xun on Gazing at Women and Other Pleasures." *Modern Chinese Literature and Culture* 16.1 (2004): 1–36.

Cheng Ju 程俱. *Bei shan ji* 北山集 (Collected works of Cheng Ju). *Siku quanshu* ed., vol. 1130. Taibei: Taiwan shangwu yinshuguan, 1983.

Chia, Lucille. *Printing for Profit: The Commercial Publishers of Jianyang, Fujian (11th–17th Centuries)*. Cambridge, MA: Harvard University Asia Center, 2002.

Chow, Kai-wing. *The Rise of Confucian Ritualism in Late Imperial China: Ethics, Classics, and Lineage Discourse*. Stanford, CA: Stanford University Press, 1994.

Chung, Priscilla Ching. *Palace Women in the Northern Sung*. T'oung Pao Monographie 12. Leiden: Brill, 1981.

Clunas, Craig. "Images of High Antiquity: The Prehistory of Art in Ming Dynasty China." In *Die Gegenwart des Altertums: Formen and Funktionen des Altertumsbezugs in den Hochkulturen der Alten Welt*, ed. Dieter Kuhn and Helga Stahl, 481–91. Heidelberg: Edition Forum, 2001.

Cutter, Robert Joe, and William Gordon Crowell. *Empresses and Consorts: Selections from Chen Shou's* Records of the Three States *with Pei Songzhi's Commentary*. Honolulu: University of Hawai'i Press, 1999.

Dardess, John W. *Blood and History in China: The Donglin Faction and Its Repression 1620–1627*. Honolulu: University of Hawai'i Press, 2002.

Davis, Natalie Zemon. "'Women's History' in Transition: The European Case." In *Feminism and History*, ed. Joan Wallach Scott, 79–104. Oxford and New York: Oxford University Press, 1996.

Delehaye, Hippolyte. *The Legends of the Saints, an Introduction to Hagiography*. Trans. V. M. Crawford. Longmans, Green and Co., 1907.

Deng Xiaonan 鄧小南, ed. *Tang Song Nüxing yu shehui* 唐宋女性與社會 (Tang-Song women and society). Shanghai: Shanghai cishu chubanshe, 2003.

Despeux, Catherine, and Livia Kohn. *Women in Daoism.* Cambridge, MA: Three Pines Press, 2003.

Dong Gao 董誥 (1740–1818) et al., eds. *Quan Tang wen* 全唐文 (Complete Tang prose). Rpt. Shanghai: Shanghai guji chubanshe, 1990.

Dooling, Amy D., and and Kristina M. Torgeson, ed. *Writing Women in Modern China: Anthology of Literature by Chinese Women from the Early Twentieth Century.* New York: Columbia University Press, 1997.

Du Xinfu 杜信孚. *Mingdai banke conglu* 明代版刻綜錄 (A comprehensive catalog of Ming editions). Yangzhou: Jiangnan guanglu guji keyin she, 1983.

Dudbridge, Glen. *The Tale of Li Wa, Study and Critical Edition of a Chinese Story from the Ninth Century.* Oxford Oriental Monographs, no. 4. London: Ithaca Press, 1983.

Durrant, Stephen W. *The Cloudy Mirror: Tension and Conflict in the Writings of Sima Qian.* Albany: State University of New York Press, 1995.

Ebrey, Patricia Buckley. "The *Book of Filial Piety for Women* Attributed to a Woman Née Zheng (ca. 730)." In *Under Confucian Eyes: Writings on Gender in Chinese History*, ed. Susan Mann and Yu-yin Cheng, 47–69. Berkeley and Los Angeles: University of California Press, 2001.

——. *The Inner Quarters: Marriage and the Lives of Chinese Women in the Sung Period.* Berkeley and Los Angeles: University of California Press, 1993.

——. "Later Han Stone Inscriptions." *Harvard Journal of Asiatic Studies* 49 (1980): 325–53.

Edgren, Sören. "The *Ching-ying hsiao-sheng* and Traditional Illustrated Biographies of Women." *The Gest Library Journal* 5.2 (1992): 161–74.

Egan, Ronald. *Word, Image, and Deed in the Life of Su Shi.* Cambridge, MA: Harvard University Press, 1994.

Eifring, Halvor. "Introduction: Emotions and the Conceptual History of Qing." In *Love and Emotions in Chinese Literature*, ed. Halvor Eifring, 1–36. Leiden: Brill, 2004.

Elliott, Mark C. "Manchu Widows and Ethnicity in Qing China." *Comparative Studies in Society and History* 41.1 (January 1999): 33–71.

Elman, Benjamin A. *From Philosophy to Philology: Intellectual and Social Aspects of Change in Late Imperial China.* 2nd ed., rev. Los Angeles: UCLA Asian Pacific Monograph Series, 2001 [1984].

——. *On Their Own Terms: Science in China, 1550–1900.* Cambridge, MA: Harvard University Press, 2005.

——. "Political, Social, and Cultural Reproduction via Civil Service Examinations in Late Imperial China." *Journal of Asian Studies* 50.1 (February 1991): 7–28.

Elvin, Mark. "Female Virtue and the State in China." *Past and Present* 104 (1984): 111–52.

Epstein, Maram. *Competing Discourses: Orthodoxy, Authenticity, and Engendered Meanings in Late Imperial Chinese Fiction.* Cambridge, MA: Harvard University Asia Center, 2001.

———. "Making a Case: Characterizing the Filial Son." In *Writing and Law in Late Imperial China: Crime, Conflict, and Judgment,* ed. Robert E. Hegel and Katherine Carlitz, 27–43. Seattle: University of Washington Press, 2007.

Er Cheng yishu 二程遺書 (Posthumously published works of the two Chengs). *Siku quanshu,* vol. 698: 1–279.

Fan Ye范曄. *Hou Hanshu* 後漢書 (History of the Later Han). 12 vols. Commentary by Li Xian 李賢. Beijing: Zhonghua shuju, 1965.

Fang Bao 方苞. *Wangxi xiansheng wenji* 望溪先生文集 (Collected works of Fang Bao). *Xuxiu siku quanshu* ed., vol. 1420. Shanghai: Shanghai guji chubanshe, 2002.

Fang Fangpei 方芳佩. *Zaiputang yin'gao* 在璞堂吟稿 (Draft chantings from the hall in uncarved jade). 1751. Academy of Sciences Library, Beijing.

Fang Xuanling 房玄齡 et al. *Jinshu* 晉書 (History of the Jin). 10 vols. Beijing: Zhonghua shuju, 1974.

Fong, Grace S. "Signifying Bodies: The Cultural Significance of Suicide Writings by Women in Ming-Qing China." In *Passionate Women: Female Suicide in Late Imperial China,* ed. Paul S. Ropp, Paola Zamperini, and Harriet T. Zurndorfer, 105–42. Leiden: Brill, 2001.

———. "Writing Self and Writing Lives: Shen Shanbao's (1801–1862) Gendered Auto/Biographical Practices." *Nan Nü: Men, Women and Gender in Early and Imperial China* 2.2 (2000): 259–304.

Frankel, Hans H. "T'ang Literati: A Composite Biography." In *Confucianism and Chinese Civilization,* ed. Arthur Wright, 103–21. Stanford, CA: Stanford University Press, 1964.

Fulian 妇联 (Women's Federation) Archives. Shaanxi Provincial Archives, Xi'an.

Furth, Charlotte. "Intellectual Change: From the Reform Movement to the May Fourth Movement, 1895–1920." *Republican China 1912–1949. Cambridge History of China* 12.1, ed. John K. Fairbank, 322–405. Cambridge: Cambridge University Press. 1983.

Gao Xiaoxian 高小贤. "'The Silver Flower Contest': Rural Women in 1950s China and the Gendered Division of Labour." Trans. Yuanxi Ma. *Gender & History* 18.3 (November 2006): 594–612.

———. "'Yinhua sai': 50 niandai nongcun funü yu xingbie fengong" 《银花赛》: 50 年代农村妇女与性别分工 ("The Silver Flower Contest": Rural women in the 1950s and the gendered division of labor). In *Bainian Zhongguo nüquan sichao yanjiu* 百年中国女权思潮研究 (Research on 100 years of feminist thought), ed. Wang Zheng and Chen Yan, 259–77. Shanghai: Fudan daxue chubanshe, 2005.

Gilmartin, Christina K. *Engendering the Chinese Revolution: Radical Women, Communist Politics, and Mass Movements in the 1920s.* Berkeley and Los Angeles: University of California Press, 1995.

———. "Gender, Political Culture, and Women's Mobilization in the Chinese Nationalist Revolution, 1924–1927." In *Engendering China: Women, Culture, and the State,* ed. Christina K. Gilmartin, Gail Hershatter, Lisa Rofel and Tyrene White, 195–225. Cambridge, MA: Harvard University Press, 1994.

Gipoulon, Catherine. "L'image de l'épouse dans le *Lienüzhuan*." In *En suivant la voie royale: Mélanges offerts en hommage à Léon Vandermeersch*, ed. Jacques Gernet and Marc Kalinowski, 97–111. Paris: École française d'Extreme Orient, 1997.

Goodrich, L. Carrington, and Chaoying Fang, eds. *Dictionary of Ming Biography*. New York: Columbia University Press, 1976.

Goyama Kiwamu 合山究. "En Bai to jodeshi tachi" 袁枚と女弟子たち (Yuan Mei and his female disciples). *Bungaku ronshu* 31.8 (1965): 113–45.

———. *Min Shin jidai no josei to bungaku* 明清時代の女性と文學 (Women's literature of the Ming and Qing). Tokyo: Kyûko shoin, 2006.

Graham, A. C. *Disputers of the Tao: Philosophical Argument in Ancient China*. La Salle, IL: Open Court, 1989.

Guangxu Wujin Yanghu xian zhi 光緒武進陽湖縣志 (Guangxu ed. of the gazetteer for Wujin and Yanghu Counties). Changzhou, Jiangsu, 1879.

Gui Youguang 歸有光. *Zhenchuan xiansheng ji* 震川先生集 (The works of Zhenchuan [Gui Youguang]). *Sibu congkan* ed. Shanghai: Shangwu yinshuguan, 1929.

———. *Zhenchuan xiansheng ji* 震川先生集 (The works of Zhenchuan [Gui Youguang]). Shanghai: Shanghai guji chubanshe, 1981.

Guo Shaoyu 郭紹虞. *Zhongguo wenxue piping shi* 中國文學批評史 (History of Chinese literary criticism). Shanghai: Xin wenyi chubanshe, 1957.

Guo Yanli 郭延禮, ed. *Qiu Jin xuanji* 秋瑾選集 (Selected writings by Qiu Jin). Beijing: Renmin wenxue chubanshe, 2004.

———. *Qiu Jin yanjiu ziliao* 秋瑾研究資料 (Research material on Qiu Jin). 2 vols. Ji'nan: Shandong jiaoyu chubanshe, 1987.

Haizhou zhi 海州志 (Gazetteer of Haizhou County). Compiled by Zhang Feng 張峯 (fl. 1550). Vol. 14 in the *Tianyi ge* 天一閣 collection of Ming dynasty gazetteers. Rpt. ed. Shanghai: Shanghai guji shudian, 1981.

Halperin, Mark. "Domesticity and the Dharma: Portraits of Buddhist Laywomen in Sung China." *T'oung Pao* 92 (2006): 50–100.

Han Feizi jishi 韩非子集释 (The annotated complete works of Han Feizi). 2 vols. Ann. Chen Qiqiu 陈奇猷. Shanghai: Renmin chubanshe, 1974.

Hanan, Patrick. *The Chinese Short Story: Studies in Dating, Authorship, and Composition*. Cambridge, MA: Harvard University Press, 1973.

———. *The Chinese Vernacular Story*. Cambridge, MA: Harvard University Press, 1981.

———. "Judge Bao's Hundred Cases Reconstructed." *Harvard Journal of Asiatic Studies* 40.2 (December 1980): 301–23.

Handlin, Joanna F. "Lü K'un's New Audience: The Influence of Women's Literacy on Sixteenth-Century Thought." In *Women in Chinese Society*, ed. Margery Wolf and Roxanne Witke, 13–38. Stanford, CA: Stanford University Press, 1975.

Hartman, Charles. "The Making of a Villain: Ch'in Kuei and Tao-hsueh." *Harvard Journal of Asiatic Studies* 58 (1998): 59–146.

———. "The Reluctant Historian: Sun Ti, Chu Hsi, and the Fall of Northern Sung." *T'oung Pao* 89 (2003): 100–48.

———. "A Textual History of Cai Jing's Biography in the *Songshi*." In *Emperor Huizong and Late Northern Song China: The Politics of Culture and the Culture of Politics*, ed. Patricia Buckley Ebrey and Maggie Bickford, 517–64. Cambridge, MA: Harvard University Asia Center, 2006.

Hattori Nankaku 服部南郭 (1683–1759). *Daitō seigo* 大東世語 (An account of the great eastern world). 5 *juan*. 2 vols. Edo: Sūzanbō 嵩山房, 1750.

He Jingming 何景明. *Da fu ji* 大復集 (The "Great Return" collection). *Siku quanshu zhenben*, 7th series, vols. 659–72. Taibei: Taiwan shangwu yinshuguan, 1977.

He Liangjun 何良俊. *Heshi yulin* 何氏語林 (He's forest of accounts). 30 *juan*. Preface by Wen Zhengming 文徵明, dated 1551. *Siku quanshu*, vol. 1041: 441–895.

Hegel, Robert E., and Katherine Carlitz, eds. *Writing and Law in Late Imperial China: Crime, Conflict, and Judgment*. Seattle: University of Washington Press, 2007.

Hershatter, Gail. "Forget Remembering: Rural Women's Narratives of China's Collective Past." In *Re-Envisioning the Chinese Revolution: The Politics and Poetics of Collective Memories in Reform China*, ed. Ching Kwan Lee and Guobin Yang, 69–92. Washington, DC: Woodrow Wilson Center Press / Stanford, CA: Stanford University Press, 2006.

———. "Local Meanings of Gender and Work in Rural Shaanxi in the 1950s." In *Re-Drawing Boundaries: Work, Household, and Gender in China*, ed. Gail Henderson and Barbara Entwisle, 79–96. Berkeley and Los Angeles: University of California Press, 2000.

Hinsch, Bret. "Reading *Lienüzhuan* (Biographies of Women) through the Life of Liu Xiang." *Journal of Asian History* 39.2 (2005): 129–57.

———. "The Textual History of Liu Xiang's *Lienüzhuan*." *Monumenta Serica* 52 (2004): 95–112.

Ho, Clara Wing-chung, ed. *Biographical Dictionary of Chinese Women: The Qing Period, 1644–1911*. Armonk, NY: M. E. Sharpe, 1998.

Holzwarth, Gerald. "The Qianlong Emperor as Art Patron and the Formation of the Collections of the Palace Museum, Beijing." In *China: The Three Emperors 1662–1795*, ed. Evelyn S. Rawski and Jessica Rawson, 41–53. London: The Royal Academy of Arts, 2005.

Hong Mai 洪邁. *Yi jian zhi* 夷堅志 (Record of the listener). Ed. He Zhuo 何卓. Beijing: Zhonghua shuju, 1981.

Hong Pian 洪楩, ed. and comp. *Qingping shantang huaben* 清平山堂話本 (Stories from clear and peaceful mountain hall). Shanghai: Shanghai guji chubanshe, [between 1995 and 1999]. Facsimile of Ming Jiajing-era ed.

Hou Wailu 侯外廬 et al. *Song-Ming lixue shi* 宋明理學史 (The Song-Ming history of the Learning of Principle). 2 vols. Beijing: Renmin chubanshe, 1984–87.

Hsiung, Ping-chen, *A Tender Voyage: Children and Childhood in Late Imperial China*. Stanford, CA: Stanford University Press, 2005.

Hsü Pi-ching. "Courtesans and Scholars in the Writings of Feng Menglong: Transcending Status and Gender." *Nan Nü: Men, Women and Gender in Early and Imperial China* 2.1 (2000): 40–77.

Hu Huaichen 胡懷琛. "Jieshao nüshihao Bo Shaojun" 介紹女詩豪薄少君 (An introduction to the great female poet Bo Shaojun). *Yijing* 逸經 29 (May 5, 1937): 4–8.

Hu Shi 胡適. "Zhencao wenti" 貞操問題 (The problem of chastity). *Xin qingnian* 新青年 5.1 (July 15, 1918): 5–14.

Hu Wenkai 胡文楷. *Lidai funü zhuzuo kao* 歷代婦女著作考 (Studies of women's writings through the ages). Rev. ed. Shanghai: Shanghai guji chubanshe, 1985.

Hu Ying. "Writing Qiu Jin's Life: Wu Zhiying and Her Family Learning." *Late Imperial China* 25.2 (December 2004): 119–60.

Hu Ying and Joan Judge. "Women's Biography and Gender Politics in Chinese History: Conference Proposal." Unpublished, 2005.

Huang Chun-chieh and John B. Henderson, eds. *Notions of Time in Chinese Historical Thinking*. Hong Kong: Chinese University Press of Hong Kong, 2006.

Huang Tingjian 黃庭堅. *Huang Tingjian quan ji* 黃庭堅全集 (Complete works of Huang Tingjian). Chengdu: Sichuan da xue chubanshe, 2001.

Huang Yuji 黃虞稷. *Qianqing tang shumu* 千頃堂書目 (A library catalog of the Qianqing hall). Taibei: Guangwen shuju, 1967.

Huang Zhangjian 黃彰健. *Mingdai lüli huibian* 明代律例彙編 (Collected statutes and substatutes of the Ming dynasty). Taibei: Academia Sinica, 1979.

Hucker, Charles O. *A Dictionary of Official Titles in Imperial China*. Stanford, CA: Stanford University Press, 1985.

Hummel, Arthur. *Eminent Chinese of the Ch'ing Period*. Washington, DC: Government Printing Office, 1944. Rpt. Taibei, 1967.

Idema, Wilt, and Beata Grant. *The Red Brush: Writing Women of Imperial China*. Cambridge, MA: Harvard University Asia Center, 2004.

Institute of Archaeology, Chinese Academy of Social Sciences. *Yanshi Xingyuan Tang mu* 偃師杏園唐墓 (Tang tombs of Xingyuan, Yanshi). Beijing: Kexue chubanshe, 2001.

Ji Dong 計東. *Gaiting wenji* 改亭文集 (Collected works of Ji Dong). *Siku cunmu congshu* ed. Ji'nan: Qilu shushe, 1997.

Jia Yi 賈誼. *Xinshu* 新書 (New texts). Beijing: Shangwu yinshuguan, 1998.

———. *Xinshu [jiaozhu]* 新書[校註] ([Collated commentary on the] New texts). Coll. and comm. Yan Zhenyi 閻振益 and Zhong Xia 鍾夏. Beijing: Zhonghua shuju, 2000.

Jiang Xinghan 姜兴汉 and Cheng Wanli 程万里. "Diyige nongmin chushen de nü yanjiuyuan Zhang Qiuxiang" 第一个农民出身的女研究员张秋香 (Zhang Qiuxiang, the first woman researcher of peasant origin). *Zhongguo funü* (October 1958): 6–7.

Jiang Yonglin, trans. *The Great Ming Code.* Seattle: University of Washington Press, 2005.

Jiang Zhu 江珠. *Xiao weimo shigao* 小維摩詩稿 (Draft poems of little Vimala-kirti). 1811. National Library of China.

Jiao Xun 焦循. *Diaogu ji* 雕菰集 (Collected works from [the Studio of] Engraved Bamboo). *Congshu jicheng xinbian* ed. Taibei: Xinwenfeng chuban gongsi, 1985.

Judge, Joan. "Blended Wish Images: Chinese and Western Exemplary Women at the Turn of the Twentieth Century." *Nan Nü: Men, Women and Gender in China* 6.1 (2004): 102–35.

———. "Meng Mu Meets the Modern: Female Exemplars in Late-Qing Textbooks for Girls and Women." *Jindai Zhongguo funü shi yanjiu* 近代中國婦女史研究 (Research on women in modern Chinese history) 8 (June 2000): 133–77.

———. *The Precious Raft of History: The Past, the West, and the Woman Question in China.* Stanford, CA: Stanford University Press, 2008.

———. *Print and Politics*: Shibao *and the Culture of Reform in Late Qing China.* Stanford, CA: Stanford University Press, 1996.

———. "Three Images of Qiu Jin: Reassessing a Cultural Icon in Light of Japanese Sources." Paper presented at the annual meeting of the Association for Asian Studies, 2003.

Kaltenmark, Max. *Le Lie-sien Tchouan.* Paris: Collège de France, Institut des Hautes Études Chinoises, 1953. Rpt. 1987.

Kawakatsu Yoshio 川勝義雄. "Edo jidai ni okeru *Sesetsu* kenkyū no ichimen" 江戶時代における世説研究の一面 (An aspect of the study of the *Shishuo xinyu* during the Edo period). *Tōhōgaku* 東方學 20 (1960): 1–15.

Ke Shaomin 柯劭忞. *Xin Yuanshi* 新元史 (New history of the Yuan Dynasty). 5 vols. Rpt of 1922 ed. Taibei: Yiwen yinshuguan, 1950.

Kegasawa Yasunori 氣賀澤保規. *Tōdai boshi shozai sōgō mokuroku* 唐代墓誌所在総和目錄 (Complete index to Tang epitaphs). Tokyo: Kyuko Shoin, 1997.

Kitchen, John. *Saints' Lives and the Rhetoric of Gender: Male and Female in Merovingian Hagiography.* Oxford: Oxford University Press. 1998.

Ko, Dorothy. "A Man Teaching Ten Women: A Case in the Making of Gender Relations in Eighteenth-Century China." In *Chûgoku no dentô shakai to kazokû* 中國の傳統社會と家族 (Chinese traditional society and family), ed. Yanagida Setsuko sensei koki kinen ronshû henshû iinkai 柳田節子先生古稀記念論集編集委員會, 65–93. Tokyo: Kyûko shoin, 1993.

———. "In Search of Footbinding's Origins." In *Tang Song nüxing yu shehui* 唐宋女性與社會 (Tang-Song women and society), ed. Deng Xiaonan 鄧小南, 375–414. Shanghai: Shanghai cishu chubanshe, 2003.

———. *Teachers of the Inner Chambers: Women and Culture in Seventeenth-Century China.* Stanford, CA: Stanford University Press, 1994.

Kobayashi Tetsuyuki 小林徹行. *Mindai josei no junshi to bungaku. Haku Shōkun no Kofushi hakushu* 明代女性の殉死と文學。薄少君の哭夫詩百

首 (Women following their husband into death and their literature during the Ming dynasty. Bo Shaojun's *One Hundred Poems Lamenting My Husband*). Tokyo: Kyoko shoin, 2003.

Kong Pingzhong 孔平仲. *Xu Shishuo* 續世說 (Continuation of the *Shishuo*). *Guoxue jiben congshu* 國學基本叢書 ed. Shanghai: Shang wu yin shu guan, 1937.

———, et al. *Qingjiang san Kong ji* 清江三孔集 (Collected works of the three Kongs from Qingjiang). *Siku quanshu* ed., vol. 1345: 177–541.

Kuhn, Philip A., and John K. Fairbank, comp. *Introduction to Ch'ing Documents*, part one, vols. 1–2, rev. ed. Cambridge, MA: Harvard University, Harvard-Yenching Institute, 1993.

Lai Zehan 賴澤涵 et al. *"Ererba shijian" yanjiubaogao* 「二二八事件」研究報告 (Research report on the February Twentieth-Eighth Incident). Taibei: Shibao Wenhua, 1994.

Lan Dingyuan 藍鼎元. *Luzhou chuji* 鹿洲初集 (Collected works of Lan Dingyuan, first collection). *Siku quanshu* ed., vol. 1327. Taibei: Taiwan shangwu yinshuguan, 1983.

"Laodong yundong de fazhan yu cunzai de wenti" 劳动运动的发展与存在的问题 (Labor model movement development and problems). Shaanxi Provincial Archives 194-8 (Nongye ting), n.d. (ca. 1950–51), 194–98.

Lee, Leo Ou-Fan. "Literary Trends I: The Quest for Modernity, 1895–1927." *Republican China 1912–1949. Cambridge History of China*, 12.1, ed. John K. Fairbank, 452–504. Cambridge: Cambridge University Press, 1983.

Legge, James, trans. *The Chinese Classics*. 5 vols. Hong Kong: Hong Kong University Press, 1960.

———. *The Chinese Classics*. Vol. 3, *The Shoo King*. Hong Kong: Hong Kong University Press, 1960.

———. *Confucius: Confucian Analects, The Great Learning and the Doctrine of the Mean*. Rpt. New York: Dover, 1971.

Levine, Ari. "A House in Darkness: The Politics of History and the Language of Politics in the Late Northern Song, 1066–1104." Ph.D. dissertation, Columbia University, 2002.

Li, Chu-tsing. *A Thousand Peaks and Myriad Ravines: Chinese Paintings in the Charles A. Drenowatz Collection*. Artibus Asiae: Ascona, Switzerland, 1974.

Li Ciming 李慈銘. *Yuemantang wenji* 越縵堂文集 (Collected works from the Yueman Hall). Taibei: Wenhai chubanshe, 1975.

Li E 厲鶚. *Songshi jishi* 宋詩紀事 (Notes on Song poetry). *Siku quanshu* ed., vols. 1484–85. Taibei: Taiwan shangwu yinshuguan, 1983.

Li Fang 李昉. *Taiping guang ji* 太平廣記. 10 vols. Beijing: Zhonghua shuju, 1961.

Li Hua 李華. *Li Xiashu wenji* 李遐叔文集 (Collected works of Li Hua). *Siku quanshu* ed., vol. 1072. Taibei: Taiwan shangwu yinshuguan, 1983.

Li Kaixian 李開先. *Li Kaixian quanji* 李開先全集 (The complete collected works of Li Kaixian), ed. Bu Jian 卜鑑. Beijing: Wenhua yishu chubanshe, 2004.

Li Mengyang 李夢陽. *Kongtong ji* 空同集 (The collected works of Master Kongtong). *Siku quanshu zhenben* ed., 7th series, vols. 487–512. Taibei: Taiwan shangwu yinshuguan, 1978.

Li Qing 李清. *Nü Shishuo* 女世說 (Women's Shishuo). 4 *juan*. Comp. early 1650s, pub. early 1670s. Nanjing Library.

Li Wenzao 李文藻. *Nanjian wenji* 南澗文集 (Collected works of Li Wenzao). *Congshu jicheng xinbian* ed. Taibei: Xinwenfeng chuban gongsi, 1985.

Li Xiaojiang 李小江, ed. *Rong nuren ziji shuohua: Qingli zhanzheng* 讓女人自己說話:經歷戰爭 (Let women speak for themselves: Experiencing war). Beijing: SDX Joint Publishing Company, 2003.

Li Xiuwa李秀娃 (pseud.). Interview with Gao Xiaoxian and Gail Hershatter, August 9, 1996.

Li Zhi 李贄. *Chutan ji* 初潭集 (Collection on the pond). 2 vols. Beijing: Zhonghua shuju, 1974.

———. *Huang Song shichao gangyao* 皇宋十朝綱要 (Chronological history of the ten reigns of the Imperial Song). *Songshi ziliao cuibian* ed. Taibei: Wenhai chubanshe, 1967.

Liang Desheng 梁德繩. *Guchun xuan shichao* 古春軒詩鈔 (Transcribed poems of ancient spring studio, 1849), app. to an ed. of her late husband's collected writings, *Jianzhi shui zhai ji* 鑑止水齋集 (Collected poems of reflection in still water studio), 1819. Harvard-Yenching Library.

Lin Jingxi 林景熙. *Jishan wenji* 霽山文集 (Collected works of Lin Jingxi). *Siku quanshu* ed., vol. 1188. Taibei: Taiwan shangwu yinshuguan, 1983.

Little, Steven. *Taoism and the Arts of China*. Chicago: Art Institute of Chicago; Berkeley and Los Angeles: University of California Press, 2000.

Liu Dakui 劉大櫆. *Haifeng wenji* 海峰文集 (Collected works of Liu Dakui). *Xuxiu siku quanshu* ed. Shanghai: Shanghai guji chubanshe, 2002.

Liu Fengyun. "Liang Duan." In *Biographical Dictionary of Chinese Women: The Qing Period 1644–1911*, ed. Clara Ho, 127–28. Armonk, NY: M. E. Sharpe, 1998.

Liu Fu 劉斧. *Qingsuo gaoyi* 青瑣高議 (Elevated discourses of the ornamented galleries). Shanghai: Shanghai guji chubanshe, 1983.

Liu, James J. Y. *The Chinese Knight-Errant*. Chicago: Chicago University Press, 1967.

Liu, James T. C. "Yueh Fei (1103–41) and China's Heritage of Loyalty." *Journal of Asian Studies* 31.2 (1972): 291–97.

Liu Jingzhen 劉靜貞 [Liu Ching-chen]. "Liu Xiang *Lienü zhuan* de xingbie yishi" 劉向《列女傳》的性別意識 (Gender perspectives in Liu Xiang's *Biographies of Women*). *Dongwu lishi xuebao* 東吳歷史學報 5 (1999): 1–30.

———. "Ouyang Xiu bixia de songdai nüxing—duixiang wenlei yu shuxie qidai" 歐陽修筆下的宋代女性—對象、文類與書寫期待 (Images of Song women in the writing of Ou Yangxiu: Subject, genre, and writing expectation). *Taida lishi xuebao*台大歷史學報 (Bulletin of the Department of History of National Taiwan University) 32 (December 2003): 57–76.

———. "Shuxie yu shishi zhijian—*Wudaishiji* zhong de nüxing xiang" 書寫與

事實之間—《五代史記》中的女性像 (Between writing and reality: Female images in *Wudaishiji*). *Zhongguo shixue* 中國史學 (Chinese history) 12 (October 2002): 51–64.

Liu Kezhuang 劉克莊. *Houcun xiansheng da quanji* 後村先生大全集. *Sibu congkan* ed. Shanghai: Shangwu yinshuguan, 1922.

Liu Su 劉肅. *Da Tang xinyu* 大唐新語 (New account of the Great Tang). Beijing: Zhonghua shuju, 1984.

Liu Taigong 劉台拱. *Liu Duanlin xiansheng yishu* 劉端臨先生遺書 (Bequeathed works of Liu Taigong). Rpt 1889. *Congshu jinghua* ed. Taibei: Yiwen yinshushe, 1970.

Liu Xiang 劉向. *Gu Lienü zhuan* 古列女傳 (Ancient biographies of exemplary women). *Congshu jicheng jianbian* ed. Taibei: Taiwan shangwu yinshuguan, 1966.

———. *Lienü zhuan jinzhu jinyi* 列女傳今註今譯 (Newly annotated and translated [ed. of the] *Biographies of Women*), ann., trans., and ed. Zhang Jing 張敬. Taibei: Taiwan shangwu yinshuguan, 1994.

Liu Xu 劉昫 et al. *Jiu Tangshu* 舊唐書 (Old history of the Tang). 16 vols. Beijing: Zhonghua shuju, 1975.

Liu Yan 劉弇. *Longyun ji* 龍雲集 (Collected works of Liu Yan). *Siku quanshu* ed., vol. 1119. Taibei: Taiwan shangwu yinshuguan, 1983.

Liu Yiqing 劉義慶. *Shishuo xinyu [jianshu]* 世說新語[箋疏] ([Commentary on] A new account of tales of the world). 2 vols. Commentary by Yu Jiaxi 余嘉錫. Shanghai: Shanghai guji chubanshe, 1993.

Liu Zhaofeng刘招凤(pseud.). Interview with Gail Hershatter, August 13, 1996.

Liu Zhiji 劉知幾. *Shitong [tongshi]*史通通釋 [(Commentary on) the compendium of history]. 2 vols. Commentary by Pu Qilong 浦起龍. Shanghai: Shanghai guji chubanshe, 1978.

Lo Jiu-jung 羅久蓉, Yu Chien-ming 游鑑明 (interviewer), and Chiu Hui-jun 丘慧君 et al. (recorders). *Fenghuo suiyue xia de Zhongguo funü fangwen jilu* 烽火歲月下的中國婦女訪問紀錄 (Twentieth century wartime experiences of Chinese women: An oral history). Taibei: Institute of Modern History, Academia Sinica, 2004.

Lo Yuet Keung 勞悅強 [Lao Yueqiang]. "Filial Devotion for Women: A Buddhist Testimony from Third-Century China." In *Filial Piety in Chinese Thought and History*, ed. Alan K. L. Chan and Sor-hoon Tan, 71–90. London and New York: Routledge, 2004.

———. "Zhen shun—Liu Xiang *Lienü zhuan* zhong de qizi" 貞順—劉向《列女傳》中的妻子 (Rectitude and compliance: Wives in Liu Xiang's *Biographies of women*). In *Qin Han sixiang wenhua yanjiu* 秦漢思想文化研究 (Research into thought and culture of the Qin-Han era), ed. Xiong Tieji 熊鐵基 and Zhao Guohua 趙國華, 355–75. Singapore: Hope Publishing House, 2005.

Lorge, Peter. "The Northern Song Military Aristocracy and the Royal Family." *War and Society* 18.2 (2000): 37–47.

Lowry, Kathryn. "Duplicating the Strength of Feeling: The Circulation of *Qingshu* in the Late Ming." In *Writing and Materiality in China: Essays in Honor of Patrick Hanan*, ed. Judith T. Zeitlin and Lydia H. Liu, 239–72. Cambridge, MA: Harvard University Press, 2003.

———. "Editing, Annotating, and Evaluating Letters at the Turn of the Seventeenth Century: Instituting Literary Forms for the Self." In *Zhongguo wenxue pingdian yanjiu lunji* 中国文学评点研究论集 (Essays in research on Chinese literary criticism), ed. Zhang Peiheng 章培恒 and Wang Jingyu 王靖宇 (John Wang), 101–28. Shanghai: Shanghai guji chubanshe, 2002.

———. "Personal Letters in Seventeenth-Century Epistolary Guides." In *Under Confucian Eyes: Women and Gender in Chinese History*, ed. Susan Mann and Yu-yin Cheng, 155–68. Berkeley and Los Angeles: University of California Press, 2001.

———. "Three Ways to Read a Love Letter in Late Ming." *Ming Studies* 44 (2000): 48–77.

Lü Fang-shang 呂芳上."Lingyizhong 'weizuzhi': Kangzhan shiqi hunyin yu jiating wenti chutan" 另一種「偽組織」:抗戰時期婚姻與家庭問題初探 (Another "fake organization": Marriage and family problems during the Sino-Japanese war). *Jindai Zhongguo funü yanjiu* 近代中國婦女史研究 (Research on women in modern Chinese history) 3 (August 1995): 97–121.

Lu Guilan 鲁桂兰. Interview with Gail Hershatter, August 15, 1996.

Lü Kun 呂坤. *Yingyin Mingke guifan* 影印明刻閨範 (Facs. of Ming ed. of *Female Exemplars*). 4 juan. Huizhou, 1617. Rpt. n.p.: Jiangning wei shi, 1927.

Lü Nan'gong 呂南公. *Guan yuan ji* 灌園集 (Collected works of Lü Nan'gong). *Siku quanshu* ed., vol. 1123. Taibei: Taiwan shangwu yinshuguan, 1983.

Lu Shen 陸深. *Yanshan waiji* 儼山外集 (Writings of Lu Shen, recent collection). *Siku quanshu* ed., vol. 883. Taibei: Taiwan shangwu yinshuguan, 1983.

Lu, Weijing. *True to Her Word: The Faithful Maiden Cult in Late Imperial China*. Stanford, CA: Stanford University Press, 2008.

———. "Uxorilocal Marriage among Qing Literati." *Late Imperial China* 19.2 (December 1998): 64–110.

Lu Xun 魯迅. "Kuangren riji" 狂人日記 (The madman's diary). [1918.] Rpt. in *Selected Stories of Lu Hsun*, trans. Yang Hsien-yi and Gladys Yang, 8–15. Beijing: Foreign Languages Press, 1960, 1972.

———. *Lu Xun quanji* 鲁迅全集 (The complete works of Lu Xun), vols. 1–18. Beijing: Renmin wenxue chubanshe, 2005.

———."Wo zhi jielie guan" 我之節烈觀 (My views on chastity). *Xin qingnian* 新青年 5.2 (August 15, 1918): 92–101.

Lü Zuqian 呂祖謙. *Song wen jian* 宋文鑑 (Mirror on Song literature). *Siku quanshu* ed., vols. 1350–51. Taibei: Taiwan shangwu yinshuguan, 1983.

Lufei Bohong 陸費伯鴻. "Lun Zhongguo jiaokeshu shishu" 論中國教科書史書 (A history of Chinese textbooks). In *Zhongguo jinxiandai chuban shiliao* 中國近現代出版史料 (Historical sources of modern and contemporary Chinese publishing), ed. Zhang Jinglu, vol. 1: 212–14. Rpt. Shanghai: Shanghai shudian chubanshe, 2003.

MacFarquhar, Roderick. *The Great Leap Forward 1958–1960: The Origins of the Cultural Revolution*, vol. 2. New York: Columbia University Press, 1983.

Mann, Susan. "Biographies of Exemplary Women [Selected by Wanyan Yun Zhu]." In *Reader of Traditional Chinese Culture*, ed. Victor Mair, 607–13. Honolulu: University of Hawaiʻi Press, 2005.

———. "Historical Change in Female Biography from Song to Qing Times: The Case of Early Qing Jiangnan." *Transactions of the International Conference of Orientalists in Japan* 30 (1985): 65–77.

——— (Man Suen 曼素恩). "Jiuzhong zhuanji: Jindai diguo rujia huoyu zhong de nüxing" 九种传记:近代帝国儒家话语中的女性 (Nine biographical types: Women in the [late] imperial Confucian discourse). In *Zhongguo xueshu yu Zhongguo sixiang shi* 中国学术与中国思想史 (Chinese scholarship and Chinese intellectual history), ed. Gong Bendong 巩本栋 et al., 121–32. Nanjing: Jiangsu jiaoyu chubanshe, 2002.

———. *Precious Records, Women in China's Long Eighteenth Century*. Stanford, CA: Stanford University Press, 1997.

———. *The Talented Women of the Zhang Family*. Berkeley and Los Angeles: University of California Press, 2007.

———. "Widows in the Kinship, Class and Community Structure of Qing Dynasty China." *Journal of Asian Studies* 46.1: 37–56.

———. "Women in the Life and Thought of Zhang Xuecheng." In *Chinese Language, Thought, and Culture: Nivison and His Critics*, ed. Philip J. Ivanhoe, 98–105. Chicago: Open Court Press, 1996.

Mann, Susan, and Yu-Yin Cheng, eds. *Under Confucian Eyes: Writings on Gender in Chinese History*. Berkeley and Los Angeles: University of California Press, 2001.

Mao Qiling 毛奇龄. *Xihe wenji* 西河文集 (Collected works of Mao Qiling). *Guoxue jiben congshu* ed. Taiwan: Shangwu yinshuguan, 1968.

Margadant, Jo Burr. "Introduction: The New Biography in Historical Practice." *French Historical Studies* 19.4, special issue, *Biography* (autumn 1996):1045–58.

———, ed. *The New Biography: Performing Femininity in Nineteenth-Century France*. Berkeley and Los Angeles: University of California Press, 2000.

Martin-Liao, Tienchi. "Traditional Handbooks of Women's Education." In *Women and Literature in China*, ed. Anna Gerstlacher et al., 165–89. Bochum: Brockmeyer, 1985.

Marwick, Arthur. *War and Social Change in the Twentieth Century*. London: Macmillan,1974.

———, ed. *Total War and Social Change*. New York: St. Martin's Press, 1988.

Mather, Richard B., trans. *A New Account of Tales of the World*. Minneapolis: University of Minnesota Press, 1976.

McLaren, Anne E. *Chinese Popular Culture and Ming Chantefables*. Leiden: Brill, 1998.

McMahon, Keith. *Misers, Shrews, and Polygamists: Sexuality and Male-Female Relations in Eighteenth-Century Chinese Fiction*. Durham, NC: Duke University Press, 1995.

Meijer, M. J. "The Price of a P'ai-lou." *T'oung Pao* 67.3–5 (1981): 288–304.

Meyer-Fong, Tobie. *Building Culture in Early Qing Yangzhou*. Stanford, CA: Stanford University Press, 2003.

Min Erchang 閔爾昌, comp. *Beizhuan ji bu* 碑傳集補 (Collected eulogies from stele inscriptions, supplement). 1931. Rpt. Taibei: Wenhai chubanshe, 1973.

Ming Chenghua shuochang cihua congkan: Shiliu zhong, fu Baitu ji chuanqi yi zhong 明成化說唱詞話叢刊 十六種附白兔記傳奇一種 (Sixteen Ming Chenghua prose-verse narratives, with the *chuanqi* play "White Rabbit" appended). Shanghai shiwenwu baoguan weiyuanhui, Shanghai Museum, 1973.

Ming Qing Women's Writings Digitization Project (McGill-Harvard website). http://digital.library.mcgill.ca/mingqing/.

Moloughney, Brian. "From Biographical History to Historical Biography: A Transformation in Chinese Historical Writing." *East Asian History* 4 (1992): 1–30.

Mou, Sherry J. *Gentlemen's Prescriptions for Women's Lives: A Thousand Years of Biographies of Chinese Women*. Armonk, NY: M. E. Sharpe, 2004.

———. "Writing Virtues with Their Bodies: Rereading the Two Tang Histories' Biographies of Women." In *Presence and Presentation: Women in the Chinese Literati Tradition*, ed. Sherry J. Mou, 109–47. Basingstoke: Macmillan, 1999.

Nivison, David S. "Aspects of Traditional Chinese Biography." *Journal of Asian Studies* 21.4 (August 1962): 457–63.

Nomura Ayuko 野村鮎子. "Ming Qing nüxing shouxu kao" 明清女性壽序考 (Prefaces to birthday greetings for women in the Ming-Qing period). In *Ming Qing wenxue yu xingbie yanjiu* 明清文學與性別研究 (Literature and gender in Ming-Qing China), ed. Zhang Hongsheng 張宏生, 19–33. Nanjing: Jiangsu guji chubanshe, 2002.

Nongye ting 农业厅 (Agricultural Bureau) Archives. Shaanxi Provincial Archives.

Nylan, Michael. "A Problematic Model: The Han 'Orthodox Synthesis,' Then and Now." In *Imagining Boundaries: Changing Confucian Doctrines, Texts, and Hermeneutics*, ed. Kai-wing Chow, On-cho Ng, and John B. Henderson, 17–56. Albany: State University of New York Press, 1999.

Ocko, Jonathan. "Interpretive Communities: Legal Meaning in Qing Law." In *Writing and Law in Late Imperial China: Crime, Conflict, and Judgment*, ed. Robert E. Hegel and Katherine Carlitz, 261–83. Seattle: University of Washington Press, 2007.

Oertling, Sewall Jerome. "Ting Yun-peng: A Chinese Artist of the Late Ming Dynasty." Ph.D. dissertation, University of Michigan, 1980.

O'Hara, Albert Richard. *The Position of Woman in Early China According to the Lieh Nü Chuan "The Biographies of Eminent Chinese Women*. Washington: Catholic University of America Press, 1945. Rpt. Taibei: Meiya Publishing, 1971.

Ouyang Xiu 歐陽修 et al. *Xin Tangshu* 新唐書 (New history of the Tang). 20 vols. Beijing: Zhonghua shuju, 1975.

Owen, Stephen. *The End of the Chinese "Middle Ages": Essays in Mid-Tang Literary Culture*. Stanford, CA: Stanford University Press, 1996.

――――. *Remembrances: The Experience of the Past in Classical Chinese Literature*. Cambridge, MA: Harvard University Press, 1986.

Ōyane Bunjirō 大矢根文次郎. *Sesetsu shingo to rikuchō bungaku* 世說新語と六朝文學 (*Shishuo xinyu* and Six Dynasties literature). Tokyo: Waseda University Press, 1983.

Pattinson, David. "The Chidu in Late Ming and Early Qing China." Ph.D. dissertation, Australian National University, 1998.

Peng Yulian 彭玉鱗 and Yin Jiajun 殷家儁, comp. *Hunan sheng Hengyang xianzhi san* 湖南省衡陽縣志三 (Hunan Province, Hengyang County gazetteer, vol. 3) (1872). Rpt. in *Zhongguo fangzhi congshu, Huadong difang, diyiyisan hao* 中國方志叢書華東地方第一一三號 (Compendium of Chinese gazetteers, South China, no. 113). Taibei: Zhengwen chubanshe, 1970.

Polachek, James M. *The Inner Opium War*. Cambridge, MA: Council on East Asian Studies Publications, Harvard University Press, 1992.

Qian Daxin 錢大昕. *Qian Daxin quanji* 錢大昕全集 (Complete works of Qian Daxin). Nanjing: Jiangsu guji chubanshe, 1997.

Qian, Nanxiu. "'Borrowing Foreign Mirrors and Candles to Illuminate Chinese Civilization': Xue Shaohui's Moral Vision in the *Biographies of Foreign Women*." *Nan Nü: Men, Women and Gender in China* 6.1 (2004): 60–101.

――――. "Milk and Scent: Works about Women in the *Shishuo xinyu* genre." *Nan Nü: Men, Women and Gender in Early and Imperial China* 1.2 (fall 1999): 187–236.

――――. *Spirit and Self in Medieval China: The Shih-shuo hsin-yü and Its Legacy*. Honolulu: University of Hawai'i Press, 2001.

Qian Shoupu 錢守璞. *Nüshi xiu folou shigao* 女士繡佛樓詩稿 (Draft poems of the woman of the embroidered Buddha tower). 1869. Harvard-Yenching Library.

Qian Yiji 錢儀吉, comp. *Bei zhuan ji* 碑傳集 (A collection of epitaphs and biographies). Taibei: Wenhai chubanshe, 1973.

Qiantang zhuren 錢塘主人 (Jiantang 鑑塘, Yan Xiyuan 顏希源), ed. *Baimei xin yongtu zhuan* 百美新詠圖傳 (New verses and illustrations of one hundred beauties). Prefaces dated 1787, 1790. Rpt. Taibei: Guangwen shuju, 1970.

Qin Guan 秦觀. *Huai hai ji* 淮海集 (Collected works of Qin Guan). *Guoxue jiben congshu* ed. Shanghai: Shangwu yinshuguan, 1936.

Qiu Jin 秋瑾. "The Man of Qi Fears Heaven's Collapse." Trans. Chia-lin Pao Tao. In *Women Writers of Traditional China: An Anthology of Poetry and Criticism*, ed. Kang-i Sun Chang and Haun Saussy, 638. Stanford, CA: Stanford University Press, 1999.

———. *Qiu Jin ji* 秋瑾集 (Collection of Qiu Jin's works). Shanghai: Zhonghua shuju, 1960, 1962.

———. *Qiu Jin shiji* 秋瑾史迹 (Historical traces of Qiu Jin). Shanghai: Zhonghua shuju, 1958.

Quan Song shi 全宋詩 (Complete poems of the Song dynasty). Beijing: Beijing daxue chubanshe, 1995.

Rankin, Mary Backus. *Early Chinese Revolutionaries: Radical Intellectuals in Shanghai and Chekiang, 1902–1911.* Cambridge, MA: Harvard University Press, 1971.

———. "The Emergence of Women at the End of Ch'ing: The Case of Ch'iu Chin." In *Women in Chinese Society,* ed. Margery Wolf and Roxane Witke, 39–66. Stanford, CA: Stanford University Press, 1975.

Raphals, Lisa. "Reflections on Filiality, Nature, and Nurture." In *Filial Piety in Chinese Thought and History,* ed. Alan K. L. Chan and Sor-hoon Tan, 215–25. London and New York: Routledge, 2004.

———. *Sharing the Light: Representations of Women and Virtue in Early China.* Albany: State University of New York Press, 1998.

"Retsujo den kei shiryō tansaku" 列女伝系史料探索 (A survey of historical documents in the genre of the *Biographies of Women*). http://www1.enjoy.ne.jp/~nagaichi/retsujo01.html.

Reynolds, Douglas R. *China, 1898–1912: The Xinzheng Revolution and Japan.* Cambridge, MA: Council on East Asian Studies Publications, Harvard University Press, 1993.

Robertson, Maureen. "Changing the Subject: Gender and Self-Inscription in Author's Prefaces and 'Shi' Poetry." In *Writing Women in Late Imperial China,* ed. Ellen Widmer and K'ang-i Sun Chang, 171–217. Stanford, CA: Stanford University Press, 1997.

Ropp, Paul S., Paola Zamperini, and Harriet T. Zurndorfer, eds. *Passionate Women: Female Suicide in Late Imperial China.* Leiden: Brill, 2001.

Ruan Yuan 阮元, ed. *Shisan jing zhushu* 十三經註疏 (Commentaries on the thirteen Chinese classics). 2 vols. Rpt. of 1816 ed. Beijing: Zhonghua shuju, 1979.

Seeley, David. 1990. *The Noble Death: Graeco-Roman Martyrology and Paul's Concept of Salvation.* Sheffield: Sheffield Academic Press, 1990.

Seo Tatsuhiko 妹尾达彦. "Caizi yu jiaren—jiu shiji Zhongguo xing de nannü renshi de xing"'才子與佳人'—九世紀中國姓的男女認識的形 (Man of talent and beautiful lady: Creating a new relationship between men and women in ninth-century China). In *Tang Song nüxing yu shehui* 唐宋女性與社會 (Tang-Song women and society), ed. Deng Xiaonan 鄧小南, 695–721. Shanghai: Shanghai cishu chubanshe. 2003.

Shaanxi Provincial Archives. Xi'an.

Shaanxi ribao 陝西日报 (Shaanxi Daily). Xi'an. 1958–59.

Shaanxi sheng minzhu funü lianhehui 陝西省民主妇女联合会 (Shaanxi Provincial Democratic Women's Federation), ed. *Shaanxi sheng funü miantian guanli jingyan jiaoliu dahui zhuanji* 陝西省妇女棉田管理经验交流大

会专集 (Special collection on the Shaanxi Province women's meeting to exchange experiences of cotton field management). N.p. [Xi'an]: Shaanxi sheng minzhu funü lianhehui, May 1956.

Shaanxi sheng nonglin ting 陕西省农林厅, ed. *Jiuyuan nüjiang wumian liqi gong: Weinan xian Shuangwang xiang Bali dian she Zhang Qiuxiang wumian xiaozu jingyan* 九员女将务棉立奇功: 渭南县双王乡八里店社张秋香务棉小组经验 (The immediate outstanding service of nine women commanders growing cotton: The experience of Zhang Qiuxiang's cotton growing group in Bali dian, Shuang Wang Township, Weinan County). Xi'an: Shaanxi renmin chubanshe, April1958.

Shaanxi sheng nongye zhanlanhui 陕西省农业展览会, ed. *Mianhua fengchan yimian hongqi: Weinan xian Zhang Qiuxiang zhimian xiaozu* 棉花丰产一面红旗: 渭南县张秋香植棉小组 (A red flag in the cotton bumper crop: Zhang Qiuxiang's cotton growing group in Weinan County). N.p., November 1958.

Shan Xiuzhen 山秀珍. Interview with Gao Xiaoxian and Gail Hershatter, June 28–29, 1997.

Shan Xiuzhen, guangrong de wuchan jieji zhanshi: Jiceng funü ganbu xuexi ziliao 山秀珍, 光荣的无产阶级战士:基层妇女干部学习资料 (Shan Xiuzhen, glorious proletarian fighter: Study material for grassroots women's cadres). Pamphlet. N.p.: Shaanxi Fulian ying, 1962, Fulian archives 178-313-001.

Shen Cheng 沈承. *Mao Ruchu xiansheng pingxuan Jishan ji liujuan fu fuke yijuan* 毛孺初先生評選即山集六卷附附刻一卷 (The collected writings of Jishan in six scrolls, annotated and selected by Master Mao Ruchu; with an appendix in one scroll). Woodblock ed., 1626. *Siku jinhui shu congkan*, vol. 41.

Shen Shanbao 沈善寶. *Hongxuelou chuji* 鴻雪樓初集 (First collection of Hongxue tower). 1836. National Library of China.

———. *Mingyuan shihua* 名媛詩話 (Poetry talks on famous women). 1845. Beijing Library.

Shen Yue 沈約. *Songshu* 宋書 (History of the [Liu-]Song). 8 vols. Beijing: Zhonghua shuju, 1974.

Shi Shuyi 施淑仪. *Qingdai guige shiren zhenglüe* 清代闺阁诗人征略 (An overview of Qing Dynasty female poets). Shanghai: Shanghai shudian, 1987.

Shi Yunyu 石韞玉. *Duxuelu yugao* 獨學盧餘稿 (More drafts from learning alone cottage). *Xuxiu siku quanshu*, vol. 1467. Shanghai: Shanghai guji chubanshe, 1995–99.

Shibao 時報 ("The Eastern Times"). Shanghai, 1904–39.

Sima Guang 司馬光. *Sima Wen zhenggong chuanjia ji* 司馬文正公傳家集 (Collected works of Sima Guang as passed down in his family). Wanyou wenku huiyao ed. Taibei: Taiwan shangwu yinshuguan, 1965.

Sima Qian 司馬遷. *The Grand Scribe's Records.* 7 vols. Ed. William H. Nienhauser Jr. Bloomington: Indiana University Press, 1994–2006.

———. *Shiji* 史記 (Records of the Grand Historian). Beijing: Zhonghua shuju, 1959.

———. "Tian Dan liezhuan" 田單列傳 (Biography of Tian Dan). In *Shiji* 史記 (Records of the Grand Historian), *juan* 82, 8: 2457. Beijing: Zhonghua shuju, 1959.

———. "T'ien Tan lieh-chuan" (Biography of Tian Dan). In *Shiji* (Records of the Grand Historian), trans. Burton Watson, 245–51. New York: Columbia University Press, 1964.

Siren, Osvald. *Chinese Painting: Leading Masters and Principles.* 7 vols. New York: Ronald Press, 1958.

Smith, Harold L. *Britain in the Second World War: A Social History.* Manchester: Manchester University Press, 1996.

Smith, Kidder, Jr., et al. *Sung Dynasty Uses of the I Ching.* Princeton, NJ: Princeton University Press, 1990.

Sommer, Matthew H. *Sex, Law, and Society in Late Imperial China.* Stanford, CA: Stanford University Press, 2000.

Song Lian 宋濂 et al. *Yuanshi* 元史 (History of the Yuan Dynasty). 15 vols. Beijing: Zhonghua shuju, 1976.

Song Meidong 宋梅洞. *Jiao hong zhuan* 嬌紅傳. In *Gudai wenyan duanpian xiaoshuo xuan ji* 古代文言短篇小說選集 (Classical-language short fiction from former eras), ed. Cheng Boquan 成柏泉, 280–323. Shanghai: Shanghai guji chubanshe, 1984.

St. André, James. "Reading Court Cases from the Song and the Ming: Fact and Fiction, Law and Literature." In *Writing and Law in Late Imperial China: Crime, Conflict, and Judgment,* ed. Robert E. Hegel and Katherine Carlitz, 189–214. Seattle: University of Washington Press, 2007.

Su Shi 蘇軾 (Dongpo 東坡). *Dongpo yuefu biannian jianzhu* 東坡樂府編年箋注 (The song lyrics of Su Shi, chronologically arranged and fully annotated), ed. Shi Shenghuai 石聲淮 and Tang Lingling 唐玲玲. Wuchang: Huazhong shifan daxue chubanshe, 1990.

———. *Su Shi wenji* 蘇軾文集 (Collected essays of Su Shi). 6 vols. Beijing: Zhonghua shuju, 1986.

Summerfield, Penny. *Reconstructing Women's Wartime Lives: Discourse and Subjectivity in Oral Histories of the Second World War.* Manchester: Manchester University Press, 1998.

Sun Qifeng 孫奇逢. *Xiafeng xiansheng ji* 夏峰先生集 (Collected works of Sun Qifeng). *Congshu jicheng xinbian* ed. Taibei: Xinwenfeng chuban gongsi, 1985.

Sun Wenguang 孙文光, ed. *Zhongguo jindai wenxue da cidian* 中国近代文学大辞典 (Dictionary of modern Chinese literature). Hefei, Anhui: Huangshan shushe, 1995.

Sung, Marina H. "Chen Duansheng." In *Biographical Dictionary of Chinese Women: The Qing Period 1644–1911,* ed. Clara Ho, 16–18. Armonk, NY: M. E. Sharpe, 1998.

———. "The Chinese Lieh-nü Tradition." *Historical Reflections* 8.3 (1981): 63–74.

Swann, Nancy Lee. *Pan Chao: Foremost Woman Scholar of China*. 1932. Rpt. Ann Arbor: Center for Chinese Studies, University of Michigan 2001.

Tan, Christine C. Y. "Prints, Seriality, and *Baimeitu* (Pictures of one hundred beauties) in Nineteenth Century China." Unpublished paper.

Tang Yaoqing 湯瑤卿. *Pengshi ouyin* 蓬室偶吟 (Casual rhymes from a modest cottage). In *Wanlin shi wen* 宛鄰詩文 (Poetry and prose from the Wanlin Studio), comp. Zhang Qi 張琦. 1840. Rpt. 1891.

Teiser, Stephen F. *The Scripture on the Ten Kings and the Making of Purgatory in Medieval Chinese Buddhism*. Honolulu: University of Hawai'i Press, 1994.

ter Haar, B. J. *The White Lotus Teaching in Chinese Religious History*. Leiden: Brill, 1992.

Theiss, Janet M. *Disgraceful Matters: The Politics of Chastity in Eighteenth-Century China*. Berkeley and Los Angeles: University of California Press, 2004.

———. "Explaining the Shrew: Narratives of Spousal Violence and the Critique of Masculinity in Eighteenth-Century Criminal Cases." In *Writing and Law in Late Imperial China: Crime, Conflict, and Judgment*, ed. Robert E. Hegel and Katherine Carlitz, 44–63. Seattle: University of Washington Press, 2007.

———. "Managing Martyrdom: Female Suicide and Statecraft in Mid-Qing China." *Nan Nü: Men, Women and Gender in Early and Imperial China* 3.1 (2001): 47–76.

Tian Han quanji 田汉全集 (Complete works of Tian Han). Shijiazhuang: Huashan wenyi chubanshe, 2000.

T'ien Ju-K'ang. *Male Anxiety and Female Chastity*. Leiden: Brill, 1988.

Tsai, Kathryn Ann. *Lives of the Nuns: Biographies of Chinese Buddhist Nuns from the Fourth to Sixth Centuries: A Translation of the* Pi-ch'iu-ni chuan. Honolulu: University of Hawai'i Press, 1994.

Tsunoda Ken 角田簡 (Tsunoda Kyūka角田九華). *Kinsei sōgo* 近世叢語 (Accounts of recent times). 8 *juan*, 4 vols. Tokyo: Shorin 書林, 1828.

———. *Shoku Kinsei sōgo* 續近世叢語 (Continued accounts of recent times). 8 *juan*, 4 vols. Tokyo: Shorin, 1845.

Tu Long 屠隆. *Bai yu ji* 白榆集 (White elm collection). Taibei: Liaowen dushu chubanshe, 1977.

Tuotuo 脫脫 et al. *Liao shi* 遼史 (History of the Liao Dynasty). 5 vols. Beijing: Zhonghua shuju, 1974.

———. *Song shi* 宋史 (History of the Song Dynasty). 40 vols. Beijing: Zhonghua shuju, 1985.

Twichett, Dennis. "Problems of Chinese Biography." In *Confucian Personalities*, ed. Arthur Wright and Denis Twitchett, 24–39. Stanford, CA: Stanford University Press, 1962.

Valussi, Elena. "Beheading the Red Dragon: A History of Female Alchemy in China." Ph.D. dissertation, School of Oriental and African Studies, University of London, 2003.

———. "Men and Women in He Longxiang's *Nüdan hebian*." *Nan Nü: Men, Women and Gender in China* 10.2 (2008): 242–78.

Van Ess, Hans. "Praise and Slander: The Evocation of Empress Lü in the *Shiji* and the *Hanshu*." *Nan Nü: Men, Women and Gender in China* 8.2 (2006): 221–54.

Waltner, Ann. "Remembering the Lady Wei: Eulogy and Commemoration in Ming Dynasty China." *Ming Studies* 55 (2007): 75–103.

———. Review of Susan Mann, *The Talented Women of the Zhang Family*. *Journal of Chinese Studies* 49 (2009): 37–41.

———. "T'an-yang-tzu and Wang Shih-chen: Visionary and Bureaucrat in Late Ming China." *Late Imperial China* 8.1 (1987): 105–33.

Wang Bi ji [jiaoshi] 王弼集校釋(Collated annotation of Wang Bi's works). Ed., coll., comm. by Lou Yulie 樓宇烈. 2 vols. Beijing: Zhonghua shuju, 1980.

Wang Cheng 王偁. *Dongdu shilüe* 東都事略 (Résumé of events of the Eastern Capital). *Songshi ziliao cuibian* ed. Taibei: Wenhai chubanshe, 1967.

Wang Dang 王讜. *Tang yulin* 唐語林 (Tang forest of accounts). 8 *juan*. Shanghai: Shanghai guji chubanshe, 1978.

Wang Duan 汪端. *Ming sanshi jia shixuan* 明三十家詩還 (Selected writings of thirty Ming writers). 1822. Rpt. 1873. Harvard-Yenching Library.

———. *Ziran haoxue zhai ji* 自然好學齋集 (Collected writings of Natural Love of Learning Studio). In *Linxia yayinji* 林下雅音集 (Collected elegant sounds of women), ed. Mao Jun 冒俊. Rugao Maoshi kanben,1884.

———. *Ziran haoxue zhai shi* 自然好學齋詩 (Poems of Natural Love of Learning Studio). Hangzhou: Wangshi Zhenqi tang, 1839.

Wang Duanshu 王端淑. *Mingyuan shi wei* 名媛詩緯 (Classics of poetry by famous women). 1667. Beijing University Library.

Wang Hsiao-po 王曉波 ed. *Ererba zhenxiang* 二二八真相 (The truth about the February 28th Incident). 2nd ed. Taibei: Haxia xueshu chubanshe, 2002.

Wang Jiusi 王九思. *Meipi ji* 渼陂集 (The collected works of Master Meipi). *Mingdai lun zhu congkan* ed. Taibei: Weiwen tushu chubanshe, 1976.

Wang Ling 王令. *Guangling ji* 廣陵集 (Collected works of Wang Ling). *Siku quanshu* ed., vol. 1106. Taibei: Taiwan shangwu yinshuguan, 1983.

Wang Meihua 王梅花 (pseud.). Interview with Gao Xiaoxian and Gail Hershatter, August 9, 1996.

Wang Ming-ke 王明珂. "Shei delishi: Zizhuan, zhuanji yu koshu lishi de shehui jiyi benzhi" 誰的歷史:自傳、傳記與口述歷史的社會記憶本質 (Whose history: Autobiography, biography, and oral history's essence in social memories). *Thought and Words* 思與言 *(Journal of the Humanities and Social Science)* 34.3 (September 1996): 147–83.

Wang Pu 王溥 (922–982). *Tang huiyao* 唐會要 (Essentials of the Tang). Beijing: Zhonghua shuju, 1998.

Wang Qubing 王去病 and Chen Dehe 陈德和, eds. *Qiu Jin nianbiao: Xibian* 秋瑾年表细编 (Detailed chronological biography of Qiu Jin). Beijing: Huawen chubanshe, 1990.

———. *Qiu Jin shiji* 秋瑾史集 (Collected historical material on Qiu Jin). Beijing: Huawen chubanshe, 1989.

Wang, Richard G. "The Cult of *Qing*: Romanticism in the Late Ming Period and in the Novel *Jiao Hong Ji.*" *Ming Studies* 33 (August 1994): 12–55.

Wang, Robin. *Images of Women in Chinese Thought and Culture: Writings from the Pre-Qin Period through the Song Dynasty.* Indianapolis: Hackett Publishing, 2003.

———. "Virtue, Talent, and Beauty: Authoring a Full-Fledged Womanhood in *Lienüzhuan* (Biographies of Women)." In *Confucian Cultures of Authority*, ed. Peter D. Herschhock and Roger T. Ames, 93–115. Albany, NY: State University of New York Press, 2006.

Wang Shizhen 王世貞. *Shishuo xinyu bu* 世說新語補 (Supplement to the *Shishuo xinyu*). 20 *juan*. Wang Shizhen's preface 1556. Chang Wen-chu 張文柱, 1585. Beijing Library, Library of Congress Collection.

———. *Yanzhou shanren sibu gao* 弇州山人四部稿 (Writings of Yanzhou Shanren, in four categories). Taibei: Weiwen tushuguan chubanshe, 1976.

———. *Yanzhou shanren xugao* 弇州山人續稿 (Writings of Yanzhou Shanren, continued). Taibei: Wenhai chubanshe, 1970.

Wang Shuizhao 王水照, ann. *Su Shi xuanji* 蘇軾選集 (An anthology of Su Shi). Shanghai: Shanghai guji chubanshe, 1984.

Wang Wan 汪琬. *Yaofeng wenchao* 堯峰文鈔 (Selected writings of Wang Wan). *Sibu congkan* ed. Shanghai: Shangwu yinshuguan, 1929.

"Wang Xianshi yiyan tu yikai" 王仙師遺言圖一開 (A picture of Immortal Teacher Wang writing her final words, one album). N.d. Palace Museum, Beijing.

Wang Xiuqin 王秀琴 and Hu Wenkai 胡文楷. *Lidai mingyuan wenyuan jianbian* 歷代 名媛文苑簡編 (Basic primer of prose works of famous women through the ages). Shanghai: Shangwu yinshuguan, 1947.

Wang Yaochen 王堯臣. *Chongwen zongmu: Fu bu yi* 崇文總目附補遺 (Chongwen general catalogue: Appendix of omissions). Shanghai: Shangwu yinshuguan, 1937.

Wang Zhaoyuan 王照圓. *Lienü zhuan buzhu* 列女傳補注 (Commentary on the *Lienü zhuan*). *Haoshi yishu* 郝氏遺書, ce 14–15. 1879. *Xuxiu Siku quanshu*, ce 515. Shanghai: Shanghai guji chubanshe, 1995–99.

———. *Lienü zhuan buzhu* 列女傳補注 (Commentary on the *Lienü zhuan*). *Guoxue jiben congshu* 國學基本叢書. Shanghai: Shangwu yinshuguan, 1937. Rpt. Taibei: Xinxing shuju, 1964.

Wang Zhenda 汪振甡. Preface to Wei Xiyuan 魏息園, *Buyong xing shenpan shu gushi xuan* 不用刑審判书故事选 (Selected stories of trials that did not resort to the use of torture), ed. Wang Zhenda, 1–7. Shanxi: Qunzhong chubanshe, 1987.

Wang Zhiwang 王之望. *Han bin ji* 漢濱集 (Collected works of Wang Zhiwang). *Siku quanshu* ed., vol. 1139. Taibei: Taiwan shangwu yinshuguan, 1983.

Wang Zhong 汪中. *Shuxue* 述學 (An account of learning). *Congshu jicheng xinbian* ed. Taibei: Xinwenfeng chuban gongsi, 1985.

Wang Zhongmin 王重民. "Li Qing zhushu kao" 李清著述考 (A Study of Li Qing's works). *Tushuguan xue jikan* 圖書館學季刊 (Quarterly of library science) 2.3 (1928): 333–42.

———. *Zhongguo shanben shu tiyao* 中國善本書提要 (Annotated catalog of Chinese rare books). Shanghai: Shanghai guji chubanshe, 1983.

Wang Zhuo 王晫. *Jin Shishuo* 今世說 (Contemporary *Shishuo*). 8 *juan*. Author's preface 1683. Shanghai: Gudian wenxue chubanshe, 1957.

Wanli dichao 萬曆邸鈔 (Wanli gazette). Taibei: Guoli zhongyang tushuguan, 1969.

Watson, Burton. *Ssu-ma Ch'ien: Grand Historian of China*. New York: Columbia University Press, 1958.

Wei Shou 魏收. *Weishu* 魏書 (History of the [Northern] Wei). 8 vols. Beijing: Zhonghua shuju, 1974.

Wei Xiyuan 魏息園 (Chengbo 程搏, Lianshang 蓮裳). *Buyong xing shenpan shu gushi xuan* 不用刑審判書故事选 (Selected stories of trials that did not resort to the use of torture), ed. Wang Zhenda 汪振廷. Shanxi: Qunzhong chubanshe, 1987.

——— (Xiyuan waishi 息園外史), comp. *Xiuxiang gujin xiannü zhuan* 繡像古今賢女傳 (Lavishly illustrated biographies of exceptional women, past and present). 9 fascicles. Beijing: Zhongguo shudian, 1998.

Wei Zheng 魏徵 et al. *Suishu* 隨書 (History of the Sui Dynasty). 6 vols. Beijing: Zhonghua shuju, 1973.

Weidner, Marsha. *The Latter Days of the Law: Images of Chinese Buddhism 850–1850*. Lawrence, KS: Spencer Museum of Art / Honolulu: University of Hawai'i Press, 1974.

West, Stephen, and Wilt L. Idema, trans. *The Moon and the Zither: The Story of the West Wing*. Berkeley and Los Angeles: University of California Press, 1991.

Widmer, Ellen. *The Beauty and the Book: Women and Fiction in Nineteenth Century China*. Cambridge, MA: Harvard University Asia Center, 2006.

———. "Border Crossing and the Woman Writer: The Case of Gui Maoyi (1762–1835/6)." In *Hsiang Lectures in Chinese Poetry*, vol. 4, 83–104. Montreal: Centre for East Asian Research, McGill University, 2008.

———. "Considering a Coincidence: The 'Female Reading Public' circa 1828." In *Writing and Materiality in China: Essays in Honor of Patrick Hanan*, ed. Judith T. Zeitlin and Lydia Liu, with Ellen Widmer, 273–314. Cambridge, MA: Harvard University Asia Center, 2003.

———. "The Epistolary World of Female Talent in Seventeenth-Century China." *Late Imperial China* 10.2 (1989): 1–43.

———. "Ming Loyalism and the Woman's Voice in Fiction after *Honglou Meng*." In *Writing Women in Late Imperial China*, ed. Ellen Widmer and Kang-i Sun Chang, 366–96. Stanford, CA: Stanford University Press, 1997.

———. "The Rhetoric of Retrospection: May Fourth Literary History and the Ming-Qing Woman Writer." In *The Appropriation of Cultural Capital:*

China's May Fourth Project, ed. M. Dolezelova and O. Kral, 193–221. Cambridge, MA: Harvard University Asia Center, 2001.

Wilhelm, Hellmut. 1962. "From Myth to Myth: The Case of Yueh Fei's Biography." In *Confucian Personalities*, ed. Arthur Wright and Denis Twitchett, 146–61. Stanford, CA: Stanford University Press, 1962.

Wolf, Margery. *Revolution Postponed: Women in Contemporary China.* Stanford, CA: Stanford University Press, 1985.

Woolf, Virginia. *A Room of One's Own.* London: Hogarth Press, 1929. Rpt. New York: Granada Publishing Limited, 1978.

Wright, Arthur F. "Values, Roles, and Personalities." In *Confucian Personalities*, ed. A. F. Wright and Denis Twitchett, 2–23. Stanford, CA: Stanford University Press, 1962.

Wright, Arthur F., and Denis Twitchett, ed. *Confucian Personalities.* Stanford, CA: Stanford University Press, 1962.

Wu Ding 吳定. *Zishiquan shanfang shiwenji* 紫石泉山房詩文集 (Collected poetry and prose from the mountain hut of the Purple-Stone Creek). 1887.

Wu Hung. "Beyond Stereotypes: The Twelve Beauties in Qing Court Art and 'The Dream of the Red Chamber.'" In *Writing Women in Late Imperial China*, ed. Ellen Widmer and Kang-i Sun Chang, 306–65. Stanford, CA: Stanford University Press, 1997.

———. *The Double Screen: Image and Representation in Chinese Painting.* Chicago: University of Chicago Press, 1996.

Wu Pei-yi. *The Confucian's Progress. Autobiographical Writings in Traditional China.* Princeton, NJ: Princeton University Press, 1990.

Wu Shijian 吳士鑑 et al. *Qing gongci* 清宮詞 (Qing palace poetry). Ed. Shi Jichang 石繼昌. Beijing: Beijing guji chubanshe, 1986.

Wu Shuping 吳樹平. "Jizhuan ti shishu zhong *Lienüzhuan* chuangshi kao" 記傳體史書中《列女傳》創始考 (A study of the origin of the "Biographies of women" in the genres of the annals and the biographies). *Zhongguo shi yanjiu* 中國史研究 4 (1987):143–50.

Wu Yuancui 伍袁萃. *Linju manlu* 林居漫錄 (Casual writings of a forest-dweller). Wanli ed., microfilm, University of Chicago.

Wu, Yenna. *The Chinese Virago: A Literary Theme.* Cambridge, MA: Harvard University Press, 1995.

Wujin Yanghu xian hezhi 武進陽湖縣合志 (Combined gazetteer of Wujin and Yanghu Counties). Changzhou, Jiangsu, 1842.

Xia Xiaohong 夏曉虹. "Qiu Jin Beijing shiqi sixiang yanjiu" 秋瑾北京时期思想研究 (A study of Qiu Jin's thoughts during the Beijing period). *Zhejiang Shehui kexue* no. 4 (2000): 114–18.

———. "Wanqing ren yanzhong de Qiu Jin zhi si" 晚清人眼中的秋瑾之死 (Qiu Jin's death in the eyes of late Qing people). In Xia Xiaohong, *Wanqing shehui yu wenhua* 晚清社会与文化 (Late Qing society and culture), 208–48. Wuhan: Hubei jiaoyu chubanshe, 2000.

Xia Yan 夏衍. "Qiu Jin zhuan" 秋瑾传 (Story of Qiu Jin). In *Xia Yan juzuo xuan* 夏衍劇作选 (Selected dramatic works of Xia Yan), 3–57. Beijing: Renmin wenxue, 1942, 1953.

Xinbian guafu lienü zhuan shiqu 新編寡婦烈女傳詩曲 (Newly edited poems and songs on widows and martyred chaste maidens). Beijing: Jintai Lu family publication, n.d. Fragment held in National Central Library, Taibei, Taiwan.

Xinhai geming Zhejiang shiliao, xuji 辛亥革命浙江史料续集 (Historical material on the 1911 Revolution in Zhejiang, sequel). Ed. Zhejiang sheng shekeyuan lishi yanjiu suo, Zhejiang tushu guan. Hangzhou: Zhejiang renmin chubanshe, 1987.

Xiong Shili 熊十力. *Han Feizi pinglun* 韩非子评论 (On Han Fei). Taibei: Taiwan Xuesheng shuju, 1978.

Xu Ji 徐積. *Jie xiao ji* 節孝集 (The faithful and filial collection [Collected works of Xu Ji]). *Siku quanshu* ed., vol. 1101. Taibei: Taiwan shangwu yinshuguan, 1983.

Xu Jian 徐堅. *Chuxue ji* 初學記 (Writings for elementary instruction). *Siku quanshu* ed., vol. 890. Taibei: Shangwu yinshuguan, 1983.

Xu Qianxue 徐乾學. *Chuanshilou shu mu* 傳是樓書目 (Library catalog of the Chuanshilou). *Xuxiu siku quanshu* ed., vol 920. Shanghai: Shanghai guji chubanshe, 2002.

Xu Shen 許慎. *Shuowen jiezi [zhu]* 說文解字[注] ([Commentary on] Interpretation of Words), comm. Duan Yucai 段玉裁. 1815. Rpt. Shanghai: Shanghai guji chubanshe, 1981.

Xu Song 徐松, ed. *Song huiyao jigao* 宋會要輯稿 (Song classified documents). Beijing: Zhonghua shuju, 1957.

Xu Weiyu 許維遹. "Hao Lan'gao (Yixing) fufu nianpu" 郝蘭皐(懿行)夫婦年譜 (Chronological record of Hao Yixing and his wife). *Qinghua xuebao* 清華學報 10.1 (1936): 185–233. Rpt. Hong Kong: Chongwen shudian, 1975.

Xu Xin 徐沁. *Minghua lu* 明畫錄 (Records of Ming painting). Shanghai: Commercial Press, 1939.

Xu Xingwu 徐興無. "Qingdai Wang Zhaoyuan *Lienüzhuan buzhu* yu Liang Duan *Lienüzhuan jiaozhu duben*" 清代王照圓《列女傳補注》與梁端《列女傳校讀本》 (Wang Zhaoyuan's "Commentary on the 'Biographies of women'" and Liang Duan's 'Annotated reader of 'Biographies of women' during the Qing period"). In *Ming Qing wenxue yu xingbie yanjiu* 明清文學與性別研究 (Studies of literature and gender in the Ming Qing periods), ed. Zhang Hongsheng 張宏生, 916–31. Nanjing: Jiangsu guji, 2002.

Xu Zaiping 徐載平 and Xu Ruifang 徐瑞芳, eds. *Qingmo sishinian Shenbao shiliao* 清末四十年申报史料 (Historical material from the Shenbao in the last forty years of the Qing). Beijing: Xinhua chubanshe, 1988.

Xu zizhi tongjian changbian shibu 續資治通鑑長編拾補 (Collected supplements to the Long Draft of the Continuation of the *Comprehensive Mirror for Aid in Government*). Beijing: Zhonghua shuju, 2004.

Xu Zongyan 許宗彥. *Jianzhi shuizhai zang shumu si juan* 鑑止水齋藏書目四卷 (Catalogue in four sections of books stored at Reflection in Still Water Studio). 1849. Harvard-Yenching Library.

Xue Shaohui 薛紹徽 and Chen Shoupeng 陳壽彭. *Waiguo lienü zhuan* 外國列女傳 (Biographies of foreign women). Nanjing: Jingling Jiangchu bianyi guanshu zongju, 1906),

Yamazaki Jun'ichi 山崎純一. "Kinsei ni okeru *Retsujo den* no hensen: Ō Ken *Retsujo den* to Asaka Shin *Reppu den* o chūshin ni" 近世における「烈女伝」の変遷:汪憲「烈女伝」と安積信「烈婦伝」を中心に (A Transition of Lieh-nü-chuan in modern times, with special reference to *Lieh-nü-chuan* by Wang-Hsien and *Leppuden* by Asaka Shin). *Chûgokukoten-Kenkyû, The Journal of Sinology* 12 (December 1964): 41–54.

Yan Heng 嚴蘅. *Nü Shishuo* 女世說 (Women's *Shishuo*). *Juanjing lou congke* ed. 娟鏡樓叢刻. Shanghai: Juzhen fangsong shuju, 1920.

Yan Xiyuan 顏希源, comp., and Wang Hui 王翽, illust. *Baimei xinyong tuzhuan* 百美新詠圖傳 (Pictorial biographies and new poetic appraisals of One Hundred Beauties). 2 vols. 1790. Rpt. Beijing: Zhongguo shudian, 1998.

Yan Yongcheng 燕永成. "Bei Song zaifu chaozheng biji yanjiu" 北宋宰輔朝政筆記研究 (Studies on the administrative diaries of Northern Song councillors). *Wenxian* 3 (2001): 105–19.

Yang Bojun 楊伯峻. *Lunyu yizhu* 論語譯注 (The *Lunyu*, annotated and translated in modern Chinese). Beijing: Zhonghua shuju, 1980.

Yang Wanli 楊萬里. *Chengzhai ji* 誠齋集. *Sibu congkan* ed. Shanghai: Shangwu yinshuguan, 1922.

Yang Zhongliang 楊仲良. *Tongjian changbian jishi benmo* 通鑑長編紀事本末 (Narratives from beginning to end from the *Long Draft of the Comprehensive Mirror*). *Songshi ziliao cuibian* ed. Taibei: Wenhai chubanshe, 1967.

Yao, Ping 姚平. "Good Karmic Connections: Buddhist Mother in Tang China (618–907)." *Nan Nü: Men, Women and Gender in China* 10.1 (2008): 57–85.

———. *Tangdai funü de shengming licheng* 唐代婦女的生命歷程 (Women's lives in the Tang dynasty). Shanghai: Shanghai guji chubanshe, 2004.

Ye Shaoyuan 葉紹袁. *Wumeng tang ji* 午夢堂集 (Collections from Mid-Day Dream Hall). 2 vols. Beijing: Zhonghua shuju, 1998.

Yeh, Catherine Vance. "Creating the Urban Beauty: The Shanghai Courtesan in Late Qing Illustrations." In *Writing and Materiality in China: Essays in Honor of Patrick Hanan*, ed. Judith T. Zeitlin and Lydia H. Liu, with Ellen Widmer, 397–447. Cambridge, MA: Harvard University Asia Center, 2003.

———. *Shanghai Love: Courtesans, Intellectuals, and Entertainment Culture, 1850–1910*. Seattle: University of Washington Press, 2006.

Yeh, Wen-hsin. "Historian and Courtesan: Chen Yinke and the Writing of *Liu Rushi Biezhuan*." *East Asian History* 27 (2004): 57–70.

Yi Zongkui 易宗夔. *Xin Shishuo* 新世說 (New *Shishuo*). 1922. Rpt. in *Qingdai zhuanji congkan* 清代傳記叢刊, ed. Zhou Junfu 周駿富, vol. 18. Taibei: Mingwen shuju, 1985.

Yili [*zhushu*] 儀禮註疏 ([Commentary on the] Manner rituals), "Sangfu" 喪服 (Mourning ritual). Comm. Zheng Xuan 鄭玄, Jia Gongyan 賈公彥. In *Shisan jing zhushu* 十三經註疏 (Commentaries on the thirteen Chinese classics), ed. Ruan Yuan 阮元. 1826. Rpt. Beijing: Zhonghua shuju, 1979, vol. 1: 1096–1128.

Yongrong 永瑢 and Ji Yun 紀昀 et al., eds. *Siku quanshu zongmu* 四庫全書總目 (Annotated catalogue of the Complete Collection of the Four Treasuries). 2 vols. 1822. Rpt. Beijing: Zhonghua shuju, 1965.

Yoshikawa, Kōjirō 吉川次郎幸. "Zang Zaidong xiansheng nianpu" 藏在東先生年普. (Chronological biography of Mr. Zang Yong). *Tōyō gakuhō* 東方學報 6 (1936): 280–307.

Youd, Daniel M. "Beyond *Bao:* Moral Ambiguity and the Law in Late Imperial Chinese Narrative Literature." In *Writing and Law in Late Imperial China: Crime, Conflict, and Judgment*, ed. Robert E. Hegel and Katherine Carlitz, 215–33. Seattle: University of Washington Press, 2007.

Yu Chien-ming 游鑑明. "Dang waishengren yudao Taiwan nüxing: Zhanhou Taiwan baokan zhong de nüxing lunshu (1945–1949)" 當外省人遇到台灣女性:戰後台灣報刊中的女性論述 (1945–1949) (When mainlanders met Taiwanese women: Female discourses in postwar Taiwanese newspapers and magazines, 1945–1949). *Bulletin of the Institute of Modern History Academia Sinica (Zhongyang yanjiuyuan jindaishi yanjiushuo jikan)* 中央研究院近代史研究所集刊 47 (March 2005): 165–224.

———. "Jinghua shuiyue bijing zhongchengkong? Nüxing koushu lishi de xuyushi" 鏡花水月畢竟總成空?女性口述歷史的虛與實 (Catching the moon in the lake? The real and unreal in women's oral history). In Yu Chien-ming, *Qingting tamen de shengyin: Nüxing koushu lishi de fangfa yu koushu shiliao de yunyong* 傾聽她們的聲音:女性口述歷史的方法與口述史料的運用 (Listening to their voices: The use and method of female oral history), 37–48. Shindian: Rive Gauche Publishing House, 2002.

———. *Qingting tamen de shengyin: Nüxing koushu lishi de fangfa yu koushu shiliao de yunyong* 傾聽她們的聲音:女性口述歷史的方法與口述史料的運用 (Listening to their voices: The use and method of female oral history). Shindian: Rive Gauche Publishing House, 2002.

———. *Tamen de Shengyin: Cong jindai Zhongguo nüxing de lishi jiyi tanqi* 她們的聲音:從近代中國女性的歷史記憶談起 (Their voices: Considering contemporary Chinese women's historical memories). Taibei: Wu-Nan Book Inc., 2009.

Yu Chien-ming 游鑑明, interviewer, and Chen Chien-hui 陳千惠 et al., recorders. "Yu Wenxiu nüshi fangtan jilu" 余文秀女士訪問紀錄 (Interview with Ms. Yu Wenxiu). In Lo Jiu-jung 羅久蓉 et al., 115–52.

Yu Chien-ming 游鑑明, interviewer, and Chu Yi-ting 朱怡婷, recorder. "Pei Wang Zhihong nüshi fangtan jilu" 裴王志宏女士訪問紀錄 (Interview with Ms. Pei Wang Zhihong). In Lo Jiu-jung 羅久蓉 et al., 185–231.

Yu Chien-ming 游鑑明, interviewer, and Huang Ming-ming 黃銘明, recorder. "Zhang Wang Mingxin nüshi fangtan jilu" 張王銘心女士訪問紀錄 (Interview with Ms. Zhang Wang Mingxin). In Lo Jiu-jung 羅久蓉 et al., 61–113.

Yu Jianhua 俞劍華. *Zhongguo meishujia renming cidian* 中國美術家人名詞典 (Dictionary of Chinese artists). Beijing: Zhonghua shuju, 1980.

Yu Jiaxi 余嘉錫. *Shishuo xinyu jianshu* 世說新語箋疏 (Commentary on the *Shishuo xinyu*). 2 vols. Shanghai: Shanghai guji chubanshe, 1993.

Yuhas, Louise. "Wang Shih-chen as Patron." In *Artists and Patrons: Some Social and Economic Aspects of Chinese Painting*, ed. Chu-tsing Li. Seattle: University of Washington Press, 1989.

Yun Zhu 惲珠 (Wanyan Yun Zhu 完顏惲珠), ed. *Guochao guixiu zhengshi ji* 國朝閨秀正始集 (Correct beginnings). 1831, sequel 1836. Harvard-Yenching Library.

———. *Hongxiang guan shicao* 紅香館詩詞草 (Draft poems of Hongxiang Studio). 1814. Harvard-Yenching Library.

———. *Langui baolu* 蘭閨寶錄. 1831. Tsinghua University Library.

Zeitlin, Judith. "The Life and Death of the Image: Ghosts and Female Portraits in Sixteenth- and Seventeenth-Century Literature." In *Body and Face in Chinese Visual Culture*, ed. Wu Hung and Catherine R. Tsiang, 229–56. Cambridge, MA: Harvard University Asia Center, 2005.

Zeng Bairong 曾白融. *Jingju jumu cidian* 京劇劇目辭典 (Dictionary of Peking opera drama synopses). Beijing: Zhongguo xiju chubanshe, 1989.

Zeng Bu 曾布. *Zenggong yilu* 曾公遺錄 (Bequeathed record of Zeng Bu). In *Ouxiang lingshi* 藕香零拾, ed. Miao Quansun 繆荃孫. Beijing: Zhonghua shuju, 1998.

Zhang Guanfa 张观发 et al. *Gudai buyongxing shenpan anli* 古代不用刑审判案例 (Ancient cases of trials that did not revert to the use of torture). Zhongguo falu shixue hui, 1981.

Zhang Guanying 張細英. *Weiqing yigao* 緯青遺稿 (Poetry of Zhang Guanying). *Wanlin shuwu congshu* ed., preface 1829. Rpt. *Jiangyin congshu* 江陰叢書, comp. Jin Wuxiang 金武祥. Suxiang shi 粟香室 ed., 1907.

Zhang Huiyan 張惠言. *Mingke wen er bian* 茗柯文二編 (Collected prose). Preface 1869.

Zhang Lei 張耒. *Ke shan ji* 柯山集 (Collected works of Zhang Lei). *Siku quanshu* ed., vol. 1115. Taibei: Taiwan shangwu yinshuguan, 1983.

Zhang Lunying 張綸英. *Lühuai shuwu shi gao* 綠槐書屋詩稿 (Collected poems of Zhang Lunying). 2 *juan*. Wanlin shuwu keben, 1845. Beijing University Library; *Fulu* 附錄 (supplement). N.d., Shanghai Library.

Zhang Qi 張琦. *Mingfa lu* 明發錄 (Record of illumination). 1840. In Zhang Qi, *Wanlin shi wen* 宛鄰詩文 (Poetry and prose from the Wanlin Studio), vol. 5. 1840. Rpt. 1891.

———. *Wanlin shi wen* 宛鄰詩文 (Poetry and prose from the Wanlin Studio). 1840. Rpt. 1891.

Zhang Tao 張濤. "Liu Xiang *Lienüzhuan* de banben wenti" 劉向《列女傳》的版本問題 (Bibliographic questions about Liu Xiang's *Biographies of Women*). *Wenxian* 文獻 3 (1989): 249–57.

Zhang Tingyu 張廷玉 et al. *Mingshi* 明史 (History of the Ming Dynasty). 28 vols. Beijing: Zhonghua shuju, 1974.

Zhang Xuecheng 章學誠. *Zhangshi yishu* 章氏遺書 (The bequeathed writings of Zhang Xuecheng). Ed. Liu Chenggan. Jiayetang ed., 1922. Rpt. Taibei: Hansheng chubanshe, 1973.

Zhang Yanxian 張炎憲 et al. *Ererba shijian zeren guishu yanjiu baogao* 二二八事件責任歸屬研究報告(Rearch report on issues of responsibility for the February 28th Incident). Taibei: Ererba shijian jinian jijinhui (February 28th Incident Memorial Foundation), 2006.

Zhao Chao 趙超. *Gudai muzhi tonglun* 古代墓誌通論 (A general history of epitaphs). Beijing: Zijingchen chubanshe, 2003.

Zhao Dingchen 趙鼎臣. *Zhu yin qi shi ji* 竹隱畸士集 (Collected works of Zhao Dingchen). *Siku quanshu* ed., vol. 1124. Taibei: Taiwan shangwu yinshuguan, 1983.

Zhao Erxun 趙爾巽 et al. *Qingshi gao* 清史稿 (Draft history of the Qing dynasty). 48 vols. Beijing: Zhonghua shuju, 1977.

Zhao Qimei 趙琦美. *Mowang guan shumu* 脈望館書目 (Library catalog of the Mowang Hall). *Hanfen lou miji* ed. Shanghai: Shangwu yinshuguan, 1918.

Zhao Ruyu 趙汝愚. *Songchao zhuchen zouyi* 宋朝諸臣奏議 (Memorials of Song officials). Shanghai: Shanghai guji chubanshe, 1999.

Zhao Zhen 趙震, comp. *Piling wenlu* 毗陵文錄 (Records of prose by writers from Piling). Changzhou, Jiangsu: Huaxin shushe, 1931.

Zhejiang Xinhai geming huiyi lu 浙江辛亥革命回忆录 (Memoirs of the 1911 Revolution in Zhejiang). Hangzhou: Zhongguo renmin zhengzhi xieshang huiyi zhejiangsheng weiyuanhui, 1984.

Zheng Guoxun 鄭國勳. *Longxi jingshe congshu* 龍谿精舍叢書. Chaoyang 潮陽, 1917.

Zhong Xing 鍾惺, ed. *Mingyuan shigui* 名媛詩歸 (A summary of poems by famous ladies). Late-Ming woodblock ed. *Siku quanshu cunmu congshu*, vol. 339.

Zhonggong Weinan xianwei bianzhu xiaozu 中共渭南县委编著小组, ed. *"Huangmao nüzi" fangchu le "mianhua weixing"* 《黃毛女子》放出了《棉花卫星》 ("Silly girls" launch a "cotton satellite"). Xi'an: Shaanxi renmin chubanshe, May 1959.

———. *Women ganshangle Zhang Qiuxiang* 我们赶上了张秋香 (We caught up with Zhang Qiuxiang). Xi'an: Shaanxi renmin chubanshe, May 1959.

Zhongguo gudai shuhua tu mu 中国古代书画图目 (Catalog of ancient Chinese painting and calligraphy). 23 vols. Beijing: Wenwu chubanshe, 1986–2001.

Zhou Shaoliang 周紹良 and Zhao Chao 趙超. *Tangdai muzhi huibian* 唐代墓誌彙編 (Collections of Tang epitaphs). Shanghai: Shanghai guji chubanshe, 1992.

———. *Tangdai muzhi huibian xuji* 唐代墓誌彙編續集 (Sequel to the collections of Tang epitaphs). Shanghai: Shanghai guji chubanshe, 2002.

Zhou Shouchang 周壽昌, ed. *Gonggui wenxuan* 宮閨文選 (An anthology of prose-writings by palace ladies and women of the inner quarters). Woodblock ed., 1846.

Zhou Xunchu 周勛初. *Tang yulin jiaozheng* 唐語林校證 (Commentary on a collated ed. of the *Tang forest of accounts*). 2 vols. Beijing: Zhonghua shuju, 1987.

Zhou Yi [*zhu*] 周易[注] ([Commentary on] Zhou Yi). In *Wang Bi ji jiaozhu* 王弼集校釋 (Collated annotation of Wang Bi's works), ed., coll., comm. Lou Yulie 樓宇烈. 2 vols. Beijing: Zhonghua shuju, 1980.

Zhou Yiliang 周一良. "Shishuo xinyu he zuozhe Liu Yiqing shenshi de kao-cha" 世說新語和作者劉義慶身世的考察 (*Shishuo xinyu* and a study of the author Liu Yiqing's life). *Zhongguo zhexue shi yanjiu* 中國哲學史研究 1981.1. Rpt. Zhou Yiliang, *Wei-Jin Nan-Bei chao shi lunji xubian* 魏晉南北朝史論集續編 (Continued collection of the essays on the history of Wei, Jin, Southern and Northern dynasties), 16–22. Beijing: Peking University Press, 1991.

Zhou Yiqun. "Virtue and Talent: Women and *Fushi* in Early China." *Nan Nü: Men, Women and Gender in Early and Imperial China* 5.1 (2003): 1–42.

Zhou Zizhi 周紫芝. *Tai cang ti mi ji* 太倉稊米集 (Collected works of Zhou Zizhi). *Siku quanshu* ed., vol. 1141. Taibei: Taiwan shangwu yinshuguan, 1983.

Zhu Dongrun 朱東潤. "Zhongguo zhuanxu wenxue de guoqu yu jianglai" 中國傳敘文學的過去與將來 (The past and future of Chinese biographical literature). *Xuelin* 學林 8 (1941): 19–29.

Zhu Shi 朱軾. *Zhu Wenduangong ji* 朱文端公集 (Collected works of Zhu Shi). 1871.

Zhu Yizun 朱彝尊. *Pushuting ji* 曝書亭集 (Collected works from the Pavilion of Sunning Books). *Sibu congkan* ed. Shanghai: Shangwu yinshuguan, 1929.

Zurndorfer, Harriet T. *China Bibliography: A Research Guide to Reference Works about China Past and Present*. Leiden: Brill, 1995.

———. "The 'Constant World' of Wang Chao-yüan: Women, Education, and Orthodoxy in 18th Century China—A Preliminary Investigation." In *Family Process and Political Process in Modern Chinese History*, comp. Institute of Modern History, vol. 1: 581–619. Taibei: Academia Sinica, 1992.

———. "How to Be a Good Wife and a Good Scholar at the Same Time: 18th Century Prescriptions on Chinese Female Behavior—A Preliminary Investigation." In *La Société Civile Face à l'État Dans la Tradition Chinoise, Japonaise, Coréene et Vietnamienne*, ed. Léon Vandermeersch, 249–70. Paris: École Française d'Extrême-Orient, 1994.

———. "Introduction: Some Salient Remarks on Chinese Women in the Imperial Past (1000–1800)." In *Chinese Women in the Imperial Past: New Perspectives*, ed. Harriet T. Zurndorfer, 1–18. Leiden: Brill, 1999.

———. "Old and New Visions of Ming Society and Culture." *T'oung Pao* 88 (2002): 151–69.

———. "Wang Zhaoyuan." In *Biographical Dictionary of Chinese Women: The Qing Period, 1644–1911*, ed. Clara Wing-chung Ho, 227–30. Armonk, NY: M. E. Sharpe, 1998.

―――. "Wang Zhaoyuan (1763–1851) and the Erasure of 'Talented Women' by Liang Qichao." In *Different Worlds of Discourse: Transformations of Gender and Genre in Late Qing and Early Republican China*, ed. Grace Fong, Nanxiu Qian, and Richard Smith, 29–56. Leiden: Brill, 2008.

Zurndorfer, Harriet, ed. *Chinese Women in the Imperial Past: New Perspectives.* Leiden and Boston: Brill, 1999.zuowen hai Dao 作文害道

Contributors

BEVERLY BOSSLER is professor of history at the University of California, Davis. She is the author of *Powerful Relations: Kinship Status and the State in Sung China (960–1279)* (1998), and served as editor of the *Journal of Song-Yuan Studies* from 2001 to 2004. She has recently completed a book manuscript on changing gender relations in China from the eleventh to fourteenth centuries, *Courtesans, Concubines, and the Cult of Wifely Fidelity: Gender and Social Change in China, 1000–1400* (forthcoming).

KATHERINE CARLITZ is adjunct professor of early modern Chinese literature and culture at the University of Pittsburgh. She is the author of *The Rhetoric of Chin P'ing Mei* (1986) and co-editor of *Writing and Law in Late Imperial China: Crime, Conflict, and Judgment* (2007). She has published many articles on the cult of women's chastity and fidelity in Ming dynasty China.

PATRICIA EBREY is professor of history at the University of Washington. Her work on kinship and gender includes *The Inner Quarters: Marriage and the Lives of Chinese Women in the Sung Period* (1993) and *Women and the Family in Chinese History* (2002). For the past decade much of her research has been on visual dimensions of Chinese history and the court of the Song emperor Huizong. These interests led both to *Emperor Huizong and Late Northern Song China: The Politics of Culture and the Culture of Politics* (co-edited, 2006) and to *Accumulating Culture: The Collections of Emperor Huizong* (2008).

GAIL HERSHATTER is Distinguished Professor of History at the University of California, Santa Cruz. Her books include *The Workers of Tianjin, 1900–1949* (1986), *Personal Voices: Chinese Women in the 1980s* (with Emily Honig, 1988), *Dangerous Pleasures: Prostitution and Modernity in Twentieth-Century Shanghai* (1997), *Women in China's Long Twentieth Century* (2007; http://escholarship.org/uc/item/12h450zf); and *The Gender of Memory: Rural Women and China's Collective Past* (2011).

HU YING is associate professor of Chinese literature at the University of California, Irvine. She is the author of *Tales of Translation: Composing the New Woman in China, 1898–1918* (2000) and various essays on the late Qing, feminism in China, and translation studies. She is completing a linked biography of Qiu Jin and her two sworn sisters, focusing on how women brought up in traditional literati culture understood and intervened in the radical cultural changes of the early twentieth century China.

WILT L. IDEMA (Ph.D., Leiden University, 1974) teaches Chinese literature at Harvard University. He has published widely in the field of late imperial Chinese literature, with an emphasis on the vernacular traditions of fiction, drama, and ballad narrative. His most important publication in the field of Chinese women's studies is *The Red Brush: Writing Women of Imperial China* (2004, with Beata Grant), a comprehensive survey of 2,000 years of Chinese women's literature. More recently he has published *Heroines of Jiangyong: Chinese Narrative Ballads in Women's Script* (2009).

JOAN JUDGE, professor in the departments of history and humanities at York University in Toronto, is the author of *The Precious Raft of History: The Past, the West, and the Woman Question in China* (2008), *Print and Politics: 'Shibao' and the Culture of Reform in Late Qing China* (1996), and of numerous articles on Chinese print culture and Chinese women's history. These include an article on women's biography published in the winter 2009 *Journal of Women's History* special double issue: *Critical Feminist Biography as Translocal History.*

WEIJING LU received her B.A. and M.A. from Fudan University, and her Ph.D. from the University of California, Davis. She is the author of *True to Her Word: The Faithful Maiden Cult in Late Imperial China* (2008). Her current research focuses on family and marital practices and private life of historical figures of the seventeenth through early nineteenth centuries. She is associate professor of history at the University of California, San Diego.

SUSAN MANN is professor of history emerita at the University of California, Davis. She is co-editor (with Yu-Yin Cheng) of *Under Confucian Eyes: Writings on Gender in Chinese History* (2001), author of *Precious Records: Women in China's Long Eighteenth Century* (1997) and *The Talented Women of the Zhang Family* (2007), and a participant in the roundtable on historians and biography in *The American Historical Review* (114.3, 2009).

NANXIU QIAN is associate professor of Chinese literature at Rice University. Recent publications include *Different Worlds of Discourse: Transformations of Gender and Genre in Late Qing and Early Republican China* (co-edited with Fong and Smith, 2008); *Chinese Literature: Conversations between Tradition and Modernity* (co-edited with Zhang, 2007); *Xue Jia yin* (Chanting following Jia), by Chen Jitong (1852–1907) (edited with an introduction, 2005); *Beyond Tradition and Modernity: Gender, Genre, and Cosmopolitanism in Late Qing*

China (co-edited with Fong and Zurndorfer, 2004); and *Spirit and Self in Medieval China: The Shih-shuo hsin-yü and Its Legacy* (2001).

ANN WALTNER is professor of history at the University of Minnesota, where she is also a member of the program in religious studies. She has published on gender, kinship, and religion in late imperial China. She also teaches and writes on gender and the family in world history. She served as editor of the *Journal of Asian Studies* from 2000 to 2005, and currently serves as director of the Institute for Advanced Study at the University of Minnesota. The chapter in this volume is part of a longer study on Tanyangzi.

ELLEN WIDMER is Mayling Soong Professor of Chinese Studies at Wellesley College. She is the author of *The Margins of Utopia: Shui-hu hou-chuan and the Literature of Ming Loyalism* (1987); and *The Beauty and the Book: Women and Fiction in Nineteenth Century China* (2006). Her edited volumes include *From May Fourth to June Fourth: Fiction and Film in Twentieth-Century China* (1993; with David Wang); *Writing Women in Late Imperial China* (with Kang-i Sun Chang, 1997); *Trauma and Transcendence in Early Qing Literature* (with Wilt Idema and Wai-yee Li, 2006); *China's Christian Colleges: Cross-Cultural Connections* (with Daniel Bays, 2009); and *The Inner Quarters and Beyond* (with Grace Fong, 2010).

PING YAO is professor of history at California State University, Los Angeles. She is the author of *Tangdai funü de shengming licheng* (Life courses of women in Tang dynasty China) and more than a dozen articles on Tang dynasty China. Currently she is writing a book on women and Buddhism in Tang China and co-editing a multivolume series introducing Western scholarship on Chinese history to academic historians in China.

YU CHIEN-MING is associate research fellow at the Institute of Modern History, Academia Sinica, Taiwan, and chief editor of *Research on Women in Modern China*. Her primary research interest is women's history in modern China and Taiwan. She is author of *Tamen de Shenyin: Congjindai Zhongguo nüxing de lishi jiyi tanqi* (Their voices: Considering contemporary Chinese women's historical memories; 2009); and *Yundongchang neiwai: jindai huadong diqu de nuzi tiyu, 1895–1937* (On and off the playing fields: A modern history of physical education for girls in eastern China, 1895–1937; 2009).

HARRIET T. ZURNDORFER is senior research scholar, Faculty of Humanities, Leiden University. She is the author of *Change and Continuity in Chinese Local History: The Development of Hui-chou Prefecture, 800 to 1800* (1989) and *China Bibliography: A Research Guide to Reference Works about China Past and Present* (1995; paperback edition 1999), the editor of *Chinese Women in the Imperial Past: New Perspectives* (1999), and she has published more than fifty learned articles and reviews. From 1992 to 2000, she was editor of *The Journal of the Economic and Social History of the Orient*. She is also founder and editor of the journal *Nan Nü: Men, Women and Gender in China*, published since 1999.

Index

417

Families *(continued)*
mistreatment by, 29–31; mourning rituals, 92–93, 314n6; protection of, 80–81; and religious practice, 223–25

Fan Ye, 75, 292, 309n8; *Hou Hanshu*, 2, 57, 72, 73–74, 77, 293

Fang Bao, 99, 101

Fang Fangpei: *Zaiputang yinguo*, 254

Fang Junmo, 304n34; epitaphs by, 33–34, 35

Fang Xuanling: *Jinshu*, 78, 292, 293

Farming: women's roles in, 38–39

February 28th Incident, 273

Female Exemplars. See Gui fan

Female personhood: role of, 111–12

Femininity: Qiu Jin's, 126–27; sexual fidelity as, 125, 324–25n3

Feng Yan: *Fengshi wenjixuan ji*, 79, 296

Fiction, 326n15; Ming dynasty, 12, 176, 183–91

Fictive tales, 8, 161, 162, 166

Fidelity, 12, 324–25n3, 327n32; of courtesans, 164–65, 168; faithful maiden cult and, 88, 90; sexual, 125, 158; of upper-class women, 171–73

Filiality, 81, 149, 152, 161, 167, 306n34, 330n18; and mourning rituals, 92–93

First Collection of Red Snow Tower. See Hongxuelou chuji

Frost in June. See Liuyue shuang

Frugality, 27–28

Funeral laments, 235–36, 339n39

Funerary inscriptions, 160, 322n1

Gao: *Lienü zhuan*, 57

Gao, Grand Empress Dowager, 193, 194–95, 196, 197, 198, 199, 200, 205, 210–11, 332n3

Gao E, 255

Gao Jin, 180

Gao Qi, 257, 258

Gao family, 115–16, 200

Gaoqing, 78

Gender, 1, 12; and literary forms, 254–55; and martyrdom, 123, 124; scholarship, 10–11

Gender relationships, 76–77, 84, 264

Gender roles, 4, 139, 148–49, 153–54, 324–25n3, 336n45; and religious practices, 221, 222–28

Gongci (palace poetry), 105

Gonggui wenxuan (Zhou Shouchang), 230

Gongsun, 152

Gongyang zhuan, 56–57

Gossip, 32, 35, 44

Gravestone inscriptions: Bao Mengyi's, 32–35; see also Epitaphs

Great Leap Forward, 45, 46

Gu Congyi, 60

Gu Guangqi, 61; *Gu Lienü zhuan fu kaozheng*, 62, 63

Gu Kaizhi, 60

Gu Yanwu, 260

Guan Panpan, 113

Guangdong, 246

Guang lienü zhuan (Liu Kai), 107

Guangxu Emperor, 67

Guanyin: devotion to, 213, 214

Guardian Dragon, 215, 226

Guchun xuan shichao (Liang Desheng): prefaces to, 251–54

Gui Maoyi, 250, 253, 256

Gui Youguang, 179, 191, 250, 251; on faithful maidens, 95, 96, 97, 98, 99

Gui fan (Lü Kun), 59, 107, 109

Guliang zhuan, 57

Gu Lienü zhuan, 58–59

Gu Lienü zhuan fu kaozheng (Gu Guangqi), 62, 63

Guo, Miss, 198

Guo Moruo, 132, 133

Guochao guixiu zhengshi ji (Yun Zhu), 247, 248, 253, 257

Guomindang (GMD), 1, 3, 268, 342n14, 343n33; during Sino-Japanese War, 273, 274

Guoyu, 65

Hagiographies, 212

Han, Lady, 76

CPSIA information can be obtained
at www.ICGtesting.com
Printed in the USA
FSOW01n1354140217
30819FS

9 780520 289734